Nineteen-forty is generally considered to be the time when political parties and factions put aside their differences to unite under Churchill and concentrate on the war. Labour's massive victory in 1945 took most politicians and commentators by surprise but Dr Addison shows that they should have been prepared for it. He traces the roots of victory from the defeats of the thirties to the growing support of coalition Conservatives for many of Labour's plans for the future; the Labour politicians' ability to control the domestic ministeries when Churchill's attention was elsewhere; and the increasing unpopularity of the Conservatives in the disasters leading up to Dunkirk. Labour's victory in 1945 was decisive.

The author has researched beyond conventional historical sources into a wider range of ephemera, drawing on newspaper reports and leaders, public opinion polls, broadcast scripts and letters and memoirs.

Paul Addison is Lecturer in History at the University of Edinburgh.

The Road to 1945

British Politics and the Second World War

Paul Addison

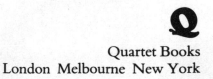

Quartet Books
London Melbourne New York

Published by Quartet Books Limited 1977
A member of the Namara Group
27 Goodge Street, London W1P 1FD

Reprinted 1982

First published by Jonathan Cape Ltd, London, 1975

Copyright © 1975 by Paul Addison

ISBN 0 7043 3154 3

Printed in Great Britain by Nene Litho
and bound by Woolnough Bookbinding
both of Wellingborough, Northants

To my Mother

Contents

Preface

The Road to 1945 is about the decline of one established order in politics, and the rise of another: Attlee's consensus replaces Baldwin's. Aspects of wartime politics with no significant bearing on the theme, however interesting in their own right, fall outside my scope. I have aimed to set the evidence out fairly, interpret it strictly, and alert readers to controversial points. But the result cannot be wholly dispassionate or detached. The war years are interesting partly because they are very much alive at the back of our minds. A book could be written about the use of wartime Britain as a point of reference for present-day attitudes. The period is still vivid not only for those who lived through it, but for those who, like myself, heard about Churchill's speeches or 'digging for victory' as they grew up, imbibing myth and nostalgia, but innocent of the misery and boredom which often accompanied the war effort. When people are still involved in recent events but want some perspective on them — as perhaps a man in his fifties will reflect again on his twenties — they write contemporary history. The contemporary historian shares much of the feeling and thought of the people he is trying to describe. It seems natural to him to ask many of the questions they asked, and he is drawn towards similar answers, expressed in scholarly form. He finds it difficult to imagine the type of question which would at once occur to an astonished visiting professor from Mars. But the fascination of contemporary history is that it also marks the beginning of a break with the past. The historian has more evidence than was available to the people he is writing about. Though he probably sympathizes with one school of thought rather than another in the recent past, he gradually becomes less interested in who was right, and more interested in explaining why people felt and acted as they did. Time already lends him some detachment, and he realizes that in certain respects he is writing about strangers whose motives and assumptions require careful reconstruction.

I began this book in 1972, by which time government papers covering the war years had become available at the Public Record Office. But I had been dabbling in the subject ever since I started research on opposition in wartime, in 1964, so I have had the benefit of help and counsel over several years. The supervisor of my doctoral research, Mr A. J. P. Taylor, has always been generous with his time and thought. The Warden and Fellows of Nuffield College elected me to a two-year studentship, and I would like to thank Mr David Butler and Mr Philip Williams in particular for valuable advice I received while I was there. I have had the great advantage of discussions over a long period with Dr Angus Calder. His imagination and expertise have been a never-failing resource and I owe him a special debt of gratitude. To Professor Arthur Marwick of the Open University, who has done so much to focus attention on the social consequences of war, and to analyse them more systematically, I am grateful for many wise observations which cleared my mind and broadened my understanding. Dr Calder and Professor Marwick both read a first draft of the book and made valuable criticisms and suggestions. I learned much about educational reform from Mr Graham Rimmer, and much about the Ministry of Information from Mr Ian MacLaine. Mr John Campbell's flair for political history has been an inspiration: he also read the proofs with a sharp eye for error. I owe a considerable debt of thanks to all the past students of my fourth year honours course at Edinburgh. I am also grateful to Miss Sara Dukes for her help in preparing the manuscript. Mr David Machin of Jonathan Cape has been an encouraging, patient and discerning critic. I have received very great help from archivists and librarians, and wish to thank in particular the staff of the Beaverbrook Library and the Library of Churchill College, Cambridge.

For granting helpful interviews I wish to thank the late Earl Attlee, Lord Boothby, Lord Ritchie-Calder, Sir Norman Chester, Lord Clitheroe, Lord Conesford, Mr Tom Harrisson, the late Sir Basil Liddell Hart, the late Sir Allen Lane, the late Lord Reith, Mr Donald Tyerman and the late Sir Horace Wilson. For access to copyright material and permission to quote from it, the author is grateful to Sir Richard Acland, Mrs Barbara Agar (diary of Euan Wallace), the Rt. Hon. Julian Amery M.P., Earl Attlee, Mrs Adele Barrington-Ward, the First Beaverbrook Foundation (Beaverbrook, Lloyd George and Hannon Papers), Lord Boothby, the British Library of Political and

Economic Science (diary of Beatrice Webb), Miss Vivian Brooks, Mr Ivor Bulmer-Thomas, Viscount Caldecote, Conservative and Unionist Central Office (Assheton committee on the Beveridge Report), Lord Croft, Mrs Elizabeth Crookshank, the Rt. Hon. Anthony Crosland M.P. (diary of Hugh Dalton), the Earl of Halifax, Mr Tom Harrisson (Mass-Observation archive), Lady Kathleen Liddell Hart, Captain Sir John Headlam, the Labour party, Lazard Brothers & Co. (Viscount Astor Papers), Liverpool University Library (Rathbone Papers), Mrs Stephen Lloyd (Neville Chamberlain Papers), Mr Nigel Nicolson, Mr Paul Paget (Templewood Papers), Reading University Library (Nancy, Viscountess Astor Papers), Viscount Simon, and Times Newspapers Ltd. The author apologizes to any holder of copyright he has failed to contact or trace. He is grateful to the Controller of Her Majesty's Stationery Office for permission to reproduce Crown Copyright material.

P.A.

Introduction

In some minds there is still an understandable belief that British politics came to a stop in World War II, and only resumed when it was over. Normal party politics were, indeed, suspended in the interests of national unity. From May 1940 to May 1945 the three main parties were in coalition under a leader of virtually impregnable authority, Winston Churchill. But it was during these years that popular opinion swung towards Labour and gave the party its 'landslide' victory at the 1945 general election. Besides, the history of consensus is more fundamental in politics (though less discussed) than the record of party strife. The national unity of the war years gave rise to a new consensus at the top which dominated Britain long after the last bomb had fallen.

Between the wars, politics were under the spell of the Conservatives and their ideas: World War II broke into the pattern. In May 1940 Neville Chamberlain's Conservative administration was overthrown in favour of a coalition in which Labour were practically equal partners. In Churchill, the descendent of Marlborough and historian of past glories, the oldest strain of ruling tradition had surfaced. Yet it was from the time Churchill came to power that the doctrines of innovation, progress and reform began to reassert themselves. 'I am quite certain', the Labour leader, Clement Attlee, told the Labour Party conference on 13 May 1940, 'that the world that must emerge from this war must be a world attuned to our ideals.'[1] Churchill's arrival marked the real beginning of popular mobilization for total war, the era of 'blood, toil, tears and sweat'. This experience in turn bred the demand for a better society when the fighting was done, lifted the Coalition on to a new place of reforming consensus, swung opinion decisively from Conservative to Labour, dismissed Churchill from office and made Attlee Prime Minister. World War II saw the reformation of British politics for a generation to come. In the book which follows I explore how and why this happened, and why it implied only very modest changes in society itself.

When Churchill met the House of Commons for the first time as Prime Minister, he announced that his government had but a single purpose: victory. This, of course, was to remain its raison d'être throughout, for the one thing of vital importance was the defeat of Hitler, without which there could be no worthwhile future of any description. But in the course of time the Coalition proved to be the greatest reforming administration since the Liberal government of 1905–14. Here, in the midst of war, was an astonishing example of the uses of adversity. Social security for all, family allowances, major reform in education, a National Health Service, Keynesian budgetary technique, full employment policies, town and country planning, closer relations between the state and industry – all these had been set on foot by the spring of 1943. By the spring of 1945 a new and wide-ranging prospectus of peacetime development was at an advanced stage of preparation within the civil service, while educational reform had already been embodied in the Butler Act of 1944 and had only to be administered. All three parties went to the polls in 1945 committed to principles of social and economic reconstruction which their leaders had endorsed as members of the Coalition. A massive new middle ground had arisen in politics. A species of consensus had existed between Stanley Baldwin and Ramsay MacDonald in the 1920s: a consensus to prevent anything unusual from happening. The new consensus of the war years was positive and purposeful. Naturally the parties displayed differences of emphasis, and they still disagreed strongly on the question of nationalization. At the hustings the rhetorical debate between state socialism and laissez-faire capitalism was renewed with acrimony. In practice, the Conservative and Labour leaders had by-passed most of it in favour of 'pragmatic' reform in a mixed economy. When Labour swept to victory in 1945 the new consensus fell, like a branch of ripe plums, into the lap of Mr Attlee.

The election gave Labour its first independent majority in the House of Commons and its largest of the post-war era to date – 146 overall. The result came as a profound shock to most of the political world which, having divined public opinion by the old techniques of im-pressionism and wishful-thinking, was convinced that Churchill's charisma would carry the day. Hence the well-known story of the lady at Claridge's who was heard to exclaim: 'But this is terrible.

They have elected a Labour government and the country will never stand for that.'[2] If one main theme of the home front is the evolution of a new consensus at the top, the other must be the movement of popular opinion below.

'Public' or 'popular' opinion has to be sharply defined. The editorials in the *Daily Mirror*, for example, are evidence only of what the editor wanted to say. The fact that three million people bought the paper is no help in discovering how many read the leaders, agreed with them, or were influenced by them. Then as now politicians and journalists made large and often partisan assertions about the way public opinion was moving. To depend on such judgments is to go hunting the unicorn. Fortunately, more systematic techniques of opinion polling and market research were already being introduced into Britain before 1939 by the Gallup poll and Mass-Observation. In 1940 the government itself set up two agencies to monitor public reactions: the Home Intelligence department of the Ministry of Information, and the Wartime Social Survey. There is, therefore, an exciting and variegated crop of evidence for the war years, to which can be added a long series of by-election results from 1941 to 1945. Judgments about the 'movement' of popular opinion have always to be tempered by the knowledge that many people never change their opinions, while some never have any to change. What changes is the relative weight of one view against another. The expression 'landslide' to describe Labour's victory can be misleading unless it is realized that it represented an average swing of 12 per cent as a result of which Labour still did not quite obtain a majority of all votes cast. But however cautiously interpreted, the evidence suggests that by the autumn of 1942 a major upheaval in public opinion had taken place. Indeed, opinion may have been further to the Left in 1942 than it was to be in 1945.

In 1939 Labour had looked all set to lose another general election: the war years represented a great revolution in the party's fortunes. But if the electoral aspect of this was the most apparent, it was not necessarily the most important. In the 1930s Labour was a party with a mission to get things done. Judged by its own rhetoric, it stood for nothing less than the conversion of Britain into a socialist commonwealth. In practice it was dominated by middle-of-the-road trade union bosses like Ernest Bevin, the General Secretary of the Transport and General Workers' Union, and Walter Citrine, the General Secretary of the T.U.C., in alliance with cautious parliamentarians—Attlee, Hugh Dalton, and Herbert Morrison. All these men were by temperament social reformers rather than leaders of the class struggle. Their political aims were moderate, but pursued with a steady bureaucratic passion: they were driven far more by the desire to achieve things than by the desire, common enough in politics, simply to be at the top of the greasy pole. The politics of the war years are unintelligible without constant reference to the absolute priority accorded by Labour between the wars to the goal of bettering the material conditions of the working classes. Poverty, mass unemployment, ill-health, absence of educational opportunity, these were the roots of the Labour passion for amelioration. Labour leaders had certain ideological commitments, chiefly towards some degree of state ownership of industry, and they believed firmly that capitalism was wasteful, inefficient and unstable. But they were far from doctrinaire. Their beliefs about means were continually changing; the end remained constant, set by the failure of the second Labour government in 1931: the next Labour government must deliver the goods in terms of tangible benefits for the working class. Electoral victory was only the preliminary: jobs, higher wages and pensions, better social services, must follow.

In the 1930s the Labour opposition faced the problem of how to make some practical use of power if and when they obtained it. Inexperienced in office, and guided by sketchy policy documents where there were any at all, they would have to wrestle with the conventional wisdom of great departments, devise new administrative agencies and techniques, and manœuvre powerful pressure-groups whose cooperation they required. They could expect sharp opposition from the Conservative Party and most of the press. How they would have fared no one can tell, but such were the terms on which they would have come to power. By 1945 resistances in Whitehall had been largely overcome, the civil service galvanized into a programme of amelioration on a wider scale than Labour had planned before 1939, the consent of the Conservative Party over much of the field secured in advance, and a team of Labour ministers schooled in office. Attlee himself had the good fortune, as Deputy Prime Minister from 1942 to 1945, to rehearse the premiership whenever Churchill was absent. So, it appears, the effect of war was to confer on Attlee a double mandate: one from the electorate, and one from within the Establishment.

If this was the main significance of the changes of the war years, what were the driving forces behind them? Why did so much happen, yet happen in a fashion so characteristic of the Whiggish and evolutionary pattern of British politics? At first sight it looks as though the later years of the war provide the best evidence. After the initial phase of 'phoney' war, there ensued between May 1940 and November 1942 a long and increasingly bleak period when the news was all of evacuations, retreats and disasters, and the overriding obsession was military events. Then, suddenly, the long tunnel of defeat was at an end. The Eighth Army defeated Rommel at El Alamein and Anglo-American troops invaded north-west Africa. Churchill ordered the church bells to be rung throughout the land in celebration of the long-awaited turn of the tide. At last there was a road back to peace, and it made sense to plan for the future. By a coincidence which seemed to emphasize the point, the government published three weeks after Alamein the famous report by Sir William Beveridge on the future of the social services. Beveridge proposed to abolish poverty, or 'want' as he termed it, by introducing a comprehensive programme of social security 'from the cradle to the grave'. Moreover his report declared that want was only one of 'five giants on the road of reconstruction ... The others are Disease, Ignorance, Squalor and Idleness.' The popular reaction was astonishing. Beveridge, a staid veteran of Edwardian liberalism, awoke to find himself a hero, the new People's William. He told a journalist: 'It's like riding on an elephant through a cheering mob.'[3] From the time of the Beveridge Report, reconstruction became a priority for the government and a major focus of political debate. The report's implications reverberated throughout the remaining years of the war.

Beveridge was certainly responsible for one of the main turning-points of political life on the home front. But for *the* critical change, we have to look back to 1940 itself. The year 1940 has gone down in our annals as the time when all sections of the nation put aside their peace-time differences, and closed ranks under the leadership of Churchill — 'their finest hour'. It should also go down as the year when the foundations of political power shifted decisively leftward for a decade. The very fact that nothing mattered beyond the task in hand explains why the change took place so easily, almost, indeed, unconsciously. The struggle for survival dictated that the Right should recruit the Left. Hence, the introduction into the War Cabinet of Labour ministers, and the installation of the T.U.C. virtually as a department of government in Whitehall. Hence, the dissemination of social democratic ideas over the B.B.C., in the army, and the information services. Hence, the new priority attaching to the morale and welfare of the working classes, and the power of popular opinion as a whole when it adopted a

Churchill or a Beveridge as its leader. Hence the new phrase on the lips of speakers: 'the people's war'.

But to think solely in terms of the effects produced by the participation of the Left in the war effort is to ignore another influential body of opinion which came into its own after May 1940: the progressive Centre. After the war the phrase might easily have applied to the majority of public figures, but in the 1930s it described a somewhat isolated minority, who felt that Labour was too socialist, and the Conservatives too rigidly capitalist. Professor Marwick has drawn attention to the existence of various pressure groups constituting 'middle opinion' before the war.[4] Logically enough, they were characterized by a belief in a mixed economy, a philosophy expounded by Harold Macmillan, an obscure backbench Conservative rebel, in his book *The Middle Way* (1938). Their patron saint was undoubtedly John Maynard Keynes, the economist and prophet of expansionist capitalism. The frustration he experienced as he watched the conduct of affairs from the sidelines is perfectly captured in his remarks about the Prime Minister, Chamberlain, early in 1939: 'If he could see even a little, if he became even faintly cognisant of the turmoil of ideas and projects and schemes to save the country which are tormenting the rest of us, his superbly brazen self-confidence would be fatally impaired.'[5] In June 1940, Keynes was given his own room at the Treasury, and the ideas and projects of 'middle opinion' found a powerful champion in high places. The Coalition itself, of course, in so far as it planned for the future, was virtually bound to plan along these lines, for it had to evolve policies which represented a compromise between Labour and Conservative sentiment.

If the Left and the Centre had their influence, it was dramatically reinforced by the social and administrative pattern of the war effort. Like the Kaiser before him, Hitler forced the British to behave according to fundamentally different rules from those which operated in peacetime. From 1940 onwards the economy, which had been allowed to operate at half-stretch with more than a million unemployed in the last year of peace, was ruthlessly planned to ensure all-out productivity in conditions of manpower shortage. From 1940, also, egalitarianism and community feeling became, to a great extent, the pervasive ideals of social life: whether or not people lived up to them, they knew that they *ought* to. The political influence of the ration book seems to me to have been greater than that of all the left-wing propaganda of the war years put together. The slogan of 'fair shares', sometimes thought to have been invented by Labour propagandists in 1945, originated in fact in the publicity campaign devised by the Board of Trade to popularize clothes rationing in 1941.[6]

Many people regarded the war as a purely evil and destructive necessity, which by its nature had no lessons to teach beyond the virtues of getting back to normal as soon as possible. Others, from Beveridge himself to the voters who swelled the support for left-wing candidates at by-elections, had their thought or attitudes changed by the experience. In his fine published diary of the war years, the journalist J. L. Hodson noted in September 1944:

> A young Radical friend said yesterday: 'We've shown in this war that we British don't always muddle through: we've shown we can organize superbly — look at these invasions of the Continent which have gone like clockwork; look at the harbours we've built on those beaches. No excuse any more for unemployment and slums and underfeeding. Using even half the vision and energy and invention and pulling together we've done in this war, and what is there we cannot do? We've virtually exploded the arguments of old fogies and Better-Notters who said we can't afford this and and musn't do that.' ... You could, were you so minded, set down a few credit items on the balance sheet of even a war as horrible as this, and an awakening of the minds of many folk and some hardening of the vigorous idealism of young people is one of those items. There are several others of a mundane sort. We've given coal-miners a minimum of five pounds a week; we've opened up shipyards that had been derelict; we've made wastelands fruitful, and cultivated millions of acres that lay idle. Our evacuation exposed hideous sores in the form of children undernourished and ill-brought up; I hope we shall be sensible enough to profit by the exposure. Our heavy taxation and our rationing of foods has, willy nilly, achieved some levelling up of the nation; fewer folk have gone hungry and fewer have gorged themselves; the poor have been a trifle better-off and the rich a little less rich.[7]

Here too are signposts to the Labour governments of 1945–51; and although the zeal for social reconstruction (of which there was a late flowering in the 1951 Festival of Britain), faded with the growth of 'affluence' in the 1950s, the foundations remained.

Churchill's part in the transformation of the war years is richly ambiguous. When he became Prime Minister he assumed a position

above party, but in October 1940 he accepted an invitation to follow
Neville Chamberlain as Conservative leader. In a sense the Conservatives could rely upon the overmighty figure at their head. He was a
convinced Conservative himself, and disliked the proliferation of
progressive causes on the home front. From time to time, when alerted
to the issue, he became anxious about the Trojan Horse of reformers
in his administration. In October 1943, for example, he vetoed the
nationalization of the coal industry for which Labour ministers were
pressing. But his efforts were more often ineffectual. He tried and failed
to wind up the Army Bureau of Current Affairs, and his attempt to
shelve the Beveridge Report was, on balance, unsuccessful. The fact
was that Churchill had given Labour very great power on the home
front while simultaneously beheading the Conservative party. There
was a Labour high command during the war: but on the Conservative
side, the old oligarchy of the 1930s, who were professional politicians
to their fingertips, had been replaced by the court of king Winston—a
little circle of eccentrics and foreign and defence experts. Lord Beaverbrook was a Conservative, but a figure detested by many in the party.
The Foreign Secretary, Anthony Eden, struck sensitive poses in
domestic politics but knew very little of the world outside the Foreign
Office. Unlike Conservative backbenchers, the Churchillian circle
were too absorbed in the heroic adventure of defeating Hitler to care
about the home front: Beaverbrook was indeed the exception, and took
a sufficiently intelligent interest to produce some answers, although
they proved to be the wrong ones in 1945.

In *The Road to 1945* I have drawn upon a wide and varied selection of
unpublished material ranging from private collections to the War
Cabinet and certain departmental files in the Public Record Office.
There is, then, a very great deal of fresh and, I hope, illuminating
material in what follows. But cautions are necessary. A definitive treatment of all the problems discussed here—from employment policy to
Churchill's political motivation, or the role of the intellectuals on the
home front—would require the labour of a lifetime. If all the problems
are ever to be exhaustively studied, the efforts of a number of scholars
will probably be needed. And if and when their work is complete,
there will still be no definitive history of Britain in the 1940s, or even
of the political history of the period. The scrutiny and publication of
the very last significant document will still leave every historian in
possession of the greatest of all unpublished sources: the ability to make
connections in thought and imagination between facts which are not

connected in a file. Controversy about the period will remain. The Marxist historian may well regard the war years, from his point of view, as a period when the conception of social justice was thwarted, and the reality of exploitation deepened by new techniques of managerialism. Although *The Road to 1945* is intended as a work of political and not of total social history, the author should forewarn readers of his own assumptions. The final outcome of the war in home affairs was that the optimists who believed that capitalism could be made to work more efficiently, and provide greater social welfare, had ousted from power the pessimists who believed that the conditions of the 1930s were decreed by iron laws of circumstance. This was far more than a contest between styles of rhetoric. At the end of the day, political change was translated into more jobs, better medical services, higher standards of social security, greater educational opportunity. J. M. Keynes argued that the problem of social organization turned not on whether people should exploit one another, but on how such exploitation should be regulated; the rules could be more, or less, civilized. In this sense the war years can be understood as a phase of genuine change in which a spirit of parsimony and caution gave way to a spirit of greater welfare and more confident management.

I The Supremacy of 'Safety First'
1922—1939

The passion for modest progress, which captured the home front during World War II, is only comprehensible as a blissful release from the frustrating circumstances which afflicted reform between the wars. In October 1922 the Conservative Party broke off its partnership with Lloyd George and his Liberal followers, and proceeded to fight and win a general election as an independent party. From then until May 1940, barring two intervals of minority Labour government in 1924 and from 1929 to 1931, the Conservatives were the masters. They seemed to have a built-in electoral advantage and a natural right to govern, like the Whigs in the age of Walpole. The latter-day Walpole, the shrewd manager of both the Conservative Party and the constitution, was Stanley Baldwin, three times Prime Minister, and Conservative leader from 1923 to 1937. The impact of war in home affairs has always to be measured by the yardstick of political life in the Baldwin era.

Under Baldwin, the Conservatives built themselves up as the most credible of the three potential governing parties, a task which was all the easier because of their rivals' difficulties. The Liberals had split after 1916 into the Lloyd George and Asquith factions. Even when the two leaders patched up their differences in 1923, Liberalism remained an ill-organized miscellany of viewpoints. Moreover, the class issue was by now a major determinant of voting. The Liberals, by trying to identify both with property and the wage-earning classes, hardly appealed to either, and gradually sank in the greatly expanded post-war electorate. As late as 1929 they won almost a quarter of the national vote: but in 1935 they were down to 6·4 per cent, with twenty-one M.P.s in the House.

The Labour Party was also handicapped. Labour became a national force for the first time in 1918, and superseded the Asquith Liberals as

His Majesty's Opposition in 1922. Ramsay MacDonald, the leader of the party from 1922 to 1931, was determined above all to prove that Labour was a respectable party of government, constitutional, competent, and gradual as the snail. The 1924 Labour Cabinet, in top hats and court dress, made the point as forcibly as possible: but however respectable Labour appeared, it was unable to win the support either of the working class as a whole, or of any substantial section of the middle class.

The inter-war years are often thought of as a period of strong working-class consciousness. After all, there were a million unemployed throughout the 1920s, and the great slump of 1929 pushed the total to a peak of three millions by 1932. This was the era of the General Strike, the Jarrow march of 1936, *Love on the Dole*, and *The Road to Wigan Pier*. Of the British volunteers who fought for the Spanish Republic against Franco, more than 80 per cent were working class. The picture is easily exaggerated. It has to be recalled that many working people, either from deference to social superiors or judgment of what would benefit them most, voted Tory. This was true in Jarrow itself, the classic blackspot of mass unemployment. The local Labour M.P., Ellen Wilkinson, wrote: 'At least 30 per cent of the workers of Jarrow vote Conservative fairly steadily.'[1] Recent research indicates that of the working-class electors who cast their first vote between the wars, about a third voted Conservative. Nor were 'trade unions' and 'working class' anything like synonymous terms. The Coles estimated in 1937 that the Trades Union Congress could claim to represent 'approximately 29 per cent of the manual and non-manual workers in the insured trades'.[2] The Labour Party had a rock-like foundation in the heartlands of basic industry — south Wales, Yorkshire and Lancashire, Tyneside and central Scotland — but found it hard to expand into agricultural areas, or into the prosperous Midlands and South-East of England.

Perhaps Labour were on the verge of a breakthrough in 1929, when they won two-thirds of the English boroughs and, for the first time, a majority of the English seats. The second Labour government seemed to have a great opportunity within its grasp. But almost at once the world slump struck Britain and demonstrated that Labour were helpless to prevent unemployment. The Cabinet collapsed ignominiously in the financial crisis of August 1931, and to the dismay of his party MacDonald accepted an invitation from the King to form a National Government of the Liberals, Conservatives, and a handful of his own

Labour supporters. The new government called an election and smashed the Labour Party proper, which secured only 30 per cent of the vote and 52 candidates returned out of 515 put up. According to David Butler's analysis of by-elections, Labour recovered its lost ground during 1932, and thereafter failed to make any headway against the Conservatives before the outbreak of war. Labour's position was, therefore, realistically summed up in the general election of 1935, when the Conservatives won 432 seats and 53·7 per cent of the vote, Labour 154 seats and 37·9 per cent of the vote. The by-election results imply that Labour would have done no better at a general election in 1939 or 1940. Chamberlain's appeasement of Hitler in 1938 did not, it must be emphasized, give Labour a new lease of popularity.[3] At the time, no one analysed election results in these terms, or paid attention to the Gallup poll, which suggested the same verdict. But it is interesting to find that towards the end of the 1930s some people in the Labour Party began to argue for a Popular Front with the Liberals, with the Independent Labour Party (I.L.P.) and the Communists included as garnishing, on the grounds that only an electoral pact with the other opposition elements could save Labour from certain defeat. Sir Stafford Cripps, who led the campaign and was expelled from the party in consequence, produced arithmetic to show that Labour would be nearly one hundred seats short of a majority if the party fought independently.[4] There might, of course, have been an electoral upset – the Conservative Chief Whip, David Margesson, thought the government might lose, or so he recalled after the war.[5] But there were no straws in the wind to show that Labour had improved its chances before the outbreak of war.

Any discussion of voting behaviour between the wars involves a large element of guesswork, but one theme is fairly clear. From 1922 to 1931 there was a three-party system in which the Conservatives and the Labour Party competed to mop up the Liberal vote. MacDonald and Baldwin sought, therefore, to hog the crown of the road, and MacDonald did it so convincingly that in 1929 Labour were on level terms with the Conservatives. The tables were turned decisively against Labour in the crisis of 1931. Baldwin had always sought to make a 'national' appeal against the 'sectional' interest of Labour. The financial collapse of August 1931 provided the perfect opportunity. At first the National government was said to be a purely temporary arrangement: once it had balanced the budget and saved the pound, the Conservative and Liberal parties, and the tiny 'National Labour' contingent under

MacDonald, would go their own ways. But the Conservatives quickly realized the value of the National government as an electoral vehicle, with a united front against Labour in the constituencies. There was a simple 'national cry' at hand to smooth over the differences within the government. The Labour Cabinet had gone up in a blaze of self-destruction, leaving the economy on the brink of ruin; all sound men, it could be argued, were putting aside their differences and pulling together in the national interest. The November 1931 election was a clever gamble which paid high dividends. The upshot of the crisis was that Liberalism disintegrated, leaving the popular following of Liberalism to be largely absorbed by the National government and thus the Conservative Party.

Baldwin had triumphantly occupied the middle ground. He had always been acutely sensitive about public opinion. Like all politicians of the day he relied on hunches and guesswork in this respect, and sometimes got the answer wrong. But he was outstanding in his responsiveness to popular feeling as he conceived it to be. In a famous speech, he confessed that in the years 1933-4, when he was Number Two in the government and anxious about the intentions of Nazi Germany, he had refrained from pressing for rearmament on the ground that it would have been too unpopular. The general election campaign of 1935, which he led as Prime Minister, was a masterly exercise in trimming. He took up the theme of rearmament, for which there had been agitation in his own party, combined it with the Labour cry of commitment to collective security through the League of Nations in foreign affairs, and underwrote the commitment with escape clauses in small print. When Chamberlain succeeded Baldwin as prime minister in May 1937, he inherited the National government and its wide-ranging appeal. And although he stirred up bitter party antagonisms, displaying none of Baldwin's remarkable sympathy for the emotions of the Labour side, majority opinion remained with him.

One of the underlying reasons for the buoyancy of Conservatism was undoubtedly the scale of economic recovery since 1931. While the areas of declining heavy industry remained blighted, stagnant, and — on the whole — loyal to the Labour Party, the Conservative Midlands and South-East of England were enjoying a remarkable burst of growth, led by the housing, electrical engineering, and motor industries. 'Britain's rapid recovery from the slump', writes one economic historian, 'put her near the top of the growth league table.'[6] The recovery owed little to government policy, but it redounded to their credit.

'Millions More!' declared the headline of a typical piece of Conservative propaganda in 1937:

> Britain's progress during the past six years under the National Government, can be measured in millions.
>
> 2¼ MILLIONS more in work
> £75 MILLIONS a year more in wage increases
> £130 MILLIONS more in exports
> 1¾ MILLION more new houses.[7]

In summing up the position of the Conservatives in September 1939 it is worth remarking that nothing is more national than war: it might well have seemed that Conservatism, as the natural vehicle of patriotism, was about to enjoy another boom in popularity like the one it experienced in World War I. Instead, World War II undermined both the popularity of the Conservatives, and the doctrines of administration for which they had stood in home affairs.

The Conservatives were not, of course, immobilists between the wars. They showed flexibility in both social and economic policy, although within well-defined bounds. Some idea of the constraints on Conservative action can be gleaned from the personality and outlook of Stanley Baldwin and Neville Chamberlain, the party's two leading ministerial figures, for if Baldwin was the chief rhetorician of Conservatism, Chamberlain was the chief policy-maker. Baldwin was a superb communicator of reassuring images and atmosphere: he brought into public life, said *The Times*, 'the fragrance of the fields, the flavour of apple and hazel nut, all the unpretentious, simple, wholesome, homely but essential qualities ... '[8] Baldwin's speeches identified the chief problem of statesmanship at home not as the raising of living standards or the cure of mass unemployment, but as the preservation of parliament and the British character from extremism. Extremism could be approximately equated with any bold experiment by the State in economic or social affairs. The responsibility of the statesman was to steer a steady course in the knowledge that any deviation carried the risk of a plunge into fascism or communism. To restrict the role of the State was, therefore, a service to a civilized community. Baldwin presented himself as a man who would do well by doing little.[9]

Baldwin may be accused of irrelevance on the grounds that he was casting himself as the saviour of a way of life which was not, in fact, threatened. Perhaps he mistook anxieties about his own stability for disorders in society at large. Whatever the cause, Baldwin's strategy was dictated by the 'thin-crust-of-civilization', or 'thus-fell-Rome' school of thought. Believing that society was held together by moral controls, he was apprehensive of appetites slipping their chains, the responsible ruler degenerating into a demagogue, and universal franchise into working-class licence. Baldwin's considerable political gifts were largely devoted to maintaining the moral controls, and if this often united happily with the promotion or preservation of his own career, it was because he knew when to release his puritanical zeal, and whom to release it against. As a minister in the Lloyd George Coalition he conceived a deep disgust for Lloyd George's character. At the right moment, the famous Conservative Party meeting at the Carlton Club in October 1922, he denounced Lloyd George in a devastating speech: 'A dynamic force is a very terrible thing; it may crush you but it is not necessarily right.' Baldwin built his reputation on his part in bringing Lloyd George down, and it seems to have been one of his primary aims after 1922 to prevent the most able and inventive politician of the age from ever again holding office.

Baldwin's conceptions of social discipline applied equally in his dealings with Labour. In the light of the Bolshevik revolution, and the severe post-war industrial unrest in Britain, Baldwin was anxious that Labour should accept its place not only in the parliamentary, but also in the capitalist system. He won the reputation of a paternal employer sympathetic to Labour grievances. In the House of Commons he befriended Labour M.P.s and undoubtedly aroused their affection. In 1925 he skilfully foiled the introduction of a Bill which would have attacked trade union political funds, ending his speech with the words, 'Give peace in our time, O Lord.' If he was ruthless and clear-sighted in defeating the General Strike of 1926, his victory was still chiefly due to the fact that the leaders of the T.U.C. hardly believed in the strike themselves. But when it came to any positive effort to revive the tradition of Tory social reform, Baldwin had little to offer but rhetoric about healing class divisions. He set his face against state intervention in the coal industry, the archaic state of which had given rise to the General Strike. He did not imagine that very much could be done to improve social conditions, and therefore deprecated large promises at election time. He believed that electors must learn to expect little. In a private letter of 1928 he wrote: 'Democracy has arrived at a gallop in England and I feel all the time that it is a race for life: can we educate them before the crash comes?'[10]

Antipathy to socialism, and the insistence that people should help

themselves rather than look to the state for solutions, were comple-
mentary doctrines. J. M. Keynes commented in 1926: 'The Conservative Party ought to be concerning itself with evolving a version of
individualistic capitalism adapted to the progressive change of circumstances. The difficulty is that the capitalist leaders in the City and in
Parliament are incapable of distinguishing novel measures for safe-
guarding capitalism from what they call Bolshevism.' When Roosevelt
came to power in the United States in 1933, and took emergency
powers to combat the depression, Baldwin commented that the regular
constitution of the United States had broken down and was giving way
to a dictatorship.[11] The values of Victorian liberalism still inhibited the
use of the State when any radical experiment was suggested.

Neville Chamberlain had none of Baldwin's aura, but all the administrative zeal which Baldwin lacked. When he took office as
Minister of Health in 1924, he laid before the Cabinet a list of twenty-
five measures which he wished to pass: twenty-one were implemented
by the time he left office.[12] However, Chamberlain was a man of
administrative, rather than social vision. An historian of British social
policy between the wars, while paying tribute to him as 'active,
courageous, intelligent and, within his limits, compassionate', none
the less comments:

> He was concerned less with what was to be done than how it was to
> be done. If social legislation is conceived as the transfer of wealth
> to needy individuals in the population, his care was for the method
> of payment rather than the alleviation of hardship. The quick
> sympathy of Lloyd George, who knew what it was to be poor
> and sought always to deal immediately with need while being only
> slightly concerned about the way in which need was met,
> Chamberlain could never understand and indeed despised.[13]

Inter-war Conservatism seldom transcended the slow evolution of
administrative logic in home affairs, which Chamberlain spent his time
in raising to the level of political principle. An inside observer, Sir
Arthur Salter, wrote of him:

> The Ministry of Health regarded him as the best Minister assigned
> to it since its creation; the Treasury as the most competent Chan-
> cellor of the Exchequer, within the limits of orthodox policy,
> since Gladstone. He was an exceptionally good Chairman of
> committees. He had all the qualities that Whitehall most desires for

its normal tasks; industry, order, precision, correctitude, decision. He was a lucid expositor, and a competent defender, of Departmental policy.[14]

The quest for 'safety first', a phrase which Baldwin actually took as his election slogan in the campaign of 1929, had its most crucial effects in economic affairs. The acid test of political thought between the wars was the existence of mass unemployment. From 1921 to 1929 the proportion of registered unemployed stood at, or just above, 10 per cent, or from one to one and a half millions. In the world slump it rose to more than 20 per cent, or nearly three millions. In spite of the subsequent economic recovery, between one and three quarter and two million men were out of work during 1938, over 12 per cent.[15] The depression began in 1921 in the basic exporting industries of Victorian Britain, whose share of world trade was fated to decline as other nations industrialized. It was exacerbated by the determination of the Bank of England and the Treasury to restore the pre-war exchange value of the pound in gold, an operation carried through by Churchill as Chancellor of the Exchequer in 1925. The effect of revaluing the pound was to increase the cost of British exports to foreign buyers by about 10 per cent. Since the export industries were in no position to cut their costs by dramatic reductions in wages, they were forced into deeper depression.

The Gold Standard apart, unemployment between the wars was partly structural, the result of a long-term decline in the demand for British exports, and partly cyclical, the consequence of a down-turn in the level of economic activity. The collapse of world trade after 1929, the most dramatic of all cyclical fluctuations, intensified the British problem. The regions of basic industry — Wales, Yorkshire and Lancashire, Tyneside, and central Scotland, suffered worst from both cyclical and structural causes. In 1938 more than a fifth of the labour force in the coal, cotton, wool, shipbuilding, and iron and steel industries, was unemployed. Not only were unemployment levels higher in the 1930s, but also there was a sharp increase in the number of people who were unemployed for years rather than months.[16]

Conservative ideas were modified, up to a point, by the slump and the financial crisis of 1931. The National government was forced to abandon the Gold Standard and devalue the pound, freeing the home economy from one of its shackles. Low interest rates, conducive to business expansion, replaced the high rates of the 1920s. The greatest innovation was the introduction of protective tariffs in 1932, an old Conservative theme, but now turned to the new purpose of state regulation of industry. The government demanded, in return for the grant of a tariff to protect an industry, that its major producers should reorganize themselves. They were encouraged to reduce capacity and keep up prices. The partnership between the government and the new federation of steel producers was a celebrated example. There was a recipe here for stability and profits, but not for the expansion of production or the creation of jobs. The Conservatives were, however, gradually casting free of the tenets of laissez-faire: between the wars they went so far as to establish outright state control of broadcasting, the generation of electricity, and overseas airways.[17]

They also made the first attempt to tackle the problem of the heavy concentration of unemployment in certain regions. The 'special areas' legislation defined four regions of high unemployment and put in charge of them commissioners with powers to attract industry and set up trading estates. The scheme was very much an experiment, and left out large tracts of blighted industrial Britain. It has been estimated that work was created for no more than 50,000 of the 362,000 men who were out of work in the special areas — largely because the commissioners had such small budgets to work with.[18]

One of the main factors inhibiting Conservatism between the wars was the taboo of economy in public expenditure, which derived from the opinions of the Treasury and orthodox economists. A balanced budget was considered to be essential for business confidence, high expenditure a diversion of funds from private enterprise, and government borrowing the primrose path to inflation, depreciation of the pound abroad, and the decline of exports. Baldwin himself, as a junior minister, gave £120,000 — one fifth of his fortune — to help pay off the national debt in 1919. The orthodox response to a downturn in the economy was to reduce taxation and expenditure. The Geddes committee set the tone by the severe cuts it recommended in 1921; and the May committee, appointed by the second Labour government, inspired a second round of reductions by the National government in 1931. Expenditure on rearmament, which did so much to restore prosperity in the late 1930s, was regarded by Neville Chamberlain, whether as Chancellor of the Exchequer or as Prime Minister, as a terrible burden which threatened inflation, industrial unrest, and the collapse of British exports. In February 1938 Chamberlain told the Cabinet that on becoming Prime Minister he had decided to make an earnest effort to improve relations with Italy and Germany. One of his major considerations had been the growing cost of armaments: 'As the Home Secretary had said the other day, some other countries did not take expenditure into account. We had not yet seen the final results of that, which must be serious. The restrictions which had already been caused had become an appreciable burden, and eventually must be a source of weakness.'[19] When rearmament had to be stepped up after the Munich crisis of September 1938, the Treasury issued a circular declaring: 'The continuing heavy cost of rearmament renders it imperative that the estimates for the coming year should be framed with the closest regard for economy, and there will be a prime need for arresting the growth in civil expenditure.'[20]

The doctrines of economy and the balanced budget ruled out any major experiment in the cure of mass unemployment. We still lack a history of the Treasury between the wars, and have to be beware of the idea that there was a simple 'Treasury view'. 'It bends so much', said Keynes, 'that I find difficulty in getting hold of it.'[21] However, Chancellors of the Exchequer put the matter in black and white terms. When Baldwin was Chancellor in 1922 he wrote: 'Money taken for Government purposes is money taken away from trade and borrowing will thus tend to depress trade and increase unemployment.' There was no way the State could increase in the long run the level of demand and thus the level of employment. Churchill said in his 1929 budget speech: 'It is orthodox Treasury dogma, steadfastly held, that whatever might be the political or social advantages, very little additional employment can, in fact, and as a general rule, be created by State borrowing and expenditure.'[22]

From within the Labour Party, proposals for the expansion of purchasing power were advanced by the I.L.P., and by Sir Oswald Mosley, as Chancellor of the Duchy of Lancaster, in the Mosley memorandum of 1930. Philip Snowden, the Labour Chancellor of the Exchequer in 1924 and again in 1929 regarded them as financial nonsense. The frankest expression of fatalism came from Chamberlain in his budget speech of 1933, when he announced that Britain must contemplate ten years of large-scale unemployment.[23] Finally, when Lloyd George unveiled a programme of public works in 1935, the Cabinet issued a statement declaring: 'It seems to the Government a misconception that a vast quantity of hitherto undiscovered work capable of giving employment to large numbers of people lies waiting to be put in hand.'[24]

In fairness to the authorities of the 1930s, it has to be said that the only two industrial powers of the day with full employment, Germany and Russia, had achieved it at the cost of massive and cruel repression. Sweden and the United States, the two democratic powers which had experimented with deficit finance, had unemployment rates of 10 per cent and 18·4 per cent respectively at the end of the 1930s.[25]

In the last days of his life, during the blitz, Chamberlain was to write, in a private letter: 'It was the hope of doing something to improve the conditions of life for the poorer people that brought me at past middle life into politics, and it is some satisfaction to me to know that I was able to carry out some part of my ambition ... '[26] There had indeed been a notable consolidation of social policy under Baldwin and Chamberlain, in spite of parsimony. Health insurance, which provided workers with sickness benefit and paid their doctors' bills, covered fifteen million wage-earners in 1921, twenty million in 1938. Unemployment insurance, which had protected eleven million workers in 1920, was expanded to cover 15·4 million by 1938. The jobless who had exhausted their entitlement to benefit were at least relieved from public funds rather than automatically thrown on the Poor Law: after 1934 they were turned over to Chamberlain's new Unemployment Assistance Board and obliged to undergo the detested household means test, which required details of all income brought into the unemployed man's home. Chamberlain also expanded old age pensions, and abolished the Poor Law Unions and their Guardians, transferring the old poor-law hospitals to the local authorities. His Housing Act of 1923 resulted in the construction of nearly half a million houses, principally for middle-class purchasers, over the next six years. The Conservatives also implemented Labour measures for working-class housing, building the best part of half a million houses for rent under the Wheatley Act of 1924, and rehousing more than a million slum-dwellers under the Greenwood Act of 1930.

The social services of Britain, taken all in all, were the most advanced in the world in 1939, and the Social Democrats in Sweden, the Labour Party in New Zealand, and the New Deal Democrats in the United States, were trying to bring about many of the improvements which Conservatism took for granted. Precisely because the social services were so well developed, reformers and radicals could envisage their 'completion' all the more easily, and a considerable gap emerged between the goals of even the most unrevolutionary variety of progressive, and the facts of administrative life. The cautious rectitude of financial policy restrained the growth of the social services, on which total expenditure increased from £490·7 million in 1919 to £596·3 million in 1939.[27] 'In the memory of those who lived through them', writes Brian Simon, 'the inter-war years were dominated by the cry for, and the practice of, economy. In the elementary schools particularly expenditure was cut to the bone, everything done on the cheap.' The elementary school, catering for children of all ages between five and fourteen, was still the typical state school of the period. The percentage of children from elementary schools who crossed the magic threshold into secondary education increased only from 9·5 per cent in 1920 to 14·3 per cent in 1938, and this chiefly because of the decline in the birth-rate. The very modest aim of reorganizing classes for children over eleven in elementary schools, to provide them with a more advanced syllabus, was yet to be realized: in 1938 under half of the pupils in elementary schools were in 'reorganized' classes.[28] The authentic period note is captured by the Royal Commission on National Health Insurance in 1926. On the one hand it concluded that since the health services must grow, the ultimate solution would be to divorce them wholly from the insurance principle, and finance them entirely out of public funds. On the other the commission recommended that no changes should be made in the immediate future which involved fresh expenditure.[29] Anyone who had proposed, against such a background, to raise expenditure on the health services from £61 million to £148 million, as envisaged in the 1944 White Paper, or the cost of social insurance from £432 million to £697 million, as Beveridge proposed in 1942, would have been laughed out of Whitehall.

The fall of Lloyd George in 1922 marked the end of truly imaginative leadership in home affairs until 1940. The pace of change was left to be determined mainly by the permanent officials of the Treasury, whom Keynes described in January 1939 as one of the main obstacles to a more progressive social and economic outlook:

> There has been nothing finer in its way than our nineteenth century school of Treasury officials. Nothing better has ever been devised, if our object is to limit the functions of Government to the least possible and to make sure that expenditure, whether on social or economic or military or general administrative purposes, is the smallest and most economical that public opinion will put up with. But if that is not our object then nothing can be worse. The Civil Service is ruled today by the Treasury school, trained by tradition

and experience and native skill to every form of intelligent obstruction ... We have experienced in the twenty years since the war two occasions of terrific retrenchment and axing of constructive schemes. This has not only been a crushing discouragement for all who are capable of constructive projects, but it has inevitably led to the survival of those to whom negative measures are natural and sympathetic.[30]

The two major alternatives to Conservative rule between the wars were the 'middle way' of imaginative reform within capitalism, personified by Lloyd George and Keynes, and the socialist way of abolishing capitalism. The socialist way had a powerful popular organization behind it, in the Labour Party, but on inspection socialism proved to be a language of ideals rather than power. The pioneers of the 'middle way' spoke the language of power, but had no big battalions behind them. They were of all parties and of none, and hence doomed to be ineffectual. The Conservatives were so committed to the rhetoric of defending capitalism, and Labour so committed to the rhetoric of attacking it, that an open and positive commitment to a mixed economy was impossible. None the less, by the end of the 1930s, the Centre was becoming more effectively organized.

In the three-party system of the 1920s, there seemed to be a natural Centre party in the Liberals. They were compelled to argue that the Conservatives were too reactionary, Labour too socialistic. But it would be misleading to represent the Liberal Party as a whole as the spearhead of progress: nostalgia for Edwardian England was the dominant note. Progressive Liberalism was the work of Lloyd George, whom the Asquithians still hated, and a small number of intellectuals. The intellectual revival began with the Liberal Summer Schools of 1922 and after. The leading lights in the movement were drawn partly from Manchester—Ramsay Muir, Ernest Simon, E. T. Scott—and partly from Cambridge—Keynes, Walter Layton and Hubert Henderson, all three professional economists. Oppressed by the decline of Britain's heavy industries, they sought a remedy in dexterous state intervention. Once Lloyd George had recovered from the major impact of his fall from power, he was instinctively drawn towards activist policies for the economy, and was one of the first Liberals to suggest a large-scale programme of public investment. In 1926 he arranged to finance a Summer School inquiry into the future of

British industry. The outcome was the Liberal Yellow Book, *Britain's Industrial Future*, a volume of nearly 500 pages which appeared in 1928. The Yellow Book's many proposals included stronger guidance by the state of monopoly enterprise, joint consultation in industry between workers and managers, and extensive public works to relieve unemployment. Of these the last is especially associated with John Maynard Keynes, the brightest star of the 'middle way' between the wars.

Keynes was the son of a Cambridge lecturer in logic and political economy. Brilliant and supremely self-confident from boyhood, Keynes could have distinguished himself in any one of several fields, whether as a man of letters like his friend Lytton Strachey, a writer on art like his friend Clive Bell, or as a mathematician, philosopher, or political scientist. In 1906 he entered the India Office and began a lifelong career as a public servant and economist. In 1919 he added a new role, that of pamphleteer and controversialist. Resigning as Treasury representative at the Paris Peace Conference, he wrote a sustained polemic condemning the reparations clauses of the Treaty of Versailles as harsh and impractical: *The Economic Consequences of the Peace*. Thereafter he began to work towards his supreme achievement, the reform of western capitalism through the revolution of economic doctrine.

From his home and early life Keynes had imbibed the virtues of the educated and cultivated bourgeoisie of late Victorian England, unashamed of their worldly advantages, confident of the moral and material lines along which society must progress, and sure of their own role as leaders of the advance.[31] The First World War dealt severe blows to British capitalism and the British Empire, and by its revelation of the worst in human beings should, perhaps, have destroyed the belief in rationally controlled progress. But the spirit of Victorian improvement survived. The energetic upper-middle-class progressive continued to be a familiar figure in public life, with Keynes as the supreme exemplar. The progressive itched to champion the League of Nations, constitutional advance in India, the relief of poverty, the planning of towns and the preservation of the countryside. In the 1930s the younger progressives, impatient of old techniques, frequently turned to Marxism as the most drastic means of rational improvement available. Keynes sympathized, but like most of his generation went on believing that his own class could introduce all the necessary reforms without disturbing the foundations of capitalism. For Soviet communism he displayed a marked contempt: 'How can I adopt a creed which, preferring the mud to the fish, exalts the boorish proletariat above the bourgeois and the intelligentsia who, with whatever faults, are the quality of life and surely carry the seeds of all advancement?'[32] Keynes explained to the Liberal Summer School of 1925 that he was a Liberal because the Liberals provided the best vehicle for scientific and intellectual expertise. The Conservatives, he argued, were satisfactorily autocratic, but unfortunately stupid. The Labour Party included intellectual elements, but owing to the democratic character of Labour, they could never be sure of exercising control over the ignorant.[33]

In the 1920s Keynes had many practical proposals to offer for economic recovery, but as yet no general theory to explain mass unemployment and its cure. Finding an outlet for his opinions in the Liberal Industrial Inquiry, he was able, his biographer tells us, 'to get endorsement for his ideas on currency management, the stimulation of domestic investment programmes, a public investment board, which would also have regard to the scale of foreign investments, an economic General Staff, greater publicity for the finance of companies, and the encouragement of the semi-public concern as an agency of industrial operation intermediate between the state and private enterprise.'[34]

Under the inspiration of Keynes and Hubert Henderson, Lloyd George launched in 1929 the celebrated Liberal election programme, *We Can Conquer Unemployment*. In a speech of 1 March 1929 he promised to reduce unemployment within a year to normal proportions, without adding one penny to local or national taxation. The centrepiece of the programme was massive public investment in roads, housing, electrification, telephones, and the renovation of the countryside. But this proved to be the last election at which the Liberals were a major force. In the aftermath of the 1931 crisis, the Liberal Party, Lloyd George, and Keynes, all flew off at different tangents, and Keynes was left without a platform for his views.

In 1936 Keynes revolutionized economic theory by the publication of his *General Theory of Employment, Interest, and Money*. Traditional doctrine, at least as politicians and civil servants interpreted it, held that the laws of supply and demand tended to create full employment: unemployment on a large scale was due to the refusal of trade unions to accept lower wages, which would increase the demand for labour. Keynes demonstrated that by stimulating consumption and investment, the government could increase demand to the level at which full employment was created. He pointed out that in themselves such conclusions made no obvious case for socialism: 'The central controls necessary to ensure full employment will, of course, involve a large extension of the traditional functions of government. Furthermore, the modern classical theory has itself called attention to various conditions in which the free play of economic forces may need to be curbed or guided. But there will still remain a wide field for the exercise of private initiative and responsibility.'[35]

One of the other conclusions to be drawn from the *General Theory* was the necessity of introducing professional economists into the government. William Beveridge had suggested an 'Economic General Staff' in 1923, Keynes had adopted the idea, and an ineffectual Economic Advisory Council had been set up in 1930. The council quickly lost all significance in Whitehall, and the *General Theory* reinforced the case for putting economists in genuinely responsible positions. Moreover, by its conquest of the economic profession in the years 1936–9, the *General Theory* prepared the way for a new élite of Keynesian advisers.

With political Liberalism in eclipse, the task of evolving the 'middle way' fell after 1931 to various pressure-groups stimulated by the catastrophe of the world slump. Among them were Political and Economic Planning (P.E.P.), established in 1931, and the Next Five Years Group formed in 1934. Arthur Marwick, in tracing the fortunes of these and similar circles in the 1930s, has pointed out that in this respect the decade we normally associate with intense divisions between Right and Left, fostered the development of 'middle opinion'.[36] In foreign affairs, supporters of all parties and of none could find common ground in supporting the League, and the cause of parliamentary democracy against fascism and communism. In home affairs they could work towards a managed economy and the expansion of the social services. Perhaps the only difficulty in talking about 'middle opinion' or the 'middle way' is the implication that here was a scheme for a half-way house between capitalism and socialism. No socialist would describe it as such, for as Marwick observes, 'the centre progressives the apostles of political agreement, still believed in the essential soundness of established society … '[37]

In March 1930 the journalist Gerald Barry, later editor of the *News Chronicle*, launched a new periodical, the *Weekend Review*. At the height of the economic blizzard in February 1931, Barry published a pioneering article by Max Nicholson entitled 'A National Plan for Britain'. Nicholson proposed among other things a reduction in the size of the Cabinet to ten members including a Minister of Defence and a Minister of Economic Development, a planning council for each industry, co-ordination of transport, fuel and power, and a new town-planning act. Before publication the article had been circulated to William Beveridge and G. D. H. Cole as progressive intellectuals, Walter Elliott and Duff Cooper as reforming young Conservatives, John Strachey and Oswald Mosley as innovators on the Labour benches, Bevin and Citrine as progressive trade unionists, and Melchett and McColl as progressive industrialists. Nicholson's article stimulated so much interest that its supporters decided to set up a research organization to advance the principles of planning. Among the founders or early activists in Political and Economic Planning were the banker Basil Blackett, the industrialists Laurence Neal, Israel Sieff and Leonard Elmhirst, the economist Arthur Salter, the zoologist Julian Huxley, and the educational pioneer and National Labour M.P. Kenneth Lindsay. The many research groups which P.E.P. set up were run almost exclusively by white-collar managers, experts, and professionals: there were no trade unionists.[38]

Like the Fabians before them, the founders of P.E.P. aimed to collect information, channel reports to the government, and permeate the Establishment with their ideas. In the 1930s they produced reports on several basic industries, as well as on housing (1934), the social services (1937), the health services (1937) and the location of industry (1939). Their influence was small in the 1930s, but they helped to prepare high-level opinion for the changes of the 1940s.

Whereas P.E.P. was strongly technocratic in outlook, committed to efficiency and modernization, the Next Five Years Group represented 'the stage army of the good': men and women of moral and philanthropic outlook who were always ready to campaign for truth, beauty, justice and liberty. Both the chairman, Clifford Allen, and the secretary, Barratt Brown, had been conscientious objectors in World War I, and the membership included many voluntary workers and pioneers of adult education, besides Lionel Curtis, R. C. K. Ensor, H. A. L. Fisher, G. P. Gooch, J. A. Hobson, Sir Oliver Lodge, Gilbert Murray, Seebohm Rowntree, Siegfried Sassoon, H. G. Wells, and William Temple, the Archbishop of York. In its recommendations, *The Next Five Years* reads like a guide to the accepted nostrums of a few years later. The proposals for the future at home included an Economic General Staff, a National Development Board, public investment in housing and electrification, the co-ordination of the social services to achieve a National Minimum, the expansion of secondary school organization, town and country planning, and the location of industry in the depressed areas.[39]

The main pressure for social reform between the wars undoubtedly came from the Labour Party, but as membership of the Next Five Years Group indicated, the precise goals were defined largely by non-party reformers and leaders of the professions. One of the outstanding personalities, for example, was Eleanor Rathbone, the Independent M.P. for the Combined English Universities and a signatory of the Next Five Years programme. The sixth in line of a dynasty of Liverpool social reformers, Eleanor Rathbone entered parliament in 1929 with the aim of championing constitutional advance in India. But the cause with which she was most closely identified was the campaign for family allowances. One of the major causes of poverty was the failure of the working-class family income to expand when the number of children increased. In 1917, Eleanor Rathbone and her friends began to campaign for the endowment of motherhood by the state and in 1924 she argued the case in an influential book, *The Disinherited Family*. She succeeded in converting another major non-party reformer, William Beveridge: but the trade union movement and the Labour Party remained cool or even hostile, suspicious that family allowances were designed to undermine trade union bargaining power.[40]

In nutritional policy the goals were set by Sir John Boyd Orr, the director of the Rowett Research Institute at Aberdeen. His book, *Food, Health and Income* (1937), demonstrated that nearly half the population had a diet inadequate for maintaining health, while the diet of the poorest 10 per cent was deficient in nearly all the known vitamins and some of the minerals.[41] The extent and causes of poverty continued to be investigated by social scientists, and several inquiries were conducted in the great industrial centres. From the surveys of London, Liverpool, Sheffield, Plymouth, Southampton, York and Bristol, carried out between the wars, Beveridge was to derive his diagnosis of 'want', and the means to prevent it, which were later embodied in his famous wartime report. Of his own great plan there was a foretaste in a pamphlet he published in 1924: *Insurance for All and Everything*.

The goals of educational advance between the wars were defined principally by the Consultative Committee of the Board of Education, with some help from Labour Party experts. In spite of its official status, the committee was in effect a high-level pressure group for the educational world. Two-thirds of its members always had to be drawn from schools, universities, and other educational bodies. In 1926, for example, it included Sir Henry Hadow, Vice-Chancellor of Sheffield University, as chairman, Alderman Percy Jackson, chairman of the West Riding of Yorkshire Education Committee, Ernest Barker, Professor of Politics at Cambridge, J. A. White, headmaster of a London central school, Lynda Grier, the economist and Principal of Lady Margaret Hall, Emmeline Tanner, headmistress of Roedean, Albert Mansbridge, the founder of the Workers' Education Association, R. H. Tawney, socialist, historian, and one of Mansbridge's leading supporters in the W. E. A., and Miss E. R. Conway, a past president of the National Union of Teachers. The committee was supposed usually to act within terms of reference provided by the Board of Education, but as the Duma of the educational world it tended to steer its own course. At the end of 1923 the Baldwin government referred to it the future education of elementary schoolchildren over the age of eleven. The committee presented a report, *The Education of the Adolescent,* in 1926. This called for the school-leaving age to be raised to fifteen, a proposal which the government at once turned down. But the government accepted the other main recommendation, that elementary schoolchildren over eleven should have special senior schools, or at least reorganized classes. Elementary schools, however, were to remain second-class institutions in terms of staffing and finance: secondary education was still to be for a minority only.[42]

Like the other social services, education was again blighted by the economy campaign of 1931–2. But in 1936, the Baldwin government introduced an Education Bill to raise the school-leaving age to fifteen as from 1 September 1939. However, the Bill took back much of what it gave through an exemption clause. In areas where manufacturers needed adolescent labour, the leaving age would remain at fourteen. Local education committees and the National Union of Teachers protested strongly. Among the government's critics on this occasion were three men whose shadows are going to loom larger in this book: the Conservative backbench M.P., Harold Macmillan, the General Secretary of the T.U.C., Sir Walter Citrine, and the Archbishop of York, William Temple. The government stuck to its guns, but even the partial raising of the school-leaving age had to be suspended at the outbreak of war. In 1934 the Consultative Committee, then under the chairmanship of Sir Will Spens, Master of Corpus Christi College, Cambridge, was asked to report on the future of secondary education. Once again, it leapt ahead of the Board of Education and the Cabinet. The Spens Report of 1938 urged the abolition of elementary schooling.

All children over eleven should have places in secondary schools, i.e.
a higher standard of teaching and financial provision. The committee
did not favour the multilateral or comprehensive school. Instead there
were to be three types of secondary school—grammar, technical, and
modern—with 'parity of esteem'. The school-leaving age should be
raised to sixteen. The main Spens proposals were rejected by the board
and the government as too burdensome to the Exchequer: in the
feverish pre-war atmosphere they sank quietly into the forgotten
depths of social policy.[43]

The British Medical Association (B.M.A.), the professional organization of the doctors, was also thinking in advance of the Baldwin and
Chamberlain governments on the subject of the health services. The
B.M.A. advocated the extension of National Health Insurance to cover
the dependents of wage-earners, and the co-ordination of the privately
run voluntary hospitals with the hospitals run by local authorities.[44]
Future experience was to underline the fact that the B.M.A., while
prepared to propose changes congenial to the medical profession, was a
jealous watchdog resentful of lay, and especially of state, regulation of
the health services. In this respect the B.M.A. was, of course, out of
line with the typical reforming lobbies of the period, bands of enthusiasts who expected the state to intervene in the name of progress.

A progressive cause dating from the end of the nineteenth century
was the garden city, an environmentalist experiment pioneered by
Ebenezer Howard, who successfully established the first garden city at
Letchworth in 1903. From the garden city movement there developed
the Town and Country Planning Association, a group who first began
to influence government policy in favour of planning the environment
towards the end of the 1930s, when the secretary of the Association was
Frederick Osborn, an early Fabian and disciple of Howard.[45] At this
date the use of land, the growth of towns, and the location of industry,
were still virtually in the lap of the gods, or rather of the developer.
In 1937 the government, worried, partly for fear of strategic bombing,
by the concentration of population in the South-East, appointed a Royal
Commission under Sir Montague Barlow on the 'Distribution of the
Industrial Population'. The Town and Country Planning Association
was invited to submit evidence, and Osborn was later to write to Lewis
Mumford, the U.S. city planner: 'I worked very hard on the doorstep
and behind the arras of that Commission, and the leading members of
the three sections [the Commission produced a majority report and
two minority recommendations] all tell me that it was my evidence

and the examination on it that got them together on the essential policy.'⁴⁶ The Barlow Report recommended that for the first time the government should take responsibility for the pattern of land use throughout the country, restricting factory development in the South-East, dispersing congested urban populations to new towns and garden cities, inspecting the plans put forward by local authorities, and encouraging the location of industry in areas threatened by unemployment. However, the majority report of the commission was reluctant to award any effective powers to the new central planning authority.⁴⁷

There was, then, a broad agenda of safe and constructive progress ready to hand by the end of the 1930s. The Conservatives were doing little about it and few indeed displayed any enthusiasm for a 'socialistic' programme of the Next Five Years variety. However, one Conservative M.P., Captain Harold Macmillan, had been active in the Next Five Years Group and even pushed aside the gentle Clifford Allen to take charge of it, and its periodical *New Outlook*, himself. Macmillan, although a well-known personality in the publishing world, was a minor eccentric in terms of Tory politics. In the 1930s there were many Conservative rebels who wanted to move the party to the right; Macmillan was among a handful who wanted to move it to the left. Even in foreign affairs, where he was a traditional patriot in most respects, Macmillan was an adamant supporter of the Labour approach of collective security through the League. In 1936 he and Vyvyan Adams were the only two Conservatives to vote against the Baldwin government's abandonment of League sanctions on Italy. In home affairs he supported the abolition of the means test, strong measures to help the distressed areas, and greater state control of industry. He advocated the nationalization of the coal mines—which he was to oppose after the war as an opposition spokesman. In 1936 he called for a new Centre Party under the leading Labour moderate, Herbert Morrison, to obtain 'a fusion of all that is best in the Left and the Right.'⁴⁸ His book *The Middle Way*, published in 1938, was a comprehensive statement of the case for a managed economy, and the expansion of the welfare state to achieve a national minimum. Macmillan took his inspiration as a pragmatic radical from Lloyd George, who remained a brilliant and constructive force in the parliaments of the 1930s; his economics from Keynes, whose *General Theory* he published; his foreign policy partly from Labour, and partly from Winston Churchill, a sombre and isolated figure in the political wilderness. This remarkable synthesis of anti-Establishment attitudes, so outlandish in the context of Chamberlainite Conservatism, appears in retrospect a bold signpost to the consensus which arose after Dunkirk. Surprisingly, the Conservative backbenches included another M.P., of more sparkling mind and erratic disposition, who was also under the spell of Churchill, Keynes, Lloyd George, and the Left: Robert Boothby. As Britain moved towards war, there was an increasing compatability between the Conservatism of Boothby or Macmillan, and the aims of the Labour Party.

The Labour movement between the wars suffered every variety of reverse. The trade unions were defeated in the General Strike of 1926; the Labour Party was defeated electorally; the second Labour government was beaten by the problems of administration and had in effect to abdicate; and last but not least, European socialism, of which Labour was a part, was crushed in Italy, Germany, Austria, Spain and Czechoslovakia. All told this was a formidable education in the necessity of modesty. By 1939, the Labour movement was grateful for small mercies.

The General Strike, led by the General Council of the T.U.C. in aid of the miners, was not so much the culmination as the last kick of the syndicalist movement for direct action. The T.U.C. leaders were reluctant to call the strike and relieved when they were able to call it off. With the collapse of the strike, the T.U.C. veered strongly to the Right under the guidance of two outstanding figures, Walter Citrine and Ernest Bevin. Citrine, the General Secretary of the T.U.C., was the archetypal trade union functionary, proud of his position in public life, anxious to understand the government point of view, knighted in 1935 by Ramsay MacDonald. Bevin, the General Secretary of the giant Transport and General Workers' Union, was in strong contrast. Aggressive where Citrine was diplomatic, class-conscious where Citrine was emollient, intellectually rugged where Citrine was meticulously-minded, Bevin was the only trade union leader of his day with the equipment of a statesman. A man of large constructive ideas derived from wide experience of practical affairs, he was contemptuous of the left-wing theorists in the Labour Party. His biographer emphasizes the breadth of his interests and the power of his imagination:

Automation and the shortening of the working week; the impact of science on industry; a comprehensive State pensions scheme;

industrial rehabilitation; the application of medical research to industrial health problems. Whatever he was engaged on, from drafting a convention on the prevention of dock accidents to the details of unemployment insurance, his imagination would open up its relation to a wider background. Behind any problem he saw people and possessed the gift of making ordinary men and women feel part of the movement of history.[49]

Bevin and Citrine never liked each other personally, but they had a common aim: to raise the status and influence of the trade unions in society. They were not very interested in the part unions would play in the socialist commonwealth of the distant future, but they did aim to improve conditions in the capitalist present. In 1928-9 the T.U.C. General Council held a series of conversations with twenty big industrialists led by Sir Alfred Mond of I.C.I.: the Mond-Turner conversations. There were few practical results, but the talks marked the acceptance by the majority of trade union leaders of the need to collaborate with the employers in the pursuit of productivity. In 1929 Bevin was appointed to the Committee on Finance and Industry under Lord Macmillan, and again broadened his horizons by acquiring a knowledge of finance and the City. When Labour came to power in 1945, his ambition was to be Chancellor of the Exchequer, not Foreign Secretary as he became.

The aims of the parliamentary Labour Party were, however, vague and confused. Of the party in the 1920s, Robert Skidelsky has written:

It suffered in those days from a split personality: on the one hand it was committed to constitutionalism; on the other it lacked a social democratic or gradualist programme without which tenure of power was bound to be rather barren of achievement. It thought in terms of a total solution to the problem of poverty, when what it was offered [in 1929] was the limited opportunity to cure unemployment. It was a parliamentary party with a Utopian ethic. It was not fit for the kind of power it was called upon to exercise.[50]

MacDonald and Snowden, the most powerful figures in the party, had written at length on the meaning of socialism. In a remarkable parliamentary debate in 1923, Snowden introduced a motion calling for the gradual supersession of the capitalist system. But it was no more possible to administer a government by reference to the canon of socialist rhetoric than by consulting Bradshaw's, or Whitaker's Almanack.

This was the discovery, and the downfall, of the second Labour government. In August 1931 the MacDonald Cabinet was obliged to put together a programme of cuts in public expenditure to prevent a run on gold and the devaluation of the pound. Having agreed on severe economies, the Cabinet split on the question of whether to include in the package a 10 per cent cut in unemployment benefits, which the T.U.C. strongly opposed. MacDonald resigned, and was re-appointed at the head of the National government. The Labour Party not only expelled him, but turned him into a scapegoat. The Labour Cabinet had had nothing to offer in place of the remedies which the National government pursued. MacDonald had only taken bankruptcy of party purpose to its logical conclusion.

The General Council of the T.U.C. observed the collapse of the Labour government with dismay. Whether or not they had the right solution themselves, they did try to put forward positive alternatives in a report to Congress which has been described as 'immeasurably superior in its economic understanding to anything that emanated from the Treasury or its orthodox economic supporters.'[51]

The Labour Party spent the 1930s recovering from 1931, and painfully evolving a new strategy. Everyone in the party could agree that the next Labour government must, at all costs, prove its potency for action. But what action? Should the aim be a sudden, dramatic, and if need be violent transition to socialism? Or should Labour settle for a first instalment of socialism, accompanied by a selection of bread-and-butter measures? Rival schools of thought quickly surfaced, personified in the figures of Bevin and Sir Stafford Cripps. After Hitler's assumption of power in Germany in 1933, the controversy spread into the areas of foreign policy and rearmament. For some time there was confusion, with the party facing distractedly in several directions at once. However, in the years 1935 to 1937, the Bevinite school of thought finally established itself in control and put the Left in quarantine. As a result, Labour was at least a more coherent force with definite aims. By the end of 1937, the party was behaving more like a potential government than ever before.

From 1932 to 1935 the Parliamentary Party, decimated by the 1931 general election, could field only a weak team of front bench spokesmen. In effect, the party was led by George Lansbury with the help of Clement Attlee and Sir Stafford Cripps. Lansbury, 'the most lovable figure in modern politics',[52] was a devout pacifist in a world turning towards aggression; Cripps a brilliant barrister of unstable outlook,

currently gripped by jejune theories of international capitalist conspiracy; and Attlee, a shy, unimpressive, clerkly figure very much under
the influence of Cripps. Cripps was a fine propagandist and much the
best known Labour politician in the country, a fact for which the
Conservative press often had reason to be thankful. His violent
rhetoric against capitalism and the Establishment was a gift for Tory
propaganda.

A fresh source of leadership in the party after 1931 was provided by
the trade unions. The General Council of the T.U.C., under the
guidance of Bevin and Citrine, 'abandoned its usual role of being the
sheet-anchor of the party and instead moved in to take the helm.'[53]
The unions had great power at their disposal under the party constitution. At the annual party conference, the system of bloc voting
ensured them a big majority over any issue on which they co-ordinated
action. Until 1937, all twenty-three members of the National Executive
of the party were elected by ballot of the conference as a whole, another
potential means of union influence. Quite apart from this, the unions
provided the Labour Party with the bulk of its funds, and at every
general election sponsored over one hundred parliamentary candidates.
By co-ordinating union action, Bevin and Citrine obtained powerful
levers of control over the party. In part they worked through the
National Council of Labour, a committee for liaison between the
T.U.C. and the party, which now acquired considerable authority.
And as G. D. H. Cole observed, they transformed the annual congress
of the T.U.C. into 'a largely political assembly which, meeting only a
few weeks before the Labour Party Conference, could define the Trade
Union point of view and marshall the Trade Union battalions behind
the official policy. That done, the decisions made at the Trades Union
Congress could be re-registered at the Labour Party Conference with
the aid of the massed Trade Union vote.'[54]

In home affairs, Bevin took the initiative in 1932 with his pamphlet,
My Plan for 200,000 Workers, which proposed to create two million
more job opportunities by raising the school leaving age to sixteen,
encouraging earlier retirement, and shortening the working week.
Over defence and foreign policy, Bevin and Citrine were anxious to
swing Labour to a policy of armed resistance to the dictators through
the League of Nations.

Trying to push the party in a different direction were the socialist
intelligentsia who were also stirred to fresh activity by the catastrophe
of 1931. Most Labour intellectuals had accepted, with some qualms, the

gradualist doctrines of Ramsay MacDonald in the 1920s. MacDonald had taught that socialism would evolve from capitalism as the oak from the acorn. This view was now thoroughly discredited. Capitalism had plunged the working class into mass unemployment, demanded cuts in the working-class standard of living, and brought a Labour government to its knees. Most socialists concluded that henceforth the only way forward would lie through a sharp and decisive transformation to socialism, at some risk of upper-class sabotage and even civil war. The main rallying-point of these apocalyptic views was the Socialist League, in which Cripps soon became the dominating personality. G. R. Mitchison, a member of the League, wrote a much-discussed book, *The First Workers' Government* (1934), advocating an enabling act under which a future Labour government would nationalize most of the economy and redistribute wealth, bringing in socialism almost overnight. Attlee himself wrote about this time: 'The moment to strike is the moment of taking power when the Government is freshly elected and assured of its support. The blow struck must be a fatal one and not merely designed to wound and to turn a sullen and obstructive opponent into an active and deadly enemy.'[55]

At the universities, the rising generation of students on the left, Labour as well as Communist, was strongly influenced by Marxism — or perhaps only by Marxism as expounded by its interpreter John Strachey in a series of books beginning with *The Coming Struggle for Power* (1932). According to this analysis, capitalism was entering its last phase. In the capitalist world, the nations were being driven to greater exploitation of the workers at home, and a bitter struggle for international markets which must end in war. British workers could take no side in a struggle among capitalist powers: the only answer to fascism in Europe was revolution at home, leading on to world socialism. Such ideas blended to some extent with the traditional Labour belief that capitalism encouraged the arms race, while the arms race led to war. Indeed, the Parliamentary Labour Party opposed the first strengthening of the R.A.F., announced in July 1934, and the first measure of general rearmament proposed in the White Paper of March 1935, on the grounds that preparations for war intensified national rivalries. However, orthodox Labour also stood for collective security against aggression through the League of Nations. Thus its foreign policy, like its home policy, was remarkably ambiguous and confused.

In 1935 the leadership of the Parliamentary Party shifted towards the centre of the Labour spectrum. When Mussolini began to threaten war against Abyssinia, the party as a whole rallied to the cause of the League, and supported a policy of economic sanctions. Cripps, however, set himself against the prevailing mood, attacked the League as an imperialist plot, and lost his place among the leaders. Lansbury himself, as a pacifist, was in an embarrassing position. When the Labour Party conference assembled, literally on the eve of Mussolini's attack on Abysinnia, Bevin in a cruel speech drove Lansbury from the leadership. In the new parliament, Labour elected Clement Attlee as leader, and as if to symbolize the party's changing line on defence and foreign policy, Labour publicity often referred to him by his First World War rank as 'Major Attlee'. Meanwhile several ex-ministers had been returned to the Labour front bench to flank him, notably Hugh Dalton and Herbert Morrison.

Dalton and Morrison were chiefly responsible for Labour's new doctrines of economic planning in the 1930s. Dalton, like Cripps, was a renegade from the upper classes—an old Etonian, the son of Canon Dalton, domestic chaplain to Queen Victoria, Edward VII and George V. Like Cripps also, Dalton retained from his early years an innate sense of superiority, a ruling mentality displaced into left-wing politics. Bursting with ambition, he loved the rough and tumble of politics, intriguing noisily, clumsily, and without a blush. He was also a convinced reformer: By profession a lecturer in economics, Dalton gathered round him in the 1930s a circle of younger economists including Hugh Gaitskell, Evan Durbin and Douglas Jay, who devoted much time to thinking out the objectives and machinery of socialist planning. Fervently anti-Marxist in domestic politics, the Dalton kindergarten was none the less profoundly influenced by the example of Soviet planning. Parliamentary democrats as they were, they were not Keynesians, but apostles of strong legal and physical controls over the economy, foreshadowing the first years of the post-war Labour government, when Dalton was Chancellor of the Exchequer. A. L. Rowse, a young Labour intellectual who stood unsuccessfully for parliament in 1935, wrote a book to prove that Keynes's *General Theory* gave Labour the method for achieving all its goals: but he was remarkably in advance of his time.[56]

Throughout the 1930s, Dalton and his disciples worked closely with Herbert Morrison in reshaping Labour policy. The son of a London policeman, Morrison never had a settled trade or profession apart from that of political organizer, but in this he excelled. He had been Secretary of the London Labour Party since 1915, leader of the opposition on the London County Council since 1925, and chief organizer of Labour's victory in the County Council elections of 1934. From then until 1940 he was chairman of the Council, administering a £40 million-a-year budget from his office at County Hall. To red-blooded socialists in the Labour movement, Morrison exhibited the stultifying qualities of the bureaucrat. Michael Foot described him, not as a careerist, but as a 'soft-hearted, suburban Stalin, for ever suspecting others of the conspiracies in which he was engaged himself'.[57] However, in Morrison's day the cause of bureaucracy was very much bound up with the cause of social reform. To every social problem, better organization at the top was thought of as the remedy, and the Labour Left surpassed Morrison in their belief in five-year plans and high-powered boards of enlightened functionaries. Modest reform through modest bureaucracy was Morrison's aim. His biographers say of him:

> Morrison was very much the spokesman of his own class. He represented the suburbs, where lived the clerk, the minor civil servant, the municipal employee, the technician, the laboratory assistant, the elementary school teacher, the commercial traveller, the small tradesman and shopkeeper and the office executive. Morrison realized their significance as a new force in politics, totally different from the middle class of the nineteenth century. In alliance with the working class they could overturn the 'established' classes and create a 'well-ordered, well-run society in which neither accident of birth nor occupation determines the status of the individual, but only the efficiency of his contribution to the social whole.'[58]

Morrison's long experience of municipal services had persuaded him of the value of public utilities in place of private enterprise. He became a missionary for the gospel of the state-controlled public corporation. Instead of a nationalized industry being run by a minister and a Whitehall department, as Labour thinking had previously envisaged, it would be conducted by a largely independent public corporation, modelled on business enterprise and staffed by professional managers. Responsible to government for the broad outline of policy, the public corporation would take its place in the development of a planned economy. Perhaps Labour leaders, Morrison in particular, thought more about the machinery of planning than about its purpose in the 1930s. This was because they were able to take the purpose for granted: if the uncoordinated decisions of bankers and businessmen led to mass unemployment and deprivation, it seemed inevitable that once the state took the power of decision to itself, these evils would be avoided. Society need not be revolutionized from below when it could be reorganized from above. The Labour leaders planned to inherit the powers of businessmen and financiers and wield them in a more enlightened fashion, like Henry VIII taking over the Church from the Pope. That such powers might in themselves be the enemy of reform was unthinkable.

In the years 1935 to 1937 the Labour Party drew itself together and set itself more definite short-term aims. The gradual recovery of the economy from the slump confirmed, as Bevin had argued in 1932, that capitalism was adapting itself and in no danger of collapse. The disappointing result of the 1935 general election suggested that Labour must groom itself to appear more credible as an alternative government. The advance of the dictators reduced the importance of domestic issues. In 1937, through the influence of Bevin and Dalton, the Labour Party at last committed itself to a definite short-term policy, designed to be carried through in the lifetime of a single parliament.

Labour's Immediate Programme, which the party conference endorsed, could be analysed into three types of domestic measure: ameliorative proposals, socialization proposals, and prosperity proposals. Under the ameliorative heading the most important items were an increase in old-age pensions and the reduction of working hours. 'Health services will be extended', the document promised, 'and special measures will be taken to reduce maternal mortality.' The industries and services to be nationalized were the Bank of England, rural land, transport, coal, electricity, gas, and armaments manufacture. Finally the principal instrument of prosperity was to be a National Investment Board, 'whose duty will be to mobilize our financial resources ... and to advise the Government on a financial plan for the full employment of our people. Large schemes of Public Development, including Housing, Electrification, Transport, and the extraction of Oil from Coal, will be carried out.'[59] This programme was in sum no more left wing than that carried out by the post-war Labour government. The majority wing of Labour were passionate moderates *before* the war, but they lacked the opportunity of demonstrating it.

The Spanish Civil War, which broke out in July 1936, was a further blow to the pacific isolationism of Labour in foreign affairs. The cry of 'arms for Spain' suggested that it was illogical to oppose arms for Britain. Up to 1937 the Parliamentary Labour Party regularly voted against the defence estimates, but in July of that year Dalton persuaded the party to reverse its decision and abstain, a symbolic acceptance of the need for rearmament.

As Chamberlain plunged into the deep end of appeasement, Labour quietly began to fall under the influence of the leading Conservative opponents of his foreign policy. Anthony Eden, who resigned as Foreign Secretary in February 1938, had always impressed Labour by his apparent loyalty to the League, and air of youthful idealism. Even Winston Churchill, who had previously been regarded as a reactionary diehard, was grudgingly admired. There was an instructive incident after the Munich crisis of September 1938, when Cripps saw Dalton and urged a common front with the anti-appeasement Conservatives: 'He thought we could agree on a programme to preserve our democratic liberties, to rebuild collective security, and for the national control of our economic life. He would put Socialism aside for the present.'[60] The 1939 Labour party conference went through the motions of preparing to fight the Conservatives at a general election. But in truth, Labour by the end of the 1930s was looking hopefully to one wing of the Conservatives to save them from the other.

II Labour at the Gates 1939–1940

At the outbreak of war in September 1939, the Chamberlain government had 418 seats in the House to the 167 seats held by the Labour Party, and an overall majority of more than 200. If parliamentary numbers were the sole test, the Conservatives were in a position to maintain a monopoly of power throughout the war. But on 8 May 1940, at the end of a two-day debate on the failure of the British expeditionary force to Norway, Labour challenged a division and, in effect, moved a vote of no confidence in the conduct of the war. Chamberlain's majority fell to eighty-one. Forty of the backbench M.P.s on his own side had joined with the Labour Party in voting against the government; about forty Conservatives may have abstained.[1] It is often said that this vote sealed Chamberlain's fate, but he was reluctant to draw this conclusion himself. He sought desperately to carry on at the head of a reconstructed administration. The final and decisive event in forcing him to resign was a telephone call from Attlee on 10 May, declaring that Labour would not serve under him. The debate over Norway was also a debate about the necessity of a Coalition government. The critics of Chamberlain wanted not only to remove him as Prime Minister but also to establish an all-party government. The prosecution of the war depended upon the wholehearted participation of the Labour movement in the war effort. Thus a small and elderly Labour Party in the House was able to dismiss a Conservative Prime Minister and enter a new government as equal partners with the Tories.

When Chamberlain entered Downing Street as Prime Minister in May 1937, he had little reason to fear Labour. The Labour Party in the House was still repeating slogans about disarmament and collective security, an entirely ineffectual exercise. The T.U.C. was a slumbering giant with which Chamberlain rarely dealt. However, there were signs of change early in 1938. Having set his course for appeasement, Chamberlain quarrelled with his Foreign Secretary, Anthony Eden, and allowed him to resign. Eden and his coterie of about twenty backbench disciples provided evidence of a split in the Conservative ranks which Labour might be able to exploit. Nor was it mere party tactics for Labour to drive a wedge through the Conservatives: Labour M.P.s believed that the fate of parliamentary democracy was at stake, both in Western Europe and Britain itself. Moreover, having swung round to support for rearmament, Labour were now a much more effective opposition. They deployed facts and figures which unsettled the government benches. Labour played an important part in driving the Secretary for Air, Swinton, from office in May 1938. In June, Attlee presented the government with a memorandum on the state of air defences. An Air Ministry memorandum observed that it contained 'a substantial amount of information as to numbers of aircraft on order and other matters which can have been derived only from deliberate disclosure of strictly confidential information by persons serving in the Air Force or employed by the Air Ministry.'[2]

The German occupation of Austria in March 1938 inaugurated a period of war crisis which was resolved only by the declaration of war itself. The more far-sighted Conservatives realized that a sustained campaign of rearmament was essential, and could only be conducted through co-operation with the trade union movement. Some, like Eden, went further, and urged that a genuinely national government should be formed so that Britain could act in foreign affairs from a basis of unity and strength. However, there was much bad blood between Chamberlain and the Labour movement. In the defeat of the General Strike, the formation of the National government of 1931, and the introduction of the means test, he had been a key figure. His closest adviser and friend, Sir Horace Wilson, had been Permanent Secretary at the Ministry of Labour in 1926. These hostile feelings came to the surface in the spring of 1938, when Chamberlain invited the General Council of the T.U.C. to Downing Street for talks about the speeding up of rearmament. When the union delegates went away and began to talk among themselves, Chamberlain's argument that Britain was militarily too weak began to excite suspicion. If more arms were manufactured, what would they be used for? Did the latest Anglo-Italian agreement imply a military commitment to aid the fascist powers? Would not the victory of General Franco in Spain mean German or Italian domination of that country? If the unions relaxed their craft rules, what guarantee was there that they would be restored? Chamberlain met the General Council representatives a second time, and gave reassuring replies on all these points: but as the government refused to intervene to secure dilution agreements in particular industries, collaboration proceeded no further during 1938. A striking feature of the discussions was the readiness of Citrine, the T.U.C. General Secretary, to sympathize with Chamberlain over the opinions of 'ill-informed' trade union leaders. But when he suggested a Council of State on which trade union leaders would serve, thus becoming better informed, Chamberlain characterized it as a 'dangerous innovation'.[3]

In the Czech crisis of September 1938, as the British government steadily yielded to Hitler's threats of force, the Labour leaders spoke the language of national resistance with growing fluency, leaving the majority Conservatives to speak of peace and conciliation. When news arrived that Britain and France were, in effect, ordering the Czechs to agree to the partition of their own country, there was a highly charged meeting of the National Council of Labour. Dalton, Citrine, and A. V. Alexander, the secretary of the Co-operative Parliamentary Committee, were among those deputed to express Labour's indignation to the Foreign Secretary, Lord Halifax. For once, Citrine spoke uncompromisingly:

> Britain and France were throwing Czechoslovakia to the wolves.
> It would mean that the British government had surrendered to
> bullying, and was showing itself utterly credulous by trusting a
> man whose word was valueless ... Sir Walter Citrine said that the
> National Council were not nervous about the future if a deter-
> mined stand was made now against Germany. From their own
> sources of information they had reason to believe that Herr Hitler's
> internal position was by no means strong, and that the alleged
> strength of German armaments was exaggerated.

A. V. Alexander 'warned the Government that they were playing with the life of the British Empire; time was on the side of the dictators and, unless a firm stand was made, this country's day was past.'[4] When a nation goes to war it is frequently the case that the 'hawks', having long championed war preparation and an abrasive foreign policy, benefit politically at the expense of the 'doves'. This happened in

Britain in the First World War, to the great advantage of the Conservative Party. By a strange exchange of roles in the late 1930s, Labour became the 'hawks', the Chamberlainite Conservatives the 'doves'.

The Munich Agreement, snatching peace from war, gave rise to a wave of popular relief, and tempted Conservative Party managers to capitalize upon the theme of 'Chamberlain the peacemaker' by holding a general election. But there was another side to the coin. Munich had exposed the inadequacy of British defences and emphasized the need for rearmament, and hence the need for Labour's co-operation. This was one of the considerations (another being an eloquent speech by a backbench member, Sir Sidney Herbert) which led Chamberlain to decide against an immediate election. The chairman of the Conservative Party, Douglas Hacking, confided to the right-wing journalist, Collin Brooks, that rearmament was impossible without the goodwill of the unions, and to achieve this it might be necessary to broaden the basis of the government. A general election would stir up bitterness and prevent co-operation: 'It may seem strange to you, with your right-wing views, that we have to tolerate such a position that we cannot defend the nation against the will of the unions, but there it is. It is part of the price we have to pay for this alleged democracy.'[5]

In the New Year of 1939 the T.U.C. collaborated with the government's voluntary National Service campaign, and discussions were held with the Ministry of Labour about the wartime regulation of wages, industrial disputes, and the supply of labour. A species of contract between Conservatism and the unions was slowly evolving. When Chamberlain introduced conscription in the spring of 1939, he pledged in return that the government would adopt a policy of 'taking the profit out of war'. There were bitter memories on the Labour side of the fortunes made by government contractors in the First World War. Chamberlain promised a wartime excess profits tax, to be levied on increases in profit above an average pre-war level.[6] (It was in fact introduced at the outbreak of war, at a rate of 60 per cent.) But the détente with the unions was painfully slow. When a Ministry of Supply was at last set up in July 1939, an advisory industrial panel consisting solely of businessmen was appointed. Labour were still so alienated from Chamberlain that Bevin was inclined almost to blame Britain rather than Germany for the war crisis. On 30 May 1939 he told the annual Labour party conference: 'Behind Chamberlain are the bankers; they are the principal supporters of appeasement for Germany. They do not want justice for the German masses – that is quite a different thing. I am anxious to prevent this movement fighting for the preservation of the Paris Bourse, the London Stock Exchange, the Amsterdam Exchange, and Wall Street.'[7]

In spite of Hitler's attack on Poland on 1 September 1939, and the British declaration of war two days later, there was remarkably little change on the 'home front', as it was now called. The peace had long been a bogus one, and the war proved to be equally bogus. Chamberlain set up a War Cabinet of nine members, and, bowing to the inevitable, included in it the prophet of Armageddon, Winston Churchill, as First Lord of the Admiralty. Anthony Eden returned to office, outside the War Cabinet, as Secretary for the Dominions. Otherwise the Old Firm remained in charge.

Hitler's forces conquered Poland in three weeks, and there ensued the 'phoney war', a phase of eerie calm in the West, with life itself muffled at the turn of the year beneath an arctic blanket of extreme winter. At home, although the stage was set by the evacuation of children to the countryside, the black-out, the carrying of gas-masks and the sandbagging of buildings, the bombs did not fall. There was no atmosphere of urgency in everyday life. At the highest level, there were hopes that the war would peter out without bloodshed. Basil Liddell Hart, the military historian and commentator, forecast that the Maginot and Siegfried lines, the defensive positions of the French and the Germans, would prove too strong for the attack, and that stalemate would persist. The government quietly encouraged the belief that victory would be achieved through economic blockade. On 8 September the War Cabinet announced that planning would proceed on the assumption of a war lasting three years. The decision was taken to build up an army of fifty-five divisions. But would there be any real fighting? Mass-Observation, in its study of the opening months of the war, concluded: 'It is difficult to over-estimate the importance of wishful-thinking in Britain. It colours every day of the war both for the masses and for the leaders. It makes it all the more difficult to deal with the reality situations and dangers in the future.'[8]

The government still found considerable difficulties in dealing with the trade unions. Whitehall had at first behaved as though they did not exist. The Ministries of Supply and Food were set up without central or local trade union representation. But after a T.U.C. deputation to Chamberlain on 5 October, Chamberlain brought about a sudden and

considerable reversal of outlook. Within the month both ministries
had agreed to plans for machinery to represent the unions, and
Chamberlain issued a circular to all government departments calling on
them to ensure the maximum co-operation with the T.U.C.[9] The
government were aware too of the need to prevent the industrial
unrest which might follow from inflation: from the New Year of 1940
subsidies were introduced to keep down food prices and stabilize the
cost of living index.

If, however, Labour felt bound to co-operate in the war effort, they
could only go so far and no further. Parliamentary leaders who collaborated in a Chamberlain government would almost certainly have
split the party: undoubtedly the cry of treason would have gone up
from the party rank and file. By the spring of 1940 there were fifty-one
resolutions on the agenda of the party conference calling for the
termination of the by-election truce. Such was grass-roots feeling that
at the annual general meeting of the Halifax Labour Party, with more
than seventy members present, a motion was passed unanimously in
favour of a negotiated peace, the risks of which 'cannot compare in
disastrousness for the workers, to a military victory by this or any other
capitalist government'.[10] There was a deep fear that if the Conservatives were left to run the war, it would end in another terrible slump,
with war workers thrown on the scrap heap. Citrine might as always
afford Chamberlain some comfort, but Bevin's was the more important
voice. The Prime Minister's policy, he declared on 9 January, was a
bankers' and rentiers' policy, which could only result in outbreaks of
labour troubles. When Keynes put forward his plan for reducing
working-class purchasing power through compulsory saving, and a
minimum standard for the poorer worker, Bevin was hostile. The
workers were being asked to lend money to prosecute the war, he
said, and they would be called upon to bear the burden of unemployment after it.[11]

In December 1939 the social reformer Seebohm Rowntree wrote to
Bevin, who was still General Secretary of the biggest union in the
country, suggesting that 'all efforts to improve living standards should,
for the moment, be set aside in the interests of the State.' Bevin
replied:

> My time has been taken up in trying to get wages commensurate
> with the cost of living. I am determined to keep them up to a
> proper level. The powers that be have won in the first round but

that is only a temporary victory for them. As our people sicken of this business they will revolt against the depression of their standards.

I disagree entirely with your thesis and the answer to it is in the last paragraph. No employer will make sacrifices unless he is compelled to. All the prices I have seen fixed, and the charges being made, indicate that taxation and everything else is included and the Employers rake off the top, and in this farcical state of Society for one class to be trying to measure another upon a fodder basis is intolerable.

Keynes, having read this letter, wrote to Lord Stamp: 'That letter of Bevin is truly shocking. Almost the worst thing I have read since the beginning of the war. However, his bark is often worse than his bite, and I should not yet despair of getting him round to some sort of rational scheme.' Chamberlain commented, on 15 January 1940: 'I fear that there is no doubt that we must expect persistent opposition from Bevin to all attempts at separating wages from cost of living.'[12] Thus the class war dragged on into the 'phoney war', stalemated like the western front.

Perhaps the most critical aspect of relations with the trade unions was the need of the government for supplies of skilled manpower in the munitions industries. In January 1940 a Whitehall committee under Humbert Wolfe had presented to the Cabinet an estimate of the additional manpower required in order to meet the targets fixed for the rate of expansion of the services. It was estimated that in certain key munitions industries, the labour force would have to be increased by 70 per cent by the period July to September 1940. At the beginning of May the Cabinet received a survey of the manpower figures for a slightly more selective group of industries. Churchill produced a powerful paper demonstrating that the existing rate of manpower expansion in these industries was one-sixth of what it ought to be. The government's Chief Economic Advisor, Lord Stamp, urged the necessity of controlling wages and the movement of labour. The Ministry of Labour had previously resisted the idea, sensing that the trade unions could only be dealt with through voluntary negotiations. At the outset of the war, the Labour Party and the T.U.C. together had emasculated the Control of Employment Act, with the result that the government had few powers over labour and hesitated to put even these into effect. But at a ministerial meeting on 8 May – the second day, as it happened, of the debate which brought Chamberlain down – the Minister of Labour, Ernest Brown, was obliged to promise that he would request from the War Cabinet powers to control the recruitment and movement of labour.[13]

On 1 September Chamberlain had invited the Labour Party to join his government. The executive of the Parliamentary Party decided unanimously against. When R. A. Butler, the Under-Secretary at the Foreign Office, asked Dalton why they had refused, Dalton replied that Labour could not enter a Cabinet in which Chamberlain and Simon were Numbers One and Two: and they would also require the influence of Horace Wilson to be eliminated.[14] As long as Chamberlain and his men held the key positions, they would be the ultimate controllers, and Labour wanted a genuine distribution of power. But they were tactically in a delicate position – They supported the war effort, and up to a point this required collaboration with the government. On 8 September, for example, the Chief Whips of the three major parties signed an electoral truce covering by-elections. By this agreement, the party which had previously won the seat would have the right, when it fell vacant, to nominate a candidate unopposed by the other two parties. Attlee had to reassure party activists that there was no *political* truce (as Conservatives sometimes alleged). But no country at war could tolerate an uncontrolled party conflict. In the House, liaison arrangements were established between the government and opposition front benches, whereby a government minister from time to time gave his Labour opposite number a confidential briefing on some aspect of war policy. Positive co-operation between local Labour and Conservative parties was required in the setting up of the Ministry of Information's local committees. In April the Labour Party agreed to take part in a joint platform campaign by politicians of the three main parties in support of the war effort.[15] All this could be seen as the thin end of the wedge. In March there was a strong rumour that Chamberlain had offered Labour three seats in the Cabinet, and that A. V. Alexander, Morrison and Greenwood were seriously considering the idea, while Attlee was against.[16] Greenwood had boasted soon after the outbreak of war that the government could not last a day without the help and co-operation of Labour. But it was obvious too that as there could be no general election, the parties in the House would in the end have to work together.

Chamberlain was peculiarly ill-suited to bring the transformation about. In the small world of the House of Commons, Baldwin had taken great care to encourage and befriend Labour M.P.s, most of whom were elderly trade unionists with an Achilles' heel of senti- mentality. But even Attlee, a far more astringent personality, had warmed to Baldwin's avuncular style. Harold Laski spoke of Baldwin as 'one of the best souls who ever breathed'. Chamberlain, however, had no emotional rapport with Labour —merely an intellectual disdain for Labour doctrines. He dreaded, he wrote once, the prospect of an 'ignorant, ill-prepared and over-pledged opposition' coming to power in a slump. A close colleague of Chamberlain, Sir John Simon, com- mented in May 1940: 'These Labour men, though many of them are very good fellows, are extremely "class conscious" in the sense that they are always watching out for rebukes supposed to be addressed to their inferior intellectual equipment ... When Chamberlain is faced with a half-baked argument, he exposes it.'[17] Chamberlain's Chief Whip, David Margesson, wrote after his leader's fall: 'He engendered personal dislike among his opponents to an extent almost unbelievable ... I believe the reason was that his cold intellect was too much for them, he beat them up in argument and debunked their catchphrases. Those of us who have lived in the country districts know how much a man whom they call "sarcastic" is disliked. It's a form of mental inferiority which produces hate.' Attlee recalled: 'He always treated us like dirt.'[18]

The Parliamentary Labour Party found themselves between the devil and the deep blue sea, inhibited from outright opposition or co-operation. They could be sure that if the war developed into a serious struggle, they would have to be called in. But would it? In December 1939 Herbert Morrison remarked to a foreign office official, Charles Peake, that 'if the war continued as it had begun he thought the Prime Minister would see it through in his present office and he doubted whether there was a better man.' On another occasion, he told Peake most of the Labour front bench were frightened of power, while few were capable of adding any drive to the government.[19] For the time being, the Labour Party acted as patriotic gadflies, offering the type of practical criticism of the organization of the war effort which often sprang from Conservative lips, while keeping up the pressure over social services and benefits. A commentator in the *Political Quarterly* shrewdly advised them to wait until the course of the war exposed to the government backbenchers the inadequacy of their leaders. A munitions crisis similar to that of 1915 was bound to arise, owing to the resistance of the civil service, and particularly the Treasury, to economic planning. Labour must have the courage to stand aside and let the government commit suicide.[20]

The seventeen Liberal M.P.s under the leadership of Sir Archibald Sinclair, a clubbable Old Etonian, ex-Guards officer, and boon companion of Winston Churchill, were in the same predicament. At the outbreak of war, Chamberlain had invited the Liberals into the government, dangling before Sinclair a post of Cabinet rank but outside the War Cabinet. The Liberals decided that they could not be expected to accept the responsibility for the decisions of the government if they had no share in the central control of policy.[21] When the story reached H. G. Crookshank, one of the younger ministers in the government, he noted: 'What a fool Chamberlain is and how mean minded—as if they could look at such an offer.'[22]

Some things about the past can never be proved, and must always be the subject of hunches and guesswork: and it is only fair for a historian to warn his readers when he is operating on a hunch. To this writer it appears that the eclipse of Conservatism in World War II began with the political misjudgments of Neville Chamberlain during the 'twilight war'. One of the mental blocks to be overcome in thinking about wartime politics is the assumption that during a great crusade against evil, calculations of personal or party advantage had to be swept aside, leaving the 'national interest' as the sole guide to action. The sources prove the reverse. No politician worth his salt could fail to believe that he could contribute more to the winning of the war than certain other persons he could name. Every government department believed that, in the interests of victory, it should have a greater voice than some less vital department on a particular committee. Political parties jostled one another to appropriate the credit for their contribution to the war effort. Churchill himself claimed, in March 1942, that when the war was won the Conservative Party would prove to have been 'the main part of the rock on which the salvation of Britain was founded and the freedom of mankind regained.'[23] To see the formation of the Coalition government of May 1940 simply as 'the nation closing its ranks' would be a mistake. The Coalition was formed in a particular fashion. It might have been formed as the result of an invitation from the Conservative leadership to Labour to join in the running of the war, in which case the Conservatives would have retained the initiative in high-level politics. In fact it resulted from the public shipwreck of a Conservative administration, and the corollary was that Labour were not in reality *given* office: they broke in and took it, on terms of moral equality. In the context of these conclusions, a hypothesis about the politics of the 'phoney war' can be advanced. Had Chamberlain been thinking in terms of another great war he would have set his course towards Coalition, with the aim of keeping events under the control oi the Conservative Party. In fact, he expected a more limited war. This is a well-substantiated point: in Chamberlain's view Hitler was only bluffing, and would not dare submit the people of Germany to the deprivations of a second conflict. He was inclined to argue, for example, that Hitler would shrink from air attack on Britain for fear of the consequences to German morale if Britain retaliated; instead, he would rely upon propaganda.[24] Chamberlain must have imagined that, since the war was turning out to be a damp squib, it would be possible to get through it without any major upheaval in the pre-war order. The Conservatives, with at the most token reinforcements from the opposition, would wind up the war on their own. There would be the minimum disturbance of normality. Hence Chamberlain, through a more or less conscious gamble on a limited war, inflicted a débâcle on his party.

Such may, at any rate, be the explanation of Chamberlain's imperviousness to high-level disquiet, often voiced by leading Conservatives, over his conduct of the 'phoney war'. At the outbreak of the war, Chamberlain's convinced critics in the party were the same handful of backbenchers who had opposed the Munich Agreement, but no longer under the leadership of Churchill and Eden, who had joined the government. The Eden group was now presided over by L. S. Amery, a privy councillor and senior figure devoted to the cause of the British Empire. Amery would gladly have taken office in September 1939, but no one took up his offer. Like Duff Cooper, the one member of the Cabinet who had resigned at Munich, Amery was forced to stay on the sidelines, bottling up his indignation. When Amery's name was suggested for a job Chamberlain 'pushed it away with an irritated snort'.[25] The Eden group continued to dine, grumble, and arrange to dine again. Perhaps Chamberlain could afford to ignore such a small group, yet with members of the calibre of General Sir Louis Spears, who had been head of the British military mission in Paris at the close of World War I, and the ambitious and overlooked Harold Macmillan, it was a potential source of trouble. More significant was Chamberlain's resistance to criticism from other quarters, and his apparent deafness to warning sounds from hitherto loyal backbenchers.

*

A month after the outbreak of war, a campaign was started by William Beveridge to establish tighter state direction of the economy. In the First World War, Beveridge had been a key civil servant in the Ministry of Munitions and later in the Ministry of Food. In the autumn of 1939 he was one of a number of economists, all of whom had been civil servants in 1914-18, who now lacked employment in government: Layton, Keynes, and Arthur Salter. Devoid of partisan feeling, they felt they had a constructive contribution to make, and from their talks resulted an article by Beveridge in *The Times* on 3 October. Sooner or later, he argued, the whole economy must be planned, and for this two agencies were required, one to collect data — an 'economic general staff'—and one to make decisions—a War Cabinet on the Lloyd George model, consisting of a few energetic ministers with no departmental responsibilities. One of them should act as Minister for Economic Co-ordination.

By tradition the Conservative Party were opposed to state intervention in the economy. But with true pragmatism they had grasped the need in 1914-18 for state control, championed it against the hesitations of Asquith, and found in Lloyd George an emergency dictator for the home front. Men like Waldorf Astor (the proprietor of the *Observer*) and Geoffrey Dawson (the editor of *The Times*) had championed Lloyd George and his methods in 1916, and now expected Chamberlain to follow in his footsteps. The ghost of Lloyd George past came back to haunt the Conservatives, and the spirit of Lloyd George present, almost as sparkling and zestful as ever, eloquently refreshed their memory. Lloyd George had done this, and done that: why was Chamberlain not doing likewise? It could also be recalled that one of Lloyd George's strokes of policy had turned out badly – the appointment of Chamberlain himself as director of national service.

There were many criticisms of particular departments during the 'phoney war' period. The Ministry of Supply, since it supplied only the Army while the other two services had their own supply organizations, was a sitting duck for critics of half-measures. There were strong attacks on the Ministry of Economic Warfare for allowing loopholes in the blockade. The Ministry of Information was the prime target of all. Set up to channel news to the press, and maintain morale at home by publicity and propaganda, the ministry at once distinguished itself by its amateurism and muddle. In October 1939 its press and censorship functions were hived off into a separate bureau responsible to the Home Secretary, and Chamberlain seriously considered winding up the ministry. When he appointed Sir John Reith as Minister in January 1940, he failed to give him any clear support or directions. The fact was that Chamberlain regarded the press with disdain, and publicity as a vulgar necessity to which he could scarcely bring himself. The Ministry of Information, he told Reith in March, was an exotic: it pertained to dictatorship; special measures had to be taken to graft it on to the democratic system.[26] The Chamberlain government was too staid to develop a flair for public relations. Symbolic of this was the ambiguous character of the slogan devised by the Deputy Secretary of the Ministry of Information, A. P. Waterfield, for its first poster campaign: '*Your* courage, *your* cheerfulness, *your* resolution, will bring us victory.'[27]

The major criticism of Chamberlain centred on his refusal to institute stronger co-ordination of the economy. In economic affairs there were several departments leading independent lives – the Board of Trade, the Ministries of Labour, Supply, Food, Shipping, and Economic Warfare. They were co-ordinated by two committees under Treasury control: an official committee under the Chief Economic Adviser, Lord Stamp, and a ministerial committee under the Chancellor of the Exchequer, Sir John Simon. As the newly elected National Labour M.P., Stephen King-Hall, observed, criticism fastened on the inability of Simon to double the roles of Minister in charge of the Treasury *and* grand strategist of the economy.[28] Some light relief was afforded by the revelation that Stamp worked only part-time, half his schedule being devoted to the affairs of the London and North Eastern Railway, of which he was a director. The demand continued for a War Cabinet minister to be placed in charge of economic affairs, supported by an economic general staff. There were questions of personality, as well as principle, at stake. The Labour Party loathed Simon, and his Permanent Secretary Sir Horace Wilson, as arch-appeasers and class enemies.

As for Chamberlain himself, the various criticisms of his methods cut very much deeper in view of his general lack of political judgment, and uninspiring style. No one had adored him more than the Conservative M.P. for Plymouth, and hostess of Cliveden, Lady Astor. But this was her account of a private speech made by Chamberlain to the Conservative backbench 1922 Committee in November 1939:

The P.M. spoke with vigour and he looked extremely well, but what he said has depressed me more than anything else since the

war began ... He said that the critics had been confounded, and the
Axis instead of working was breaking ... he implied that the
Government's policy had been definitely planned and carried out,
and that we had entered upon the war fully prepared, when
everyone knows that the Russian–German alliance altered the whole
face of things. He sneered at the Labour Party for not coming in,
and said we were better off without them. Worse than all, he said
that some people were talking about what we would do after the
war, but there could only be one thing before us – winning the
war ...

I am sure that he meant it to be a fighting speech, but its effect on
me was to make me wish that Winston were P.M. (This was
only momentary, and I know it was wrong, but that was my
reaction!)[29]

Chamberlain's appointments sometimes created real astonishment in
the small world of parliamentary politics. That Chatfield should be
made Minister for the Co-ordination of Defence in January 1939,
Leslie Burgin put in charge of Supply in July, or Sir John Gilmour
made Minister for Shipping in October, means little to us now, but at
the time they were examples of breathtaking indifference to informed
opinion. Hoare wrote, in retrospect (and self-justification): 'Undoubtedly his two worst advisers were Horace Wilson and David
Margesson, both of them determined to keep everything in their own
hands and to keep out of the Government any one who was not in their
particular swim. The worst appointments were invariably due to
them.'[30]

Waldorf Astor was one of the first to lose faith in Chamberlain.
Having been Lloyd George's Parliamentary Secretary in 1918, he felt
strongly about the discrepancy between Lloyd George's methods and
Chamberlain's, and was soon arguing in private that Churchill must be
Prime Minister. At *The Times* Dawson consistently pressed for a
reformed War Cabinet and economic co-ordination along the lines
proposed by Beveridge. 'The P.M. was rather worried by *The Times*
on the Economic Front', he noted after an important debate on the
subject.[31] Another dissonant voice was raised by Wilson's predecessor
as permanent head of the Treasury, Warren Fisher. Having become
disillusioned with Chamberlain since 1937, he was convinced that the
Prime Minister and his friends were mediocrities. In his new job of
Regional Commissioner for the North-West, where he was in touch

with the Manchester business community, he accused the government in a public speech of 'showering spanners and monkey wrenches into the industrial machine' and called for the appointment of a Cabinet minister to provide real economic planning.[32] On the eve of a debate in December on the export trade, the Vice-President of the Federation of British Industries, Lord Dudley Gordon, called on the President of the Board of Trade, Oliver Stanley. He showed him a draft press statement in which the Federation called for the appointment of a single minister for economic policy. Stanley persuaded him to shelve the statement for the time being, and wrote to Chamberlain telling him that he wholeheartedly agreed with the Federation's proposal. But in the debate Stanley was obliged to make a bantering speech on the theme that all was well, arguing a case he did not believe in.[33]

From the government's backbenches a new gadfly appeared: Clement Davies, a Liberal M.P. in the parliament of 1929-31, who had followed Simon into the National Liberal group, and acquired a directorship in Unilever. (Davies was eventually to be leader of the Liberal Party from 1945 to 1956.) After the outbreak of war Davies became chairman of the All-Party Parliamentary Action Group, a forum organized by Eleanor Rathbone in which M.P.s could discuss frankly the progress of the war, and act as a ginger-group to the administration. One of the founder members of the group was Robert Boothby, an he, unlike Miss Rathbone, wanted to hitch the group to the fortunes of Lloyd George, and convert it into an engine for the overthrow of the government. Perhaps it was Boothby who introduced Davies to the group: at any rate Davies suddenly appeared there as chairman. Boothby then tried and failed to carry a resolution 'to separate the sheep from the goats', and the group carried on as an open forum for M.P.s of all parties. Nevertheless Davies, Boothby and Lloyd George kept in close touch, as they were to do in the critical debate which brought Chamberlain down. Davies and Boothby were both active in the group's economic sub-committee, whose members dined regulary at the Reform Club with figures such as Keynes, Layton, Salter, and the financier Robert Brand, a director of *The Times*.[34] Davies' prescription for the home front was the usual one of a Lloyd George style War Cabinet assisted by an economic general staff. In December he wrote to Chamberlain resigning the Government whip on the grounds that the administration lacked 'the resolution, policy or energy demanded by the country and the situation itself'.[35]

Trouble was developing in curious quarters. Wing-Commander A. W. H. James, one of General Franco's more open admirers in Britain, was disgruntled by the government's failure to keep down wages. He wrote to Simon: 'You must not be surprised—and I say this as a former loyal supporter of the National Government—if the time is not far distant when many of us will feel obliged to seek the defeat of the Government in order to obtain its reconstruction.'[36] Ralph Glyn, Conservative M.P. for Abingdon and a man with important business interests and connections, told his constituents in the New Year that parliament had reassembled with an increased lack of confidence in certain ministers, notably the Ministers of Agriculture and Food. In the manufacturing centres, he continued, there was a well-founded belief that the economic war was not being prosecuted with sufficient vigour. Many members' support for the government was being severely strained, and might snap unless the Prime Minister made a drastic reconstruction of the Cabinet.[37]

Chamberlain made some effort to appease his critics. A beginning was made in the establishment of a small Central Economic Service, to assist Stamp. The Prime Minister even tried to remove Simon. Montagu Norman, the Governor of the Bank of England, wanted him sacked. On 2 January Chamberlain invited Stamp to become Chancellor, and proposed the extraordinary expedient of taking away Stamp's peerage by Act of Parliament. He assured Stamp that he would be able to remove Simon without creating bad feeling. The Hore-Belisha affair probably accounts for Chamberlain changing his mind and keeping Simon on. Under pressure from the military top brass Chamberlain was planning to move Hore-Belisha from the War Office to another job. Hore-Belisha refused to be moved, and resigned. He and Simon were the two leading National Liberals in the government, with about thirty followers. They could not both be axed at once.[38] Simon remained, an increasing liability.

Chamberlain reshuffled the Cabinet after Hore-Belisha's departure, bringing in Sir Andrew Duncan, Chairman of the British Iron and Steel Federation, as President of the Board of Trade, and Sir John Reith, the former Director-General of the B.B.C., as Minister of Information. The reshuffle was generally well received, but *The Times* pointed out that it was only an interim measure. Chamberlain would have to return one day to the question of the size and character of the War Cabinet, and the case for greater co-ordination of the economic front.[39]

Labour decided to force a debate on the issue and on 1 February

Herbert Morrison, in his most emollient mood, introduced a motion calling for a Cabinet minister to be put in charge of economic affairs. It was a good tactic, isolating Chamberlain from his party. The *Manchester Guardian* lobby correspondent wrote that apart from the Treasury, there was no support for Chamberlain's line: parliament, the press, economists and industrialists all agreed with Labour. Chamberlain refused, however, to take his critics' proposals seriously, and was rebuked by *The Times* and the *Daily Telegraph*.[40] 'We are bound', wrote Hoare to Lothian, 'to go cautiously with labour questions such as the introduction of women and dilution, at a time when the fighting has not started and labour and industry are not keyed up to the extreme sacrifices of a war effort.'[41] There was also a simple reason for skirting around the problem, which Chamberlain had candidly advanced during the debate: '... the existence of a Minister who was a dictator over all those Departments ... would challenge the position of the Prime Minister, because I do not quite see what the Prime Minister would have to do by the time this gentleman had given his orders to all the Departments ... '[42]

Many Conservative M.P.s judged the state of war production by their knowledge of shortages of equipment in the Army and the R.A.F. By January 1940, sixty-two government backbenchers were on active service in the Army, sixteen with the R.A.F., and seven with the Royal Navy. There was indeed a Serving Members Committee, with Major Victor Cazalet as chairman and Flying Officer Hamilton Kerr as secretary, to discuss service problems. These were undoubtedly worst in the Army. The government had decided only in the spring of 1939 that in the event of war a British Expeditionary Force should be sent to the Continent. At about the same time, the size of the Territorial Army had been doubled at a stroke, from thirteen to twenty-six divisions, as a political gesture to appease backbench anxieties. In consequence, hardly a unit of the B.E.F. went to France properly equipped during the 'phoney war', while the Territorials were acutely short of supplies. When the first parliamentary secret session of the war was held on 13 December 1939, a number of serving M.P.s sought leave from their regiments to air their complaints. Amery recorded how Chamberlain, replying to his critics 'with an extraordinary unconscious naïveté, explained that it was absurd to complain of inadequacy of supplies when he had only begun to think of having an Army on the Continent, even of five divisions, as late as March, of anything more after we had guaranteed Poland in April, of anything required to equip a really substantial force after we had accepted universal service.'[43]

In January, Fleet Street tried to create a sensation on behalf of the Secretary of State for War, Leslie Hore-Belisha, when Chamberlain dismissed him on the prompting of Generals Ironside and Gort, the C.I.G.S and Commander of the B.E.F. Most M.P.s, believing that Hore-Belisha had been misleading the public about the state of the Army's equipment, were well content to see him depart.[44]

The winter of 1939–40 was marked by an episode which, in retrospect, seems wholly irrational. The Russian attack on Finland at the end of November created a wave of sympathy for Finland in Britain and France, and in government circles plans were drawn up to assist the Finns. On 12 March 1940 the Cabinet actually decided to send a British expedition across Norway and Sweden to Finland. This is not the place to discuss the motivation of these plans, except to note that at the time Germany was receiving considerable economic benefit from her pact with Russia, while the British expedition was also intended to seize the iron ore mines in northern Sweden from which Germany derived most of her supplies. Attlee and Greenwood expressed to the Foreign Secretary, Lord Halifax, their great anxiety lest assistance to Finland escalate into war with Russia. But the Labour leadership was split. The General Secretary of the T.U.C., Walter Citrine, and Philip Noel-Baker, a front bench spokesman, had visited Finland on a Labour Party delegation and become ardent for all possible help to this tiny nation menaced by Stalinism. Halifax told the Cabinet that they 'evinced the strongest hostility against the Soviet Union'. With one squadron of Hurricane fighters about to be sent to Finland, Noel-Baker urged Halifax that a second should be sent, as it would 'do tremendous havoc among the Russian aircraft in the Isthmus'. While personally urging the dispatch of R.A.F. pilots to Finland, Noel-Baker noted that there was 'a certain nervousness on this point in some sections of the Labour party … ' Citrine, reporting to Chamberlain on his visit, urged a special committee of supply chiefs to speed munitions to the Finns.[45] Fortunately for all those involved, Finnish resistance collapsed before British troops were dispatched to Scandinavia, and Finland made peace without losing its fragile independence.

Ironically, no doubt, the armistice between Finland and Russia was held to be fresh evidence of the government's lack of drive. In France, the Daladier government fell; in Britain there was renewed pressure on Chamberlain to reconstruct his government. Early in April Chamberlain put through the type of reconstruction which reminded everyone that he was not prepared to make any important changes. The chief feature was an exchange of jobs between two particularly uninspiring old political hands, Kingsley Wood, who became Lord Privy Seal, and Samuel Hoare, who returned to the Air Ministry, an office which he had held in the 1920s. 'This seems fantastic,' Crookshank confided to his diary. 'P.M. must be mad.'[46] A few days later, disquiet among certain government supporters was crystallized into a body under the guidance of Lord Salisbury, and known as the 'Watching Committee'. The Committee combined peers and M.P.s, opponents of Munich and more recent critics of Chamberlain, and had an initial membership of twenty-six. Through Clement Davies, this little group was in touch with Attlee, but Attlee pointed out that nothing could be done to change the government until Conservatives openly challenged Chamberlain's authority.[47]

For most people, life during the 'phoney war' continued largely along the grooves of peacetime routine. The major upheavals had yet to come, so it is not surprising to detect few references to changes in the climate of ideas. There was some apprehension among the well-to-do that war taxation would eventually sweep away their privileges. Harold Nicolson and Vita Sackville-West almost enjoyed a masochistic sensation that by fighting the war against Hitler, the cultivated classes were sealing the doom of their own way of life.[48] Lord Brocket, a pre-war amateur diplomat specializing in contacts with Nazi circles in Germany, wrote to Chamberlain in January 1940 urging a speedy end to the war, and observing: 'Middle and upper class people here see no hope for the future owing to the appalling taxation which a long war makes necessary ... '[49]

The one significant upheaval at the start of the war was created by evacuation. In the first days, one and a half million people, mostly women and young children, were evacuated from industrial areas where they were thought to be in danger of bombing, to reception areas in the countryside. Here they were billeted on the local inhabitants. The evacuees were often the victims of slum conditions, habituated to low standards of health and diet, and ignorant of such normal domestic conveniences as sheets to sleep in, or a table to eat at. The 'condition of England question' was literally brought home to the middle classes. At this stage of the war, however, the evacuees probably awoke more resentment than constructive concern. The cry of horror was shrill and angry. Moreover, this first evacuation was short-lived: by December, owing to the absence of bombing and indeed to the unpopularity of the evacuees, nearly 90 per cent of the mothers and children had returned home. Nevertheless verminous children did not fit the Conservative Party's assumptions about the material progress of the working classes and there was, among thoughtful people, an early revelation of self-doubt. Chamberlain, who it will be remembered had himself been Minister of Health from 1924 to 1929, wrote in a private letter: 'I never knew that such conditions existed, and I feel ashamed of having been so ignorant of my neighbours. For the rest of my life I mean to try to make amends by helping such people to live cleaner and healthier lives.'[50] Hoare, as Lord Privy Seal, said in the House that there were lessons to be learnt from the experience: there must be higher standards of health in the more backward industrial areas.[51]

There were younger Conservatives who sensed that big changes were inevitable. Eden declared: 'The war will bring about changes which may be fundamental and revolutionary in the economic and social life of this country.' The deputy-editor of *The Times* was talking in February with R. A. Butler (still Under-Secretary at the Foreign Office), about 'the new social revolution that is making its way, and how to anticipate and meet it.'[52] Outside the government, Boothby, whose social imagination was the strongest of all, wrote to Lloyd George:

Nothing is more certain than that this war will mark the transition from monopoly capitalism to socialism. By that I mean that the ultimate control of all basic monopolistic industries, of the Central Bank, of money, and of credit, will pass definitely and finally into the hands of the state.
... You cannot hope to go through a world convulsion of this magnitude without fundamental changes in the social as well as the economic structure. It is inconceivable to me that our present hereditary system, or our 'caste' system of education, can survive the struggle without drastic modification. In the case of Churchill any diminution of the power of the governing class will involve a clash between his natural instincts and his imagination. But is there anyone else in the present-day set-up who possesses sufficient imagination even to see the issues involved?[53]

This was very close to Labour thinking. The war could not be organized without state direction of economic resources. Once Labour and the working classes were mobilized for a total war, they would insist on making the change permanent. This was the gist of the amendment to the address moved by Greenwood on 5 December 1939: Labour regretted the absence of proposals for organizing the human and material resources of the nation to the full, or for the solution on the basis of social justice of the problems which would arise at the peace. As Morrison pointed out, the two considerations could not be separated.[54] Harking back to 1918, *Labour's Aims in War and Peace*, a declaration of policy drawn up during the 'phoney war', declared:

> The Labour Party demanded then, and it demands now, that wartime organization shall be undertaken in the full knowledge that there can be no going back; that, after the war, the national war effort must be turned to the building of a new Britain.
>
> While planning the war, the Government must plan for peace and a new society. Instead of regarding each item of state control as a temporary infringement of the normal, the occasion should be seized to lay the foundations of an efficient economic system.[55]

Brave words, which have to be taken with a large pinch of salt. Attlee and Greenwood confided their pessimism in March 1940 to President Roosevelt's special emissary in Europe, Sumner Welles. They believed that if the war were prolonged and became a war of devastation, it would reduce to ruins many of the social gains for which Labour had fought, and postpone any hope of economic recovery: nevertheless there was nothing for it but to go on and defeat Hitler.[56]

The very fact that war was so destructive was probably an incentive for people of constructive outlook to seek the means of turning it to at least some beneficial end. Beveridge was deeply involved in the Utopian project of a European federal union. Keynes discovered the possibility of social change in the reform or wartime finance. To avoid inflation it was necessary to reduce working-class purchasing power as the volume consumer goods was reduced. Keynes advocated that instead of rationing consumption and holding down prices, the government should impose on the working classes a scheme of compulsory saving by deferring a portion of the pay packet until after the war. The saving would be so great as to bring about a redistribution of property, and the National Debt, instead of building up as a credit to the rich, would be held by workers. But he was unable to swing Labour and trade union opinion behind the plan; and the home front remained in a state of suspended animation. [57]

III Churchill's Breakthrough 1939–1940

The growth of Labour's moral authority in the late 1930s was paralleled by the rehabilitation and triumph of Winston Churchill. After May 1940, Churchill and his circle on the one hand, and the Labour leaders on the other, were to act as twin centres of power in the Coalition, with Churchill at the head of the military and diplomatic machine, and Labour as the chief—though not the sole—animating force in civilian affairs.

In 1931, while the Conservatives were still in opposition, Winston Churchill resigned from his party's front bench and broke into open rebellion against the bipartisan policy of Dominion status for India. Thus he excluded himself from office when the National government was formed, and all three Prime Ministers of the 1930s, MacDonald, Baldwin and Chamberlain, were determined to keep him in the political wilderness. The ruling politicians of the day saw in Churchill's career and character a huge canvas, splashed irregularly with genius, but with the overall effect spoiled by lurid strokes of wild impulse and egotistical fantasy. They regarded him as a man who would have been great but for his flaws of temperament, and who was now slipping into the role of ageing adventurer. He had rebelled over India; after 1934 he campaigned against the government for accelerated rearmament in the air; at the end of 1936 he shocked the pillars of society and threw away his remaining prestige by intervening on behalf of King Edward VIII in the Abdication crisis. Finally, in 1938, he rebelled against appeasement, and after the Munich Agreement condemned Chamberlain's policy with all the anger and oratorical skill he could muster. In the Conservative Party he was an isolated and rejected figure, supported only by Brendan Bracken M.P. and a handful of others. His constituency association was torn by rebellion and only sustained him, in the winter of 1938–9, by three votes to two.

As war grew more likely, his political stock began to recover, and by the summer of 1939 there was considerable agitation to include him in the Cabinet. His line over rearmament and appeasement was being vindicated by events, and Churchill was beginning to establish himself as the prophet who had been right all along. Paradoxically, however, the imminence of war reinforced the suspicion with which the established politicians regarded him. Churchill had the reputation of being at his most dangerous and irresponsible in the conduct of war: a gimcrack strategist whose pugnacity was likely to overwhelm his judgment. He was the man of Gallipoli. Possibly, the authorities believed, he might be useful in a subordinate position under careful control, but he must if possible be prevented from becoming Prime Minister.

Perhaps the Labour front bench shared these apprehensions. But Churchill's main problem with Labour was his reputation as a class enemy. To begin with there was a legend in the Labour movement that Churchill, as Home Secretary in 1910, had ordered troops to fire on striking miners in the village of Tonypandy in the Rhondda Valley. In fact Churchill on this occasion had at first specifically forbidden the dispatch of troops, insisting that police be used instead. Subsequently, however, he had authorized the stationing of troops in the valley, albeit on strict instructions not to intervene between police and rioters.[1] This *moral* use of the military to restore law and order was no doubt the origin of the Tonypandy story. Churchill's militant opposition to the General Strike of 1926 was an established fact. In December 1938, when there were rumours that Labour might co-operate with Churchill, Bevin issued a powerful counterblast. He listed six actions taken by Churchill as Chancellor of the Exchequer in the era of the General Strike which branded him as an enemy of the trade union movement. 'Is it any wonder', he concluded, 'that he makes no appeal to us!' At the annual conference of the Labour Party in June 1939, Arthur Greenwood was still speaking of 'the grim figure of Mr Winston Churchill, the man who tried to beat us in the Great Strike.' On the eve of Churchill's premiership in May 1940, Attlee is said to have suggested that Labour would not accept him because of Tonypandy.[2] In international affairs, Churchill's record was deplorable from the left-wing point of view. This was the man who had wanted military intervention to suppress the Russian revolution in 1919, who had ridiculed Mahatma Gandhi, praised Mussolini, and condemned the 'Reds' in the Spanish Civil War. After Munich, the editor of the *Daily Herald*, Robert Fraser, wrote to Dalton: 'There is only one danger of Fascism, of censorship, the unification of parties, of national "discipline", and that will come if Chamberlain is overthrown by the Jingoes in his own Party, led by Winston, who will then settle down, with his lousy and reactionary friends, to organize the nation on Fascist principles for a war to settle scores with Hitler.'[3]

Churchill had made some ground with the Left in the late 1930s, in spite of the lingering suspicion of him as a fire-eating militarist. From 1936 onwards he had based his attack against appeasement upon a defence of the Covenant of the League of Nations. The General Secretary of the T.U.C., Walter Citrine, had shared a public platform with him, and later on urged Chamberlain to appoint Churchill Minister of Supply.[4] The private pressure-group known as 'Focus', formed in 1936 to provide Churchill with support, included some Labour M.P.s and radical journalists. Among them was the editor of the *New Statesman*, Kingsley Martin, who also published a long interview with Churchill, in a series on the future of democracy, in January 1939.[5]

Churchill's standing in popular opinion before the war is impossible to define very closely. In the spring of 1938 the Midlands M.P., Ronald Cartland, took Churchill to visit the Austin aeroplane factory in Birmingham, and recorded: 'The men were thrilled to see him. I've never seen such enthusiasm. It's not surprising—he has such presence— such personality—also the man in the street realizes that he has been right in everything he has said since 1933. Those in high places say he's finished—I don't believe it. He has a following in the country far bigger than those in Westminster think.'[6] But the west Midlands were a justly celebrated home of working-class Conservatism, and we can only wonder what reception Churchill would have received in south Wales or on Clydeside. An opinion poll in May 1939 gave some firmer indication: 56 per cent were in favour of asking Churchill into the Cabinet, 26 per cent against. In the summer he was contracted to write a series of articles for the *Daily Mirror*, the rising left-wing tabloid, which described him as 'the most trusted statesman in Britain'. Meanwhile the Home Secretary, Sir Samuel Hoare, was confiding his belief that four out of five Conservative backbenchers were against Churchill joining the Cabinet.[7]

At the outbreak of war, Chamberlain felt obliged to invite Churchill into the War Cabinet, and appointed him First Lord of the Admiralty. The War Cabinet contained, in Chamberlain and Churchill, two natural driving forces. Chamberlain possessed no great vision or imagination, but he was masterful in administration, swift in the assimilation of detail and the execution of policy, and above all, stubborn. The powers of the Prime Minister were at his disposal, and he could rely for the time being on the steady solidity of the Conservative Party in the House. An opinion poll in April 1940 recorded 57 per cent approval of his premiership.[8] Although unspectacular and uninspiring as a leader, Chamberlain may well have benefited from the appearance he gave of quiet, middle-class assurance and decency. Churchill's resources were also varied. In the War Cabinet his animal spirits and fluent tongue made him formidable. His department was a major asset: of the three services, only the Navy at that time, before the Battle of Britain, possessed any glamour. Moreover it was the only service in a position of superiority in relation to its German opposite number, and therefore offered the best launching pad for the aggressive tactics which Churchill had in mind. Churchill could rely, outside the confines of Whitehall, on powerful support from the popular press and indeed upon a groundswell of genuine popularity.

Had they agreed on everything, Churchill and Chamberlain would still have been natural rivals in the execution of policy. The fact that they often disagreed made the situation potentially explosive. Churchill's extraordinary brain and energy did not fit well into the punctilious system of war administration which Chamberlain, supported by his colleagues, the service chiefs, and leading civil servants, insisted upon. For eight months the pre-war oligarchy succeeded in containing and harnessing Churchill. Then, at the very moment when Whitehall judged Churchill to have disgraced himself, and been thoroughly put in his place, he escaped from control. Eluding his captors, he not only broke down the resistance on the Conservative side, but fused Right, Left, and popular feeling into a government of national unity which opened a new chapter in British politics.

Churchill built up his reputation during the 'phoney war' at an astonishing pace. Of his first speech as a minister on the progress of the war, Harold Nicolson wrote on 26 September:

His delivery was really amazing and he sounded every note from deep preoccupation to flippancy, from resolution to sheer boyishness. One could feel the spirits of the House rising with every word.

It was quite obvious afterwards that the Prime Minister's inadequacy and lack of inspiration had been demonstrated even to his warmest supporters. In those twenty minutes Churchill brought himself nearer the post of Prime Minister than he has ever been before. In the Lobbies afterwards even Chamberlainites were saying, 'We have now found our leader.'[9]

Following up this first success, Churchill made a world broadcast on 1 October. At once the left-wing popular press seized on the opportunity of creating a Churchill boom. The main topic of discussion the following week, Hamilton Fyfe of *Reynolds News* noted privately, was how soon Churchill would take over. In the *Daily Herald* Maurice Webb wrote of a sharp slump in Chamberlain's stock, with Churchill as the clear favourite to succeed him. William Connor, the *Daily Mirror*'s 'Cassandra', wrote: 'It is hardly premature to say that in popular imagination Churchill has already ousted Chamberlain as the dominant war figure.' The *Sunday Pictorial*'s front page carried a picture of Churchill with the headline: 'This is the man that Hitler fears.'[10]

Against the banal landscape of the 'phoney war', Churchill's eighteenth-century splendour was bound to stand out. He and the Admiralty took great care over their public relations. The Admiralty, unlike most other government departments at the time, enjoyed excellent relations with the press, feeding them succulent items of news which the Ministry of Information was unable to obtain, and the other services could not produce.[11] The Director of Naval Intelligence, Admiral Godfrey, felt that Churchill paid far too much attention to publicity and even distorted the facts for the sake of effect. Churchill had the trick of holding up the release of good news until he could announce it in a speech. Vice-Admiral Hallett of the press section was posted to sea after releasing news items which Churchill wanted to announce himself, and the section was reorganized as a division directly responsible to the Vice-Chief of Naval Staff. Admiral Godfrey wrote of Churchill: 'He did not hesitate not to tell them [the public] the truth or to paint a rosy picture that had no connection with reality ... I think he knew that soon he would be Prime Minister and guessed that he would be the most potent single force against Hitler and needed to become the popular hero of the British and her [sic] allies.'[12] These sweeping and even bitter remarks were the fruit of Godfrey's battle with Churchill over the true state of the war against the U-boat. On 18 January 1940

Godfrey circulated figures to show that of the sixty-six U-boats with which Germany had begun the war, nine only had definitely been sunk. On 20 January Churchill claimed in a speech that it was 'pretty certain' that half of the U-boats had been lost. In a personal minute to Godfrey, he claimed that thirty-five sinkings was 'the lowest figure that can be accepted'. Indisputable evidence appeared in April to show that German losses even by that date numbered only twenty-two.[13] Churchill gave enormous attention to his broadcasts, and Ogilvie, the Director-General of the B.B.C., described how the First Lord was determined to get the best times and the largest public. Asked if he would not contribute to the regular Wednesday broadcasts by ministers he replied: 'What! Stand in a row with that rabble!'[14]

Battles fought and won made the best propaganda, and Churchill came to be associated with exploits such as the battle of the River Plate in December 1939, which ended in the scuttling of the *Graf Spee*, and the seizure off Norway in February of the German ship *Altmark*, with the liberation of the British sailors on board.

A British Institute of Public Opinion (BIPO) opinion poll of December 1939 showed Churchill catching up with Chamberlain in public esteem. Thirty per cent said they would prefer him to Chamberlain as Prime Minister, 52 per cent were loyal to Chamberlain. The breakdown of support was revealing. Chamberlain's support was strongest among women, elderly people, and the better off. Churchill's was greatest with men, the lower income groups, and people between twenty-one and thirty. The majority of Labour supporters preferred Churchill.[15] When newsreels were shown in the cinemas, Churchill got the biggest applause, and a Mass-Observation inquiry reported that he was the clear popular favourite as next Prime Minister. Cecil King of the *Daily Mirror* reported this to Churchill in person.[16] There was some evidence too that not only the general public, but the Tory grassroots, were inspired by the First Lord of the Admiralty. The Conservative M.P. Somerset De Chair made inquiries, early in 1940, of the party secretaries in ninety polling districts in his constituency, asking who were the most popular ministers. Churchill was named by 63 per cent, Chamberlain by 53 per cent.[17] By April 1940, Churchill had achieved something of the popular standing enjoyed by Lord Kitchener as Secretary for War in the Asquith Cabinets of 1914–16. Kitchener's colleagues, at first admiring, had become increasingly disillusioned about his capabilities: but he had been too popular to dismiss. Outside the highest circles, Churchill was being regarded as a candidate for the premiership, but the gap between his popular standing and his credibility in Whitehall was considerable—as Chamberlain reflected in moments of exasperation.[18]

From the start of their wartime partnership, Churchill sought a special relationship with Chamberlain, and tried to win his confidence by a series of letters advising on many aspects of the war. Chamberlain would not answer them, arguing that he and Churchill met every day at the War Cabinet. Churchill of course longed to escape the limitations of formal procedure and thrash out the issues in unbuttoned private gatherings.[19] Chamberlain would have none of it. Despite his attempt to damp down Churchill's correspondence, he continued to receive daily letters on subjects ranging far beyond the work of the Admiralty. Was this an intrigue? Was Churchill preparing a case for resignation? Chamberlain sent for Churchill and talked frankly to him: the flow of letters ceased.[20]

The Admiralty was a formidable responsibility. It may even have been calculated that it would confine Churchill's energies. Boothby wrote to Lloyd George on 18 September: 'As a member of the Government, who shall be nameless, put it to me last week, "We fixed him when we sent him to the Admiralty."'[21] A false assumption, for Churchill took a comprehensive view of the responsibilities of a Cabinet minister. Almost at once after arriving at the Admiralty, Churchill summoned his scientific adviser, Professor Frederick Lindemann, to join him as head of a new Statistical Section. Lindemann explained to Roy Harrod, one of the economists recruited to the section, that Churchill regarded it as his positive duty to keep himself well informed on all matters on which the Cabinet had to decide. Accordingly, the Statistical Section acted as a private intelligence agency for informing Churchill of what was going on in Whitehall, and thus strengthening his hand in Cabinet. Harrod gives a revealing account of Lindemann's efforts to prove that the Ministry of Shipping was underloading the ships bringing in imports. When the question came up in Cabinet on 17 November 1939, Churchill vigorously attacked the Director-General of the Ministry, Sir Cyril Hurcomb, while Chamberlain and Simon defended him.[22]

The Admiralty was the hub of the strategic war effort, and thus bound up with foreign affairs in many ways. On 11 September President Roosevelt wrote to Churchill initiating their celebrated correspondence. Churchill told the Cabinet on 5 October that Roosevelt took an immense pride in his rank as Commander-in-Chief, and was personally responsible for many of the movements of his ships.[23] Chamberlain and Halifax approved of the correspondence and knew of its contents. The fact remains that Churchill was in effect negotiating a secret understanding with Roosevelt of the highest importance in foreign affairs, and by-passing from time to time the British embassy in Washington. Churchill also stepped into the sphere of relations with Russia. In his broadcast of 1 October he argued that by advancing into eastern Poland, Russia had rendered a service to the Allies by blocking the path of Hitler's advance, and that self-interest was the key to Russian policy. This decisively improved Anglo-Soviet relations; for the time being at least the Soviet Ambassador, Ivan Maisky, found himself *persona grata* in London society.[24]

The foreign policy pronouncements in Churchill's speeches were often made on the authority of no one but himself. In the eyes of the world, the British government had spoken. In the eyes of the British government Churchill was trumpeting personal views. Thus he said in a broadcast of 12 November: 'You make take it absolutely for certain that either all Britain and France stand for in the modern world will go down, or that Hitler, the Nazi regime, and the recurring German or Prussian menace to Europe will be broken and destroyed.'[25] But the speech had not been 'vetted' beforehand by the Foreign Office, and the under-secretary, R. A. Butler, had to tell the Italian Ambassador that 'Churchill's speech was in conflict with the Government's views not only in the present instance. As a matter of fact he always spoke only as Mr Churchill.' The Government *were* willing, said Butler, to examine any serious proposals for peace put forward by the German government.[26]

Here was evidence of one of the many issues during the twilight war on which Churchill differed from the ruling group in the War Cabinet. It was the most fundamental question of all. The formal position of the British government on peace had been stated by Chamberlain on 12 October 1939: 'Either the German Government must give convincing proof of the sincerity of their desire for peace by definite acts and by the provision of effective guarantees of their intention to fulfil their undertakings, or we must persevere in our duty to the end.'[27] There was no word here of proscribing Hitler or his regime as such, although Chamberlain had spoken earlier of the elimination of 'Hitlerism' as the war aim. Neither Chamberlain nor Halifax expected Hitler to become a reformed character, but Chamberlain especially clung to the belief that a total war could be avoided. Somehow or other Hitler would disappear, and the war end without fighting. Hitler, as he was to say in April 1940, had 'missed the bus'. Churchill, in absolute contrast, knew from the start that a long war lay ahead and that there was no way to avoid an all-out struggle. He told Roosevelt's envoy Sumner Welles, in March 1940:

> The objectives of the German people had not changed and would not change. These were world supremacy and military conquest ... There could be no solution other than the outright and complete defeat of Germany; the destruction of National Socialism, and the determination in the new Peace Treaty of dispositions which would control Germany's course in the future in such a way as to give Europe, and the World, peace and security for 100 years.[28]

This difference of attitudes towards Germany was part of something bigger. Chamberlain, Simon, Hoare and Halifax still dealt in the liberal Conservatism of the inter-war years. They had learnt to accept the limits of British power and to equate retreat with peace and morality. When challenged by the Congress Party in India, by Mussolini in the Mediterranean, or by Hitler in central Europe, they had generally taken the line of appeasement. Even so they were extremely reluctant to yield up the great hoard of British power, and it is wiser to regard them as foxes than as fools: they conserved the Empire by deviousness. Churchill's entry into the Cabinet meant the intrusion of rugged, leonine patriotism of the pre-1914 school. After the Munich Agreement, Churchill had called for 'a supreme recovery of moral health and martial vigour.' Though he too could operate by stealth and masterly delay, Churchill had an irrepressible urge to fly the flag and bang the drum. Anxious to prove his loyalty to the Chamberlain team, and thus to work his passage back to respectability, Churchill none the less had a habit of bursting into the language of Palmerston or Disraeli. Without seeking to write the military and diplomatic history of the 'phoney war', we can observe the points over which Churchill diverged from the majority of the Cabinet.

In April 1938 Chamberlain had negotiated an agreement with De Valera, the Irish Prime Minister, whereby the naval bases secured to Britain by the Free State Treaty of 1921 were restored to Ireland. Churchill had strongly attacked this agreement on strategic grounds. In the first two months of World War II, Churchill and the Admiralty came round to the view that the ports should, under some pretext, be seized by force. At Cabinet on 24 October, Churchill contended that as a member of the Commonwealth Ireland could not legally declare itself neutral. Britain should challenge Ireland on this point, and after the forthcoming repeal of the Neutrality Act by the United States, insist on the use of the harbours. His main critic in Cabinet was Eden, the Secretary for Dominions, who recognized Churchill's arguments as no more than a thin smokescreen for international lawlessness. Oliver Harvey noted: 'A. E. is beginning to doubt whether Churchill could ever be P.M. so bad is his judgment in such matters.'[29]

One of these matters was India. With his entry into the War Cabinet, Churchill resumed his long rearguard action against the dissolution of British power in India, which the war was hastening on. He did not hesitate to speak in the most frank terms:

> The First Lord said that he did not share the anxiety to encourage and promote unity between the Hindu and the Moslem communities. Such unity was, in fact, almost out of the realm of practical politics, while, if it were to be brought about, the immediate result would be that the united communities would join in showing us the door. He regarded the Hindu-Moslem feud as a bulwark of British rule in India.[30]

The distinctiveness of Churchill's views was most apparent in his attitude to neutral states. He accepted always the need to cosset American opinion, for the United States was a great world power which Britain must have on her side. But he refused to treat small European neutral states with the same care. His argument was that their 'opinion' as a moral factor did not count—they would side with whichever power they feared most. This was a constant bone of contention during the long debates of the winter of 1939–40 over intervention in Scandinavia. On 20 January 1940 he delivered another world broadcast at a moment when the British and French governments were angling for support from Norway and Sweden in a joint programme to help Finland resist Russia. Churchill was annoyed by the refusal of the neutrals to take sides, and still more annoyed because the Foreign Office, by arguing for the rights of neutral states, had recently played a large part in suppressing his plan for halting the traffic of iron ore to Germany through Norwegian waters. Churchill urged the neutrals to take sides before it was too late: 'Each one hopes that if he feeds the crocodile enough, the crocodile will eat him last.'[31] The Scandinavian states and the Low Countries were thrown into deep indignation by the broadcast, which had again been made by Churchill off his own bat. 'I can hardly emphasize strongly enough', wrote the British Minister at the Hague, 'the deplorable effect which the First Lord's speech has had in this country.' Churchill was obliged to offer Halifax an apology in the light of such reactions:

My dear Edward,

This is undoubtedly a disagreeable bouquet. I certainly thought I was expressing yr. view and Neville's. To make certain I asked Sir O. Sargeant to look through what I had written; but I did not take his advice on one point – viz. the reference to the L. of N. In this I was wrong. For the rest I never intended to make any pronouncement on Foreign Affairs, least of all one differing from yours.[32]

Churchill was the *enfant terrible* of the War Cabinet in more ways than one. Not only was he, from the point of view of Chamberlain, a boy wonder whose performance was variable – he was also a troublesome boy who must be kept in his place. Churchill was difficult to control in many of his activities, such as his speeches, and pet Admiralty projects. But on the main issues of the day which came before the Cabinet he found himself again and again in a minority of one. Not until April 1940 was Churchill able to make a partial escape from his warders.

Of course Chamberlain and his colleagues were not uniformly sceptical of all Churchill's ideas. In November 1939, for example, he wanted to seize Germany's exports in reprisal for German acts of illegality at sea. He won support from his colleagues, and on 27 November an Order in Council was made for the seizure of German exports.[33] It seemed to be an unwritten maxim of Whitehall that Churchill could only be managed by talking out his big ideas while promoting his lesser and often more valuable ones. This was the method of the Sea Lords within the Admiralty. Arthur Marder describes how Pound, the First Sea Lord, tackled Churchill:

Pound decided early that he would fight Churchill only on the really vital matters. The first sea lord was a master-hand at patiently weaning or diverting Churchill from his wilder, or shall we say more imaginative, projects, usually perfectly desirable tactically or strategically, but completely impracticable from entire lack of resources. This was, in the judgment of a postwar first sea lord,

Sir Charles Lambe, Pound's greatest accomplishment. The *modus operandi* was never to show any obstructive response, but to indicate that the proposition would be fully investigated.[34]

On 6 September 1939 Churchill began to initiate planning for an expedition into the Baltic, 'Operation Catherine'. This plan never got out of the Admiralty. It was sabotaged by a masterly programme of expert obfuscation, which carried Pound safely through to April 1940, after which events ruled it out.[35]

In April 1940 the Chamberlain government committed itself to a disastrous campaign in Norway. How was this decision reached? Both Churchill and his critics would like us to believe that he was the driving force. Churchill claims that the operation failed because the Cabinet delayed so long in carrying it out. His critics argue that it was a foolhardy idea, implemented only because Churchill overcame his colleagues' resistance. Liddell Hart, for instance, pins the Norwegian expedition on Churchill by claiming that after the Russian defeat of Finland, Churchill

> reverted to the plan of action on the Atlantic coast of Norway, to gain control of that neutral area. But a small German invading force forestalled and upset the plan ... Churchill's dream-castles had thus tumbled down in succession. Yet the blame fell on Chamberlain, as Prime Minister, and his enforced resignation opened the way for Churchill to take his place. It was the irony, or fatality, of history that Churchill should have gained his opportunity of supreme power as the result of a fiasco to which he had been the main contributor.[36]

There is still a variety of expert opinion about the arguments for and against intervention in Norway, and the consequences of the expedition. But the rights and wrongs of the affair take us away from the main question in political history. Was Churchill responsible for the intervention?

Churchill's *attempts* to achieve this are celebrated. In September 1939 he launched his plan for naval action alone, to cut off Germany's supplies of iron ore, which travelled in winter from the port of Narvik. He argued that this would be a major victory in economic warfare. The Cabinet vetoed the scheme. After the beginning of the Russo-Finnish war on 30 November a new prospect opened. The French and British planners developed the idea of landing a force in northern

Norway which, under the pretext of going to the aid of the Finns, would seize the iron ore mines of Gallivare in Sweden. Churchill raised once more his own proposal for naval action against the iron ore traffic, which he now believed would result in German intervention, and the development of a major war in Scandinavia. Again, the Cabinet outmanœuvred him. In January 1940 the Churchill plan was turned down, this time on the grounds that if Britain offended Norway and Sweden by action against the iron ore traffic, this would prejudice the 'larger plan' of intervention at the request of Finland, which required the support of the other two powers. It is a matter of great doubt whether Chamberlain believed more than half-heartedly in the 'larger plan'. Certainly Halifax did not. But under the guise of supporting it, it was possible to keep Churchill from action which would probably expand the war. The collapse of Finland left the naval plan as the only remaining possibility. The *Altmark* incident provided Churchill with a favourable opportunity to urge it once more on the war Cabinet. Chamberlain, still very much the master, turned the idea down, to the relief of his colleagues, on 29 February. On 12 March Finland collapsed, and with it the unreal scheme for a war in the north. Chamberlain ordered the dispersal of the forces which had been gathered for intervention.

Then a new factor entered — deriving from the internal problems of French politics. The Daladier government, reeling from the collapse of Finland, proposed action in Norwegian waters on 15 March, with the aim of inviting a German response. On 21 March the Daladier government fell and was succeeded by the more bellicose administration of Paul Reynaud. It was Reynaud who brought about the Norwegian campaign, as he claimed:

Je suis l'Homme de la route du feu.
C'est sur moi seul que pèse la responsabilité d'avoir entrainé l'Angleterre à frapper le Reich 'au Nord, en plein coeur', suivant l'expression d'Hitler en personne.[37]

Reynaud pressed Chamberlain to accept a gigantic expansion of the war, to include action against the iron-ore traffic, the seizure of Norwegian ports, the dispatch of submarines to the Black Sea and the bombing of Russian oil sources in the Caucasus. Chamberlain 'went through the ceiling' when he read these proposals.[38] Chamberlain and Halifax dealt with this French warmongering by shelving the major proposals and adopting what they believed to be minor ones — the British idea, Churchill's brainchild, of dropping 'fluvial mines' in the Rhine to disrupt its traffic; and the mining of Norwegian territorial waters. At the Supreme War Council on 28 March Chamberlain dominated the proceedings and dished Reynaud. Ironside, the British Chief of Staff, recorded with admiration how Chamberlain 'took all the thunder out of Reynaud's mouth and left him gaping with no electric power left. All the "projects" that Reynaud had to bring forward, Chamberlain took away. It was most masterly and well done.'[39] The meeting decided to launch the fluvial mines – an operation which in the event was held up until May—and to mine Norwegian waters.

Chamberlain had acted on his own initiative, without asking Churchill's advice. The Cabinet authorized the preparation of British retaliatory measures should Germany intervene. But Chamberlain did not believe Germany *would* intervene. He had told his Minister of Information, Reith, on the day the Cabinet accepted in principle the mining of territorial waters, that he believed the war would go on more or less indefinitely as a war of nerves, the Germans being too afraid to risk an adventure. In private he was inclined to disbelieve intelligence reports of a pending German offensive – there had been so many reports before.[40] The best evidence of Chamberlain's attitude was his speech of 4 April to the Central Council of the Conservative Party. Was it not, he asked his listeners, extraordinary that in the opening months of the war Hitler had made no effort to overwhelm them? 'Whatever may be the reason – whether it was that Hitler thought he might get away with what he had got without fighting for it or whether it was that after all the preparations were not sufficiently complete – one thing is certain: he missed the bus.'[41] Chamberlain had once more miscalculated Hitler's intentions. Unbeknown to Chamberlain, the Germans had been planning the conquest of Scandinavia. When news came through on 9 April of the German invasion, Caldecote noted in his diary: 'Hx [Halifax] was against the Norway minefield. P.M. and the Ch. of Ex [Simon] and Hankey thought (as it turns out wrongly) that there would be no retaliation by Germany.'[42]

Summing up, it appears that Churchill had *not* got his own way over Norway. The need to humour the French had propelled Chamberlain into two gestures of belligerence, neither of which he believed would lead to any extension of the war. Once more it was Hitler whose actions determined the course of events and of British politics.

Once the War Cabinet found itself in charge of daily operations, Churchill's position changed. As early as 1936 Churchill had been tipped for the job of Minister of Defence, and soon after war broke out in 1939 the idea was again in the air. The Chamberlain War Cabinet in September 1939 included the three service ministers and Lord Chatfield, the Minister for the Co-ordination of Defence. *The Times* urged, in October 1939, that this arrangement made little sense. The three service ministers should be outside the War Cabinet, and Churchill inside with a general oversight for strategic problems – in effect, Minister of Defence.[43] Chatfield realized that there was nothing very much for him to do, and wrote to Chamberlain offering to resign; but Chamberlain kept him on and succeeded in inventing functions for him.[44] He was a shield against the demand for the promotion of Churchill. In January 1940 Hoare noted 'Winston wishing to be Minister of Defence', and in March Eden advised Halifax that when the Cabinet was reconstructed, Chamberlain should give Churchill the job.[45] At the beginning of April 1940 Chamberlain reshuffled the Cabinet, but with a minimum of change. Chatfield departed, and the title of Minister for the Co-ordination of Defence lapsed. Churchill was given the responsibility of presiding over the Military Co-ordination Committee, which consisted of the three service chiefs and the three service ministers. This gave him nominal responsibility without any executive authority: bowing to Churchill's popularity while keeping him in fetters.

Churchill had scarcely received this double-edged promotion when, on 8 April 1940, German forces overran Denmark and began to seize points along the Norwegian coast. The War Cabinet at once decided to mount an expedition to thwart the German thrust in Norway, and Churchill burst into action as a strategist and would-be supremo. His behaviour precipitated a crisis in Whitehall, and had the politician involved been anyone but Churchill, he would probably have been shifted to another job, under a cloud. But Churchill, by an outburst of anger which deeply alarmed Chamberlain, emerged the winner. From 8 to 15 April Churchill took the chair at meetings of the Military Co-ordination Committee, of which Colonel Hastings Ismay was the Secretary. There was pandemonium. Ismay told the staff at Downing Street 'in despairing tones of the confusion caused by his [Churchill's] enthusiastic irruptions into the peaceful and orderly deliberations of the Military Co-ordination Committee and the Chiefs of Staff. His verbosity and restlessness made unnecessary work, prevented real planning and caused friction.'[46]

On 14 April the Secretary for War, Oliver Stanley, went to see Chamberlain to protest at this method of conducting affairs.[47] The source of the trouble was that Churchill was no longer allowing the Chiefs of Staff to meet together as a sub-committee, frame their views, and submit them in writing to the War Cabinet. Instead they found themselves sitting as part of the Military Co-ordination Committee, bombarded with advice and demands from Churchill. In the War Cabinet, ministers had no formal expert advice to go on: the service ministers were reporting by word of mouth the advice given by the Chiefs of Staff under pressure from Churchill. The Joint Planning Staffs, who advised the three service chiefs, were being pushed out of the picture altogether. The crisis came to a head on 16 April, when the official world mutinied against Churchill. At this point the main subject under discussion was the tactics of a proposed assault from the sea against Trondheim. Churchill told Ismay that he disagreed with the Chiefs of Staff about their plan, and Ismay went to see Bridges, the Secretary of the War Cabinet, to tell him 'that there was every chance of a first-class row' if Churchill took the chair at the Co-ordination Committee that day. When the Chiefs of Staff had met that morning, Ismay had cleared the room of secretaries and implored the service chiefs to keep their tempers. 'He told them that, if there was a row at the meeting, he was afraid of a first-class political crisis.'[48]

After the meeting of the War Cabinet on the morning of 16 April, Simon, representing Hoare and Hankey besides himself, saw Horace Wilson and told him they were agreed that it was wrong 'that the Cabinet should be invited to acquiesce in naval and military operations which were obviously of a hazardous character, having before them only oral statements made at the Cabinet and not having the customary written appreciations by the Chiefs of Staff.'[49] Chamberlain therefore took the chair himself at the meetings of the Co-ordination Committee, and orderly procedure was restored. It looked as though Churchill was deflated, and Chamberlain could feel justified in his efforts to contain the First Lord. But Churchill drew the inevitable moral that Chamberlain had not given him *enough* authority to make the arrangement work. A week later he drafted a letter to Chamberlain proposing that Chamberlain appoint someone with the specific responsibility for defence policy:

> If you feel able to bear this burden, you may count upon my unswerving loyalty as First Lord of the Admiralty. If you do not feel you can bear it, with all your other duties, you will have to delegate your powers to a Deputy who can concert and direct the

general movement of our war action, and who will enjoy your support and that of the War Cabinet unless very good reason is shown to the contrary.[50]

Chamberlain, hearing of Churchill's discontent before this letter was sent, called Churchill to see him, and gave in substantially to Churchill's demands. Churchill describes the incident with his usual blandness, but it was none the less *force majeure* on his part. Chamberlain's government could not last a day if Churchill resigned on the issue of the conduct of the war. Churchill was the most loyal of ministers, and had told the press that he would sink or swim with Chamberlain.[51] But even if he stayed on, such a clash of opinion was unlikely to remain secret for, Churchill's friends were less scrupulous than he was, and ready to tell stories. Chamberlain had no choice. The two other service ministers, Hoare, by then Secretary for Air, and Stanley, threatened to resign if Churchill was given responsibility for defence, but Chamberlain silenced them by threatening to resign himself. The new arrangements provided Churchill with the power to give guidance and direction to the Chiefs of Staff on behalf of the Co-ordination Committee. This principle was qualified by a series of checks and balances which would have done credit to the founders of the United States Constitution, and it was still unclear how much executive authority would pass into Churchill's hands. There would always be provision for stopping him, but he was to have considerable scope until he was stopped. Churchill adopted the plan with some enthusiasm, and at once set about planning a private defence staff of his own, to include Professor Lindemann. Ismay was again alarmed.[52]

The collapse in central Norway, followed at the end of April by the inevitable decision to evacuate, set the scene for a political crisis. The Chief Whip thought it would be the greatest since August 1931.[53] But opinions differed about when it would come to a head: the majority held that Chamberlain would weather the immediate storm, the debate on the motion to adjourn the House on 7 and 8 May.

The Whitehall belief that Churchill was not to be trusted at the helm had been greatly strengthened by the events of the previous three weeks. John Colville, a member of Chamberlain's secretariat, has recalled how 'the mere thought of Churchill as Prime Minister sent a cold chill down the spines of the staff at 10 Downing Street ... Our feelings ...,

were widely shared in the Cabinet Offices, the Treasury, and throughout Whitehall.'⁵⁴ Although it was Chamberlain who had taken the
decision to mine Norwegian territorial waters, Churchill was known to
have championed an extension of the war to Scandinavia, and created
upset during the military operations. Among insiders, therefore,
there was a tendency to pin the blame on him. Simon wrote on 8
May:

> It will certainly be an odd result if Churchill ... who is more
> directly responsible for recent decisions on tactics and strategy in
> Norway than any of his colleagues, should be elevated into
> the P.M.'s place. My own observation of him during the last
> eight months makes me admire his talents more than ever,
> but I think that his judgment is at its worst when things go
> badly.⁵⁵

Hoare drew up a list of seven mistakes which Churchill had made
since his entry into the War Cabinet: apart from 'complete wobbles'
over Norway they included his pro-Zionist outlook in Palestine, and
opposition to a conciliatory policy in India.⁵⁶ Chamberlain spoke to
Reith, the Minister of Information, with unusual candour. He referred
to Churchill's great (and by implication inflated) reputation, and said
that if Churchill were to be debunked he, Chamberlain, could not do
it.⁵⁷

If Chamberlain could not do the job personally political allies
could. 'Chips' Channon, M.P. for Southend—the delighted chronicler
of Society glitter and gossip—noted on 25 April: 'Dunglass [Chamber-
lain's parliamentary private secretary, later Sir Alec Douglas-Home]
pumped me: did I think that Winston should be deflated ... ? Ought he
to leave the Admiralty? Evidently these thoughts are in Neville's
head.'⁵⁸ Harold Nicolson heard some days later that the Government
Whips were putting it about that Norway was all Churchill's fault and
another of his failures. It was said, too, that Churchill was too old and
feeble to stand the strain of the premiership. Sir Edward Spears, one of
the few who wanted a Churchill government, was alarmed that
Churchill would be too damaged by Norway to become Prime
Minister.⁵⁹

Looking back on the parliamentary crisis of May 1940 with the aid of
hindsight, we must remark how uninevitable the 'inevitable' seemed
to be at the time. Many experienced commentators expected the
Chamberlain government to survive. The critics were uncertain of

success. Their candidate to succeed Chamberlain was Lord Halifax, or even Lloyd George, rather than Churchill, although there were exceptions. As would-be Cabinet makers, they tended to share the inside view of Churchill as a delinquent genius who should not be trusted with the very top job. In the House of Commons there was fear that Hitler was about to attack in the west, but no one could foresee the fall of France and the need for a leader of inspiration to defend the last ditch. In the event, the political crisis was resolved as though in anticipation of Dunkirk and the Battle of Britain.

News of the decision to evacuate central Norway became known in political circles on 29 April. The following day, before the decision had been made public, the Liberal leader, Sinclair, made a speech at Edinburgh calling on the government not to 'scuttle away' from central Norway. Sinclair had been making political use of confidential information. It so happened that his home in Caithness was, for military reasons, an area of special security. One of Sinclair's tapped telephone conversations had been reported to Chamberlain, who called Sinclair to Downing Street and rebuked him.[60]

On 2 May Clement Davies with about fifteen of his associates in the All-Party group of M.P.s decided to make the debate on the Whitsun adjournment the occasion for a trial of strength with Chamberlain. Both Davies and L. S. Amery believed that it was best to make an overt assault, instead of relying on the 'palace revolution' which Beaverbrook was predicting. Davies tried to persuade Attlee to put down a motion of no confidence, but Attlee thought the Conservatives would feel freer to show their discontent if the debate took place on the motion for the adjournment. None the less, the Labour leaders began to campaign against the government. In weekend speeches before the debate, Morrison called on Chamberlain, Simon, and Hoare to resign, and Dalton for the departure of Simon and Chamberlain. The problem facing Labour was not whether to oppose Chamberlain, but what tactics to adopt.[61] The crucial question, as the *Manchester Guardian's* political correspondent noted on 4 May, was whether the central mass of Conservative M.P.s would compel a crisis: the opponents of Munich within the party were more passionate than ever, but they had always proved powerless in the past, and they now had a new factor against them, the presence in the government of Churchill as a strong supporter of Chamberlain. On the eve of the debate, none of the editorials in Conservative or pro-government newspapers called for Chamberlain's resignation. On the contrary, they supported him vigorously, and

Fleet Street in general predicted his survival. On the night of 8 May, when the House divided and the government's majority crashed, the first editions of the next day's *Daily Herald, Manchester Guardian*, and *The Times*, were all appearing with leaders criticizing Labour's decision to call a division on the grounds that it would only solidify the government ranks.

On the first day of the debate, Chamberlain opened with an unconvincing defence, harassed by Labour members who interrupted with cries of 'Hitler missed the bus'. The Prime Minister had only one card to play, the announcement that greater powers had been conferred on Churchill, who was now 'authorized by the Cabinet on behalf of the Military Co-ordination Committee to give guidance and direction to the Chiefs of Staff Committee, who will prepare plans to carry out the objectives which are given to them by him.'[62] At first Chamberlain would only say, under questioning, that the new arrangement had been made 'since 11th April'. This would have created the impression that Churchill was personally responsible for events in Norway. It was Herbert Morrison who established that the change had come about since the Norwegian operations. Attlee voiced the basic criticisms of the conduct of the campaign, but emphasized that Norway was only one incident in a long record of failure, which was the true subject of the debate. He turned Chamberlain's card against him by declaring that it was unfair to burden Churchill with so much responsibility. Winding up his speech, Attlee made a severe attack on the government front bench as a whole, and called on the Conservatives to overcome their loyalty to the Chief Whip and enable different men to take the helm.[63]

The speech of the Liberal leader, Sinclair, was very different, perhaps due to Chamberlain's lecture a few days earlier. He devoted most of his time to particular criticism of the Norway campaign, but disclaimed all criticism of the government for having withdrawn its forces from central Norway. He urged that a War Cabinet should be established on the Lloyd George model, and called for parliament to speak out, but instead of calling for ministers to depart, he ended: 'Let us insist upon and rally to a policy for the more vigorous conduct of the war.' This was no clarion call. But Sinclair claimed that he was playing a tactical game to unsettle the Conservatives, writing to Lord Cecil of Chelwood: 'Violent attacks always disconcert them, but if *we* sing in a low key *they* are more likely to sing out … '[64]

The first damaging speech against Chamberlain from the government side came from Admiral Sir Roger Keyes, Conservative M.P. for Portsmouth North. During the Norway campaign, Keyes, a hero of World War I who was now on the retired list, had pleaded with the Admiralty and the War Cabinet to be allowed to lead an attack through the Trondheim fjord. His appeals had been rejected. Keyes appeared in the House in his full admiral's uniform with six rows of medal, and announced that he was speaking for the officers and men of the fighting navy against the incompetence and caution of the naval staff. He specifically excluded Churchill from his criticisms on the grounds that he was the prisoner of circumstances. Nicolson described the impact of Keyes's intervention: 'The House listens in breathless silence when he tells us how the Naval General Staff had assured him that a naval action at Trondheim was easy but unnecessary owing to the success of the military. There is a great gasp of astonishment. It is by far the most dramatic speech I have ever heard, and when Keyes sits down there is thunderous applause.'[65]

A second devastating speech from the government benches came from Amery. Seeing that the House was filling up as he spoke, and sensing how M.P.s were warming to his theme, he decided to conclude with the words used by Oliver Cromwell in dismissing the Long Parliament: '"You have sat too long here for any good you have been doing. Depart, I say, and let us have done with you. In the name of God, go."'[66] This outburst derived much of its force from the fact that Amery was an old colleague and friend of Chamberlain, and a disciple of his father Joseph Chamberlain. Yet even after this speech it was not yet certain that there would be a division. Amery noted in his diary: 'Went on to a gathering of Clem Davies' [All-Party group] conclave combining with our own [Eden] Group and arranged for speakers for the morrow and also trying to get as many votes as possible if there were a Division. On the other hand we were on the whole inclined to deprecate a Division and gathered the Labour leaders themselves were doubtful of its advisability.'[67]

As can be seen, the Tory rebels and Labour were in close touch, comparing notes on the likelihood of a sizeable Conservative defection. Sinclair also took some part. On the morning of 8 May he was writing of the Conservative backbenches: 'As a matter of fact a strong movement did develop among them yesterday, and it is Attlee's opinion, as well as my own—which we expressed to Amery and Dick Law in an informal conversation in the corridor—that if they could undertake to produce twenty votes in the Lobby we should divide the House.'[68] Even at Munich, not a single Conservative had *voted* against Chamberlain, so twenty votes appeared to be a useful catch.

The executive of the Parliamentary Labour Party met on the morning of 8 May to decide whether to put down a motion against the adjournment, thus dividing the House. According to Attlee in 1954, it was he who recommended the executive to challenge a division. Morrison in 1960 claimed that none of the Labour front bench apart from himself had decided what to do: they were shocked when he proposed that they divide the House. In 1961 Francis Williams, on the basis of conversations with Attlee, wrote that both Attlee and Morrison favoured a division. Dalton, in his diary kept at the time, noted that a majority of the executive, including Morrison and Lees-Smith, were for a division, but Tom Williams, Pethick-Lawrence, Wedgwood Benn, and Dalton himself, were against. Dalton opposed the decision in the belief that only twelve or fifteen Conservatives would vote against the government, in which case the result would consolidate Chamberlain's position. What the respective roles of Attlee and Morrison were it is still hard to say — but the decision was taken. It was then put to a meeting of the full Parliamentary Labour Party, and, curiously perhaps, opposed by the spokesmen for the *Tribune* Left, Aneurin Bevan and George Strauss. A week before they had told George Orwell that there was no chance of removing Chamberlain.[69] At the same time as Labour were taking their decision, Lord Salisbury was strongly advising the M.P.s who belonged to his Watching Committee not to vote against the government if there were a division. No doubt he believed, as a Conservative elder statesman, that it would be more seemly to engineer the change behind the scenes, but the M.P.s concerned decided to ignore his advice once they discovered how far the rebellion had spread.[70]

Morrison opened the second day's debate and announced that Labour would challenge a division. Chamberlain rose to accept the challenge and, in a bad tactical mistake, called upon 'my friends', adding 'and I have friends in the House', to vote for him. According to the somewhat hypocritical conventions of debate, he had reduced an inquest on the nation to an affair concerning his personal fate. Yet this is exactly what, in many respects, it was. Chamberlain had made many enemies and the debate offered the chance to settle old scores. Lloyd George had long regarded Chamberlain with contempt, and efforts were made by a number of people to get him to speak against the government. These two notes reached him, the first from Eleanor Rathbone:

> There is terrific lobbying going on to get Conservatives to vote against the Government. They say the Tories are shocked by N.C. making this into a personal vote for or against him.
>
> E.

> It is a direct challenge now. The P.M. has appealed to his 'friends' — as against the interests of the country. And there is to be another Maurice division. I think we may get as many as 40 Conservatives into our lobby. In any case he is done; because any kind of national unity under his leadership is now impossible.
>
> R. BOOTHBY[71]

Lloyd George decided to speak, and apart from attacking his old enemy Chamberlain he made sure of protecting his old friend Churchill, arguing that the First Lord was not entirely responsible for what happened in Norway. When Churchill rose, and declared that he accepted his full share of the responsibility, Lloyd George replied: 'The right hon. Gentleman must not allow himself to be converted into an air-raid shelter to keep the splinters from hitting his colleagues.' Macmillan recalls that the whole House was reduced to laughter by this sally. And once again, Churchill had been exempted from the general attack on the government. Lloyd George ended bitterly: 'I say solemnly that the Prime Minister should give an example of sacrifice, because there is nothing that can contribute more to victory in this war than that he should sacrifice the seals of office.'[72]

Subsequent speakers continued to rub in Chamberlain's *faux pas*, and the Government Whips could produce no backbenchers, beyond certain loyal warhorses who had seen better days, to swing the debate in the other direction. By the time Churchill appeared, to wind up loyally and forcefully for the government at the end of the day, the damage was irreparable. Boothby and Davies had made certain that the rebel M.P.s were organized. Well before the vote, a meeting was arranged of the Eden group and the All-Party group: Amery, as the senior ex-minister, took the chair, and acted as leader of all the dissidents on the government benches. The decision was taken to vote against Chamberlain.[73]

After Munich, the House had approved Chamberlain's action by a vote of 366 to 144, a majority of 222. On 8 May the voting was 281 for the government and 200 against — a technical victory and crushing moral defeat. Forty Government backbenchers voted against Chamberlain and with Labour. The number who abstained is difficult to estimate. By corresponding with surviving M.P.s, the political scientist Jorgen S. Rasmussen has established that thirty-two government backbenchers were unable to be present. Another fifteen were paired; so that, of eighty-eight government backbenchers whose names did not appear in the voting lists, no more than forty-three could have been at the debate and abstained. If we plump for a figure of eighty government backbenchers who voted against the government or abstained, we have just over one-fifth of the total of government backbenchers categorized as dissidents.[74] Only the most intense outbreak of collective anger could account for the flouting of a three-line whip on this scale. When the result was announced, the emotions surfaced in a remarkable scene in which Harold Macmillan and the Labour M.P. Josiah Wedgwood tried to sing 'Rule Britannia', and were howled down.

The collapse of the government's majority was the result of several elements among the backbenches. First of all the pre-war critics of appeasement were hardened in their opinions and accounted for nineteen of the votes cast against Chamberlain. Secondly a number of backbenchers had joined the services and been shocked into rebellion by the deficiencies they encountered. During the debate Captain Quintin Hogg declared that not one serving M.P. believed in the continuation of Chamberlain's premiership. And yet thirty-two serving M.P.s voted for the government, and only sixteen against. A good half dozen of the sixteen had a strong enough record of opposition to appeasement to be accounted rebels on that score alone, so that only ten votes can definitely be accounted for by virtue of the fact that an M.P. was on active service. The eleven other rebels cannot be categorized: they included well-known Commons personalities such as Hore-Belisha, Winterton, and Lady Astor.[75] No definite list of abstentionists is possible, but the list of those who for one reason or another did not vote discloses the names of hitherto loyal backbenchers who had never made a name for themselves in foreign affairs or defence, or created a splash. The middling ranks had broken.

After the vote there were two questions to decide. The first was whether Chamberlain could reconstruct his government by bringing in the Conservative rebels, the Labour Party, or both. The second was, who should succeed him if he failed. After the division, Chamberlain told Churchill that he could no longer go on as Prime Minister and that he must make way for a national government. Churchill — who had skirmished with Labour backbenchers during his own speech —advised Chamberlain to fight on with his diminished majority. Churchill's account of his advice to Chamberlain is sharply confirmed by Chamberlain's remarks the following day to Simon: 'Winston had apparently originally taken the view that the Labour people had nothing to contribute, and that the way to broaden the government was to bring in a selection of last night's rebels instead, together of course with Archie Sinclair, with whom Winston has long been in close relations.'[76] This option was firmly closed by the actions of the Tory rebels. On the morning of 9 May the Watching Committee and Clement Davies's group held separate meetings and both decided that a coalition government was essential. A comprehensive meeting of the rebels in the early afternoon, with Amery as chairman, adopted the formula of agreeing to support any prime minister who enjoyed the confidence of the country and could form a national government. This statement was given to the press. Thus Chamberlain was put to the test of trying to persuade Labour to accept office under him.[77]

Among the last minute efforts to keep Chamberlain in power were those of one of Chamberlain's most loyal supporters, a fellow Midlands M.P., Sir Patrick Hannon. At the House on 9 May Hannon discussed with Chamberlain's opponents their intense dislike of Simon and Hoare, and he subsequently wrote to Chamberlain: 'So far as I can gather from Attlee, Greenwood and Sinclair they are prepared to serve under you if the two statesmen whom I have mentioned will be eliminated ... ' In later years Clement Davies recalled that Attlee was, at this time, prepared to serve under Chamberlain, in view of the expected German attack: he and Greenwood argued with Attlee for two hours before converting him.[78]

At 6.30 on 9 May, Chamberlain, Halifax and Churchill jointly received Attlee and Greenwood and urged them to accept office under Chamberlain. Attlee told Chamberlain that neither the Labour Party nor the country would have him. But he added that the matter would have to be referred to the Labour Party executive, which was then in Bournemouth for the annual party conference. Attlee promised to put to the executive two questions: were they prepared to serve under Chamberlain, and were they prepared to serve under someone else?[79]

At dawn on 10 May the Germans invaded Belgium and Holland. Chamberlain took fresh heart, convinced that there was now a case for him to stay on. He wrote to Beaverbrook that 'we cannot consider changes in the Government while we are in the throes of battle', and

Sir Archibald Sinclair issued a statement for the Liberals endorsing this position.[80] Dalton drafted a statement issued by Labour which re-affirmed the need for 'a drastic reconstruction of the government'. The Labour Party National Executive met at the Highcliffe Hotel in Bournemouth at 3.30 in the afternoon and resolved that the party would take 'its full and equal share as a full partner in a new Government under a new Prime Minister which would command the confidence of the nation'. At 5.0 Attlee spoke over the phone to Downing Street and gave Chamberlain's secretary the answer to the two questions: No to the first, Yes to the second. Within an hour, Chamberlain was at Buckingham Palace to tender his resignation.[81]

In anticipation of Labour's veto, the Conservative high command had already determined the leadership question. At 4.30 on 9 May, Chamberlain, Halifax, Churchill, and the Conservative Chief Whip David Margesson, gathered to decide. Chamberlain opened the discussion by saying that in view of Labour's attitude he would have to go and make way for Halifax or Churchill, and would serve under either. He implied that after the scene in the House between Churchill and Labour, Churchill might not be able to win Labour support.[82] Margesson then spoke — but what exactly did he say? According to Halifax, Margesson did not pronounce as between Halifax and Churchill. According to Beaverbook's record of a conversation with Margesson in 1960, Margesson said that the Conservative Party would prefer Halifax. In 1963 Margesson commented that he must have said that 'some Conservatives' would.[83] Churchill has the date of the meeting wrong in his account, but is compelling on one point. When the moment came for him or Halifax to speak, there was 'a very long pause' which seemed longer to Churchill than the two minutes' silence of Armistice Day. This was the decisive moment: by refusing to offer to serve under Halifax, Churchill claimed the succession for himself. Then Halifax spoke and said that as a member of the Lords he could not hope to conduct a government when the real source of authority lay in the Commons. Was this his deepest reason? It would have been possible, as the King suggested, to suspend his peerage. Churchill recalled in his account of 1949: 'I could tell that he had thrown in his hand.'[84]

In the succession of Churchill instead of Halifax a deeper force was at work than appeared in the discussions, as Beaverbrook demonstrated in an article prepared in 1963. Who wanted Churchill? Not the King or the politicians, Beaverbrook replied, but the people. George VI thought that Halifax was the 'obvious man'. Chamberlain had written in March that he would rather have Halifax succeed him than Churchill. Margesson had indicated that the Conservatives' preference was Halifax, and Dalton had wanted a Halifax government with Churchill as Minister of Defence.[85] Beaverbrook could have added that Herbert Morrison, Lord Salisbury, and Lloyd George, had all expressed themselves in support of Halifax, while Cripps, acting on Lloyd George's advice, wrote to the *Daily Mail* proposing a Halifax government, but doing so under the guise of 'a British politician'.[86] A point of interest to historians, perhaps, is that A. L. Rowse wrote to *The Times* in support of a Halifax government. Voices for Churchill included the Labour front-bencher A. V. Alexander, the Liberal economist Walter Layton, and General Spears and Harold Macmillan among Conservative M.P.s.[87] But there was never any organized support for Churchill. He himself seems to have been prepared at first to accept office under Halifax. The story that it was Brendan Bracken who encouraged Churchill to seize his opportunity was very quickly in circulation, and later recorded by Moran and Beaverbrook.[88] But the main force behind Churchill was that obscure and owlish-looking figure, Kingsley Wood, the Lord Privy Seal.

Kingsley Wood had some standing as the politician most in contact with the grassroots of the Conservative Party. The journalist Colin Coote, who knew him well at the time, has recalled how he began to swing away from Chamberlain, being 'an extremely barometrical politician'. At lunch with Churchill and Eden on 9 May Wood argued that Churchill should make known his willingness to take over, and say nothing if asked to serve under Halifax. Eden was shocked by Wood's change of allegiance.[89] The connection between Churchill and Wood may have been in operation for some time. An undated, unsigned document in the Beaverbrook Papers, headed 'Kingsley Wood, Question and Answer', records this exchange:

'Did you decide that Chamberlain ought to be supplanted by Churchill? and if so, when did you start working to that end?'

'Quite soon after the start of the war Chamberlain himself told me he would have to give way to Churchill. He never intended that Halifax should be Prime Minister, he always intended Churchill to be his successor. By the end of the year it had become obvious that the change was not far off, and I started negotiations with Churchill which resulted in the change.'

The statement about Chamberlain must be discounted, for it goes against the evidence: after all, Wood warned Churchill on 9 May that Chamberlain did want Halifax to succeed him. But Wood may have wanted to disguise his disloyalty to Chamberlain, while taking credit for far-sightedness.[90] When Chamberlain tried to renew his tenure in office after the German attack on Belgium and Holland, Wood told him that he must make way. Horace Wilson commented many years later: 'He [Chamberlain] was misled by Kingsley Wood in the latter months. I didn't realize how far Kingsley Wood had gone in his association with the opposition. He didn't warn Chamberlain.'[91] Beaverbrook was therefore not quite right in saying that the people made Churchill Prime Minister. Churchill's authority rested ultimately on his popular standing in the country, but he did not choose to base himself on extra-parliamentary support alone: he only acted when he felt he had powerful party backing. The new firm of Churchill and Wood became the main Conservative axis in the new Coalition. The change of Government in May 1940 was a defeat for the Establishment of the day, but an incomplete one as subsequent events were to show. Conservatism was not the dominating spirit of the home front during the war, but with its complete control of parliament the party imposed important checks.

But the fall of Chamberlain was also one of those critical moments when patronage and initiative begin to pass from one set of hands to another. The critics of the National Government — the Labour movement, the stage-army of philanthropists and social engineers and the anti-appeasement Conservatives — had finally got the better of their old opponents. They were able to cast themselves in the crisis as a national fire-brigade, saving an Empire as great as that of Rome from the feeble grip of Chamberlain, a Birmingham Nero. Such was the way in which Morrison, Keynes, and Churchill, bore themselves. It was extraordinary that Labour, and a variety of social reformers, should find themselves playing the patriotic card against orthodox Conservatism. But this was not to be the end. Having, as they believed, been summoned to help the nation, they soon began to assert the right to change it.

IV New Deal at Dunkirk

Between 10 May and 17 June 1940 there occurred the greatest catastrophe of the war in the west. The Germans overran the Low Countries, almost trapped the British Expeditionary Force as it struggled to escape across the Channel from Dunkirk, and broke French resistance. On 17 June France sued for peace, and the British were left alone to await Hitler's onslaught. These events, when combined with the changeover to the new government at home, marked the first great shock to the political order over which Baldwin had presided. Indeed the tempo of change was so rapid in the weeks following 10 May, and public life so overwrought with emotion beneath the surface, that many of the judgments of the time have an apocalyptic ring. Was the world coming to an end? Lord Hankey, who had been the most powerful civil servant of the Baldwin era, imagined that the new government was a positive danger:

> God help the country which, at the beginning of the supreme crisis of its fate, suddenly replaces half of the eight key leaders by men without experience of war or of public affairs (other than very sordid politics) or of administration, most of whom have consistently opposed all war preparation, and which commits its future existence to the hands of a dictator whose past achievements, even though inspired by a certain amount of imagination, have never achieved success ... [1]

The disintegration of the French army prompted Field-Marshal Ironside, the Chief of the Imperial General Staff, to remark: 'This is the end of the British Empire.'[2] The intellectuals of the Left were the most apocalyptic of all. Orwell noted in his diary on 20 June: ' ... if we can only hold out for a few months, in a year's time we shall see red militias

billeted in the Ritz, and it would not particularly surprise me to see
Churchill or Lloyd George at the head of them.'[3]

Judgments of this kind now appear wildly inaccurate, but they have
their significance. They serve as reminders that patriotism, rage against
the Nazis, and the fear of invasion, were powerful tides of feeling.
Why was there in June 1940 a sudden wholesale internment of aliens, a
rash of prosecutions for spreading 'alarm and despondency', a gro-
tesque campaign by the Ministry of Information for citizens to form a
'silent column' against rumour? As Nicolson observed, only an element
of panic in the minds of the service chiefs could account for these
actions.[4] The politics of the inter-war years may be explicable in
terms of economic man, but from May 1940 the passions of collective
aggression were the main force for change. The brief era of Dunkirk
and the Battle of Britain was to have as great an impact on the domestic
future as the great slump of 1929. The leading Conservatives of the
1930s found themselves made into the scapegoats of defeat, a reverse
from which their reputations were never, in their lifetime, to recover.
The demand for social reform at home sprang up as suddenly as a gust
of wind on a still day, and continued to blow with increasing force.
The Labour Party discovered, in Ernest Bevin, a leader with the
ability and ambition to reverse the defeat which organized labour had
suffered in the General Strike. Political life was on the move.

On taking office, Churchill faced the remarkable predicament, for a
Prime Minister, of having no party to command in the House of
Commons. He had asked Chamberlain to continue as the leader of the
Conservative Party, and Chamberlain did so until fatal illness forced
him to retire in October. Churchill formed his War Cabinet on a
strictly party basis. Apart from himself it consisted of Chamberlain and
Attlee, the party leaders, and their chief henchmen, Halifax and Greenwood. For the time being the old ruling circle of Conservatives
was extremely powerful. As Lord President, Chamberlain built up the
committee of which he was chairman into the decisive authority on the
home front.[5] The majority of Conservative M.P.s continued to cheer
him when he walked into the chamber of the House, greeting Churchill
in silence. Halifax, as Foreign Secretary, still preserved the aplomb to
dispute with Churchill at length, during the evacuation from Dunkirk,
about the hypothesis of a negotiated peace with Hitler, which Halifax
treated as a real possibility.[6] Kingsley Wood, rewarded no doubt for his

switch to Churchill, became Chancellor of the Exchequer. Margesson was joint Chief Whip for the Coalition. Lord Caldecote, who as Sir Thomas Inskip had been Minister for the Co-ordination of Defence from 1936 to 1939, was Secretary for the Dominions. Simon became a viscount and sat on the woolsack as Lord Chancellor. Hoare alone was penalized, and sent on a most dangerous temporary mission to Madrid. The distinctively Churchillian Tory appointments were fairly discreet: Boothby, Macmillan and Nicolson as junior ministers; Amery at the India Office, Lord Lloyd at the Colonial Office, Eden as Secretary for War, Duff Cooper as Minister of Information, and Beaverbrook as Minister for Aircraft Production. Lindemann — 'the Prof' — naturally became Churchill's chief scientific adviser, and Bracken his P.P.S.

The Liberal party, which had 21 M.P.s in the House, could scarcely have fared worse than under the leadership of Churchill's old friend Sinclair, who in recent years had belonged in effect to the Churchill faction. The Liberal Chief Whip wrote in his memoirs:

> I was severely criticized for the character of the Liberal representation. But I had taken no part in the negotiations; in fact I was not even consulted by Archie [Sinclair], and the first I knew of the names of the Liberal ministers was when I read them in *The Times*. Several of my colleagues had special claims and qualifications to be included. Graham White had been a junior minister in 1931, had a wide knowledge of social problems and was respected by members on all sides. Kingsley Griffith, too, would have made an excellent minister: he was one of the best speakers in the House and had a good parliamentary style.

The Liberals won two ministerial appointments. Sinclair became Secretary for Air: but since Churchill intended to dictate strategy himself, without paying much attention to the service ministers, and had also hived off the task of aircraft production into the new ministry under Beaverbrook, Sinclair's job was now of lesser importance. Sinclair's greatest friend, Harcourt ('Crinks') Johnstone, had been at Eton with him, shot and fished with him, helped with his speeches and also supplied the Liberals with much of their finance. Like Sinclair, Harcourt Johnstone was a member of the Other Club, which Churchill and Birkenhead had founded in 1911. In the new government he became Secretary for Overseas Trade at the Board of Trade.[7] The one junior minister from the Liberal ranks was Dingle Foot, Parliamentary Secretary to the Ministry of Economic Warfare.

On the Labour side, there was a major recruit from outside the House: Ernest Bevin. In his speech in the great debate on 8 May, Churchill had described Bevin as 'a friend of mine, working hard for the public cause, and a man who has much help to give', and it was Churchill who decided on the experiment of appointing the general secretary of Britain's biggest trade union as Minister of Labour. (A vacant Labour seat was quickly found for Bevin, who thus became M.P. for Central Wandsworth in June 1940). Attlee and Churchill easily agreed on the other Labour appointments. Charles Edwards became joint Chief Whip with David Margesson; A. V. Alexander, First Lord of the Admiralty; Herbert Morrison, Minister of Supply; Hugh Dalton, Minister for Economic Warfare. The office of Solicitor-General went to Sir William Jowitt, one of the political world's most nimble survivors: first a Liberal M.P. (1922–9), then a Labour Attorney-General (1929–31), a National Labour candidate (1931), and finally a Labour M.P. again in 1939.

All told, Labour held sixteen offices in the new government, the Conservatives fifty-two. At the top, Labour's frontbench representatives enabled the party to deal on virtually equal terms with the Conservatives, but Labour representation was weak among the lesser ranks, owing to a shortage of promising younger personalities. In the lifetime of the Coalition, Attlee was to see Labour's position considerably improved, partly due to his own patient efforts. In June 1940, Labour occupied eight ministerial and eight junior ministerial posts; by March 1942, eight ministerial and fourteen junior ministerial posts; and by April 1945, ten ministerial and seventeen junior ministerial posts. But the key to Labour's influence has also to be found in the party's representation on the Cabinet sub-committees concerned with the social and economic aspects of the war effort. In May 1940, for example, Attlee as Lord Privy Seal was also chairman of the Food and Home Policy Committees, while Greenwood, Minister without Portfolio, was chairman of the Economic Policy Committee and the new Production Council.*

Churchill had good reason to resent the treatment he had received from the Chamberlainites in the past. But from the beginning of his premiership he made it plain that he had no intention of trying to base himself on the anti-appeasement faction of the party, or of forming some new combination. The majority elected in 1935 became in-

* See Appendix on Labour in the Coalition.

creasingly out of touch with public opinion outside Westminster, but Churchill inevitably based himself on the realities of parliamentary politics. Temperamentally he had no quarrel with Conservatism, and although he gradually broke up and dispersed the old circle of appeasers, it was chiefly for the practical purposes of substituting his own men, rather than from any desire to settle old scores. 'He will not smash the Tory Party to save the country, as I smashed the Liberal Party,' Lloyd George told Tom Jones.[8]

On 25 May 1940 the commander of the B.E.F., Lord Gort, recognizing the imminent danger that his forces would be surrounded and captured by German divisions, ordered the B.E.F. to march to the sea. Under constant threat of air attack, the B.E.F. retreated to Dunkirk, and from there 225,000 British troops and over 100,000 French troops were evacuated between 26 May and 4 June. General Mason-Mac-Farlane, the Director of Military Information with the B.E.F., told an assembly of war correspondents at Lille that 'history provided many examples of a British Army being asked to operate under appalling handicaps by the politicians responsible for British policy. But I doubted if the British Army had ever found itself in a graver position than that in which the Government of the past 20 years had now placed it.'[9] He explained to the new Parliamentary Secretary to the Ministry of Information, Harold Nicolson, that he was determined, for the sake of the British Army's reputation, that the blame for Dunkirk should be placed where it belonged – on the French, and on the British politicians. On 29 May he broadcast, anonymously, an account of the evacuation, and departed from his script to level these very accusations. After this he was 'warned off the air'.[10]

The soldiers themselves spread appalling tales of their experiences, centring on the absence of R.A.F. support during the retreat. The Home Intelligence unit of the Ministry of Information was at this period reporting daily on public opinion from thirteen regional offices. On 3 June, to take an example, no fewer than six of the regions reported strong criticisms by returning troops, sometimes associated with a reaction against the politicians held responsible.[11] A clamour arose to make scapegoats of the appeasers. The demand for their resignations was voiced across the whole range of Labour opinion, and there were signs of similar disturbances among the Conservatives. In *Tribune* Aneurin Bevan called for an inquiry into Dunkirk, and the impeachment of those responsible: Chamberlain, Kingsley Wood, Caldecote (Inskip), and Simon, should depart at once.[12] The *Daily*

Mirror called for the removal of the survivors from 'the old loitering gang' who brought about Dunkirk, and the *Daily Herald* took a similar line, with more tact.[13] On the Conservative side the *Daily Mail* joined in the hue and cry, and the editor of the *Observer*, J. L. Garvin, was moved to write to Simon: 'I have as little appetite for personal recriminations as any man alive; but no man in this land has given more study to German war-history and war-method than I have done for 50 years ... And when I think of how much more might have been done especially since 1935, my very soul is sick; and it can't be otherwise.'[14]

In their anger, men forgot their own responsibility for Dunkirk. Bevan had wanted no armaments. In February 1937 he attacked the Defence White Paper on the ground that the National government was incapable of using arms in the workers' interests, and he opposed Labour's decision to endorse rearmament later in the year. The *Daily Mail* under Rothermere had been a major apologist for Nazi Germany. Garvin had indeed campaigned for stronger defences. But he had also acted as one of the chief loudspeakers of appeasement, applauding the Italian conquest of Abysinnia, and justifying the conciliation of Germany down to March 1939.

Dunkirk created fresh disturbances among the serving M.P.s. A large number of them were reported to be feeling that the B.E.F. had been let down by inadequate supplies of tanks and aircraft. A secret session was imminent and there was open discussion of the dismissal of Chamberlain and Wood. Chamberlain approached Churchill and offered to resign, but Churchill replied that he wanted him to stay. After the meeting of the War Cabinet on 6 June, Churchill lectured the Labour leaders, and Sinclair, on the importance of calling off attacks on members of the previous government. The next day he summoned the chairman of the *Daily Mirror*, Cecil King, and told him that if the newspapers continued their attacks the government would fall—he would have to resign with Chamberlain as jointly responsible for the conduct of affairs since the outbreak of war.[15]

The political atmosphere of the time, with France collapsing and the prospect of invasion looming up, was charged with tension and irrationality. Churchill prevented a witch-hunt and preserved political continuity. The Labour leaders at once fell into line: Greenwood told Clement Davies that as the House had given the new government a unanimous vote of confidence there was no cause to alter its composition. Both he and Attlee gave Chamberlain an assurance that they would try to muzzle the agitators in the Labour Party.[16]

The irrational pitch which feelings had reached was, however, illustrated in a curious episode which came to be known as the 'Under-Secretaries' plot'. Boothby, Macmillan and Amery had joined the government, but none of them in an important capacity. Having helped to bring down Chamberlain they felt deeply frustrated to discover that he and his allies were still in charge above them. They feared also that with the 'old gang' entrenched there were unknown perils ahead. Boothby wrote a remarkable letter to Churchill arguing that a revolutionary situation was developing in the country, and proposing drastic changes:

(i) The War Cabinet should be replaced by a Committee of Public Safety in which absolute and omnipotent power should be vested —and would be vested—by Parliament. Such power to be ruthlessly exercised.

(ii) Ministers should be given dictatorial powers over policy and personnel in their Departments, subject only to the overriding control of the Committee of Public Safety.

(iii) The authority of the Commander-in-Chief—who again would be subject only to the direction of the Committee of Public Safety—should be strengthened by a declaration of martial law.

(iv) Parliament should be summoned only as occasion requires, for the purpose of hearing statements on behalf of the Government, of debating general policy in secret, and of granting the necessary supplies. The activities of the Select Committee on War Expenditure should be curtailed or suspended.

(v) Private Members of Parliament, not otherwise engaged in national service, should be requested to assist in the organization and direction of local efforts in their constituencies ... In a secret memorandum which I sent to the War Cabinet on 20th March last I wrote: 'It is this incredible conception of a *movement*—young, virile, dynamic and violent—which is advancing irresistibly to overthrow a decaying world, that we must continually bear in mind; for it is the main source of the Nazi strength and power.'[17]

On 17 June, Amery, Davies, Macmillan, Boothby, Arthur Salter, Horabin, and their hero Lloyd George in person, assembled at Amery's home. Macmillan had drafted a memorandum for them to send to Churchill, proposing that members of the War Cabinet individually should be in charge of a group of ministers, that ministers should have

fuller control over their departments and be able to appoint and dismiss
civil servants without Treasury sanction (in other words independently
of Sir Horace Wilson), and that the personnel of the War Cabinet
should be changed. In the end it was agreed that Amery should present
the group's views personally. When Amery saw Churchill, Churchill
told him that it was every minister's duty to get on with the job he had
been appointed to: 'If anyone in the Government wished to criticize
its workings or its composition they should resign and criticize from
outside. He was going to make no changes of any kind and would
sooner resign himself than be forced to do so ... '[18] This dashed the
'Under-Secretaries' plot'. On 18 June Churchill told the House that an
inquest into the past would be 'a foolish and pernicious process. There
are too many in it. Let each man search his conscience and search his
speeches. I frequently search mine.'[19] Clement Davies persisted in his
efforts for a while. But when he assembled an all-party meeting of
M.P.s on 3 July, to discuss changes in the government, 180 loyal
Conservatives packed the meeting and expressed their support for
Chamberlain in no uncertain terms.[20]

'The attack on Neville and the "Men of Munich" comes to nothing',
wrote Beaverbrook soothingly to Hoare on 6 July. But on the previous
day three Beaverbrook journalists, Peter Howard of the *Daily Express*,
and Michael Foot and Frank Owen of the *Evening Standard*, had
published under the pseudonym 'Cato' the classic political satire
Guilty Men. Written in four days during the evacuation from Dunkirk,
Guilty Men accused the men who had ruled Britain from 1931 to 1940
of exposing the British Army to disaster by failing to rearm. It consisted
of a series of brilliant and unfair character assassinations of Baldwin,
Chamberlain, Inskip and others. Despite the fact that it was banned
from distribution by W. H. Smith's and Wyman's it sold over 200,000
copies. 'Inspiration from Beaverbrook himself had not been lacking',
his biographer remarks.[21]

The success of *Guilty Men* suggests that while the appeasers continued
to club together in the House, their reputation with the public had been
severely undermined. Mass-Observation conducted a survey which
recorded that 62 per cent wanted Chamberlain sacked from the
government: a BIPO survey showed that 77 per cent thought so.[22]
But how could he be removed? Frank Owen gathered together a
number of trade union leaders who were ready to demand a purge of
the appeasers, in the belief that a widespread demand by the unions
could not be ignored. The National Union of Railwaymen had passed a

resolution against the 'men of Munich', and Owen was also in touch
with Harry Pollitt of the Communist Party, who argued that Soviet
friendship could only be secured by dismissing the appeasers. But
Communist involvement only served to discredit the campaign in the
trade union movement. When a party stalwart, Arthur Horner,
proposed at the Mineworkers' Federation a motion calling for
Chamberlain to go, he was defeated by 430,000 votes to 160,000.
Citrine, the General Secretary of the T.U.C., put in a word for
Chamberlain by proclaiming the novel doctrine that the Conservatives
had the right to appoint the man they trusted.[23]

What were the implications of the 'guilty men' thesis? In the short
run, the campaign to purge the government failed. Chamberlain was
only to resign office because he was dying of cancer. In the long run,
and in his own time, Churchill dispersed the appeasers to foreign parts
or gracefully retired them. Although he was undoubtedly out of
sympathy with the campaign against the 'guilty men', it eased his way
to the enjoyment of untrammelled power. He could scarcely have
packed off his Foreign Secretary, Halifax, to be Ambassador in
Washington in December 1940, had not Halifax been under a cloud.
But the effect on high-level politics was not all that important:
Churchill was bound to be master in his own house once he was Prime
Minister. The main impact was on popular feeling. Historians may
argue for many years to come about the degree of responsibility which
Baldwin, Chamberlain and their colleagues should bear for the
appalling situation of 1940, when Britain had barely the means to
defend itself, let alone to attack. But in the circumstances of the hour,
the Conservatives were bound to take much of the blame. The Left, the
very people who were campaigning against the 'men of Munich',
might have been even more wrong in the past. But the Conservatives
had been in power, and it had been their duty to protect the security of
Britain. No matter why they had failed, they *had* failed: they had left a
perilously narrow margin between survival and defeat. Parties find it
difficult to blame themselves for their own shortcomings, and Conservatives have often claimed that they were undermined by left-wing
propaganda. The record suggests that the 'guilty men' thesis derived
from the troops who were at Dunkirk, and was spread by word of
mouth before it was put into print. But was it not, in any case, a
most obvious reaction to defeat? What could be more natural than
to seek a scapegoat when disaster takes place? In private, some Conservatives were quite clear who was to blame. Waldorf Astor wrote

to a correspondent in the United States during the retreat from
Dunkirk that Chamberlain had been

> disastrous as Prime Minister in a dangerous world. We looked on
> the Munich settlement as the right get out of a situation in which
> we had been caught unarmed and without anti-aircraft defence or
> aircraft. He looked on it as, in itself, a triumph.
>
> Subsequently on every important occasion his prophecy and
> judgment as to the course of events proved wrong. He was
> unable to grasp the need for full urgent rearmament ...
>
> Chamberlain is a very capable mediocrity, a pacifist, a narrow
> party politician, incapable of greatness or Statesmanship, with a
> mind clear on detail but with no vision ... [24]

Another Conservative M.P. of normally loyal outlook, confided to his
diary on 1 July 1940:

> The losses in material of every description in France have been
> appalling and apparently there were no supplies in existence at
> home to replace them — or, at any rate, not nearly enough. This is
> pretty disgraceful and one feels that there has been no real drive
> behind our war effort for the last nine months. Chamberlain will
> have to bear the blame for this — for he should have realized, when
> the Labour people refused to come in with him, that it was useless
> to carry on. Unless they would cooperate, he could not count
> upon the full support of the trade unions and a whole-hearted
> effort by the workers. He should, therefore, have resigned long
> ago. [25]

In World War I the Conservatives had figured, with Lloyd George, as
the supreme patriots who would deliver the knock-out blow against the
Hun. In World War II the new folklore of the period made them out
to be incompetents and obstacles in the path of victory. The 'guilty
men' thesis, as a later chapter suggests, was only the beginning of the
erosion of their credibility. [26]

The 'guilty men' controversy was rooted in the divisions of the 1930s.
Meanwhile the party leaders were learning to co-operate with each
other in the government. From the vantage point of high office, the
quarrels of yesterday were irrelevant to the flow of urgent decisions
which had to be taken. Soon Chamberlain was writing in a private

letter: 'I have some reason to believe that my colleagues, Attlee, Greenwood & Alexander have considerably revised their ideas of my value in the government.'[27]

When the Coalition was formed it had yet to be established that it represented a genuine partnership between the two main parties. Without any effective leadership, Labour might easily have lapsed into a purely subordinate and technical role as experts on labour questions and social conditions. Attlee himself proved to be as enigmatic a figure in office as in opposition. No one was impressed by his speeches, and although he was a competent committee chairman, good at summing up conclusions, he was never among the big men of power in wartime Whitehall. As a politician Attlee resembled the frog who sits motionless on a stone, occasionally snapping up an insect with its tongue. If it came to the point he could take sharp decisions with no fuss or self-advertisement. Dalton's diary records Attlee describing how he chose the Labour members of the Coalition: 'A. says that he left out Pethick [Pethick-Lawrence] because too old, Lees-Smith because too slow, W. Benn because too recent, and Phil [Noel-Baker] because too unbalanced in his judgments, increasingly so these last few months. Also a balance had to be maintained between bourgeois and working-class M.P.s.' On 8 June Dalton noted: 'Lunch with C.R.A. He is a very good G.S.O. 1 [General Staff Officer, 1st Grade]. He is doing a lot of push on home front, e.g. for communal feeding, rational restriction of imports etc.' Dalton soon had reason to be grateful for Attlee's 'push'. Attlee fought doggedly, through an epic Whitehall intrigue, to ensure that the new secret department of political warfare went to Dalton in addition to his existing job. The function of the department was to stimulate resistance in Europe, and Attlee argued that this was a task best accomplished 'from the Left'.[28]

Of the other Labour leaders, Morrison had only mixed success in his first assignment, at the Ministry of Supply, while Alexander at the Admiralty was divorced from the home front, and Greenwood, the victim still of a sad drink problem, proved ineffectual. Labour's one giant was Bevin. Bevin had a solid basis of power in the trade union movement, for whom he could speak, but his force of mind and character did the rest. Alan Bullock has described how Bevin, after three days as Minister of Labour, produced for the War Cabinet a bold programme of action, the essence of which was Bevin's claim to unify responsibility for all manpower and labour questions under his own authority. By accepting his proposals, the Cabinet transformed the Ministry of

Labour into one of the commanding heights of the home front. Chamberlain, as Lord President, drafted an Emergency Powers Act which proclaimed the right of the government to conscript not only property but labour. Men would be ordered to work in a particular factory in the same way as conscripts were ordered to bear arms. Bevin determined to maintain the voluntary principle so far as possible.[29] In this and other respects he knew his own mind, and his presence quickly made itself felt. H. F. Crookshank, a Conservative whom Churchill had appointed as Financial Secretary to the Treasury, noted on 22 May: 'Ctee on O.A. Pensions at 5, where Kingsley [Wood] gave way to Bevin, a sign of the times.'[30]

Bevin knew that by participating in the war effort the Labour movement could help win the war and at the same time claim the rights which must flow from its participation. On the eve of Dunkirk he told a special emergency conference of trade union executives: 'If our Movement and our class rise with all their energy now and save the people of this country from disaster, the country will always turn with confidence forever to the people who saved them. They will pay far more attention to an act of that kind than to theoretical arguments or any particular philosophy.'[31] Pressing boldly on, he announced that he was ready to raise the wages of agricultural labourers and railwaymen, a prerogative which no Minister of Labour had claimed before. Chamberlain was worried, and sent for Citrine. 'What are we to do with this man Bevin?' he asked him.[32] But there was no stopping Bevin on this occasion. Nor was it ever easy to impede a man of such fiery temper. A sense of how formidable Bevin could be when ranting at full blast is conveyed by an incident early in July. Bevin was attending a sub-committee of the Civil Defence Executive. The subject under discussion was the powers to be exercised by the thirteen regional commissioners who were deputed, in the event of invasion, to take over the functions of government in a particular area. One of the commissioners had suggested that they be given a 'trial run' by the acquisition of certain powers over the railways. Bevin, according to another member of the meeting, referred to the proposal

> as likely to produce a 'revolutionary condition' among the workers and suggested that it was simply a plot on the part of right-wing Conservatives and big business interests to prevent Labour having a say in works management. This happy condition of affairs now prevailed under Bevin's joint committee representing the T.U.C.

and employers and if it were to be set aside he could not continue to be responsible for delivering the goods. He referred to the inability of soldiers to make up their minds ... He went on to ask where was this public opinion of which Findlater Stewart had spoken except in 'The Times' and the 'Evening Standard' and followed it up with an attack upon Beaverbrook [the minister of aircraft production] as a man who had gone behind the agreement for the control of skilled labour and was quite unable to work in a team! He said that the collapse of France had been due to assumption of power by soldiers and prophesied the loss of the war if his work were interfered with.[33]

Through the Coalition, the Labour leaders had seized the initiative in the mobilization of the war effort on the home front. In the House of Commons, Labour ministers and backbenchers began to make the running. After the debate on the defence regulations at the end of July 1940, the Conservative M.P., Sir Cuthbert Headlam, wrote:

It was mainly conducted (as all debates now are) by the Labour Party — it is odd how the Conservatives, even the stock bores who usually keep talking, have faded out of the picture ... I feel that we are mistaken and ought not to allow the Socialists such a free run. There is of course a 'party truce', but it is only observed by one side. Every speech made by the Labour people in the H. of C. is a party speech and is propaganda ... It is altogether a bad look out for the future and it looks as if everything we ought to stand for will go by default.[34]

The advent of Bevin and the Labour Party coincided with the need to tighten up economic controls and expand the welfare of the civilian population. The pressures of expediency, and the doctrines of economic planning and social justice, became intermingled and difficult to unscramble. What some regarded as pragmatic measures for the emergency, others insisted might provide the embryo of a superior social system. The *New Statesman* argued on 1 June that a democratic revolution had begun:

... The result of the collaboration of Tories prepared to sacrifice private interests for the empire, and Labour, is seen in every Order in Council now issued.
We cannot actually achieve socialism during the war, but we can

institute a whole series of Government controls which after the war may be used for Socialist ends.[35]

A symbol of the times was the raising, in the week of Dunkirk, of the rate of tax on excess war profits from 60 per cent to 100 per cent. This, the official historian of financial policy recalls, was 'essentially a political decision, hastily taken in the heat of the new political climate'.[36]

Throughout the 1930s the Treasury had been the power-house of conservative financial policies repugnant to the Labour Party. With the change of government it began to be eclipsed, largely from expediency but much to Labour's satisfaction. The historians of the British war economy observe:

> Before May 1940 the Government thought of 'financial and economic plans' and put the accent on the first word. The new Government shifted the order of words and put 'economic' in front of 'financial'. It continued and indeed carried further its predecessor's anti-inflation policy; nor did it despise budgetary arithmetic; but it shifted the emphasis of planning to the simpler arithmetic of import programmes and stocks and the supply of skilled engineers.[37]

The eclipse of the Treasury was due to the fact that in total war it was essential to plan resources first, leaving the financial side to be adjusted accordingly. In peacetime the Treasury imposed its criteria of what the government and the taxpayer could afford. These criteria were already in decline before May 1940, and they were swallowed up altogether when catastrophe struck. And limits on spending gave way for welfare almost as readily as for war. R. M. Titmuss, in his *Problems of Social Policy*, drew attention to the importance of Dunkirk in the growth of the social services. Before the war they had been built up to assist the socially underprivileged, Titmuss maintained; but since the whole population had to endure the rigours of participating in the war effort, the government had to cater for the welfare of all. The turning-point was the crisis of 1940. In June, for example, Attlee's Food Policy Committee approved a scheme for free or subsidized milk to mothers and their children under five years of age, which had been ruled out in August 1939 as financially impracticable. In July, the Board of Education decided that free school-meals, which had hitherto been supplied only to undernourished children, should become generally available.[38]

During Dunkirk there were still 645,000 men and women registered as unemployed: by the time of the Normandy landings in June 1944 the figure was down to 54,000. Britain in the summer of 1940 had some way to go before the economy was fully planned and mobilized. But the need to plan was obvious, and with it the need to recruit all the talents into administration. Greenwood, as chairman of the Economic Committee, recruited several economists from the universities to expand the Central Economic Information Service. By the summer of 1940 it included Harry Campion, Alec Cairncross, D. N. Chester, Ely Devons, Stanley Denison, John Jewkes, James Meade, Lionel Robbins, Austin Robinson, Richard Stone and Harold Wilson.[39] In June Kingsley Wood invited the most eminent of economists to join his consultative council, and the following month Keynes was given the room at the Treasury in which he was to do most of his work, as an unsalaried freelance, until his death in 1946.[40]

A more ponderous new broom in Whitehall was Beveridge, whose outstanding administrative abilities were, as before, liable to be frustrated by the fact that most of the important people found his conceit intolerable. Bevin invited him to take charge of the new Welfare Department of his ministry. Beveridge declared that he wanted to organize manpower, thus losing his first opportunity only to discover that Bevin denied him the second. Neither Bevin, nor Sir Thomas Phillips, the permanent secretary at the Ministry of Labour thought Beveridge a congenial colleague. None the less Beveridge became a temporary civil servant in the department in June 1940, engaged in a not very important manpower survey. Beveridge, however, still had ambitions to direct manpower policy, and in contrast to Bevin he stood forth as an advocate of compulsion. It is fascinating to observe how the catastrophe of 1940 had swung him decisively in favour of strong centralized planning, not only for the war, but for the peace to follow. His old Fabian mentors, Sidney and Beatrice Webb, were still living at their Hampshire home, Passfield Corner, where Beveridge arrived one day in August. Beatrice Webb recorded:

> Poor Beveridge was in a state of collapse: I have never seen him so despondent about public affairs, so depressed about his own part in bettering them. The collapse of France and the obvious incompetence of our own government and governing class to foresee this catastrophe ... has overthrown his old confidence that the Allies would win the war and dictate the peace.
> ... What is more interesting is that Beveridge realizes that if the

war is to be won, and still more if the industrial state of Great Britain is to be saved from decay, *planned production and consumption has to be undertaken*. But as of old, Beveridge is obstinately convinced that he and his class have to do the job, and the Trade Unionists have to be ignored and the wage-earner *ordered* to work; the where, when and how, to be settled by a civil servant, with or without a profit making employer as intermediary. He agrees that there must be a revolution in the economic structure of society; but it must be guided by persons with training and knowledge —i.e. by himself and those he chooses as his colleagues.[41]

The home front organized for war was becoming a model, and an inspiration, for the reorganization of the peace. The implications were bound to be disquieting for the more traditional type of Conservative, who instinctively distrusted talk of a better world beyond the horizon: hence the controversy which began, during the Battle of Britain, over the broadcasts of J. B. Priestley. The B.B.C. had started a regular Sunday evening series of talks, featuring various speakers, under the title 'Postscripts'. Priestley, who was already well-known as a novelist and playwright, began to broadcast in the series on 5 June, with an elegiac tribute to the pleasure-steamers which had sailed into the inferno of Dunkirk to rescue the troops of the B.E.F. His warm Yorkshire voice stood out from the dead level of B.B.C. English, and his mastery of colour and detail, conveyed by a few vivid strokes, breathed life into propositions which had all too often died on the lips of politicians. B.B.C. audience research reported that on average one adult in every three listened to his talks (for Churchill the average was about two out of three, but to do half as well as Churchill was to be an outstanding success.)[42] As Priestley got into his stride, he introduced into his vignettes of wartime life a new and idealistic theme: the idea that there could be no going back to the social conditions of the 1930s. In his 'Postscript' of 21 July he concluded:

> Now, the war, because it demands a huge collective effort, is compelling us to change not only our ordinary, social and economic habits, but also our habits of thought. We're actually changing over from the property view to the sense of community, which simply means that we realize we're all in the same boat. But, and this is the point, that boat can serve not only as our defence against Nazi aggression, but as an ark in which we can all finally land in a better world.[43]

Priestley touched only occasionally on the theme, but enough to stir up his critics. In a hitherto unpublished entry in his diary, Nicolson noted that at a dinner which Herbert Morrison had attended 'Somebody disclosed the fact that David Margesson had been round today to the B.B.C., and complained that J. B. Priestley's talks on the wireless (which have immense popular appeal) were "leftish". This annoyed Morrison ... who said "Margesson should realize that he is Government Chief Whip and not a Conservative Chief Whip."' Margesson and his Deputy Chief Whip, James Stuart, emphasized their disquiet directly to Nicolson in September.[44] However, Priestley survived, and continued his talks into October. The belief that he was 'forced off the air' in the autumn of 1940 is mistaken. Perhaps the best tribute to Priestley's talks came from Graham Greene, who confessed that he had regarded his novels and plays with venom: 'He became in the months after Dunkirk a leader second only in importance to Mr Churchill. And he gave us what our other leaders have always failed to give us—an ideology.'[45]

The thesis that war was the midwife of social progress was common to a wide spectrum of opinion. If Priestley was a socialist, his socialism was of a cheerfully idiosyncratic kind, a vision of a more warm-hearted and egalitarian way of life. More typical of the Labour Left of the period was Harold Laski, who shared the Marxist conviction that capitalism was coming to an end, and the equally fervent if contradictory belief that the reactionary forces were about to triumph. He partially resolved the contradiction by arguing that the revolution would come about if Attlee would call on the workers to rouse themselves, but that Attlee was letting them down by compromising with capitalism. Attlee and the Labour leaders found him extremely tiresome, but he was a popular member of the National Executive of the party and one of the chief exponents of socialism in the country. During the evacuation from Dunkirk he began to argue that immediate social reform was essential to prove to the working classes that the governing classes recognized the need for a people's war. Soon he was arguing at the Labour Party Policy Committee that morale would be raised by the nationalization of the land and the Bank of England. Several of the trade unionists on the committee replied that whatever the arguments were in favour of such action, raising morale was not one of them. Dalton noted: 'This is better done by Air Force victories, by full employment, by better dependent's allowances, by improvements in Workmen's Compensation, and by modifications in the

Means Test. He [Laski] goes away with his little tail between his little legs.'[46]

Conservatives who recall the war years often speak as though the ideological content of the war had been introduced exclusively by the Left Book Club intelligentsia. But the Centre (including some Conservatives) was just as active. The post-war reconstruction group at Political and Economic Planning (P.E.P.), in a paper of 12 July which was circulated in the Ministry of Information, argued:

> Wartime conditions have already compelled us to make sure, not only that the rich do not consume too much, but that others get enough. The needs of war production call for new measures for improving the housing, welfare and transport of workers. The evacuation scheme should give the impetus to radical improvements in our educational system and social services. The wartime measures to protect the standard of living point the way to a planned population policy. The mobilization of manpower should spell the end of mass unemployment. War measures for rationalizing the distribution of various products should lead to a remodelling of distribution as a whole, so as to transform increased productivity into increased consumption on a higher standard.[47]

At the same moment *The Times* was beginning to express the influence of the two men who were to shape its editorial policy after the retirement in 1941 of Geoffrey Dawson as editor. R. M. Barrington-Ward, the deputy editor, and E. H. Carr, at that time an occasional writer for the paper on international affairs, had both been leading apologists for the policy of appeasement. Barrington-Ward had defended it on moral grounds of pacifism and justice for Germany; Carr, in his *Twenty Years Crisis* (1939) on grounds of *realpolitik*. The same contrast is evident in their desire to accommodate to the social upheaval of wartime Britain. Barrington-Ward placed the emphasis on idealism and justice for the underprivileged, Carr on the need to plan the community and weld it into a powerful modern state. It was Carr who wrote the eloquent leading article of 1 July on 'The New Europe':

> If we speak of democracy, we do not mean a democracy which maintains the right to vote but forgets the right to work and the right to live. If we speak of freedom, we do not mean a rugged

individualism which excludes social organization and economic planning. If we speak of equality we do not mean a political equality nullified by social and economic privilege. If we speak of economic reconstruction, we think less of maximum production (though this too will be required) than of equitable distribution.

Barrington-Ward was probably more influenced than influencing in his relations with Carr. 'I agree with Carr', he wrote in his diary, '—planned consumption, abolition of unemployment and poverty, drastic educational reform, family allowances, economic organization of the Continent etc ... '[48]

In governing circles, too, Dunkirk and the fall of France gave the first clear impetus towards the consideration of social and economic reconstruction: no doubt P.E.P., *The Times*, and other sources, did something to encourage the process. Some of those in authority (though not Churchill) believed that it was important for the sake of raising popular morale to announce promises of a better post-war Britain. No one knew how to define morale, measure it, or affect it, but all were agreed that it was there: it was the woolliest and most muddled concept of the war.[49] Moreover, as an issue it shaded into the problems of overseas propaganda. The morale of the peoples of occupied Europe, and of the friends of the British cause around the world, had also to be considered. The favourite argument of the lobby which demanded a statement of war aims from the government, was that the champions of liberty everywhere would take heart when they learned what Britain was fighting for.

On 18 June 1940 the Director General of the Ministry of Information, Sir Kenneth Lee, raised at a policy committee meeting 'the question whether opportunity should be taken of an all-party government to make some promise as to social reforms after the war.' A poignant question, or an absurd one, on the day after France had sued for peace? The Germans were beginning to proclaim the birth of their New Order in Europe. Both the political warfare section of the Foreign Office, and the Ministry of Information, expressed the desire for some counter-stroke of propaganda from London. According to Nicolson, Attlee felt 'that we should put before the country a definite pronouncement on Government policy for the future. The Germans are fighting a revolutionary war for very definite objectives. We are fighting a conservative war and our objects are purely negative. We must put forward a positive and revolutionary aim admitting that the

old order has collapsed and asking people to fight for the new order.'
Nicolson, as Parliamentary Secretary to the Minister of Information,
Duff Cooper, prepared a draft declaration of war aims calling for
federalism abroad and social reform at home.[50]

The Foreign Secretary, Halifax, tended to think in the language of
the nineteenth century, but he was obviously impressed when Bevin
and others talked to him in more down-to-earth terms, for he wrote to
Duff Cooper:

> It was suggested that talk about Nationalism, Liberty and Inde-
> pendence was not sufficient and was indeed almost Gladstonian in
> relation to the whirling pace at which thought is moving. We
> were all conscious as the talk proceeded of the contrast between the
> readiness of the Nation, and particularly of the Treasury, to spend
> £9 million a day in war to protect a certain way of life and the
> unwillingness of the administrative authorities in peace to put up,
> shall we say, £10 million to assist in the reconditioning of Durham
> unless they could see the project earning a reasonable percentage ...
> I am quite certain that the human conscience in this country is not
> going to stand for a system that permits large numbers of unem-
> ployed, and that the masses of the population in foreign countries
> are also likely to be powerfully affected by whether or not we, with
> I hope the United States, are able to put up a counter plan in the
> economic field to Hitler's.

He was increasingly conscious from the Foreign Office angle, he wrote
a few days later, of the need for the government to have some definite
programme.[51]

On 23 August Duff Cooper persuaded the War Cabinet to set up a
sub-committee on war aims. Its terms of reference were:

> (1) To make suggestions in regard to a post-war European and
> world system, with particular regard to the economic needs of the
> various nations, and to the problem of adjusting the free life of
> small countries in a durable international order.
> (2) To consider means of perpetuating the national unity achieved
> in this country during the war through a social and economic
> structure designed to secure equality of opportunity and service
> among all classes of the community.[52]

The War Aims Committee, set up ten days after the opening of the
Battle of Britain, was a minor preoccupation of the government at the

time. But it was the first of an unbroken relay of committees, each of which handed on the baton of reconstruction to the next, reaching all the way through to the last meeting of the principal Reconstruction Committee in May 1945.

Having set the committee on foot, Duff Cooper consulted Halifax and Attlee, and picked the brains of Professor Arnold Toynbee, the historian (six volumes of his *A Study of History* had appeared by 1939) and since 1925 Director of Chatham House, the research institute in international affairs. Toynbee produced a long manifesto of proposals, which was not ready until after the beginning of the blitz on London in September. He called for a statement by the government setting out what it was already doing and what it promised to do for the future. On the domestic side, it would be announced that plans for rebuilding bomb-damaged areas were already in hand, and that demobilization plans would be drawn up. The government were inquiring into family allowances.[53] The social services ought to be made available to all who needed them; the voluntary hospital system might have to be superseded, health insurance would be extended, and there would be greater equality between all classes in the quality of medical services and treatment. The state would control capital investment at home and abroad. There must be equality of opportunity in secondary education.[54]

We can take it that Toynbee's paper had virtually no influence over the subsequent course of events, yet it reads like a brilliant piece of crystal-gazing. How did he manage to anticipate the future? Surely because the ideas he expressed were becoming the conventional wisdom of governing circles whenever the question of reconstruction cropped up. They had been the common coin of the progressive Centre before 1939. Now, in the aftermath of a more broadly-based government, and glowing in the reflected light of the war effort, they were circulating freely in Whitehall. The Labour leaders, who were keen to promote the idea that progress must go hand in hand with victory, were happy to encourage middle-of-the-road reform, and the middle-of-the-road reformers were at last in positions of influence on the inside.

Duff Cooper asked Chamberlain to take the chair of the War Aims Committee, and Chamberlain agreed — but a few days later his health finally broke down, and on 22 September he resigned from office. The consequent changes gave the Coalition a new and more enduring shape. The Home Secretary and Minister of Home Security, Sir John

Anderson, had been severely criticized in the opening weeks of the London blitz (which began on 8 September), for the chronic failures of local government to organize emergency services. This was not especially his fault, but it was politically convenient to move him away to the post of Lord President, where he became in effect a non-party Prime Minister of the home front. Herbert Morrison became Home Secretary in his place. At the Ministry of Supply, Morrison had had to deal with the men and machinery of industrial production, a world in which he was a novice. At the Home Office and Ministry of Home Security he was in his element as a gifted bureaucrat in charge of a galaxy of public services — including Civil Defence and the Police — and constitutional regulations concerning civil liberties and censorship. The London that he knew so well bulked large in his responsibilities. He made a very great success of his job and became in consequence a Labour minister almost as powerful as Bevin. Since, however, Bevin hated Morrison, they were not likely to form an axis; indeed personal relations among the chief Labour figures were so troubled that it is a wonder they exerted the collective influence they did. Bevin himself joined the War Cabinet in Churchill's reshuffle. He told Dalton: 'I thought it would help the prestige of the trade union movement and the Ministry of Labour if I went in. No one has ever put the Ministry of Labour in the forefront like this before.'[55] To balance the inclusion of Bevin, Kingsley Wood, the natural heir to Chamberlain's principles, was also nominated to the War Cabinet. Other significant appointments were those of Sir John Reith as Minister of Works and Planning, responsible not only for repairing the damage caused by the blitz but for planning the renewal of Britain's towns, and of Churchill's old friend Oliver Lyttelton to be President of the Board of Trade.

The blitz (whose impact on town and country planning is discussed later on) encouraged the press to keep up a flow of lofty talk about reconstruction. 'In opposing Hitler', declared the *Manchester Guardian* on 3 October, 'we must call upon the feeling for liberty and human right all over the world and make ourselves its champion as France made herself the champion of equality in 1792. The clock must not be put back to 1939.'[56] The Labour leaders threw out many broad hints about a changing world. Bevin told the Bristol Rotary Club in November that after the war, service to the community, and social security, must be the main motives of national life. This caused a former Conservative minister, Lord Londonderry, to write to Halifax:

This is nothing but a piece of Party propaganda and I should have thought that a leading member of the Government should refrain from expressing his own Party views at a time when we are engaged in a tremendous struggle for our existence ...

I am frankly disturbed by Bevin's rise to power, not that in his proper place he is [not] more than useful, but as a director cf British policy I see nothing but disaster.[57]

In vain, for at that very moment Halifax was heeding Bevin's overtures for the reform of the Foreign and Diplomatic Service, yet another sign, though a minor one, of the times.

Changes there might be, but the prophets of a British millenium soon had to agree that they were mistaken. Priestley said in the last of his series of 'Postscripts': ' ... the high generous mood, so far as it affects our destinies here, is vanishing with the leaves. It is as if the poets had gone and the politicians were coming back.'[58] When Churchill accepted the leadership of the Conservative Party early in October 1940, the Left sensed that the promised land was once more receding from view. 'It is a million pities', wrote Aneurin Bevan in *Tribune*, 'that he should have chosen to give new vigour to elements in our national life which must be progressively weakened if we are to gather sufficient strength to win through.'[59]

Churchill had been a Conservative since 1924, quite apart from his early career in the party at the turn of the century, so it made no difference to his philosophy that he was now the Tory leader. But it was a blood transfusion for an exhausted and demoralized party. He had acquired a parliamentary machine, they a hero fit to stand with Pitt and Wellington.

The committee of the War Cabinet on war aims met for the first time, under the chairmanship of Attlee, on 4 October 1940. Halifax, retreating from his previous ideas, drew up a memorandum of moral and spiritual principles under three headings. Bevin proposed a fourth, 'the direction of our economy to achieve social security and the provision of a reasonable standard of living and social welfare.' Duff Cooper found Halifax's paper so inadequate that he said nothing for fear of being impolite, as he put it. He suggested to Attlee that the Halifax and the Toynbee drafts should both be sent to Churchill: 'It seems to me that Arnold Toynbee's paper, dated Nov. 23rd., is a much more business-like and satisfactory document. There is no conflict between the two, but Toynbee's paper does put forward certain definite proposals and does give a sensation of solid ground rather than of airy visions.' In the event a compound of the two memoranda was worked out, sent to Churchill, and sunk almost without trace.[60]

Churchill, when he could be persuaded to think about the subject for a moment or two, had fairly generous Whig sentiments about 'the forward march of the common people'. Addressing the boys of Harrow, his old school, on 18 December 1940 he declared: 'When this war is won, as it surely will be, it must be one of our aims to establish a state of society where the advantages and privileges which have hitherto been enjoyed only by the few shall be far more widely shared by the many, and by the youth of the nation as a whole.'[61] But Churchill's inclination was to absorb himself completely in one thing at a time. In his view the peace would have to be framed after the war was won, or almost won. Talk of the future would divert attention from the terrible urgency of the immediate crisis, and stir up political controversy. Moreover he found such questions humdrum, gruel after the champagne of grand strategy. Bevan wrote: 'His ear is so sensitively attuned to the bugle note of history that he is deaf to the raucous clamour of contemporary life ... '[62] Reconstruction, then, could not come about through Churchill. But gradually it flowed around and past him, like a tide cutting off an island from the shore.

V Two Cheers for Socialism 1940–1942

Between Dunkirk and the battle of Alamein there were many signs of a movement to the left in popular opinion. The reaction against the 'guilty men'; the slogan of equality of sacrifice on the home front; the popularity of the Soviet Union after its entry into the war; the success of left-wing candidates at by-elections; the prestige enjoyed by figures such as J. B. Priestley, or the 'people's Archbishop', William Temple; all suggested a leftward trend: and the evidence accumulated by Mass-Observation and Home Intelligence confirms it. This steady groundswell of feeling had notable repercussions on high politics. Stafford Cripps, appearing fresh from the snows of Russia in the New Year of 1942, was swept up as though by a magic carpet to heights of popularity which made him giddy. At the end of the year a similar experience befell William Beveridge when he produced his report on the social services. In the longer run, of course, the leftward swing was to pave the way for Labour's success in the 1945 general election.

The phrase 'swing to the left' implies only that some people, probably a minority, changed their views. Mass-Observation estimated that by December 1942 about two people out of five had changed their political outlook since the beginning of the war.[1] Naturally, there was no room in this desperate phase of the fighting for most of the normal competition between parties. Such rivalries as there were had to be settled within the Coalition and behind closed doors. There was little publicity for political parties, and no open attempt by the party organizations to proselytize voters. Hence the swing to the left by-passed the question of party choice: neither students of popular opinion, nor voters themselves, could think realistically about a general election that was light years away. The trend was essentially one towards left-wing attitudes, with the Labour Party as the natural beneficiary whenever party politics revived.

Any discussion of the origins of the move to the left inevitably puts us on controversial ground. Both during the war and after, Conservatives complained strongly about the quantity of leftish propaganda disseminated in the war years. Sometimes the complaint was given a legalistic turn through the allegation that the Left were guilty of 'breaking the political truce'. But there never was a political truce in that sense. The only formal agreement among the parties to limit controversy was the arrangement of September 1939 to avoid contests in parliamentary by-elections. All three parties observed the by-election truce throughout the war, although occasionally Labour, Liberal, or Conservative Party members gave assistance to Independent or minor party candidates, who were themselves under no obligation to the truce. The co-operation of the three parties in the Coalition placed obvious limits upon formal party activity, but there was no specific agreement to avoid controversy. Attlee or Churchill were free if they wished to make party points in their speeches, and did in fact do so. Thus Churchill urged the Conservatives, in March 1942, to establish their claim as 'the main part of the rock on which the salvation of Britain was founded.'[2]

Taking the war years as a whole, however, the Right was politically quiescent while the Left kept up a barrage of activity and propaganda. After his party's defeat in 1945, the Conservative chairman Ralph Assheton wrote: 'Throughout the war the Socialists have never ceased to preach their materialistic gospel in season and out ... This theme (with variations) was plugged in their popular Press, in yellow-backed books and pamphlets, on platforms and at street corners, and, above all, by ardent disciples in guard rooms and wardens' posts, on fire watches and at factory benches.' Meanwhile, he continued, the Conservatives had suspended all political activity and concentrated on expounding government policy.[3] In June 1947 the Conservative Party organized an exhibition in London which included a section entitled: 'How the People were told a Story'. This illustrated how 'Socialist propaganda was "put across" in spite of the Party Truce.' A rogues' gallery of propagandists included pictures of the *Daily Herald* correspondent Hannan Swaffer; the proprietor of Penguin Books, Allen Lane; and the co-author of *Guilty Men*, Michael Foot.[4]

The legitimate boundaries of propaganda on the home front make an absorbing problem. The Conservative case was that, by all the accepted rules of the British political tradition, the Left had committed a foul by stirring up controversy in a national emergency. But as with football, the spectator sees that although fouls are illegal, they are constantly committed by both sides. They are as much a part of the game as the formal rules. By the standards established in World War I, when Conservative propagandists were active, the behaviour of the Left in World War II was unexceptionable. When does a fact become an opinion, an opinion a distortion, a distortion a divisive and unpatriotic act? Fascinating as it would be to referee the war of words in World War II, it would only lead us to the conclusion that politicians will be politicians, and that everyone in fact behaved in an extremely British manner.

There is also a danger of exaggerating the significance of pamphlets and radio talks. Whatever importance is attached to the influence of progressive ideology, it has to be recalled that in many respects the character of the war effort provided the most important propaganda of all. In the Britain of 1939, the Labour way of looking at things was already deeply rooted; perhaps it only required the eloquence of circumstances to make it blossom. Did private soldiers need lectures from leftish army education officers to put them into a disgruntled frame of mind with 'Them'? Did voters need Sir Richard Acland to explain to them the virtues of 'fair shares for all'? Was it only through hearing Harold Laski speak that workers could understand the advantages of maintaining the full employment brought about by the war? Were people grateful for the Russian war effort simply because Communist Party workers extolled the Red Army? The record of underground popular thought is sparse indeed. But perhaps there was sufficient freedom of mind in Britain for many people to be able to construe the facts without the aid of rose-coloured spectacles provided by professional commentators.

Among the wartime population, egalitarian conditions which had found no place in peacetime were, of necessity, the order of the day. The roots of class remained untouched, but above ground there was much levelling and trimming. The need to reduce private consumption resulted in an era of austerity and the rationing of essential commodities, a partial blow against the privileges accompanying superior spending power. After March 1942, for example, the basic petrol ration was available only to people who needed a car to travel to work. The high levels of taxation on personal incomes also had a levelling effect, leading several commentators to argue that fee-paying public schools were doomed to extinction because no one would be able to afford the cost after the war. Meanwhile, wage-earners enjoyed both an absolute and relative improvement in their position. Although wage-rates did not overtake the rise in the cost of living until July 1943, unemployment was virtually abolished, and wage packets increased rapidly because of overtime. Largely as a result of the war, the average wage income rose by 18 per cent between 1938 and 1947, while the average income from property fell by 15 per cent, and from salaries by 21 per cent.[5]

The war effort also hurled together people of different social backgrounds in a series of massive upheavals caused by bombing, conscription, and the migration of workers to new centres of war industry. Over the war as a whole there were sixty million changes of address in a civilian population of about thirty-eight million, while more than five million men and women were drawn into the three armed services. There were one and a half million in the Home Guard, and about the same number in the various Civil Defence services, by the end of 1940. More than one and a quarter million evacuees, over half of them children, were billeted on families in the reception areas in February 1941. The number of women working in industry increased by 1,800,000 between 1939 and 1943.[6] In air-raid shelters, air raid warden's posts, Home Guard units, and overcrowded trains where soldiers barged into first-class compartments, class barriers could no longer be sustained. 'It is quite common now', Lord Marley was reported as saying in 1941, 'to see Englishmen speaking to each other in public, although they have never been formally introduced.'[7]

Of course, the British people were not changed overnight into ideal citizens of a Socialist Commonwealth. In the spring of 1942 the city journalist Nicholas Davenport wrote:

Not a week passes without the Ministry of Food prosecuting hundreds of food offenders and the board of trade dozens of offenders against clothes rationing and quota laws. Cheating the excess profits tax is now so universal and so well-tried that accountants and income-tax inspectors no longer trouble to cross-question ... When food rationing was introduced it was considered smart to circumvent the law. When clothes rationing came in June 1941 it was thought clever to dress round the rules, convert crépe-de-Chine sheets into dresses or blankets into coats, buy up loose coupons from street vendors, purchase clothes without coupons at dishonest shops, and in general cheat the Board of Trade.[8]

But however much individuals evaded the rules, the social pressure for 'equality of sacrifice' was consistent and powerful, and its implications far-reaching. In peacetime there was no obvious yardstick for determining the social distribution of rewards, beyond the established values of the market-place. Socialists criticized inequality by reference to abstract principles, but it was not easy to convince an unemployed man that doctrinal beliefs had any relevance to his circumstances. There was a working-class sense of defensive solidarity, but expectations were low and the depression appeared to be the natural order of things. The sense of being deprived in relation to higher-income groups was either absent, or feebly developed: there was no point it seemed, in thinking along such lines.[9]

The war effected a quiet revolution in standards of comparison. The increase in the working-class standard of living, and especially the rising money wages commanded by labour in a period of shortage, created rising expectations. Moreover, the war effort provided an acid test for judging the social equity of rewards. The moral code of a society at war demanded that no one should benefit unduly from a collective effort in which men were getting killed. The case was never pushed to a logical conclusion, nor was it solely a question of working-class resentment against the rich. Soldiers resented their low pay and allowances by comparison with wages in the munitions industry. Coal miners were inevitably bitter as their industry fell to fifty-ninth place in the league table of industrial earnings.[10] However, the economic privileges of the managerial and upper classes did become a major source of grumbling.

In World War I the dominant ethos was one of traditional patriotism, with the emphasis upon the duty each man owed to his king and country. The searchlight of social disapproval was turned on the conscientious objector, or the munitions worker suspected of drinking too heavily. In World War II the prevailing assumption was that the war was being fought for the benefit of the common people, and that it was the duty of the upper classes to throw in their lot with those lower down the social scale. Whenever there was a military setback, or a crisis in war production, resentment would break out against the 'vested interests', people who were alleged to be clinging to their privileges at the expense of the common good.

In the ascendant demonology of the war period, the upper classes were usually to blame because they were rich, because they were obsolete in their ideas, or because they were both. To illustrate the point, it is worth dipping into the radical folklore of the period to examine two satirical inventions of the Left which, originating in the 1930s, flourished in the war years. One was 'Colonel Blimp', the creation of the New Zealand-born cartoonist David Low. Launched in the *Evening Standard* in 1934, Blimp was a rotund, bald figure with drooping walrus moustaches, a symbol of military incompetence and political reaction. 'Gad sir,' Colonel Blimp would remark, 'the only way to teach people self-respect is to treat 'em like the curs they are.' Blimp became a standard term of reference in radical journalism, and in 1942 the film director Michael Powell decided to bring him to life on the screen in a feature film, with Roger Livesey in the leading role. The aim was to tell the life story of a fictional British officer who had first seen action in the Boer War, and subsequently risen, by 1939, to the rank of general. There was to be a clear message: that modern warfare could not be conducted by the obsolete ideas and gentlemanly methods of Colonel Blimp. While the film was still in the production stage, news of it reached Churchill who wrote the following minute for the Minister of Information, Brendan Bracken, in September 1942: 'Pray propose to me the measures necessary to stop this foolish production before it gets any further. I am not prepared to allow propaganda detrimental to the morale of the Army, and I am sure the Cabinet will take all necessary action. Who are the people behind it?' Subsequently, however, the script of the film was vetted and passed by the Ministry of Information. Possibly Churchill's moral pressure had some effect, for the film, while stating its message clearly enough, dealt indulgently with its Blimp hero, General Wynne-Candy. Jeffrey Richards, in his study of the cinema of empire, has commented: 'The Blimp of David Low's wartime cartoons, petty-minded, choleric, anachronistic, achieves in this film the status of a tragic hero. He is the gentleman and sportsman who suddenly discovers that his style of life and war have gone out of fashion.' *The Life and Death of Colonel Blimp* had great success at the box-office. Churchill then tried, again unsuccessfully, to prevent it from being exported.[11]

Another vigorous creation of left-wing propaganda was the celebrated 'Cliveden set'. In November 1937 the Communist journalist Claud Cockburn revealed in his privately circulated paper *The Week* that British foreign policy was being decided behind the scenes by Lord and Lady Astor and their friends at their country house at Cliveden. By exaggerating a grain of truth, Cockburn brilliantly symbolized the thesis that the wealthy classes were plotting to sell the pass of democracy to Hitler, in return for protection against communism. It is remarkable how the Cliveden myth lived on. In March 1941, for example, *Picture Post* interviewed Lord Astor's gardener, who boasted that there were fifteen gardeners on the staff, that the estate produced for the house and not for the market, and that the Astors were not going to plough up their golf course but keep it. Under wartime conditions, these were all embarrassing allegations of anti-social behaviour. Lord Astor vigorously denied them, and received letters of apology from the editor and proprietor of *Picture Post*. Lady Astor was the target of a malicious whispering campaign in the services to the effect that she was making speeches insulting the troops. In particular she was supposed to have described the British soldiers in Italy, after the allied landings in Normandy, as the 'D-Day Dodgers'.[12] The Eighth Army had a well-known song, to the tune of Lili Marlene, called 'The Ballad of the D-Day Dodgers'; it is still sung, immortalizing an entirely baseless rumour.

The 'guilty men' thesis, in one form or another, reverberated in political debate throughout the war. In a famous incident in 1942, Baldwin tried to appeal against the requisition for scrap of the garden gates of his country home. In the House of Commons, a Conservative M.P., Captain Alan Graham, interjected at question time: 'Is the honourable member aware that it is very necessary to leave Lord Baldwin his gates in order to protect him from the just indignation of the mob?' About the same time the chairman of the Home Counties Conservative Association was complaining: 'It is not easy for us in the constituencies to lie down under constant attacks upon our Party — especially so when those who fought tooth-and-nail for years against rearmament seek to fasten upon pre-war Conservative Governments all the blame for entering the war ill-prepared.' An anonymous Conservative commentator admitted in 1943: 'I should say that the young people in the services and industry, when they look backwards, have a feeling that the politicians ought to have "rumbled" Hitler sooner than they did, that they ought to have known more about what was going on in Russia, and that if they had set about rearming sooner there would have been no "Munich" or it would have had a different result ... '[13]

One of the more imponderable influences in the erosion of conservative attitudes was the popularity of the Soviet Union. The German invasion of Russia on 22 June 1941 came at a moment when it was becoming difficult to see how victory could be won. It opened up a new vista of hope. Churchill took the lead in a great speech in which he promised all possible aid to Stalin and the Russian people ('I see the ten thousand villages of Russia ... where maidens laugh and children play'), while reaffirming his hatred of communism. The titanic struggle between Russia and Germany dwarfed the British campaign against Rommel in the Middle East. The British public knew that Russia was bearing the brunt of the war against Hitler, and that Russia desperately needed help. The fear of a Russian collapse was ever present from the day of Hitler's invasion until the New Year of 1943. It is no wonder that the 'Tanks for Russia' week inspired by Beaverbrook at the Ministry of Supply evoked a renewed effort in the factories. Home Intelligence recorded on 3 February 1942: '"Thank God for Russia" is a frequent expression of the very deep and fervent feeling for that country which permeates wide sections of the public.'[14]

What were the political effects of the association between Britain and Russia? The authorities feared that popular admiration for Russia would too often crystallize into communism. The British Communists would seize the chance of propagating their gospel under the guise of enthusiasm for the war effort. Popular opinion would be swayed. The trade union movement would be subverted. Such calculations hardly required conscious expression: they were instinctive.

The B.B.C. had broadcast, until the invasion of Russia, a programme consisting of the national anthems of the allies. This went on the air on Sunday evenings before the nine o'clock news and was a popular feature. The B.B.C. refused to add the Internationale to the list after 22 June. Trivial as the matter was, it had a symbolic importance and the B.B.C. was severely criticized in the press and the House. After trying to compromise by playing the Kutusov 1812 march, the B.B.C. scrapped the programme.[15] Eden's Private Secretary, Oliver Harvey, minuted on 11 July: 'The P.M. has issued an instruction to the M. of I. [Ministry of Information] that the Internationale is *on no account* to be played by the B.B.C.' Churchill maintained the ban until January 1942 when Eden told him that it was becoming increasingly embarrassing, since the Russians played 'God save the King' on every conceivable allied occasion in Russia, while the British were forbidden to return the compliment. 'All right', Churchill minuted with ill-disguised disdain:

and from 22 January the Internationale could be broadcast and played on official occasions.[16]

On the broad issue of containing domestic communism Churchill instructed the Ministry of Information 'to consider what action was required to counter the present tendency of the British Public to forget the dangers of Communism in their enthusiasm over the resistance of Russia.' R. H. Parker, the director of the ministry's home division, had already diagnosed the problem as follows, in July 1941:

> The Russians are operating against the Germans beyond expectation, so that we cannot call Communism in itself inefficient. The control by Government in this country of industry, the levies made upon earnings and upon capital are all integral parts of the Bolshevik theory, and the combination of all these factors ... is bound to educate the public into assuming that Communism ... is either a reasonable alternative to the pre-war system of democratic theory or is a logical sequence to the wartime system of control ...[17]

Soon after Churchill's directive, Parker's division of the ministry issued a general instruction defining its policy. Perhaps the most intriguing feature of this was the suggestion that the best people to contain the British communists were their masters in Moscow:

> ... it is the policy of this Ministry to attempt to curb exuberant pro-Soviet propaganda from the Left and to anticipate criticism inspired by Communist Party action and to prevent initiative from falling into or remaining in the hands of the Communist Party ... It is intended to develop a close liaison between this Ministry and the Soviet Embassy which will greatly assist us in dealing vigorously with the English Communist Party since the attitude of the Soviet Government is almost cynically realist about the war position ... We shall hope, therefore, in the case of each week or exhibition, to obtain the assent of the Soviet Embassy and to publicize such demonstrations as being under the joint aegis of the Soviet Embassy and this Ministry.[18]

The regional information officers of the ministry were quietly encouraged to take over local campaigns begun by the Communist Party. Ian MacLaine describes how the local Communists in Manchester organized an Anglo-Soviet committee to raise funds for Russia. Prompted by the North-West regional information officer, the lord mayor gave the committee his blessing but persuaded it to disband so that he could form one of his own with ministry representation.[19]

The alliance with Russia was bound to bring with it the blooming of a thousand committees and societies to publicize the Soviet cause and encourage friendship between the two nations. The Foreign Office was as watchful as the Ministry of Information in its desire to see this movement in safe hands. Sir Orme Sargent explained to the Secretary of the Cabinet, Sir Edward Bridges, that the Foreign Office was giving its blessing to a new body, the Anglo-Soviet Public Relations Committee, because it was 'a sensible organization including M.P.s of all parties, interesting itself in Anglo-Soviet matters and tending to become the most authoritative and representative of all such organizations which have a habit of falling into the wrong hands.'[20] Right-wing trade unionists were as anxious as any Foreign Office official to keep the communists in check. The General Secretary of the T.U.C., Citrine, realized that there would have to be some organization to provide contact between British and Russian trade unions. In August 1941 he therefore approached the Foreign Secretary, Eden, who in turn wrote to Churchill:

> You know Citrine's feelings about Communism, which he expressed again with undiminished emphasis, even going so far as to say that, were he given a choice between life under a Nazi or Soviet rule, he would be in doubt as to which to choose ... Citrine said he would carefully choose the men to be so employed and that he thought it was wiser to take the initiative in the matter than to be forced into it, as he almost certainly would be at the next Trade Union Conference.[21]

Before long Citrine was in Moscow arranging with his opposite number, S. M. Shvernik, to set up an Anglo-Soviet Trades Union Committee. In January 1942 a Russian trade union delegation visited Britain and conducted a triumphal tour of mines, factories and shipyards. Workers gave these burly experts in the regimentation of labour a naïvely warm-hearted reception, chalking up the hammer and sickle and the 'V' sign side by side. Shvernik put salt on the tails of the British trade union leaders by closing his visit with a press conference at which he urged management to pay more attention to the views of shop stewards.[22]

The immense popularity of Russia was bound to acquire political overtones. On the negative side, circumstances dictated a moratorium on the stock criticisms of the communist system. This was no time, for example, for the former British spy in Russia, and anti-Bolshevik publicist, Sir Paul Dukes, to be lecturing to the forces: he was banned from doing so. A case of unofficial censorship was the rejection by T. S. Eliot at Faber and Faber of the manuscript of Orwell's satire on the Russian revolution, *Animal Farm*, on the grounds that it was not 'the right point of view from which to criticize the political situation at the present time'.[23] Eliot's political views were strongly right-wing, but he too collaborated in the whitewashing of Britain's ally — without whom the war might be lost.

The official authorities would have liked to de-politicize enthusiasm for Russia by concentrating on the military, patriotic, and anodyne aspects of Russian life, but in practice this was very difficult. The two politicians who presented themselves to the public in 1942 as champions of Russia, Cripps and Beaverbrook, were· both convinced anti-communists. Yet both found themselves singing the praises of the Soviet system. Beaverbrook resigned from the War Cabinet in February 1942 in order to campaign for the opening of a Second Front in Europe to help Russia in her hour of peril. In his first speech throwing down the gauntlet, Beaverbrook justified the treason trials of the 1930s and denied the existence of religious or racial persecution in Russia.[24] Today the horrific nature of Stalinism is as clearly understood by the British Left (apart from old-fashioned Communists), as by anyone. But in the war years it was still an article of faith among 'progressives' — people who were not Marxist, but optimists for mankind — that the Soviet system was a great and inspiring experiment in science and democracy. Such was the doctrine of the surviving Edwardian giants, Bernard Shaw and H. G. Wells, and indeed of Lloyd George; or at least, it was one of his doctrines. Progressive Liberals found their hopes of Russia mirrored in the outlook of a national newspaper, the *News Chronicle*. The Fabian colonial expert Leonard Barnes could still write a book arguing that British administrators in tropical Africa had much to learn from the practice of Soviet rule over the peoples of central Asia.[25] Even people who had followed the communist line in the 1930s as 'fellow-travellers', and in many cases been soured and disillusioned by Stalin's pact with Hitler, and the opposition of British Communists to the war, still in some sense believed in Russia. The founder of the Left Book Club, Gollancz, sponsored in 1941 an exposé of the defeatist tactics of the British Communist Party before Russia entered the war. But then he became secretary of the

Anglo-Soviet Public Relations Committee. This organization, although encouraged by the Foreign Office and presided over by the royal physician Lord Horder, was none the less a distinctively progressive bandwagon: Eleanor Rathbone and Phillips Price were the vice-chairmen, and the committee included Acland, Addison, Bevan, Brailsford, Seymour Cocks, Creech-Jones, Laski, Low, Kingsley Martin, John Parker, Priestley, Mervyn Stockwood, Strauss, Tanner, Wells, Wintringham and Woolf.[26] Thus, quite apart from the activities of British Communists, the Soviet system was guaranteed much favourable publicity. 'Twenty-five years of Soviet progress' was the title of an exhibition held in London in November 1942, opened by the Soviet Ambassador, Maisky, and the President of the Royal Academy, Sir Edwin Lutyens. Talks were included by leading British authorities on the Soviet worker, Soviet women, art, agriculture, theatre, music, and the Red Army—presenting Russia as a society distinguished by its civic virtues.[27]

The favourable image projected of the Soviet Union was reinforced by the near monopoly which communists and fellow-travellers possessed over the supply of information and publicity material about Russia. What was the most comprehensive work of reference in English on the subject? It was Sidney and Beatrice Webb's *Soviet Communism: A New Civilisation*, originally published in 1935 with a question mark at the end of the title, later dropped from the 1937 edition. Films, photographs, posters, and other display material, derived almost exclusively from Soviet propaganda and its British outlets. Thus the Society for Cultural Relations with the U.S.S.R., a fellow-travelling organization, came into its own. In the first year of the Anglo-Soviet alliance, its assistance was called upon by six government departments, the United States embassy, and the B.B.C.[28] To mark the first anniversary of the alliance of Britain and Russia a demonstration and pageant were arranged at the Empress Hall, Earls Court, in June 1942. Of the three bodies which organized the meeting two—the Joint Committee for Soviet Aid, and the Russia Today Society—were under Communist direction. The collection appeal was by the Communist Pat Sloan, and the script of the pageant was the work of another Communist, Montagu Slater. But the chairman of the meeting was the Bishop of Chelmsford, music by the band of the Coldstream Guards, and the main speaker was Cripps, a member of the War Cabinet. 'May God bless Russia', said the Bishop, extending the Popular Front to heaven itself.[29]

The authorities, as has been said, tried hard to take control of the new currents of friendship with Russia. The Foreign Office successfully steered the Boy Scouts Association away from the lure of the Anglo-Soviet Youth Friendship Committee, a Communist Party 'front' organization which, according to Scotland Yard Special Branch, had been set up by a meeting at Ley On's Chop Suey restaurant near Piccadilly.[30] But in the course of 1942 both the Communist Party and Beaverbrook organized mass demonstrations in favour of the launching of a Second Front in Europe, gathering crowds of 50,000 in London and Birmingham respectively.[31] This gave the authorities fresh cause to be anxious, since it threatened to undermine both them and their strategy. In October 1942 the Cabinet decided to stage demonstrations to salute Russia's resistance. These meetings, wrote Bracken, the Minister of Information, to Eden, 'would serve a double purpose. First, to show the Russians that all sections of political opinion are genuinely behind our Alliance with Russia; second, to get in ahead of the Communist Party in organizing authoritative and impressive demonstrations in the main centres of population.' The twenty-fifth anniversary of the formation of the Red Army, 23 February 1943, was chosen as a suitable occasion, and a dozen demonstrations arranged in large towns up and down the country, each addressed by a minister. Nothing like this had been seen since the coronation of George VI. The full panoply of civic celebration was brought into play and the platforms groaned beneath the full cast of British bigwigs. At the Albert Hall Malcolm Sargent conducted the London Philharmonic, Basil Dean produced the 'show', and Louis MacNeice contributed a short play, 'Salute to the Red Army'. MacNeice's script was read with gloom and irritation by foreign officials. Sir Alexander Cadogan complained: 'This is sorry stuff, but I am glad to see that there are *some* references to Britain's part in the war.' Sir Reginald Leeper was more despairing: 'What has happened to the people of England if they can really stomach this?' In a letter to the Director-General of the Ministry of Information Sir Orme Sargent expressed the disquiet of the Foreign Office:

We feel that Section 10 of the script should be omitted or so radically altered that it does not, as at present, imply that the 'upper class man and woman' took a very poor view of Russia's chances in 1941, whereas the working class men and women did not do so. My Secretary of State also thinks that the Internationale should not be sung at the end of the programme as proposed in Section 27 but that it should only be played.[32]

Unlike Priestley's 'Postscripts', MacNeice's play was vapid and forgettable, but interesting as a minor revelation of a major wartime phenomenon, the tension between the Conservative mind in authority and the left-wing intellectual hired to fight the war of words. When Russia began to win the war, and the Second Front movement died away, the words and celebrations were gradually turned off. Bracken told the War Cabinet that the festivities arranged to mark Red Army Day 1944 would be greatly reduced by comparison with the previous year.[33]

The effect of pro-Russian feeling on domestic political attitudes is impossible to measure. In spite of all the years of anti-Bolshevik propaganda before the war, most people seem to have been pro-Russian, or so two opinion polls would suggest:

December 1938
Q: If there were a war between Germany and Russia, which side would you rather see win?
A: Germany, 15 per cent; Russia 85 per cent.
January 1939
Q: If you HAD to choose between Fascism and Communism which would you choose?
A: Fascism, 26 per cent; Communism, 74 per cent.

These results accord well with Orwell's observation, late in 1941, that all the more thoughtful members of the working class were 'mildly and vaguely pro-Russian', and would be so long as Russia made even the pretence of being a workers' state.[34] But the Russian alliance dramatically increased membership of the Communist Party. The highest pre-war figure for membership was 18,000, in the first half of 1938; by June 1941, owing to the party's anti-war line, it was down to about 12,000. There followed a surge of recruitment among industrial workers in the big war factories. Membership may have been as high as 65,000 in September 1942, although it tailed off slightly later on.[35]

Pro-Russian feeling had two important repercussions for the Conservatives. The successful resistance and recovery of Russia were taken to vindicate the communist system: they seemed to show that socialism could organize industrial production and inspire the hearts of a people. Secondly the Conservatives were vulnerable to the charge of despising and underrating Russia, both before and during the war. A Conservative minister, Colonel Moore-Brabazon, who had taken over from Beaverbrook as Minister of Aircraft Production in May 1941, said privately in the presence of trade unionists that it would be best for Britain if Germany and Russia fought each other to a standstill. The secretary of the Amalgamated Engineering Union, Jack Tanner, caused a sensation by letting this particular cat out of the bag at the T.U.C. conference in September. Home Intelligence soon noted that Moore-Brabazon was one of the ministers who 'are constantly mentioned as names which inspire foreboding in the public mind', and Churchill dismissed him in the reshuffle of February 1942.[36] The Second Front campaign, conceived initially as a movement to ginger up the government, soon turned into an attack on 'men in high places' for letting Russia down, once it became clear that there was to be no Second Front in 1942. In politics a distinctive outlook is usually compounded from a host of values and ideas which have become associated, and reinforce one another. The pro-Russian element in wartime radicalism was one piece of the jigsaw. At the post-mortem held by Conservative candidates after the party's defeat at the 1945 general election, Captain Aubrey Jones declared:

> At meeting after meeting questioners would get up and say: 'Look what nationalization has done for Russia, and how strong and great she has become ... We had very properly and rightly concluded an alliance with Russia; but to my mind, we, as Conservatives, interpret that alliance so blindly that we have no longer said what should have been said about the internal working of the Communist State. How then could we hope to win an election on an anti-Socialist issue'[37]

The popularity of Russia probably worked in favour of the Labour Party, in spite of the profound hostility of its leaders to communism. In this respect and many others the war ripened public opinion while the Labour Party machine lay rusting and the voice of Labour was stilled. Labour was clearly in the lead when the first opinion polls on the subject of a general election were resumed in June and July 1943, but it was only after the summer of 1943 that party organization and propaganda began slowly to recover.

The war effort made party activity in the constituencies extremely difficult. The shortage of halls and speakers, and the claims of the services and essential war work on the time of members and officials, the black-out, air-raid warnings, the restriction on motoring after dark, all were obstacles. A memorandum by the Labour Party staff at Transport House in March 1942 summed up the state of organization as follows:

(a) Individual membership has declined and continues to do so.
(b) Propaganda by public meetings is far less practised.
(c) There has been a large reduction in the output of printed propaganda.
(d) Constituency and local Labour Parties in many cases are meeting less often and are not as active as they were.
(e) Federations of Constituency Parties act only when prompted by Headquarters.
(f) Social activities are reduced, and although continued in some cases have virtually ceased altogether elsewhere.[38]

In July 1942 the National Agent circulated a report surveying eighty-eight Midlands constituencies and recording that there were only six with full-time secretaries or constituency agents. The absorption of women into war work from the end of 1941 eroded the activities of the women's sections.[39] This picture is very much what we might expect to find, but it is important to establish it because of the persistent Conservative misconception that the swing to the left arose partly because Labour kept its organization going at a high pitch of efficiency due to the fact that many trade unionists were in reserved occupations and thus stayed at home, while Conservative agents were in the armed forces. The individual membership of the Labour Party, which had stood at 408,884 in 1939, was past its low point by 1943, but still reduced to 235,501.[40]

While the party's organization seized up, official propaganda for the party was taboo. Bevin boasted, with only a slight exaggeration, that his first party speech after the formation of the Coalition was in April 1945. [41] The official party line, especially at the height of the war effort, was that considerations of national unity forbade activities which might disturb relations with the Conservatives. A National Executive memorandum of January 1942 argued that as long as Labour was in the government, there could be no campaign based on 'party aggrandisement, inter-party controversies, persistent and destructive criticism of the government, naval or military tactics'. What would the Labour Party say if the Conservatives were to launch a widespread campaign demanding the maintenance of capitalism? 'The answer is certain. We should counter-attack at once.' Rejecting the dreams of Laski, Attlee told the National Executive in April 1942 that he and his Labour colleagues held the view that Labour should not try to get socialist measures passed under the guise of winning the war.[42] After March 1942 Independent candidates began to defeat government Conservative candidates at by-elections. Local Labour parties were under orders from Transport House to co-operate in the return of Conservative supporters of the government, or at least take no part against them. The rank and file found this a most galling discipline and at the Party Conference in May 1942 a National Executive motion endorsing the truce was barely accepted by a majority of 1,275,000 to 1,209,000. There were party 'rebels' such as Emanuel Shinwell, Richard Stokes, and Bevan, who criticized the Churchill government's conduct of the war and continued to denounce the Conservatives, but generally speaking the Labour Party steered clear of party controversy and acted in the spirit of the contemporary slogan: 'Be like Dad: keep Mum.' The first reassertion of party feeling came in February 1943 when the Parliamentary Party rebelled against the government's lukewarm treatment of the Beveridge report. And in July 1943 the party's National Executive decided to launch a campaign, beginning that autumn, to recruit membership and expound party policy.[43]

In the years 1940 to 1942 the main source of radicalizing propaganda was certainly not the official Labour apparatus, but the leftish intelligentsia. During the 1930s several of the intelligentsia became Marxist, but the predominant type of radicalism among the intellectuals was more pragmatic—progressive on the great questions of fascism in Europe and social reform at home, but following in the footsteps of Wells or Lloyd George rather than Lenin. Both Marxists and progressives became obsessed by the problem of communicating with the mass of the public, and equally with the effort to explain to the middle classes how the working classes lived. There was a movement, part literary and political, part commercial, to radicalize domestic communications. The growth of the documentary film movement under John Grierson, the formation of Mass-Observation by the poet Charles Madge and the anthropologist Tom Harrisson, the establishment of Penguin Books by Allen Lane and of *Picture Post* by Edward Hulton and Stefan Lorant, the transformation by Cecil King and Guy Bartholomew of the *Daily Mirror* from a right-wing paper for women into a left-wing *vox populi*, all occurred during the 1930s and were all related developments. The most lonely and original pioneer in the field was Orwell himself. This mission by the progressive middle classes to educate democracy and increase social understanding between the classes was to come into its own after the outbreak of war. Having expressed his loathing of imperialism in his novel *Burmese Days*, Orwell was drawn into war work broadcasting to India, and this was symbolic of a more general phenomenon, which he described in 'Poetry and the Microphone' (1943):

> The British Government started the present war with the more or less openly declared intention of keeping the literary intelligentsia out of it; yet after three years almost every writer, however undesirable his political history or opinions, has been sucked into the various ministries or the B.B.C. and even those who enter the armed forces tend to find themselves after a while in public relations or some other essentially literary job ... No one acquainted with the Government pamphlets, Army Bureau of Current Affairs lectures, documentary films and broadcasts to occupied countries which have been issued during the past two years can imagine that our rulers would sponsor this kind of thing if they could help it.[44]

The progressive intelligentsia did succeed in conveying something of their ideals through official services, although of course they had to pick their words with care. The leaders of the documentary film movement, notably Basil Wright, challenged the Films Division of the Ministry of Information to adopt a propaganda policy, by which they meant a set of war aims in line with their own left-wing inclinations: not surprisingly, no such policy was adopted.[45] The relationship between the progressive writer and the official authorities in wartime was likely to be delicately balanced between the need of the authorities to avoid controversy, and the writer's need to express his feelings. The Right were constantly on guard and ready to call for a tightening up of communications. When Priestley returned to the air in January 1941 with another series of 'Postscripts' and began by calling for a declaration of war aims, he was at once censured by Sir David Hay of the Glasgow Unionist Association. Priestley, banking perhaps on his own popularity, became more and more an aspiring political leader. In a talk to the National Trade Union Club in March 1941 he openly called for the Left to take the gloves off before the Right administered a knock-out: 'I am walking a tightrope every Sunday evening. I doubt if it will be possible to continue, because you people give me no assistance. It is time you wakened up. You are being sold.' He spoke of the callousness of the ruling classes towards the sacrifices being made by Labour to win the war, and warned that he would soon be pushed off the air because of right-wing hostility.[46] The Conservative 1922 Committee had indeed protested once more against his broadcasts. Asa Briggs, the historian of the B.B.C., writes: 'It was plain ... that there was a real conflict of views in 1941 between Priestley and the Government not only about domestic social policy but about international war aims.'[47] Three left-wing luminaries, Julian Huxley, Professor Joad, and later in the war Barbara Ward, were among the most popular performers on the 'Brains Trust', one of the most successful B.B.C. programmes in wartime. The members of the team answered listeners' questions on a host of factual as well as speculative matters, but there was fairly strong censorship of the content to prevent controversy.[48]

Although Priestley was off the air the B.B.C. remained uncomfortably leftish in the eyes of some Conservatives. In April 1942 the Under-Secretary at the War Office, Lord Croft (formerly Sir Henry Page Croft), a Tory of diehard outlook, was agitated by the problem and expressed his anxiety to the Government (and Conservative) Chief Whip, James Stuart. It was not so much, he wrote, that the B.B.C. was purveying left-wing propaganda, as elevating left-wingers into positions of eminence. Having 'listened in' on five successive evenings, Croft had heard

a long talk from Mr Harold Laski as an interpreter of American opinion: a long talk from Mr G. D. H. Cole on Social Problems, who informed us that he was acting for the Government; the oft repeated Mr Joad as the star of the Brains Trust ... long reports of the extremist views of the Teachers on the denial of the right of people to give their sons such education as they are prepared to pay for, and extracts from at least five speakers on this theme.[49]

Similar reactions developed to Army education. Two separate organizations were involved: Army Education proper, and the Army Bureau of Current Affairs. Army Education was the job of the Army Education Corps. By the outbreak of war in 1939 it was practically defunct, and the first instinct of the War Office —typical of the blinkered outlook of the 'phoney war' —was to wind it up. But there were strong arguments in favour of educational activities as the Army was built up. At best they engaged the troops' interest, improved morale, and imparted new skills. At worst they provided a safety valve and harmless diversion. In the New Year of 1940 a powerful academic body, the Central Council for Army Education, was set up to channel teachers from schools and universities into extra-mural lectures and courses for the Army, with the Army Education Corps administering the scheme. In August 1940, however, there were still only 113 officers and 238 instructors in the Corps. As in so many aspects of the wartime revolution, the fundamental change began in the summer of 1940. A War Office Committee under Sir Robert Haining produced a report in September advocating voluntary education carried out by the soldier in his spare time in the humanities, 'utilities', arts and crafts—in fact in anything he wanted to take up.[50] Meanwhile Churchill's Under-Secretary for War, Lord Croft, had grasped the need to improve morale. The Army faced a long winter of inactivity ahead, and had only the glorious retreat of Dunkirk to look back upon. Page Croft wanted education and entertainment to be provided on a grand scale—travelling cinemas, technical classes, correspondence courses, and plenty of stirring stories of the Empire and regimental tradition.[51] A Director of Education was appointed to implement these plans, and the Army became a voluntary part-time university for those who wanted it. By the winter of 1943–4 more than 110,000 courses, lectures and classes were in progress. To the voluntary programme a small compulsory element was added in the winter of 1942. One of the compulsory hours was occupied by a course in citizenship, whose curriculum was laid down in a monthly pamphlet: 'The British Way and Purpose'.[52]

The Army Education Corps had a mildly left-wing reputation. The left-wing intellectual going into the forces was likely to find the job of education officer an attractive one, while the main pre-war adult education organization, the Workers' Educational Association, had strong bonds of sympathy with Labour and reformers in general. Harold Laski, tirelessly making the rounds of Army and R.A.F. camps, often found that the education officers were his former pupils from the London School of Economics.[53] On the whole the Army Education Corps was extremely moderate and strictly educational in its aims, steering clear of controversy. But education in current affairs was in itself objectionable to the strict Tory interpretation of the war—which enjoined that all domestic debate should be set aside in the interests of military unity. When, for example, an education officer suggested to the Conservative M.P. Maurice Petherick a number of topics on which he might address the troops, Petherick was furious at the ideas suggested – the Beveridge Report, the future of Germany, 'everything connected with Russia', the problems of employment. Writing to Churchill's P.P.S., Harvie Watt, he said:

> I am more and more suspicious of the way this lecturing to and education of the Forces racket is run ... I maintain most strongly that any of these subjects which tend towards politics, even if the lecturers are Tories, are *wrong*!
> ... The object, therefore, is to avoid all subjects which lend themselves to politics and for the love of Mike do something about it, unless you want to have the creatures coming back all pansy-pink.[54]

There were a few political activists in the Education Corps. In the spring of 1942 the government's attention was drawn to the activities of two education officers, Major George Wigg and Major Gilbert Hall. Hall and Wigg were discontented with the way Army Education was run, and Hall sent a memorandum to Cripps, who had just then entered the War Cabinet, which according to the Secretary for War appeared to advocate 'the introduction of the commissar system into the Army.' Wigg's ideas were in line with Hall's, and the pro-Communist M.P. D. N. Pritt had been sent a copy of the paper. Shortly afterwards the War Office received a request from Northern Command for Pritt to lecture to the troops; the source of the request was Wigg. Pritt had already slipped through the unofficial embargo on his lectures twice at the invitation of Hall. In explaining the background of the Pritt case to Churchill, the Secretary for War, P. J. Grigg, wrote:

> I must say I am shocked that people of this sort should have found their way into the A.E.C., but as the work of both had been well reported on, and Cripps would not allow me to use the only clear piece of evidence we had of a breach of regulations, I could do no more than give instructions that both should be watched and specially reported on in six months time.[55]

The Cabinet approved the War Office's informal ban on Pritt – and Wigg and Hall survived the episode.[56]

One of the suggestions of the Haining Report of 1940 was that officers should give informal talks and lectures. From this idea germinated the Army Bureau of Current Affairs (A.B.C.A.), established in June 1941 with W. E. Williams as its director. A pillar of the Workers' Educational Association, and Secretary of the British Institute of Adult

Education, Williams had also joined with Allen Lane in the hazardous adventure of Penguin Books, and pioneered the Penguin Special series, which consistently attacked appeasement. Lord Croft, while disliking his political affiliations, recognized in him 'a very vital personality' and 'a man of ideas as well as push and drive.'[57] The heart of the A.B.C.A. scheme was a compulsory weekly session of the troops at platoon level, with the officer in charge leading off a discussion on a pre-arranged topic. The Bureau itself prepared two regular bulletins which appeared on alternate weeks from September 1941: 'War', on the latest military events, and 'Current Affairs'. These provided a framework of topics, though officers were not obliged to stick rigidly to them. A.B.C.A. was intended to raise morale, especially by improving relations between officers and men, but also to educate for education's sake. The 1943 A.B.C.A. handbook proclaimed the ideal set forth by Cromwell of the citizen soldier who 'must know what he fights for and love what he knows'. The topics suggested for discussion in 'Current Affairs' began by ranging across the world, but from the end of 1942 they reflected the increasing preoccupation with domestic life at home after the war.

It was not so much the content of A.B.C.A. bulletins which upset its critics—for they were generally cautious and uncontroversial—but the very idea of political discussion and debate in the Army. Churchill was the most powerful of its opponents. The most conscientious and paternal of officers in World War I, he could not bring himself to accept that an officer should encourage debates which might undermine his own authority in the eyes of his men. On 6 October 1941 he minuted the then Secretary for War, Margesson: 'Will not such discussions only provide opportunities for the professional grouser and the agitator with a glib tongue?' Margesson could only reply that the Army Council had unanimously approved the scheme, and refer to the real danger of boredom among the troops. Bracken, the Minister of Information, fed Churchill's suspicions: 'Out of 10 young officers who essay to lead their men in these political discussions, 9 are going to get hopelessly tied up with two or three of the men who really know something about politics or public affairs ... '[58]

Such forebodings were disproved. Discipline did not suffer. According to the first A.B.C.A. report of April 1942 troublesome incidents were rare, and usually caused by a foolish officer. Some 60 per cent of units were operating the scheme, and while some officers contented themselves with reading out the weekly bulletin, most were more enterprising and their general level of performance higher than was expected. Both officers and men had welcomed A.B.C.A.[59]

What was the political significance of Army Education? It is only possible, without specialized research, to rely on careful guesswork. The weekly A.B.C.A. session must have been sweet relief for many a bored and fatigued private soldier: the chance of a quiet cigarette and a discreet nap. Nor, to glance ahead to 1945, does the assumption that the troops voted Labour necessarily reflect the influence of Army Education. As Duff Cooper wrote: 'To the private soldier the government is the War Office and the War Office is the sergeant-major. The exercise of the franchise gives to the private soldier a brief and blessed opportunity of expressing his opinion of the sergeant-major.'[60] Nor was the formal education provided in current affairs much guide to political choice. Both A.B.C.A. and the Army Education Corps had to work within strong constraints against controversy. To seek for a Labour message in the pages of 'Current Affairs' or 'The British Way and Purpose' would be a fruitless quest. The political significance of Army Education lay in the circumstances of the war, the bias in content imparted by the type of liberal progressive who was active in educational activities, and most of all in the stimulus given to the informal discussion of politics.

Because the war followed on the heels of a long phase of Tory supremacy, political education was bound to involve the use of Chamberlain's England as a chopping-block. Page Croft, being on the right of the Conservative Party, was particularly sensitive to this inevitable technique. He wrote in 1943:

When we first discussed the promotion of talks on current affairs our main object was to create an interest among all serving soldiers in the course of this war; knowledge of the Dominions, India and the Colonies and a broad outline of British citizenship, the Constitution and methods of government and administration.

Since that time discussions on material provided by A.B.C.A. and to an extent by British Way and Purpose, on all home affairs have tended all the time in the following directions:
(a) the promotion of criticism upon financial, economic and social structure existing in this country at the outbreak of war.
(b) the suggestion that all soldiers should regard material considerations as they concern themselves as the most important factor in life.

(c) the suggestion that the pre-war way of life must never be consented to and that something much better is coming.

(d) that the old kind of job in which the man was serving is possibly inadequate and unsuitable and not one to which he would wish to go back to.[61]

In the eyes of Page Croft, to question whether something was right or inevitable was to stoke up discontent. But to men concerned with a liberal education, citizenship began only when people could ask intelligent questions and weigh alternatives. In this sense A.B.C.A. could only be subversive, all the more so because it encouraged open-ended discussion. A very frank and informed account of A.B.C.A., which *The Times* published in September 1942, let the cat out of the bag and deserves lengthy quotation:

> Of the dozens of topics so far promoted for discussion in the Army a few stand out in popularity. Reconstruction themes are well up. Although they develop plenty of debate about such bread-and-butter matters as post-war security, they also reach broader issues like 'What's wrong with democracy?' 'Do we deserve our Empire', 'Town planning', 'How should our schools be run?' Far from being incompatible with concentration on winning the war, there is abundant evidence that the most martial and efficient units are the keenest to debate these questions. A.B.C.A.'s official bulletins are necessarily cautious, detailed, and objective documents. Yet many units go much farther into controversy, and often pick their own subject rather than sample the 'Chef's own choice'. The War Office is sufficiently Nelsonian to turn a blind eye if a unit is disciplined enough and well enough led to tackle such thorny topics as electoral reform or the second front ... Rash as it is to look too far ahead, the A.B.C.A. habit may develop in the demobilized soldiers such a social consciousness as may make them a shrewder electorate than their fathers were.'[62]

A.B.C.A., in fact, was only the most prominent instance of the widespread wartime hobby of the discussion group or 'brains trust'. In the London Fire Service, discussion groups on current affairs were introduced at about the same time, and involved some 15,000 men and women in weekly meetings of between ten and thirty people.[63]

On 17 October 1942 Churchill minuted the Secretary for War on the subject of A.B.C.A.: 'I hope you will wind up this business as quickly and as decently as possible, and set the persons concerned to useful work.' But A.B.C.A. was too deeply entrenched by this date. Churchill continued to express anxiety about it, threatening a Cabinet inquiry in the spring of 1943, and requesting the Lord President, Sir John Anderson, to make a special report. Anderson gave A.B.C.A. a clean bill of health.[64]

No one will ever be able to measure the significance of A.B.C.A. in forming the political opinions of the troops. On the eve of the 1945 election the journalist J. L. Hodson, accompanying British forces into Germany, recorded a conversation between three officers which takes us as close as we are likely to get to a conclusion:

First officer: 'The men are so sick of five years of officer rule they'll swing violently to the Left.'
Second ditto: 'But they're not really politically-minded – they don't realize that Belsen and what's behind Belsen is what the war is really about.'
Third ditto: 'In fifteen months in the ranks I never heard politics mentioned.'
First ditto: 'Yes, but A.B.C.A. teaches them something is wrong, and that changes are needed. They'll vote Labour, although they couldn't give you the names of three Labour politicians.'[65]

The role of the press and publishing in the leftwards swing is also difficult to measure. From about 1930 onwards there was a marked shift towards the left in the world of printed communications. This was evident in the national press. The *Daily Herald*, which began the 'circulation war', pushed up its share of sales among the major national dailies from 13·1 per cent in 1930 to 20·4 per cent in 1937.[66] At the end of the decade came the transformation of the *Daily Mirror* to a mass circulation working-class paper thriving on new techniques of 'human interest' and sensationalism, and tub-thumping anti-Tory politics. Its circulation rose from 1,750,000 in 1939 to 3,000,000 in 1946. And although much of this additional circulation was balanced by a loss of sales by the two other left-wing dailies, the *News Chronicle* and the *Daily Herald*, the swing of the *Mirror* to the Labour side shifted the balance of the national press from about 1938 onwards. Taking the eight principal morning newspapers, and categorizing them a little roughly as 'Right' or 'Left', the long-term share of national sales changed as follows:[67]

| | percentage of national daily sale in | |
	1930	1947
Right-wing dailies	68·6	51·5
Left-wing dailies	30·0	48·1

The abrasive political style of the *Mirror* is a familiar subject. After denouncing Munich, it did its bit in building up Churchill, harried the 'guilty men' after the fall of Chamberlain, championed the Beveridge Report, and Labour in the 1945 general election. Its fundamental line was populist agitation against 'Colonel Blimp, the Old School Tie, Vested Interests' and the other archetypes of radical demonology. Its vendetta against the military authorities eventually led the government to threaten its suppression in February 1942.

While the *Mirror* created most noise, radical journalists were quietly achieving influence in other Fleet Street offices. The 1930s was the decade of the radical journalist, whether it was Ritchie Calder reporting the Jarrow march for the *Daily Herald*, or Vernon Bartlett the Munich Agreement for the *News Chronicle*. First-hand contact with events, especially with events in Europe, was bound to harden sheltered liberals into more adamant left-wingers. Vernon Bartlett moved a long way between 1933, when he wrote something very close to an apologia for Hitler, *Nazi Germany Explained*, and 1938, when he won the Bridgwater by-election in opposition to the Munich Agreement. Michael Foot too, went left between 1934, when he was proclaiming 'Why I am a Liberal', and 1940, when he wrote *Guilty Men*.[68] It was a refugee from Austria, Stefan Lorant, who launched the new weekly *Picture Post* as editor in 1938. The property of Edward Hulton, a radically-minded Liberal, *Picture Post* created the highest standards of photographic journalism. It specialized in light entertainment and high thinking. In the summer of 1940 Lorant left for the United States and Tom Hopkinson took over as editor. About the same time *Picture Post* began to take a strong line on post-war reconstruction. More than any other medium, *Picture Post* was the popularizer of the views of intellectuals and progressive politicians. Here Quintin Hogg could expound the case for Tory reform, and A. J. P. Taylor, supported by Robert Boothby, argue that Russia had a right to the Baltic states.

The *News Chronicle*, owned by the Liberal Cadbury family, had passed in 1936 into the hands of Gerald Barry as editor. With colleagues

like Bartlett, Paul Winterton and A. J. Cummings, Barry moved the
paper further left. It was pro-Popular Front before the war, and to
Churchill's great irritation pro-Second Front in 1942. In the 1945
general election it was nominally Liberal but in fact cheering on
Labour. In the Beaverbrook stable, the London *Evening Standard* was
given greater political latitude than the *Express*. Under the editorship of
Frank Owen (1938–42) and Michael Foot (1942–4), both passionate
left-wingers, it was anti-appeasement and pro-Second Front. Of course
Beaverbrook championed the Second Front, but there can be no doubt
that Owen and Foot did so from their own political standpoint. Since
1934 the paper had carried, without any interference from Beaverbrook,
the cartoons of Low – among the finest propagandists the Left ever
produced. The new regime at *The Times*, following the departure of
Geoffrey Dawson in 1941, has already been discussed. Barrington-Ward
and Carr, prompted discreetly by Stanley Morison, clothed themselves
in mandarin pink, while introducing other radical writers like François
Lafitte, David Owen, and Donald Tyerman, to the staff. Less well-
known is the change at the *Observer*. In February 1942 the proprietor,
Waldorf Astor, sacked J. L. Garvin, the great Conservative sermonizer
who had edited the paper since 1910. In theory he was sacked because
he supported Churchill's retention of the Ministry of Defence, which
Astor opposed. In fact he was getting too old and fixed in his ways.
The new editor was a Liberal sympathizer, Ivor Brown; but the paper
was increasingly under the influence of Astor's heir, David Astor, whose
sympathies were with Labour.[69]

The changes in the press found their parallel in publishing, with the
rise of Penguin Specials, the political series sponsored by Allen Lane's
Penguin Books, and the Left Book Club, which had been founded in
1936 and continued through the war, ending in 1947. And there were
many other tributaries of the stream, not least the documentary film
movement, which, having grown up under the aegis of John Grierson
in the 1930s, was to provide an idealistic portrait of Britain to itself
during the war.

How can we assess the impact of the new radical propaganda? The
professional communicators involved – Allen Lane, Tom Hopkinson,
Edward Hulton and so forth – knew one another well and formed a
fairly conscious network. 'We were anti-They,' Allen Lane recalled.
'We were against the privileged classes.'[70] On the shelves of second-
hand bookshops there can still be found the Penguin Specials in their
orange stripes, and many polemical works from Gollancz – *The Trial*

of Mussolini by 'Cassius', for example. That works of this type created
an ideology for a generation of Labour activists is impossible to doubt.
Indeed the second-hand copies of Laski, Cole, Brailsford and others
often have annotations from painstaking disciples, struggling to make
sense of the world in a nutshell. But as Muriel Spark's heroine Miss
Jean Brodie remarked, on the subject of Brownies and Girl Guides, 'For
those who like that sort of thing, that is the sort of thing they like.'
Radical ideas were for a minority who enjoyed abstraction, and wanted
to think critically about society while still holding on to optimistic and
reassuring beliefs. To read the left-wing propaganda of the late 1930s
and war years is to enter a thought-world of certainty in which intelligence and justice, however outraged for the time being, are bound
to triumph. For a moment we might almost be re-living the convictions
of the English Puritans in the 1630s, on the eve of their triumph and
subsequent defeat. In a diluted fashion, the Marxist vision of the rise of
the industrial working class prevailed: and the war seemed to prove
that the day of the common people had arrived. But how does intellectual fashion relate to the massive working-class vote for Labour in
1945? Perhaps the intelligentsia were accurate prophets, and World
War II was in some respects a victory of the working classes in Europe
over fascism. Perhaps left-wing ideas, popularized and translated into
stock phrases by the press, A.B.C.A. and so forth, carried the day
indirectly. After 1945 the radical intelligentsia claimed to have won the
election for Labour: but we shall never know whether their influence
was great or small.

The advantage of turning to the by-elections of the period is in discovering the way in which the discontents of wartime tended to be
expressed at the expense of the Conservatives. In the early days of the
war, under Chamberlain, by-elections had been contested, if at all, by
fringe anti-war candidates who picked up few votes. The formation of
the Coalition government in May 1940, and the psychological unity of
the heroic days which followed, rendered by-election contests still
more superfluous from the average voter's point of view. But from the
spring of 1941, when the failure in Greece was followed by the humili-
ating loss of Crete, independents at by-elections were able to tap a new
current of frustration, deepened by guilt about Russia, difficulties over
production, and stalemate in the Middle East. The first by-election
defeats for Conservative supporters of the government, at Grantham
in March 1942 and Rugby in April 1942 followed the Japanese conquest
of Malaya and a string of other disasters. Between the spring of 1941

and the end of 1942, nineteen Labour seats fell vacant and two of them were contested. Twenty-eight Conservative seats fell vacant, nineteen were contested, and three lost. In other words, the by-election independent knew his trade—blame the Tories—and the voters responded. Some of this discontent must have been temporary, but given the evidence of a swing away from the Tories in 1940–2, and the statistical harmony between the by-elections of 1941–2, and their successors of 1943–5, the moral must be that these obscure and even comic contests were the harbingers of Labour victory in 1945.

In which case Noel Pemberton Billing, unfurling his banner at Hornsey in May 1941, was the first. This was ironic, since he was also a lone throw-back to the jingoism of the First World War, during which he had been the first candidate to succeed in defying the electoral truce at the East Hertfordshire by-election of March 1916. A champion of air power before the R.A.F. existed, Billing later in the war figured as the hero of a libel case in which he alleged that the Germans had a black book listing perverts in high places in English society. In World War II he campaigned for reprisals against German air action, and victory by bombing alone. Travelling in a yellow Rolls-Royce, and bellowing out the cry of vengeance, Billing also introduced into his campaigns a general anti-Tory note, stressing Conservative misdeeds, and the need for full employment in peacetime. Fighting Conservatives at four by-elections, he gained between 24 per cent and 44 per cent of the vote.[71] He was followed into the lists by Reg Hipwell, founder of *Reveille*, the private soldier's counterblast to the Sergeant-Major and the War Office. At Scarborough in September 1941 he stood on the programme of better pay for servicemen and their wives and a 20 per cent increase in old age pensions. He accused the President of the divisional Conservative association of quitting Dunkirk ten days before his men, and the Conservative candidate, who only had one leg, of shirking military service, (which Hipwell himself had never experienced). Hipwell pointed out that the fighter pilot Douglas Bader had no legs at all. A frivolous candidate, Hipwell told a Mass-Observer: 'I only came up here for a holiday—something to make a change.' Nevertheless he struck the authentic period note of vague, bloody-minded resentment: 'For Democracy, not Vested Interest', 'For Equal Opportunity, not Old School Tie', ran his slogans. Later Hipwell contested Hampstead, by this time equipped with an 'eight-point programme' calling, among other things, for a Second Front, the dismissal of the 'men of Munich', and a 'square deal' for servicemen and their families. His assistant Winifred Henney contested Harrow on the same programme in December.[72] In these early contests of 1941 the Conservative share of the poll was almost 6 per cent higher on average than in the 1935 general election. Despite the shifts of population brought about by the war, and the fact that the electoral register had last been compiled in March 1939, the pro- and anti-Conservative breakdown of the electorate could still be discerned. Despite the climate of national unity and the injunctions of Churchill and sometimes Attlee to vote for the government candidate supporting the all-party Coalition, the old pattern of Left and Right remained.

By-elections told a steady tale of the welcome given to anyone who could provide left-wing or radical credentials. The first Independent to defeat a government candidate, Denis Kendall, stood at Grantham in March 1942, proclaiming in one of his leaflets: 'Denis Kendall is another Stafford Cripps. Independent yet Churchillian.' Kendall was the manager of a local engineering firm noted for its high wages and welfare benefits: the local leaders of the Amalgamated Engineering Union were among his allies. Kendall announced that he was a 'production man', with no other aim in politics but the speeding up of the munitions industry. Once a member of the local Labour Party, he had failed to secure nomination at the by-election in the Conservative interest. He argued that the state should take over inefficient firms, attacked the 'cost-plus' system whereby government contractors were awarded a fixed percentage of profits in relation to costs of production, and stressed his membership of the War Cabinet Gun Board. The local Labour Party decided to restrain their candidate, or party workers, from helping Kendall. But Reg Hipwell and *Reveille* gave him support. The Communist Party called on voters to support the Conservative candidate, Sir Arthur Longmore, whom Churchill had recently retired from the command of the R.A.F. in the Near East.[73] On election day Kendall won 50·8 per cent of the poll, reducing the Conservatives' share of 1935 by 9 per cent.

When Churchill reshuffled his government in February 1942 he dismissed one of the remaining 'men of Munich', David Margesson, the Secretary for War. With Margesson ennobled as a viscount, his seat of Rugby, a gilt-edged Conservative property, was vacant. The Conservatives put up Sir Claude Holbrook, fifteen years chairman of their local association. On the eve of poll he wrote an article for the local press entitled 'Why I Won'. A few days before, however, a carpet-bagger had arrived in the shape of W. J. Brown, a complete stranger to the constituency. Brown, a Labour M.P. in the parliament of 1929, had broken with the party to flirt with Oswald Mosley's New Party, and subsequently fought a personal campaign against all party machines. He was best known as a broadcaster, and General Secretary of the Civil Service Clerical Association. W. J. Brown's programme, as communicated to the *Birmingham Post*, deserves quotation as a guide to the many discontents which an independent candidate might try to play on:

> (1) total efficiency in total war effort; (2) reconstitution of the Government on a non-party basis; (3) breaking through the contradictions in production, the Civil Service, politics and propaganda, which hinder the war effort; (4) maintenance of the freedom of the public Press and of public criticism against the growing tendency of the Government towards repression; (5) democratization of the Army; (6) real equality of sacrifice.
>
> As to the post-war situation, he stands for (1) a non-party approach to the problem of reconstructing Britain; (2) such alterations in the social set up of Britain as are necessary to achieve the abolition of unemployment, the ending of the slums and the banishing of economic insecurity from the minds of men; and (3) a peace settlement which deals with all factors which must be dealt with if peace is to be permanent—economic, political, and social.[74]

Despite a resolution by the National Council of Labour condemning him, the local Labour Party was split by Brown's candidature. But it was plainly not organization which gave Brown his triumph, reducing the Conservative share of the vote by over 13 per cent compared with the result in the 1935 general election.

On the same day that Brown defeated the Conservative at Rugby, 29 April, another Independent achieved an even greater upset at Wallasey, where George Reakes reduced the Conservative share of the vote by 35 per cent. Reakes was a local councillor of twenty years' standing, who had drifted away from the Labour Party by championing conscription, rearmament, and appeasement under Neville Chamberlain. He stood at the invitation of certain Conservatives who feared that an outside candidate would be foisted on them. In fact the local organization chose as their man Alderman Pennington, another long-serving councillor. Reakes and Pennington were good friends, and the contest was therefore devoid of any great controversial interest, except that provided by Stafford Cripps's brother Leonard, a wealthy right-wing shipowner, who effectively disguised whatever aims he had in mind beneath a mask of platitudes. Reakes attributed his victory partly to the migration of thousands of better-off voters from the constituency to avoid bombing. 'Above all', he concluded, 'there was the firm resolution, formed by many at the time of Dunkirk, that they would take the first opportunity of registering a protest against those who had brought the fortunes of the nation so low.'[75]

Reakes's campaign had been enlivened by the missionary zeal of Sir Richard Acland, a quixotic Christian socialist of deep sincerity, and one of the minor wonders of the war years. Acland's father, grandfather and great-grandfather were Devonshire baronets who sat as Liberal M.P.s in the House of Commons. Indeed, Sir Francis Acland, the thirteenth baronet, was still M.P. for North Cornwall when his son Richard was elected M.P. for Barnstaple in 1935. Acland became a convert to socialism in 1936, and in 1940, after reading John Hadham's book, *Good God*, he underwent a 'physically compelling' conversion to Christianity. For Acland, the war had to be nothing less than a crusade against selfishness, a renunciation of the economic motive in favour of truth, love, and service. This was the message argued passionately in his book *Unser Kampf* (1940), and such was the response that Acland gathered together a band of disciples in a new movement called Forward March. Strange to say, Acland hoped that Churchill would put himself at the head of it and lead the way to the socialist millennium. Acland recognized in Reakes a comrade of the Left, but he suspected the credentials of Kendall and Brown, and was eager to prevent the return of opportunist candidates.[76]

Also ready to enter the field was J. B. Priestley's newly-formed 1941 Committee, a network of progressive intellectuals who wanted to give the war effort a leftward turn (see pp. 188–9). In May 1942 they issued a Nine-Point Declaration to serve as a platform for the Left at by-elections. Setting out the current radical prescription for victory, the declaration advocated:

(1) Greater equality of work, payment, sacrifice and opportunity;
(2) Transfer to Common Ownership of services, industries and companies in which managerial inefficiency or the profit motive is harming the war effort; (3) Reform of the Government Supply

Organizations ... (4) Establishment of effective Works Councils
... (5) Elimination of Red-Tape in the Civil Service ... (6)
Maximum freedom of expression ... (7) British initiative in planning an Offensive Grand Strategy ... (8) Repudiation of any policy
of Vengeance ... (9) Preliminary Post-war plans for the provision
of full and free education, employment and a civilized standard of
living for everyone.[77]

Among the members of the 1941 Committee was the editor of
Picture Post, Tom Hopkinson, and it was he who suggested to a fellow
journalist, Tom Driberg, that he should stand in support of the Nine-
Point programme at Maldon, another Conservative seat where a by-
election was due. Driberg was best known as the creator of the 'William
Hickey' gossip column in the *Daily Express*. He decided to stand, he
told the historian A. J. P. Taylor at the time, in order to express the
viewpoint of the ordinary servicemen. Driberg's campaign workers
included local Conservatives as well as Labour supporters, and from
outside the constituency came leading members of the 1941 Committee
to appear on his platform: J. B. Priestley, Tom Wintringham, and
Vernon Bartlett, the *News Chronicle* correspondent. Acland appeared
once more in the lists, and Driberg observed gratefully that 'despite his
almost George Washington reputation for Christian integrity' he was a
master of electioneering tactics.[78]

The Conservative candidate, a taciturn farmer, had the fates against
him. A few days before polling day, 25 June 1942, news arrived of the
fall of Tobruk, regarded at the time as one of the worst disasters of the
war. Whether this won Driberg the seat is uncertain, for there was
already powerful discontent with Britain's failure to take the offensive,
but *The Times* observed that he exploited the news of the defeat. Of all
wartime by-elections, Maldon recorded the highest turn-out, and the
Conservative share of the vote fell by 22 per cent. Simultaneously,
Forward March and the 1941 Committee announced that they were
about to merge into a new political party, Common Wealth, with
Priestley as chairman.

By the autumn, Priestley had withdrawn from the life of politics,
leaving Acland as the undisputed leader of the party. Common Wealth
never had more than about 10,000 members, and at the zenith of its
fortunes, only four M.P.s in the House of Commons: Acland, and three
members who defeated Conservatives in by-elections at Eddisbury
(April 1943), Skipton (January 1944) and Chelmsford (April 1945). It

came into existence only because the Labour and Liberal Parties were unable to contest Conservative-held seats owing to the by-election truce, and it is unlikely that many voters regarded it as a serious force in its own right. Again it can be argued that there was nothing essentially new about Common Wealth: it was reminiscent of the Left Book Club or the League of Nations Union, and for some at least of its active members, like Peggy Duff or George Wigg, it was no more than a staging-post along the highway of left-wing causes. The organizing secretary, R. W. G. Mackay, in post-war years a Labour M.P. noted for his devotion to the cause of a socialist United States of Europe, certainly regarded Common Wealth as no more than a stand-in for the Labour party.

In this he was a-typical. Common Wealth was an idealistic movement whose ideals were brought into full blossom by the peculiar conditions of wartime society. When Acland made over his family estate to the National Trust in 1943, he was not seeking to avoid death-duties: he was living up to his belief that service to others, not private gain, should be the mainspring of social action. In time of war, the ideal of service to the community had a special appeal. But as the social profile of Common Wealth revealed, that appeal had a distinctively middle-class resonance. The typical Common Wealth activist, Dr Calder explains in his illuminating and definitive study of the party, was the suburban professional employee – a teacher, manager, or civil servant. Whereas Labour thinking was permeated by the demand for higher wages, and the built-in conflict between employer and worker, Common Wealth's appeal was overwhelmingly ethical, summoning up co-operative in place of economic man. The ethos of Common Wealth was conveyed, for example, in the slogan of Flight-Lieutenant Moeran, one of its candidates in 1943: 'Human Fellowship, not In-human Competition; Service to the Community, not Self Interest; the Claims of Life, not the Claims of Property.'[79] The Common Wealth movement aimed at a libertarian form of socialism in which all property beyond what was necessary for personal use would be taken into common ownership. Like a violinist playing in a brass band, it took up in a more sensitive rendering the basic wartime theme of 'fair shares for all'.

It is sometimes alleged that wartime austerity measures were unpopular: Churchill thought so, and struggled against many a proposal to extend rationing, or curtail amusements, under the impression that this would be bad for morale. Thus he wrote to his economic adviser, Lord Cherwell, early in March 1942: 'I deprecate the policy of "misery first", which is too often inculcated by people who are glad to see war-weariness spread as a prelude to surrender.'[80] But later in the month Sir Stafford Cripps, who had recently entered the War Cabinet, announced a new round of cuts in civilian consumption. The regional offices of the Ministry of Information reported to Home Intelligence that 'an "almost pathetic gratitude" had been the main reaction to the new restrictions on clothing and fuel, both of which are regarded as real steps towards total war.'[81]

The demand for 'equality of sacrifice' ran like a thread through the weekly Home Intelligence reports. In the week of Cripps's announcement, Home Intelligence reported the feeling that *it did not go far enough*:

> There is a growing evidence of a feeling among certain sections of the public that 'everything is not fair and equal and that therefore our sacrifices are not worthwhile.' In particular, there is some belief that the rich are less hit by rationing than 'ordinary people' for the following reasons:
> (a) They can eat at expensive restaurants.
> (b) They can afford to buy high priced goods in short demand, such as salmon and game.
> (c) They can spend more on clothes and therefore use their coupons more advantageously.
> (d) They receive preferential treatment in shops, as 'people giving large orders' are favoured and the poorer people wanting 'little bits' are refused.
> (e) They receive preferential treatment as regards petrol rationing. To quote a Postal Censorship report: 'we can see the Big Bugs riding in their posh cars and poor beggars can't get petrol for business.'[82]

Whatever term we choose—jealousy, sense of justice, awareness of relative deprivation—the social drive towards egalitarianism was obviously a powerful force. Hence the general principle of rationing was always popular. In June 1942, for example, nearly 3,000 housewives were asked which of the food schemes then in operation they would like to see retained after the war. The majority wanted to maintain food rationing, points rationing, the national and priority milk schemes, and even the non-profitmaking, state-run British Restaurants. A survey in the summer of 1942 disclosed that 90 per cent of those interviewed approved food rationing, more than 60 per cent giving as their reason the belief that it ensured fair shares.[83]

There were early signs that levelling ideals were being projected, at least by some, into the post-war future. In January 1941 the Postal Censor made a special report on the attitude of lower-middle and working-class correspondents to the question of the peace and the future at home. He commented: 'They are looking forward confidently to a post-war levelling of class-distinction and a redistribution of wealth ... They anticipate a post-war Government which is either "national" (with a strong socialist complexion) or labour, with either Mr Churchill or Mr Bevin as Prime Minister.'[84] J. B. Priestley, who spent three years from the summer of 1940 as an itinerant speaker up and down the country, recalled: 'In hotels, camps, factory canteens, hostels, railway trains, bars, restaurants, I listened and talked and argued. Topic Number One was probably the state of the war at the particular time; but Topic Number Two, running Number One very close, was always the New World after the war. What could we do to bring our economic and social system nearer to justice and security and decency? That was the great question ... '[85]

It is very difficult to believe that the Conservative Party would have won a general election at any point after June 1940. The Labour leaders were not popular figures in the same sense as Churchill, nor is vaguely left-wing sentiment the same as a commitment to the Labour Party. But it is not far removed. In the spring of 1942 Mass-Observation conducted a poll in three separate areas of the country in which people were asked who they thought would win the next general election. About half would express no opinion: they were not, after all, being asked how they *intended* to vote. The remaining results were as follows:

	Expecting win by	
	Conservatives	Labour
	per cent	
London	12	27
Midlands	14	33
North	17	26

These figures are either wrong, or they show that Conservatism was in far worse shape in 1942 than in 1945.[86]

About the same time as these results were collected, a careful study of the state of public opinion was conducted by Home Intelligence, intrigued by a phrase which had occurred in one of the regional summaries: 'home-made socialism'. Every region was asked to report, without making any special inquiries, whether they had any evidence of such a phenomenon. All but two of the thirteen regional offices reported that something of the kind was in the making. The Northern Region, commenting on 'a strong tendency towards the ideal of socialism in all classes', suggested as explanations

    (a) A levelling up of classes, resulting from bombing and rationing.
    (b) The Russian successes.
    (c) The blaming of vested interests for 'ills of production'.
    (d) The fear that conditions of the last post-war period may be repeated.

The South-Western Region, underlining the rather vague quality of the trend, spoke of 'a distinct swing to what is vaguely called "the Left" ... It does not appear to be on Labour Party or Socialist lines, but it does seem to be directed against the Conservative Party, in so far as this represents the so-called "Men of Munich", "the old gang", "Colonel Blimp" and similar diehard types.' Summing up the various regional reports, Home Intelligence concluded that the chief characteristics of the movement were

    (a) Its non-political character.
    (b) The impetus it has received from the Russian successes.
    (c) A general agreement that 'things are going to be different after the war'.
    (d) A revulsion against 'vested interests', 'privilege', and what is referred to as 'the old gang'.[87]

VI Blueprints from Above 1940–1942

There is a paradox to the war years in domestic politics. The popular swing to the left presaged the defeat of the Tories by Labour, and the resumption of party strife. But simultaneously there was emerging among the parties, as the result of their partnership in the Coalition, a common approach to the long-term future. From this distance in time (1975), the new wartime consensus appears more significant than the particular verdict of the electors in 1945. For the war inaugurated an era of consensus, sustained later on by the growth of 'affluence' in the 1950s and 60s.

Since the days when Disraeli defined a sound Conservative government as 'Tory men and Whig measures', the word consensus has had a wide range of possible meanings. The modern party system could never have developed without a fundamental consensus between the parties over the rules whereby they competed for power and governed the country. Had the Conservatives supported a military rising by the Ulster Protestants against Home Rule, as seemed possible before 1914, or had Labour backed a successful General Strike in 1926, the parliamentary system would in effect have broken down. By encouraging direct action outside Westminster, parliamentarians would have been abdicating their own authority in favour of rival leaders. They had a professional, as well as a civilized interest, in the peaceful resolution of problems through their own mediation.

At a higher level, consensus implies that the two front benches in the House of Commons are in substantial agreement about the way government should be managed, and can win the support of the rank-and-file of their membership for such policies. But this does not exhaust the definition. There appeared to be a consensus in the 1920s between the Conservatives under Baldwin and Labour under MacDonald: the

Labour goverments of 1924, and 1929 to 1931, were distinguishable only by a dim and flickering light from their Conservative surroundings. In practice, the Labour Party of the day was the prisoner of circumstances. It was hemmed in by the lack of a majority, by its leaders' inexperience and sense of inferiority, and by a powerful Establishment hostile to experiment. By August 1931 the Labour Cabinet had virtually to admit that it was helpless, and MacDonald was only behaving with ruthless logic in joining with the Conservatives. But it is surely inaccurate to speak of the consensus between a prisoner and his gaol. Consensus presupposes a more equal meeting of minds and a more genuine fusion of purpose.

The new Labour leaders of the 1930s were more self-confident and effective figures, and they shared the bitterness which the party as a whole derived from the experience of the means test, the Spanish Civil War, and the appeasement of Hitler. As has been remarked before, the Churchill Coalition was therefore a genuine partnership in which the Conservatives gave a great deal of ground in home affairs. The Labour Left, whose spokesmen were Laski, Bevan, and Emanuel Shinwell, steadfastly refused to look this fact in the face, and could only repeat that their leaders had 'sold out' to the Conservative party machine.

Churchill, who liked to think of himself as a national leader, and had no great love for the Conservative machine, was very much in favour of continuing in peacetime the co-operation which the parties (including the Liberals, for whom he had a soft spot) had begun in war. Addressing a Conservative gathering in March 1941, he deplored the prospect of a general election at the end of hostilities. He continued: 'I may say, however, that some of the ties and friendships which are being formed between members of the administration of all parties will not be very easy to tear asunder, and that the comradeship of dangers passed and toils endured in common will for ever exercise an influence upon British national politics far deeper than the shibboleths and slogans of competing partisans.'[1] For Labour, Arthur Greenwood declared in June 1941: 'Among my colleagues representing other political points of view I have found a strong and sincere wish, not merely to avoid the mistakes made after the last war, but to co-operate in the fullest measure in working together to restore the shattered fabric of our civilization ... '[2]

All three parties to the Coalition can claim to have contributed to the programme of wartime reforms. Two Conservative ministers,

R. A. Butler and Henry Willink, piloted the schemes for education and the health services respectively, Keynes. the originator of the 'full' employment policy, and Beveridge the author of the social security programme, are frequently identified with Liberalism. On the Labour side. Greenwood was the first minister to be given specific responsibility for reconstruction, and the Labour team were to dominate the powerful Reconstruction Committee between 1943 and 1945.

Such an explanation, redolent with goodwill to all sides, hardly cuts very deep. Among the Conservatives, enthusiasts for reform were always in a minority, except possibly in the field of education. Neither Butler nor Willink could claim to have originated the schemes which they championed. The Labour Party, meanwhile, came forward with most of the petrol to fill up the tank of reconstruction, but strange to say played only a negligible part in the design and development of the engine. The Liberal claim to include Beveridge and Keynes in the party pantheon has to be regarded with vigorous scepticism. Beveridge and Keynes were first and foremost powerful technocrats, experts in certain areas of policy who looked upon all parties and governments as potential vehicles for their influence. Keynes was a convinced and lifelong Liberal, but he made his impact as an economist, and it would be foolish to assume that his economic doctrines were inspired by the traditions of a particular party. Beveridge had no formal links with the Liberals until September 1944, when he became the Liberal candidate for Berwick-on-Tweed.[3] Keynes and Beveridge can more usefully be regarded as the greatest of the social and administrative experts, usually of no party at all, who provided the technical blueprints for reconstruction in World War II.

So there is less of a paradox to wartime politics than appears at first. The growth of consensus in the realm of government was not in contradiction to the popular swing to the left. Both represented a loss of initiative by the Conservatives in home affairs, and a repudiation of the record of the National government of 1931-40. Naturally, they were linked: Beveridge, for example, sensed the popular demand for change while also reinforcing it by the publication of his report. We have to picture the Conservatives by 1945 as victims of the wind and tide, driven off course, and apprehensively dropping anchor in strange Keynesian waters.

*

At the close of 1940 the War Aims Committee of the Cabinet, under Attlee, had failed to agree on a declaration of war aims and handed the matter back to Churchill. In January 1941 Churchill announced that Arthur Greenwood, Minister without Portfolio, had been moved from his job in charge of production and would henceforth be responsible for the study of post-war problems and reconstruction. He was to work on the assumption that the Coalition would continue for about three years after the war, and prepare practical measures of advance in 'four or five great spheres of action.'[4] Greenwood was a sad figure whose career was sinking. Although a popular character in the Labour Party (he was elected treasurer by the party conference in 1943, defeating Morrison), Greenwood no longer had enough grip on the daily round of administration to survive in a key job. The Reconstruction Committee over which he presided until he was dismissed in February 1942 met on only four occasions. His appointment, in fact, indicated that reconstruction had a very low priority in Whitehall in the second winter of the war.

Greenwood began with a great fanfare from the press, and at the first meeting of his committee on 27 February 1941 circulated a grandiose memorandum which classified every possible goal at home and (blithely assuming the acquiescence of the Foreign Office), abroad. For example, among the long-term issues at home which required action were:

(1) Economic problems
   (a) National finance and taxation.
   (b) Banking, investment and credit policy.
   (c) Foreign trade and commercial treaties.
   (d) The stabilization of employment. The location and organization of industry. Reconstruction of basic industries.
   (e) Development of new industries and the place of rural industries; availability of labour.
(2) Social problems
   (a) National minimum.
   (b) Reform and consolidation of social services.
   (c) Equality of opportunity and reform of educational system: facilities for enjoyment of leisure.
   (d) Planning of town and country.[5]

Yet Greenwood's committee could only co-ordinate the work of the various departments: it had no powers to compel action. Greenwood was so restricted in what he could do that he did not even support a proposal, of which he approved in principle, for the B.B.C. to broadcast a series of talks on the problems of the post-war world: he feared Churchill's opposition.[6]

In a letter to the editor of the *New Statesman*, Kingsley Martin, in December 1940, Keynes accused him of 'attempts to exploit the war in favour of something you want anyhow on the bogus ground that it will promote the winning of the war when quite likely it won't.'[7] But at that very moment Keynes, who had been asked by the government to draw up a declaration of war aims as a counterblast to Hitler's propaganda about a new order, was writing his own philosophy into his manifesto. As completed in January 1941, Keynes's declaration would have opened with an attack on the peace-makers at Versailles for having ignored economic questions, and continued: 'The British Government are determined not to make the same mistake again. Mr Bevin said recently that social security must be the first object of our domestic policy after the war. And social security will be our policy abroad for the peoples of all the European countries not less than at home.' The government would also commit itself 'to radical remedies for our own unemployment', and the adoption of an international currency to restore world trade.[8]

Keynes's paper, although never published, marked the beginning of the policies of social security for all and full employment. In May the Foreign Secretary, Anthony Eden, repeated in a speech the pledge that social security must be the first object of policy both at home and abroad. In August, after the meeting of Churchill and Roosevelt off Newfoundland, the two leaders promulgated that cloudy mass of phrases known as the Atlantic Charter, a declaration of peace aims by the leaders of democracy. The War Cabinet persuaded Churchill to insert a clause dealing with social security. This theme, therefore, had been built firmly into British propaganda.[9] But would anyone ever breathe life into it?

In February 1941 the T.U.C. sent a deputation to meet the Minister of Health, Malcolm MacDonald (Ramsay MacDonald's son), and the Secretary for Scotland, Ernest Brown. The main aim of the T.U.C. was the strictly limited one of reforming the national health insurance system, the rotten plank in the structure of social insurance. The cash benefits obtained by workers when they were sick were lower than benefits paid during unemployment, an illogicality which would have to be ironed out. The medical benefit under health insurance provided for the attention of a doctor, but not for diagnostic, specialist or hospital services. Both cash benefits and medical entitlement varied, as they were administered by a large number of 'approved societies', often branches of the big commercial insurance firms. The approved societies were obliged to be non profit-making, but some had bigger funds and offered superior benefits. Unemployment benefit varied according to the size of the unemployed man's family, but health benefits were again illogical in taking no account of dependents and their needs. The T.U.C. delegation also pointed out the growing poverty of the voluntary hospitals, and called for an overhaul of the hospital system.[10] On 22 May 1941 the Minister of Health announced the formation of an inter-departmental committee of officials 'to undertake, with special reference to the inter-relation of the schemes, a survey of the existing national schemes of social insurance and allied services, including workmen's compensation, and to make recommendations.' It was an unspectacular brief for the sorting out of a mass of red tape. Bevin, who was glad to find a way of easing Beveridge out of the Ministry of Labour, suggested to Greenwood that Beveridge should be chairman of the committee.

Greenwood, who still retained his political flair, at once saw the opportunity which had come his way. He inspired Fleet Street to write up the committee as the harbinger of social security for all, and shrewdly alerted opinion in the United States and Canada by a timely broadcast. Beveridge, however, at first regarded the committee as a technical chore diverting him from problems of manpower. It may have been his secretary and future wife, Janet Mair, who convinced him that it offered great opportunities. The committee was set up on the eve of the German invasion of Russia. Six months later came the Japanese attack on the American fleet at Pearl Harbor. On the face of things, the period was a grim and barren season for thinking about the shape of the peace. Yet on 11 December Beveridge circulated to his committee of officials the first outline of his new welfare state. Social insurance would be designed to create a national minimum, and would involve three fundamental assumptions: a National Health Service, family allowances, and the maintenance of employment.[11] Thus Beveridge had decided what he wanted before the committee began to hear evidence from interested parties. The civil servants on the committee were technical experts with no power to gainsay him even if they had wanted to. They had been chosen on the assumption that administrative codification was the chief aim. Now that Beveridge was proposing to advise the War Cabinet on major political questions, it no longer made sense for relatively minor civil servants, with no authority to speak for their departments on questions of policy, to sign the report. Hence the Treasury, under Kingsley Wood, insisted that Beveridge alone should sign, taking the sole responsibility for the report's recommendations.[12]

• Keynes's great innovation of 1941 was the reform of the budget. In wartime the main method of economic planning was by the use of physical controls: the fixing of import quotas and the allocations of raw materials to industry, the rationing of consumer goods, the compulsory shrinking ('concentration') of less essential industries, and the direction of man- and womanpower. Physical planning culminated with the introduction of the first manpower budget in December 1942. Since manpower was the ultimate limiting factor in the mobilization of the war economy, it eased life for the government to budget by fixing the levels of manpower necessary in the services, civil defence, war industry, and the rump of the peacetime economy. The manpower budgets became 'the main force in determining every part of the war effort from the numbers of R.A.F. heavy bombers raiding Germany to the size of the clothing ration.[13] But there remained a financial dimension which it was also vital to plan. In this respect the overriding aim was to prevent inflation, with the industrial strife and angry queues of housewives at the shops which must follow.

Keynes, as will be recalled, had tackled the inflationary demon in the first weeks of the war in a series of articles for *The Times*, later expanded into his book *How to Pay for the War*. Even before Keynes was given his room at the Treasury, the government was influenced by his approach and employed the budget to damp down demand. But they had no means of measuring the amount by which demand had to be reduced. Inflation resulted from the gap between effective money demand and the value of goods and services. Excess demand could be removed partly by voluntary savings: the remainder had to be taken away compulsorily through taxation. But what was the size of the gap? Only an estimate of the future level of demand and savings, taking account of the taxation and spending of the government, could provide the answer. In the winter of 1940–41 Keynes, and two of his disciples in the economic offices of the Cabinet, James Meade and Richard Stone, pioneered the first official statistics of national income and expenditure. Before then Chancellors of the Exchequer had dealt exclusively in the figures of government revenue and outgoings. The new statistics were a little hazardous, but they transformed the budget into the key regulator of the market economy. The budget introduced by Kingsley Wood on 7 April 1941 was a triumph for the Keynesians. 'We drank champagne that night', Stone recalled, 'and felt we had accomplished something.'[14] The methods of forecasting and regulating aggregate demand were introduced for the immediate purpose of helping the war effort, but their application was permanent. When the war ended, and physical controls were gradually abandoned, they would plainly become the chief instrument of economic management. They also opened up the vista of maintaining demand at the level necessary to prevent mass unemployment. At a moment in the summer of 1941 when the British military authorities were predicting the collapse of Russian resistance, Meade produced a paper in which he proposed four main techniques for the maintenance of peacetime employment: banking, investment, consumption, and budgetary policies. Meade's paper fired the imagination of the deputy head of the Treasury, Sir Richard Hopkins, and gave rise eventually to the 1944 White Paper on employment policy.[15]

Keynes argued that the budget for 1942 should concentrate on social needs. Both he and his fellow Treasury economist, Hubert Henderson, put the case for the introduction of family allowances. This and other ideas came up against the opposition of the Inland Revenue Department, which argued that 'the purpose of the income tax is not the redistribution of income.'[16] At this stage of the war, the main ideas of reconstruction were in their first bloom, but largely, also in a state of suspended animation. Like the sleeping beauty, they awaited the prince's kiss. In almost every field of reconstruction, Beveridge's report of December 1942 was to be the decisive breath of life.

The impetus towards educational reform was very nearly destroyed early on by Churchill. In the summer of 1940 the President of the Board was an unspectacular figure, Herwald Ramsbotham, who gave the impression of being firmly guided by his officials. The Permanent Secretary, Sir Maurice Holmes, in a note on post-war reconstruction circulated on 5 November 1940, commented that various bodies and individuals were putting forward proposals for educational reform, and that it was up to the Board to lead rather than to follow. Discussions within the Board began at once, energetically pursued by the Deputy Secretary, R. S. Wood. A note by him written on 17 January 1941 conveys his sense of the atmosphere in Whitehall at the time:

There are straws to be found in Cabinet papers and elsewhere which indicate the way the wind is blowing, and we may assume that responsibility for the direction of the nation's effort in the immediate post-war years will remain in the hands of a National Government prepared to face radical changes in our social and economic system and contemplating not merely restoration or a return to normality, but reconstruction in a very real sense ...

While policies will have to command the support of the main elements in all parties, it is clear that the war is moving us more and more in the direction of Labour's ideas and ideals, and the planning for a national 'New Order' will be more towards the Left than may generally be imagined now.[17]

R. A. Butler, who succeeded Ramsbotham as President of the Board in June 1941, has very properly been credited with the implementation of educational reform, a task which required great political subtlety and persistence: but he himself agreed that it was the Board, that is, its civil servants, who originated the plan before his arrival.[18] In May 1941 the Board's detailed proposals, set forth in a Green Book, were circulated to local educational authorities and professional associations. Except in relation to the proposed settlement of the religious issue in the schools, the Green Book represented the package of reforms as brought forward in the Education Act of 1944. But it was a long road from the blueprint to the statute book. The Board were, in 1941, chancing their arm. They could not tell whether they would obtain political sanction for their proposed scheme. The foreword to the Green Book stated that the proposals were only for discussion: they did not commit the Board.

R. A. Butler understood the domestic consequences of the war better than any other Conservative minister. In June 1941 Churchill offered him the choice of a diplomatic post or the Board of Education. In Churchill's eyes the Board of Education in wartime was a political backwater of no possible significance, and he thought Butler peculiar for wanting to take it on. Butler, however, saw things differently. If there was one field where the existing arrangements were clearly trailing behind informed opinion, it was education. The Hadow Report of 1926 and the Spens Report of 1938 had set up the goal of the division of the school system into primary, secondary and further education. The bulk of this reorganization remained to be carried out, and although it was slowly developing, there were so many loose ends and administrative obstacles that the time was ripe to take the matter in hand and legislate. Butler was already chairman of the Conservative Committee on Post-War Problems, and he kept in close touch with developments at home: it is interesting that Samuel Courtauld, the reforming industrialist, was his father-in-law. His family had strong educational traditions and had produced many Cambridge dons and Masters, and two headmasters of Harrow. The key to Butler's strategy may have been suggested to him by a conversation with H. G. Wells in October 1941: 'in a period of convulsion any plan which was ready and thought out was apt to be accepted and put into force by the ruler or rulers of the day.'[19]

The obstacle in the way was Churchill, with his insistence on setting aside all potentially controversial questions until the end of the war. On 12 September 1941 Butler wrote to Churchill suggesting a Joint Select Committee to discuss the various questions of educational change which were before the Board. A number of them were controversial: a Joint Committee would represent the various points of view while keeping controversy from developing into a parliamentary dogfight.[20] Churchill was deeply alarmed. Both the Roman Catholics and the Anglicans were seeking increased state support for their schools, which still comprised more than half the schools in the country, while demanding that they should remain under their own denominational control. The less that was conceded to the Church of England, the more discontent would appear in that quarter: the more that was conceded to them, the greater the possibility that Nonconformists, who objected to the basic principle of supporting denominational schools from public money, would echo the cry they had raised in 1902 against 'religion on the rates'. The great controversy at the dawn of the century was still fresh in Churchill's mind, and Butler's letter with less than his usual skill played up the possibilities of trouble. 'We cannot have party politics in wartime,' Churchill replied on 13 September, and vetoed a new Education Bill. As Butler records, his two senior civil servants, Holmes and Wood, were inclined to accept Churchill's veto and reserve educational reform for the post-war period. Butler carried on with his efforts: 'having viewed the milk and honey from the top of Pisgah, I was damned if I was going to die in the land of Moab. Basing myself on long experience of Churchill over the India Bill, I decided to disregard what he said and go straight ahead.'[21] He was taking a political risk. If he could defuse the controversial aspects of reform, Churchill would accept it. In his original letter to Churchill, Butler had raised the question of the role of the public schools. If it was ever intended to include legislation on the public schools in the general plan of reform, this was now dropped, thus eliminating one major source of controversy. It remained for Butler to get an agreed settlement of the religious question: and this, by well-conceived negotiations, mainly with the Church of England, he achieved.[22] By the end of 1942 the proposals of the White Paper on Education were proceeding through the Lord President's Committee.[23]

Reformers in the educational world were fortunate in having a Conservative minister to lead them. Butler's ideas were scarcely controversial from a party political point of view, and he was able to work in close partnership with a Labour under-secretary, James Chuter-Ede, a former schoolteacher. But through Butler the majority party could claim credit for a major initiative which might well have been eyed with suspicion coming from a non-party or Labour politician.

The town and country planning lobby were in a far more difficult position than educational reformers. Their proposals were necessarily controversial, and the discussion about how to implement them bristled with technical difficulties which laymen found it hard to understand. Before 1939, such town and country planning as existed, under legislation of 1909 and 1932, was of marginal significance. Legally, local authorities had the right to prevent undesirable development of land, but found it hard to do so because of the high cost of compensating owners for the loss they suffered when they were forbidden to develop. On the positive side the local authorities had the power to draw up schemes of development. But there was nothing to compel them to do so, and the use of this power was generally limited to the planning of new suburban estates. There was no means of ensuring, as a town expanded, that the new areas had a balance of housing, industry, and amenities. In June 1942 only 3 per cent of Britain was covered by operative planning schemes.[24] Of a national planning policy, there was barely a shadow beyond the legislation to encourage employment in the depressed areas. After Labour won control of London in 1934, Herbert Morrison as chairman of the London County Council pioneered the green belt, 'the first attempt since the days of Queen Elizabeth to stop the expansion of London'.[25] In this, he was in advance of his fellow politicians.

Some reference has already been made to the progress of the Town and Country Planning Association, originally founded at the turn of the century. The dominating personality of its early years was Ebenezer Howard, the founder of Letchworth and Welwyn Garden City, and co-founder in 1918 of the New Towns Group, which argued for a government policy of locating properly designed new towns in the regions. The Group included Frederick Osborn, estate manager at Welwyn Garden City from 1919 to 1936, and thereafter secretary of the Town and Country Planning Association. But neither the new town idea nor the more general cause of planning had much influence between the wars. As in so many other areas of policy, planning was distrusted. The career of Patrick Abercrombie, Professor of Civic Design at Liverpool from 1915 to 1935, and subsequently Professor of Town Planning at University College, London, is a case in point. Lord Holford wrote of him, in the *Dictionary of National Biography*: 'Looking through some thirty pre-war reports, all delightfully presented but now largely superseded and dust-laden, one is made aware of Abercrombie's immense industry and fertility; but also of the fact that although they were persuasive, and beginning to be influential, they were not yet backed by administrative power or by economic incentives.'[26]

As was mentioned earlier, the appointment of the Barlow Commission in 1937 marked the beginning of the planners' breakthrough. Abercrombie was himself an influential member of the commission. He and two other members produced a minority report which agreed with the majority about the aims of planning, but called for a ministry with strong executive powers to see them carried through.[27] The Barlow Report appeared in January 1940 — and at the time appeared to have little relevance in the circumstances of war.

'A Ministry of the Future, Please', was the title of an article by Philip Jordan in the *News Chronicle* soon after the opening of the blitz on London, and it was typical of a rash of articles on the same theme. By destroying large areas first of London and then of other great cities, the blitz gave the word reconstruction an obvious practical meaning. The press itched to cheer up its readers with visions of the new cities of the future, and soon Frank Lloyd Wright was projecting a superlative new London with a chessboard of green spaces and built-up areas.[28] In October 1940 Churchill appointed Sir John Reith at the head of the new Ministry of Works, with responsibility for repairing bomb-damaged buildings, and 'consulting the departments and organizations concerned' about the post-war rebuilding of cities. For a man with Reith's desire to build the New Jerusalem, these were constricting terms of reference. They did not, said *The Times*, 'yet quicken the eye to see, not far off, an England of well-designed, clean and slumless towns and an architecture of public buildings and private homes on which civil and personal pride might justly dwell.'[29]

Readers today, beset by the ugliness and destructive power of urban development, can only wonder at the faith that new would necessarily prove better. How wisely the new town and country planning powers were used is a vexed question, and can only be answered by examining the way in which Coventry, Plymouth, Glasgow and so on were rebuilt, and the rest of Britain planned, in the aftermath of the war. The only certainty is that the machinery and powers of planning were introduced, and largely because of a movement led by Reith in the years 1940 to 1942.

Reith's career proclaimed him to be a Calvinist technocrat imposing order through the State rather than the Church. Having begun his career as a mechanical engineer, Reith was appointed general manager of the British Broadcasting Company in 1922, and after its conversion into a public corporation became the first Director-General. In 1938 Neville Chamberlain put him in charge of the reorganization of Imperial Airways into a state corporation, and in January 1940 introduced him into politics as Minister of Information. Churchill, who held Reith personally responsible for keeping him off the air in the 1930s, moved him first to the Ministry of Transport, and subsequently to the Ministry of Works. To Churchill, Reith was an unfathomable creature, towering over him in puritanical zeal as well as physical stature. Once, when Reith had departed after a difficult interview, Churchill remarked: 'Thank God, we have seen the last of that Wuthering Height!'[30] To the end of his life, Reith found Churchill equally unsympathetic. He detested the circle of exotic adventurers with which Churchill surrounded himself, and it was moral contempt which led him to disparage Churchill's greatness as a war leader. 'A whole lot of people could have done it better and more cheaply,' he remarked in later years. After Churchill's death, Reith could not bear to pass by a commemorative plaque in the floor of Westminster Abbey inscribed: 'Remember Winston Churchill'.[31]

One of Reith's first actions as Minister of Works in 1940 was to appoint a panel of consultants to advise him on post-war planning. Of the twenty-one members of the panel, ten were members of the Town and Country Planning Association, and Osborn, the secretary of the Association, was appointed as an under-secretary in the department. Reith swiftly drew up a statement of planning objectives for the approval of the War Cabinet. He proposed a central planning authority whose goals would be 'controlled development of all areas and utilization of land to the best advantage; limitation of urban expansion; redevelopment of congested areas; correlation of transport and all services; amenities; improved architectural treatment; preservation of places of historic interest, national parks and coastal areas.' In February 1941 the War Cabinet approved Reith's ideas in general terms.[32] But Reith spent a whole year battling to reach agreement on the definition of the new central authority—becalmed in the Sargasso Sea of Arthur Greenwood's Reconstruction Committee.

Among the many initiatives which Reith took to accelerate planning was the appointment, by agreement with the London County Council, of Patrick Abercrombie and the L.C.C. architect J. H. Forshaw to prepare a plan for post-war rebuilding over the whole area of the county of London. (*The County of London Plan* appeared in 1943, and was followed by another report commissioned by Portal, Reith's successor in office: the *Greater London Plan* of 1944). To stimulate the development of national policy, Reith established committees under Mr Justice Uthwatt (January 1941) and Lord Justice Scott (October 1941). The Scott Committee was to consider the future of the countryside, the Uthwatt Committee the highly abstruse problems of compensation and betterment, which would have to be tackled before planning could be implemented.

Reith's struggle to establish a central authority for town and country planning was brought to a successful conclusion at last with the approval by the War Cabinet on 9 February 1942 of proposals to confer the new powers on the Ministry of Works, translating it into the Ministry of Works and Planning. On 21 February Churchill dismissed him from the government. After the fall of Singapore and other disasters the government was unpopular and a major reshuffle became essential. A handful of Conservative backbenchers had complained to the Conservative Chief Whip about him; Reith had no party to speak for him; and his fate was sealed.[33]

The new minister, Wyndham Portal, was a Conservative, a self-made millionaire, and one of Churchill's intimates. The Portal family business printed notes for the Bank of England: Portal, after a distinguished war record in World War I, had made his fortune and flirted with Sir Oswald Mosley's New Party in Mosley's pre-fascist phase. Portal pursued a policy of masterly procrastination at the Ministry of Works and Planning until, to his very great relief, the town and country planning responsibilities were hived off into a separate ministry.[34] But while Reith himself was gone, he left behind him the legacy of the Uthwatt Committee, whose final report on compensation and betterment appeared in September 1942.

The most controversial aspect of planning policy was its effect on property values. If a local authority forbade an owner to develop his land, how much compensation should be paid to him for the loss of the gain he would otherwise have made? And once land was developed, and was rising in value because of the activities of the community where it was sited, should not some of the betterment value be taken back by the community? The Uthwatt Report (Cmd 6386), recommended that the state should nationalize the development rights in all land which had not yet been built up. Subsequently, whenever land was required for development, the state would buy it for a price which reflected its existing use, and either develop it directly or lease it to a private developer. All the land required for development was to be valued at a single sum, and the amount divided among all those who claimed the right to compensation for nationalization of development rights. Developed land would pass in perpetuity to the state.[35]

From the outset, there were two powerful currents of hostility to the Uthwatt Report. Although it rejected nationalization of land as a whole, nationalization of development rights was in itself a powerful blow against private property, and the Conservative Party was thoroughly hostile to the principle. Secondly, the attempt to define and evaluate development value involved almost baffling technical problems. Whatever the justice of the Uthwatt Report, it was fiendishly complicated from the administrative point of view, with the result that ministerial arguments over its niceties were interminable. Another acute problem, of purely bureaucratic origin, was the relationship of the new Ministry for Planning to the many other Whitehall departments affected. When W. S. Morrison was designated to head a new Ministry of Town and Country Planning in December 1942, it was an open question what powers he would be given. The Labour Party stood for the outright nationalization of land, but welcomed Uthwatt; the Conservatives opposed Uthwatt and stood for no nationalization at all. Consensus was difficult to achieve when property rights were at stake.

The reform of the health services caused less controversy between the parties, at least during World War II. There was a consensus of opinion among doctors before 1939 that the existing system of National Health Insurance, which paid the doctor for treating the wage-earner, should be revised to include the wage-earner's family, and the provision of specialist services. There was agreement also that the existing hospital system, divided between local authority hospitals providing nearly three-quarters of the beds, and independent voluntary hospitals which relied upon flag-days, private endowments and legacies, ought to be integrated administratively. This was the programme set out by the British Medical Association (B.M.A.) in 1938 in *A General Medical Service for the Nation*. But the government of the day was preoccupied with the crisis in Europe.

The war struck directly at the existing hospital system, obliquely at general practice. With the outbreak of war there sprang into activity a new centralized state agency, originally intended to provide medical treatment solely for the victims of air-raids: the Emergency Medical Service (E.M.S.). Its doctors and nurses were directly employed and paid by the government. In the hospitals the old health services and the new E.M.S. functioned side by side. Since it commandeered both public and voluntary hospitals it brought about a limited unification of the two systems. Meanwhile the category of patient cared for by the E.M.S. was expanded to include sick servicemen, unaccompanied evacuee children and others. By September 1941 the E.M.S. had added 153,000 hospital beds to the previous total of 292,000. It owned the beds and the temporary buildings in which many of them were placed: and the influence of the E.M.S. naturally began to spread through the hospitals in which it had an interest. Here was another demonstration of the virtues of centralized planning, and the E.M.S. had a powerful impact as a model structure.[36] The new vision developing in Whitehall was notably expressed by the Deputy Permanent Secretary of the Ministry of Health, A. N. Rucker, who had been Principal Private Secretary to Chamberlain until his fall from power. In February 1941 he recorded the main objectives of health policy on which he felt there was general agreement in the Ministry's Office Committee on Post-War Hospital Policy:

(a) A complete health service to be available to every member of the community.

(b) This health service to include the services of a medical practitioner.

(c) The medical practitioners so employed to be based on clinics which would in turn be based on a net-work of hospitals. The clinics would be, in effect, out-patient departments of hospitals, whether or not they were attached to a hospital.

. . .

(e) The network of hospitals would be planned for a region and so

drawn as to provide for the population of the region all forms
of diagnosis and treatment including adequate laboratory and
ambulance services.[37]

Hospital policy became the immediate priority, and this for a pressing
practical reason. A paper by the Permanent Secretary of the Ministry
of Health, Sir John Maude, pointed out in August 1941 that the
expansion of the E.M.S. had made the voluntary hospitals financially
dependent on the government; when the E.M.S. was wound up at the
end of the war they would therefore be in difficulties. Meanwhile the
voluntary hospitals, sensing the effect the war would have, had taken
the lead. The Nuffield Trust, set up at the end of 1939, was campaigning vigorously for co-operation between the two hospital systems on
terms designed to safeguard the voluntary hospitals. This campaign was
in turn beginning to upset the local authorities, and the government
was therefore forced into a public declaration of policy.[38] On 9 October
1941 the Minister of Health pledged the government to adopt after the
war a National Hospital Service, with local authorities having a large
say in the running of the voluntary hospitals.

The trend towards planning had also affected the thinking of the
medical profession. In August 1940 the B.M.A., the Royal Colleges,
the Royal Scottish Corporations, and the Medical Officers of Health,
set up the Medical Planning Commission to prepare for the post-war
world. The date itself is revealing, confirming the great impact of 1940.
The deputy secretary of the commission, Charles Hill, has explained
the motivation behind its work: 'The war had compelled the temporary integration of hospitals in the Emergency Medical Service and
no one could expect a return to pre-war conditions. Those who
planned first would be more likely to influence the final form.'[39]

The commission reported its interim proposals in May 1942. They
suggested a National Health Service available to all, without income
limits to exclude the wealthy; the building of health centres in which
doctors would operate group practices; the payment of general
practitioners in part by salary, instead of exclusively by fee as before;
the gradual disappearance of the tradition of buying and selling
practices; and the unification of hospitals under regional administra-
tions. In each of these respects the proposals were notably more radical
than the B.M.A. programme of 1938. In later years a suspicion was
voiced that two or three socialist Medical Officers of Health had planted
a left-wing programme on the commission. But as Hill has recalled, the

true explanation lay in the general climate of opinion, which favoured generous and radical measures. The B.M.A. itself, while referring back the idea of part payment through salary, accepted in outline in September 1942 several principles which it began fiercely to attack after 1944.[40]

If the Planning Commission was designed to get the medical profession's blow in first, it succeeded. A Ministry of Health paper on the future of general practice, and contemplating a salaried service, was drawn up in March 1942, but in general the ministry was slow to produce comprehensive plans.

It will already be apparent that the politicians were escorted along the road to reconstruction by a volunteer army of post-war planners, some in the civil service, most in various organizations outside. There was a South Sea Bubble of reconstruction projects, launched with high hopes, but fated for the most part to an obscure end. One of the most ambitious was the Nuffield College, Oxford, Reconstruction Survey. G. D. H. Cole, a member of the College committee, proposed the idea, and won the support of Arthur Greenwood and Sir John Reith in the winter of 1940–41. The Treasury was persuaded to provide a grant, and the Nuffield Social Reconstruction Committee came into being in February 1941. By the end of 1941 the problems of economic reconstruction alone were being investigated by Nuffield College, Political and Economic Planning, the National Institute of Social and Economic Research, the Oxford Institute of Statistics, and the London School of Economics. As for town and country planning, it would be a simple matter to list two or even three dozen ardent bodies circulating memoranda.[41] The reconstruction campaign also had strong allies in Fleet Street—Gerald Barry at the *News Chronicle*, Cecil King at the *Daily Mirror*, Waldorf and David Astor at the *Observer*, Barrington-Ward and Carr at *The Times*.

All three main parties set up reconstruction committees. The Liberals were first in the field in the autumn of 1940, and eventually had sixteen committees on different aspects of post-war planning. E. H. Carr, Seebohm Rowntree and Geoffrey Crowther were among the members.[42] The Conservative and Labour Parties followed suit in the summer of 1941. The Labour Party National Executive set up thirteen sub-committees of which the most prominent, on the social and economic transformation of Great Britain, had Shinwell as chairman and Laski as secretary.[43] The Conservative central committee on post-war problems was under the chairmanship of R. A. Butler, and the sub-committees dealt with demobilization, agriculture, industry and finance, education and the social services, constitutional and administrative reform, and national security.[44]

Some of the reports of party committees find a niche in the history of reconstruction, but the parties were following events rather than setting the pace. In every area of policy-making the main principles of advance had been defined before 1939 by non-party experts. Professional bodies like the B.M.A. and the Town and Country Planning Association, centre pressure-groups like Political and Economic Planning and the Next Five Years Group, advisory committees like those of Spens and Barlow, the school of Keynesian economists, the social investigators of poverty and malnutrition like Rowntree and Boyd Orr —these were the architects of reconstruction and consensus. Perhaps true power resides not with the occupants of high office, but with the people who define the agenda for them. In any case, most ministers were so overburdened with the task of running the war that they could only think vaguely about the 'better Britain' promised in the papers. In a sense this was very fortunate for the Labour Party. When Laski drew up one of his memoranda calling for 'socialism now', Attlee told the National Executive that: 'With his colleagues in the government he held the view that the Labour Party should not try to get Socialist measures implemented under the guise of winning the war.'[45] But socialist measures apart, the Coalition would have been placed under severe strain had the Labour ministers borne the onus of devising and proposing reforms. This would have set up a party game, with Attlee lobbing ideas over the net, and Churchill returning his serve. Instead, the Labour team could applaud and encourage the work of Butler, Beveridge, Reith, Keynes and others. Thus they obeyed the rules of Coalition punctiliously, while gratifying their appetite for amelioration. The system had one other feature helpful to Labour. Most Conservative M.P.s still thought of themselves as the governing party. The opposition in the House of Commons consisted mainly of the Labour backbenchers, and the Leader of the Opposition was always a Labour member: Lees-Smith from May 1940 to November 1941, Pethick-Lawrence until February 1942, and Greenwood, after dismissal from office, for the remaining lifetime of the Coalition. At some risk of internal division, Labour could lead a double life, taking the credit for its part in the government *and* for opposing the government when it was under a cloud. For example, when Greenwood was sacked in

February 1942, responsibility for reconstruction was handed to a Labour minister, Sir William Jowitt. For almost two years, Jowitt announced the Coalition's progress on post-war planning while Greenwood urged the Government to move faster.

Only on the surface did reconstruction consist of separate problems in watertight compartments. It was the cry of a broad movement of progressive thought. Indeed, we are bound to be struck by the muscular faith in reason and progress displayed by its protagonists. The traditional philanthropic drive to perform good works was allied to the modernizing, technocratic motive. The condition of Britain between the wars, above all the phenomenon of mass unemployment, had profoundly disturbed the public-spirited businessman or professional person. Economic inefficiency and human deprivation spurred on both the technocrat and the social idealist. The new ideology of 'the middle way' spoke always of the rational and centralized control of resources, and the priority which must be given to social welfare. The war appeared to vindicate these principles by requiring their application of the home front. If they were matters of obvious common sense, why not plan to embody them in a programme for post-war Britain?

The campaign for reconstruction wore the guise of sweet reason, but it was impelled also by highly subjective and irrational motives. The liberal, educated civilian had learned in World War I to regard war as an unmitigated evil, and was at heart anti-war. In the early months of World War II this demonstrated itself in the overt pacifism of part of the intelligentsia. But the mainstream of pacifism went underground, and resolved itself into a passion to turn the war, with all its depravity, to humane and constructive ends. The present generation would suffer so that future generations would have life in greater abundance. There had to be 'war aims', or 'peace aims' as they were sometimes called. Was there some irony to this? Surely Britain never fought a war which could more easily be justified on moral and humanitarian grounds than the war against Nazi Germany.

In the case of the academic or journalist, who lived by words and ideas, reconstruction had another function. In a society at war, self-respect dictated that he should do his utmost for victory. But how? While factory workers were building tanks, and soldiers learning to handle them on the battlefield, he was likely to feel dissatisfied with the contribution he could make. Usually of comfortable background and liberal persuasions, he most likely felt a sense of guilt before the war at the conditions of the working classes. Now the underdog was a hero of the blitz, or a hero of war industry. How could he be rewarded? At this point the intellectual could cast himself as the manufacturer of the moral weapon against Hitler. By designing an idealistic programme of war aims, he could at once reward the working classes, and by inspiring them to even greater efforts take his own place in the front line as the man who built the moral Spitfire. Thus Laski wrote in the summer of 1940: 'The way to victory lies in producing the conviction now among the masses that there are to be no more distressed areas, no more vast armies of unemployed, no more slums, no vast denial of genuine equality of educational opportunity.'[46] Barrington-Ward, forwarding an idealistic draft of war aims to Churchill in April 1942, contended: 'It is not hard to imagine the stirring effect of some such appeal ... I venture to believe that, in a crucial phase of the war in which the national endurance must in all probability be required to support heavier trials than it has known even yet, it would add hope to fortitude and imagination to energy in the factories and in the field, strengthen national unity and give resolution a still keener edge.'[47] Beveridge, in a broadcast at about the same time, put the message in a nutshell: 'A war of faith is what the world is waiting for.'[48]

In the making of post-war plans there was the suggestion that We should reward Them. Laski, in an unconscious slip of the pen, explained that one of his books had been partly inspired by 'the pride every *citizen* of this country is bound to have in the amazing heroism and endurance in the *common people* [italics added] he has witnessed day by day during the blitz ... '[49] The historians of the war economy, W. K. Hancock and Margaret Gowing, put the point as follows:

> There existed, so to speak, an implied contract between Government and people; the people refused none of the sacrifices that the Government demanded from them for the winning of the war; in return, they expected that the Government should show imagination and seriousness in preparing for the restoration and improvement of the nation's well-being when the war had been won. The plans for reconstruction were, therefore, a real part of the war effort.[50]

But it could just as easily be argued that the public were led to expect a new deal by men and women who were, no doubt unconsciously, trying to find a role in the war effort for themselves and the reforms they wanted. Hitler suffered a million deaths by typewriter.

The importance of reconstruction plans in raising morale was greatly exaggerated by the post-war lobbyists. Though it could be one factor among several it could scarcely be the decisive one as was so often maintained. Stephen Taylor, the head of Home Intelligence at the Ministry of Information, analysed morale in depth in a paper of 1 October 1941. In his view the factors determining morale could usefully be divided into the material and the mental. The material factors were more important, and consisted of food; warmth; work; leisure, rest and sleep; a secure base; and safety and security for dependents. The mental factors were: belief that victory is possible; belief in equality of sacrifices; belief in the efficiency and integrity of leadership; and belief that the war is a necessity and our cause just. On reconstruction Taylor commented, indirectly: 'The public is unimaginative. It is unable and has, apparently, no great wish to picture the details of the post-war world. It speculates relatively little about the end of the war.'[51] Home Intelligence had no scientific definition of morale, or of the means by which it could be assessed, so Taylor's conclusions were at best impressionistic. But one cannot help reflecting that a square meal and a good comedy programme on the radio must have meant more to morale than any promise about post-war conditions; moreover the promises that were made later on by Churchill and others were greeted with a scepticism reserved for the utterances of politicians.[52]

The arguments used on behalf of reform by vaguely liberal improvers on the one hand, and thoroughgoing state socialists on the other, were remarkably similar, and the personalities involved so mixed up in each other's company that no boundary could be drawn between them. It was as though the Popular Front against the Conservatives, which had failed to come about before the war, had at last got into its stride. As the ideas of the Left stood no chance of adoption by the Coalition, the Left fell back to the front line represented by the Scott and Uthwatt Reports, and did battle against the Conservatives there. Labour's major reconstruction committee, guided by Shinwell and Laski, produced for the 1942 conference a document entitled 'The Old World and the New Society'. On generalities it echoed the dogmatism of Laski about the inevitable decline of capitalism, but the particulars had a familiar ring:

We must organize now
    to provide full employment;
    to rebuild a better Britain;
    to provide social services to secure adequate health, nutrition, and care in old age, for everybody;

to provide full educational opportunities for all.[53]

In the late 1930s, when the Communists were trying Popular Front tactics, the 'red dean of Canterbury', Dr Hewlett Johnson, would appear as the 'representative of the church'. The invisible Popular Front for post-war planning, by contrast, had much genuine backing from church dignitaries. The Cardinal Archbishop of Westminster, Arthur Hinsley, encouraged in the summer of 1940 a new social Catholic movement, The Sword of the Spirit, which enjoyed a brief life. About the same time an Anglican body, the Industrial Christian Fellowship, conceived the idea of a conference on reconstruction to consider 'the new society that is quite evidently emerging' and discuss how Christians could try to shape the spirit of the times. On 21 December *The Times* carried a joint letter from the Archbishops of Canterbury and York (Lang and Temple), the Archbishop of Westminster and the Moderator of the Free Church Council, setting out five agreed standards for social organization:

1. Extreme inequality in wealth and possessions should be abolished.
2. Every child, regardless of race or class should have equal opportunities for the development of his peculiar capacities.
3. The family as a social unit must be safeguarded.
4. The sense of a divine vocation must be restored to man's daily work.
5. The resources of the earth should be used as God's gift to the whole human race, and used with due consideration for the needs of the present and future generations.

In the New Year of 1941 the conference proposed by the Industrial Christian Fellowship was held at Malvern College. Fifteen bishops, nearly 400 clergy, and such notables as Middleton Murry, T. S. Eliot, Dorothy Sayers, and the then Liberal M.P. for Barnstaple, Sir Richard Acland, were present. Acland spoke out on the last day of the conference in favour of common ownership, adding one more element of confusion to a disorganized conference. At the last minute William Temple, the Archbishop of York, invented a series of conference conclusions which came as a surprise to most of those who had taken part. Acland insisted on a clause condemning the morality of private capital, and a formula was accepted to the effect that the private ownership of the principal industrial resources of the community *might* be a stumbling-block to Christian lives. The findings of the conference, exaggerated by the press with its love of 'red' dukes, duchesses and deans, had a surprising popular impact. The two pamphlets containing the Malvern proceedings sold, together, more than a million copies. Temple set to work on a book, *Christianity and the Social Order*, which sold 139,000 copies as a Penguin Special in 1942.[54]

Temple was the son of Frederick Temple, headmaster of Rugby and Archbishop of Canterbury, and followed his father into both of these high posts. A distinguished theologian, Temple had always been sympathetic to Labour, and had joined the party for a period in 1918. Hitherto, while prominent in church reform, the ecumenical movement, and social work for the unemployed, Temple had never struck out as a Christian leader intervening in politics. The war emboldened him, as it did other temperamentally liberal figures like Beveridge, or Barrington-Ward, to take the plunge in favour of immediate social reform. By the time that Cosmo Gordon Lang, the Archbishop of Canterbury, announced in January 1942 that he was about to retire, the prospect of Temple as his successor made a number of Conservatives uncomfortable. The M.P. for Newcastle North, Cuthbert Headlam, wrote:

> I found in the H. of C. last week that Conservative members were much exercised in their minds as to the succession—a very strong feeling—which I share—against William Ebor. Of course the man is among the other bishops a triton among minnows—but it always seems to me that he lacks the judgment and a sense of proportion in political matters and his open adherence to the Socialist or Christian Socialist programme is all wrong for an Archbishop ... I had a word with Brendan Bracken (who is Winston's bishop-maker!) the other day. He told me that it was a very difficult business. W. Ebor is the outstanding man among the bishops and none of the others appears to wish to stand in his way.[55]

So, in February 1942, Temple became Archbishop. His religious principles, in so far as they were translated into politics, certainly made him an unorthodox primate of the Church of England. Believing that no one should ask more than a just reward for his services to the community, he thought it wrong for banks to make private profit from the supply of credit, wrong that shares could be inherited, and wrong that dividends, rather than wages, should be the first charge on industrial profits. To this extent he was a Christian socialist. He also advocated family allowances, better housing, holidays with pay, and a higher school-leaving age. In making these proposals he consulted Keynes and R. H. Tawney — a nice indication of the blend of his mind.[56]

The agitation for reconstruction arose from the joint frustrations of the Centre and the Left, frustrations which applied with equal force in the years 1941 and 1942 to the conduct of the war. The student immersed in wartime polemics sees, in his overheated imagination, Colonel Blimp being pursued through a land of Penguin Specials by an abrasive meritocrat, a progressive churchman, and J. B. Priestley. A curious forum of these various schools of thought was the 1941 Committee, a ginger group designed to collect informed criticism and communicate it to the government. The committee met at the home of its sponsor, Edward Hulton, the owner of *Picture Post*, under the chairmanship of Priestley. The character of the committee emerges vividly from a list of some of the more notable figures associated with it:

RICHARD ACLAND   Christian socialist, erstwhile Liberal M.P., and founder of Forward March

DAVID ASTOR   *Observer* journalist and heir apparent to the paper

THOMAS BALOGH   Economist

GERALD BARRY   Editor of the *News Chronicle*

RT REVD A. W. BLUNT   Bishop of Bradford, self-declared socialist

RITCHIE CALDER   *Daily Herald* reporter and science correspondent

ELIZABETH DENBY   Specialist in the problems of low-cost housing and estate planning. Designer (1942) of Army Bureau of Current Affairs 'Homes to Live In' exhibition

VICTOR GOLLANCZ   Left Book Club publisher

LADY HINCHINGBROOKE   Wife of viscount Hinchingbrooke M.P., later co-founder of Tory Reform Committee

EVA HUBBACK   Pioneer of adult education

DOUGLAS JAY   Former journalist with *The Times* and the *Economist*, temporary civil servant at Ministry of Supply, Labour politician

FRANÇOIS LAFITTE   Social scientist, deputy-secretary of P.E.P., adopted son of Havelock Ellis

KINGSLEY MARTIN   Editor of the *New Statesman*

CHRISTOPHER MAYHEW   Economist, temporary civil servant at Ministry of Economic Warfare, Labour politician

DAVID OWEN   Social scientist, secretary of P.E.P., aide (1942) to Sir
  Stafford Cripps

A. D. PETERS   Literary agent

LANCELOT SPICER   Businessman, active Liberal, and founder in
  1940 of Liberal Action ginger group

PETER THORNEYCROFT   Conservative M.P., later co-founder of
  Tory Reform Committee

RICHARD TITMUSS   Social scientist

TOM WINTRINGHAM   Ex-communist and former commander of
  the British battalion of the International Brigade in Spain

KONNI ZILLIACUS   Left-wing polemicist, former member of
  League of Nations secretariat at Geneva

H. G. Wells, who belonged for a while to the committee, described it
as a 'well-meaning (but otherwise meaningless) miscellany of people
… earnestly and obstinately going in every direction under their
vehement professions of unity.'[57] The 1941 Committee was probably
never very effective, but it remains a perfect snapshot of the new progressive Establishment rising from the waves, contemptuous of all the
muddle which had arisen from the lack of planning and scientific
expertise, and pregnant with all the higher muddles which arise from
their application. Hard on the heels of the committee came a prophet
of this new order, Sir Stafford Cripps.

VII Stafford Cripps's Progress

From the end of 1940 Churchill, through his intimates and appointees, commanded the key positions in the military and diplomatic machinery of war. There were many quarrels in the Churchillian circle —such as the battle between Bracken and Eden over the control of Political Warfare —but all were agents of Churchill's premiership, driven along as members of his team. On the home front things were very different. In the domestic affairs of the country there was a chief administrator, Sir John Anderson, but no big political figure to carry public opinion, not even Bevin or Morrison. By the beginning of 1942 the vacuum in home front leadership was severe. For a moment it looked as though Beaverbrook would fill the gap as the first head of the new Ministry of Production. In the event he was to resign almost at once to campaign for Russia. A golden opportunity presented itself to Sir Stafford Cripps. Arriving in Britain in January 1942 after eighteen months as Ambassador to Russia, he was acclaimed as though sent by providence to set the world right. He was thought of as a man of the Left, who would compensate for the fact that Churchill belonged to the Right. He was thought of as the man to run home affairs while Churchill attended to the war. But Cripps did not see himself in this light. While still a progressive in outlook, he accepted the realities of power at once, and was soon being gossiped about as a possible Conservative leader. Nor did he believe the war should be left to Churchill. Instead of seizing the opportunity which was given him, he fell for the illusion that he could supplant Churchill and run the war more scientifically. He wanted to share power with Churchill in Churchill's own domain. The attempt to rival Churchill led straight to failure. What had become of Cripps?

By temperament Cripps had always been both a technician and a moralist. Although his father's family, the Parmoors, were a traditional landed family, he had marked himself out very early in life by deciding to read chemistry at university, and by turning down a scholarship at Cambridge in favour of a place at University College, London, to work under Sir William Ramsay. During the First World War he worked under Lloyd George and eventually Churchill at the Ministry of Munitions, as assistant superintendent of the largest explosives factory in the country: Churchill wrote that he had filled the post 'with remarkable efficiency'.[1] But before the outbreak of war Cripps had already embarked on a career in the law. In the year of the General Strike, having built up a remarkable expertise in the law of patents, he became the youngest K.C. in the country, and thereafter commanded princely fees. In the late 1930s he received a fee of £30,000 from the Westminster Bank in a celebrated case. While the law was his professional vocation, he loved expertise of almost every kind: political, social, economic. On his tour of India and China in the winter of 1939–40 he was fascinated by all the data and outward signs of modernization — factories, technical institutes, banks, local government offices. He was capable of the same kind of approach to political life. In 1939 he wrote a programme for the expediting of parliamentary business: *Democracy up to Date.* This combined proposals for speeding up parliamentary business, and thus enabling parliament to achieve more, with the idea of specialist committees of the House to supervise the administration of government departments, and the vetting of Orders in Council. Cripps proposed up to a dozen of these committees, in the belief that there were scores of backbench M.P.s ready to take the same busy scalpel to the details of administration and law as he himself. It is difficult to think of any twentieth-century politician with as wide a range of intellectual curiosity as Cripps. What other wartime minister would have bothered to seek out George Orwell and other writers for an evening's discussion?

The foundation of Cripps's moral beliefs was, throughout his life, Christianity. He did not enter the Labour Party until 1929, when he was forty. Despite the fact that his father, Lord Parmoor, and his uncle by marriage, Sidney Webb, both held office in the 1924 Labour government, Cripps for most of the 1920s directed his efforts in public life to the building of international Christian understanding, through the 'World Alliance to promote international friendship through the Churches'. From 1923 to 1929 he was a member of the Church of England National Assembly and delivered scores of speeches on the theme of the Christian duty to organize for world peace, the moral co-ordinate, as he saw it, of the League of Nations. Drawn into the Labour Party by Herbert Morrison, and appointed Solicitor-General in 1930, Cripps appeared to be the very pearl of MacDonaldism, with its Establishment ethos and belief in gradu; l improvement. But with the fall of the Labour government in 1931, Cripps's upward zeal drove him into a phase of Marxism which lasted at least until 1938. This was the period in which he became infamous in the eyes of the press as a revolutionary intellectual. He proclaimed the inevitable collapse of capitalism, warned that a future Labour government might face opposition from Buckingham Palace as well as from the bankers, called for the abolition of the House of Lords, and denounced the League of Nations as a conspiracy of capitalist governments against the interests of the workers. In 1937 he launched a campaign for a United Front of the Labour Party, the I.L.P., and the Communist Party, through the organization of which he was president and chief financial backer, the Socialist League. The Labour Party excommunicated and destroyed the League and with it the United Front campaign. *Tribune*, a weekly paper founded largely with Cripps's money to run the campaign, survived.

During 1938 Cripps swung back to a more orthodox liberal-progressive line, endorsing rearmament and calling for collective security through the League of Nations. Ironically, he was finally expelled from the Labour Party in January 1939 for moderation. Arguing that Labour could not win the next general election alone, he put forward the strategy of a Popular Front alliance with the Liberal Party, to gather together all the anti-appeasement elements in British politics. Whereas previously he had argued that the working class provided the one and only basis for resisting fascism, his new gospel was one of national unity, based on a social programme more limited than that of the Labour Party's short-term programme of 1937. Cripps was expelled from the Labour Party for distributing a memorandum on the argument for a Popular Front to constituency organizations, and thereafter refusing to abandon his campaign. Following his expulsion, he organized the National Petition campaign, which through committees up and down the country was supposed to create the pressure necessary for a Popular Front government. So tender was Cripps towards Liberal feeling, that his programme contained no mention of nationalization: only of the 'control' of armaments and other key industries. Keynes signed the Petition and wrote him a letter of support.[2]

This new campaign also failed, and was formally abandoned in June 1939. Cripps switched again. This time he began to approach leading Conservatives – Baldwin, Churchill and Halifax – to argue for a broadening of the government, the same plan which Halifax himself had favoured since Munich. His aim was to get rid of the inner ring of appeasers, Chamberlain, Simon and Hoare: his new hope was that the more enlightened Conservatives would make Halifax Prime Minister.[3] Halifax was again to be his candidate in the crisis of May 1940. Cripps had come down from the clouds with a vengeance. He felt that the only issue now was to save the nation by gathering together everyone who was prepared to resist Hitler. 'I don't think,' he wrote to his aunt Beatrice Webb in June 1939, 'that "party politics" in the old sense will have any meaning in this country for a very long time to come. They are discredited and useless as a means of directing policies in times like these.'[4]

There were excellent tactical reasons for shelving the question of socialism in the crisis of 1939. There remains the problem of how far and how fast these new tactics modified Cripps's basic beliefs. From the time of the Popular Front campaign onwards, Cripps's views were indistinguishable from those of unaligned radicals who believed in more planning at home and an alliance with Russia against Germany in world politics. Cripps was no longer a member of the Labour Party. No one, he told Beatrice Webb, was interested any longer in their outworn programme; if they fought a general election they might get as few as fifty seats.[5] From 1931 until 1937 Cripps had tried to achieve power by resort to the people. By the outbreak of war he had decided to stay clear even of the Labour Party and pursue his course as an Independent. Henceforth he behaved as a thoroughly pragmatic reforming politician.

This is not to say that he became an orthodox careerist or Conservative. The moment war broke out his instinct was to plan the advance of mankind. His diary for 26 September noted: 'I am trying very tentatively to organize an all-party group of persons who are prepared to devote themselves to a new beginning at the end of the war.' One of his biographers tells us that there were several meetings of this kind, where there appeared to be little difference between the views of the younger Labour and Conservative politicians.[6]

In the winter of 1939–40 Cripps, with considerable prescience, visited India, China, Russia and the United States. He explored the minds of as many of the leading men of these countries as would see him, and gathered facts remorselessly. He could see that the future of the war depended upon these powers, although he overestimated the importance of India and China. Above all, he sought to repair the relations between Britain and Russia, obstructed by the Russo-German pact, and destroyed by the Russo-Finnish war. In February 1940 he flew from Sinkiang to the Russo-Chinese border, and from there on to Moscow to an audience with Molotov. The journey from Singkiang and back took him 6,000 miles through the wilderness of central Asia, and the meeting with Molotov was an unprofitable affair lasting only two hours.

Cripps had travelled relatively little before: he now thought of himself as an actor on a global stage, mobilizing the progressive forces of the world. For he remained a fervent believer in moral and political progress; nothing else accounts for his sense of mission. He remained markedly pro-Russian by comparison with his former colleagues in the Labour Party—who were condemning Russia for aggression against Finland at the very moment when Cripps was talking to Molotov — and his views contrasted markedly with the sceptical attitude of the Foreign Office.

In May 1940 Halifax and the War Cabinet under Churchill decided that it would be useful to make contact with Russia by sending Cripps on a special temporary mission to Moscow, announcing at the same time that an ambassador would be appointed later. The Russians, however, refused to accept any emissary except an accredited ambassador: and thus Cripps was appointed in place of Sir William Seeds. He arrived in Moscow in June 1940.

It is sometimes suggested that Cripps's period in Russia did a great deal to disillusion him in socialism and the Soviet system. There is little evidence of this, but a great deal to show that the longer he stayed there, the more convinced he became that the failure to establish good Anglo-Soviet relations was due to the reactionary resistance of the Foreign Office and the upper class. In a letter to Halifax of 10 October 1940 he argued that there would never be any improvement in Anglo-Soviet relations so long as the Russians believed that Britain was interested, not in permanent friendship, but only in extracting temporary advantages. In Cripps's view it was vital to make an imaginative bid for Russian friendship by offering goodwill in the present and future partnership in world reconstruction. Commenting on Cripps's outburst, the Northern Department of the Foreign Office declared that it was Russia which did not want continuing partnership with Britain, a capitalist country. Later Halifax wrote, emphasizing his view that Russia was entirely realist, and took no notice of Britain as long as Britain did not appear to count as a force to be reckoned with.[7]

Cripps conceded that Russia was inefficient, backward, and cruelly repressive under Stalinism. But, he wrote, 'the whole tradition and bias of the Foreign Office is violently and unreasoningly anti-Russian ... one can either look upon them [the Russians] as a people broadly groping after something which is in the right direction or as wicked and malevolent destroyers of world civilization.'[8] In mid-October 1940 the War Cabinet authorized him to put forward in Moscow a far-ranging offer of friendship based on proposals Cripps himself had drafted. They were at once overtaken by Molotov's visit to Berlin, and never referred to by the Russians again. But Cripps's bitterness was still directed against the Foreign Office. In a remarkable indiscretion he told the United States ambassador in Moscow that there were 'individuals in the British Government who were so hostile to the Soviet Union that they would prefer to risk the Empire rather than permit a rapprochement to take place.'[9] Despite the replacement of Halifax by Eden in December 1940 there was no improvement in Anglo-Russian relations between then and the German invasion of Russia on 22 June 1941. Cripps continued to behave with cantankerous independence: in April 1941 he aroused Churchill's anger by refusing to deliver a message from Churchill to Stalin, on the grounds that it would cut across a message he himself had prepared on the need for a revision of Russian policy.[10]

As wartime frustrations tended to be directed against the social and political symbols of Conservatism, so there was a demand for distinctively leftish leaders, a current which ran crystal clear in 1942. The year opened with more disaster as the Japanese conquered Malaya and Singapore, and advanced into Burma, and it continued in a depressing stalemate until November, when the Anglo-American landings at one end of North Africa, and Montgomery's victory at the other, marked the light at the end of the tunnel.

At the lowest ebb of his personal popularity, after the fall of Tobruk in June 1942, Churchill was supported by 78 per cent of the opinion poll sample. As the military leader he was felt to be indispensable. But there were other discontents. The government as a whole, by contrast with Churchill, was remarkably unpopular, as another Gallup poll series revealed during 1942:[11]

Q: Are you satisfied or dissatisfied with the Government's conduct of the war?

	Satisfied	Dissatisfied
17 March	35	50
17 April	50	38
18 May	63	24
16 June	57	26
20 July	41	42
22 August	45	38
20 September	41	37

Over the same period four Independent candidates defeated Conservative supporters of the government at by-elections. There was room for another man of action, especially one who would concentrate on the domestic aspects of the war effort. The Left, too, found itself without leadership. Strange as it now seems, Churchill himself had been the hero of the Left in 1940–41, to the exclusion of the Labour leaders. The three founders of the Left Book Club had fallen at his feet. Laski wrote in *Tribune* of the popular faith in Churchill: 'In twenty-five years' knowledge of our movement I have known no leader to whom that faith has been given in greater measure or from a fuller heart.'[12] Strachey, his biographer tells us, regarded criticism of Churchill as 'scarcely conceivable'.[13] Gollancz wrote that Churchill was such a great patriot that he would win the war by and for socialism rather than lose it—but Attlee and Bevin were ineffectual men with little following.[14]

During 1941, however, it was gradually realized by the Left, and by the advocates of *ad hoc* radicalism, that Churchill was conservative both socially and in his approach to administration. There was no repetition of the system of 1916–18—inspired dictatorship by outsiders. The rogue elephants, Beaverbrook, Bracken and Lindemann, were kept on a close rein. Above all Churchill eschewed all traces of populist radicalism, presenting himself solely as the chief warrior. A Lloyd George, with his nose for currents of opinion, impatience with bureaucracy, and cottage-bred oratory, might have combined supremacy in the military field with mastery of the home front. But if there was no one of this calibre who could replace Churchill, there was still scope for a leader at home who could appeal to the two main currents of discontent—the call for abrasive efficiency and the popular groundswell of left-wing feeling. The Lloyd George disciples were again becoming restless. Waldorf Astor returned to his advocacy of a Lloyd George

War Cabinet and wrote impatiently to Garvin, the editor of the *Observer*, in July 1941: 'I wired you that this seemed psychological moment to advocate ministerial reorganization. It has grieved me and disturbed me for some time that the *Observer* was not giving a lead as it used to in former days.'[15] In the House of Commons, Clement Davies was the unofficial organizer of the ginger opposition: outside it was expressed by the 1941 Committee. Harold Macmillan, who was then Under-Secretary to Beaverbrook at the Ministry of Supply, wrote a deeply perceptive and prophetic letter on the need for home front leadership to Beaverbrook in October 1941. No doubt he felt Beaverbrook might fill the gap. His letter deserves a lengthy quotation:

> The political system is bad.
> The House of Commons is very restive.
> The Press is hostile.
> The reasons are:
> 1. Our impotence to help Russia by direct military effort causes us to search our hearts again.
> 2. A sense of lack of grip by the Government on internal questions —labour supply, production policy, etc.
> 3. The 'old gang' are unpopular. (Halifax, Simon, Kingsley-Wood, E. Brown.) The 'new gang' are largely regarded as failures. (Greenwood, Attlee, Duff Cooper.)
> The Bureaucratic method of Whitehall is becoming known in wider circles: Government by Committee; the Lord President's elephantine slowness; the difficulty of getting decisions.
> 4. All the symptoms are developing which marked the end of the *Asquith* coalition (a coalition of parties) and the formation of the *Lloyd George* coalition (a coalition of personalities).
> But in this case the second coalition must be under the same leadership. The Prime Minister's personal position is as high as ever. But he is thought to be let down by his loyalties.
> 5. The War Front and the Home Front should be divided. We want a leader for all that comes under the Home Front. This must *include* Labour, which with Raw Materials and Machine Capacity forms the Trinity of Production.[16]

Beaverbrook as Minister of Supply made the attempt to become the home front leader himself, taking the leadership of factory workers and shop stewards, and appealing to them to work all out for the cause of Russia. In September 1941 he flew on a much publicized visit to Russia to agree on war supplies with Stalin; in the secrecy of the Cabinet room he was urging the case for larger supplies to Russia against the opposition of the Chiefs of Staff, and arguing for a Second Front. But a millionaire press baron of militant if idiosyncratic Tory outlook was unlikely to fill the bill if there was anyone with a better public image. Cripps easily eclipsed him in the New Year of 1942. On 23 January he arrived in Britain after eighteen months as Ambassador to Russia. He was said to be credited by the public with having brought Russia into the war, and with the Anglo-Soviet alliance of July 1941. Political insiders knew full well how inaccurate such ideas were, and it looks as though the press to some extent built up Cripps for reasons of morale. But he was also of course the white hope of the progressive intelligentsia and their friends in journalism. The 1941 Committee, on his first return from Russia, had deputed David Astor and Tom Harrisson, as the young men of the future, to go and represent its views to him.[17]

Cripps's rise to power on the Russian issue had a public side to it, apparent at the time, and a private side which has not been pointed out before. Like Churchill before him, Cripps opportunely filled a critical role in the maintenance of morale, and relied on the press and the public (for he had no party backing) to impose him on the party politicians. At the time of his arrival from Moscow, morale was in decline, discouraged by the fall of Singapore and the astonishing events of 12 February 1942 when three German warships, the *Scharnhorst*, the *Gneisenau*, and the *Prinz Eugen*, slipped through the English Channel en route from Brest to Germany, evading the Royal Navy and the R.A.F. The Weekly Intelligence Report spoke of 'the blackest week since Dunkirk.'[18] A new leader was in demand to restore general confidence in the direction of the war effort. There was no thought of Bevin, who had made such a success of the Ministry of Labour, or Morrison, the admirable Home Secretary, for they were familiar names with no glamour attached. But Cripps was a dramatic new figure on the domestic scene, and carried with him all the public admiration which centred on the Russian war.

His association with Russia also gave him an important private hold on the government. Beaverbrook's championship of Russia has often been contrasted with the failure of Cripps, the theoretical left-winger, to get on with Stalin or press the Russian case. There is the story of how Cripps was recalled to London on the eve of the German assault on Russia. On the day of the German attack, he was pessimistic about Russia's chances of holding out, while Beaverbrook took the more robust view.[19] While, however, Beaverbrook became the champion of sending the maximum supplies to Russia, and thus cut across the ideas of the Chiefs of Staff, Cripps outdid him by consistently demanding a thorough-going Anglo-Russian partnership. The British Ambassador became increasingly restless and threatening in his communications to London. On 4 September he telegraphed that Britain must cease regarding the Russo-German war as no responsibility of hers, and throw everything in.[20] At the end of the month Beaverbrook arrived in Moscow with the United States envoy Averell Harriman, to arrange the Anglo-American supply programme for Russia. Beaverbrook struck up an unholy camaraderie with Stalin and impressed him with the generosity of his decisions: Cripps was by-passed. Cripps complained strongly that the conference should have embraced strategic issues. If, he wrote to Churchill, there had been concerted action with the Greeks earlier in the year when they were threatened by the Germans, why could there be no similar relations with the Kremlin? 'It appears to me that we are treating the Soviet Government without trust and as inferiors rather than trusted Allies. This attitude is similar to that which we have adopted ever since the revolution ... '[21]

On 25 October he called for the dispatch to Russia of an army corps with R.A.F. support. The Russians, he said, were obsessed by the suspicion that the British were ready to fight to the last drop of Russian blood. Churchill replied with a strong condemnation of Russian policy since 1939: 'If they harbour suspicions of us it is only because of the guilt and self-reproach in their own hearts.' Twice in November Cripps cabled that he would resign unless a whole-hearted alliance with Russia, covering the post-war future, was adopted: 'I came here to do a special job and not as a professional diplomatist and it was understood that when the job was at an end I should leave. Owing to the policy of His Majesty's Government, the job is now at an end and there is nothing more that I can do.' Churchill commented to Eden: 'Cripps is evidently preparing his case against us.'[22]

Here was a potential political sensation, dangerous for Churchill at home, and for Anglo-Soviet relations. Cripps had not just come home from Russia for a change of scene; he had in effect resigned in protest at the government's failure to establish closer relations with Stalin. At first Cripps did not play his Russian card. He and Lady Cripps lunched with Churchill, Churchill offered him the Ministry of Supply, without a seat in the War Cabinet, and on 29 January Cripps rejected the offer.[23]

Having first rejected any reconstruction of the government, Churchill reluctantly changed his tune, in particular meeting the clamour of the press for a Minister of Production by announcing the appointment of Beaverbrook to the job on 4 February. The failure to provide for Cripps in the reshuffle created disappointment—not least to Cripps himself. On 8 February he played his Russian card in a speech at Bristol. He declared that he had returned to Britain with one main purpose:

> We must get rid of the idea that there are two separate wars in Europe; that we are fighting one of them and the Russians the other ... We must treat the Soviet Union as our allies in a single war ... If we do that; if we work with 100 per cent effort; if we give to Russia all the support we can, then, in my view, there is every chance of Germany being defeated by this time next year.[24]

The same evening he delivered one of the evening talks in the 'Post-scripts' series which had launched J. B. Priestley in 1940. It consisted of a cleverly drawn comparison between the sacrifices and hardships being endured by the Russians, and the relative comfort of Cripps's audience by the fireside, a severe critique of the slackness of the British war effort.[25] The effect of the broadcast, according to Tom Harrisson, was sensational. From that day on Cripps had a firm grasp on the public, and people felt that he would be the guiding leader on the home front, leaving Churchill free for strategy. He was also thought of as the only credible successor to Churchill apart from Eden: he left his Labour rivals standing:[26]

Q: If anything should happen to Mr Churchill, whom would you like to succeed him as Prime Minister?

	Nov 41	Apr 42	Jul 42	Nov 42
		percentage replying		
A: Eden	38	37	34	39
Cripps	1	34	28	24
Attlee	3	2	3	3
Bevin	7	2	3	4
Morrison	2	1	1	2

On 23 February 1942 it was announced that Cripps was to become a member of the War Cabinet as Lord Privy Seal and leader of the House. In his first speech as a member of the government he spoke of the funeral of 'the late and not lamented Colonel Blimp'. This struck a

promising note, but Cripps had at once adapted to the realities of power. Having entered the War Cabinet on the cry of better relations with Russia, Cripps seemed to fall silent on the question. The War Cabinet often discussed the problem of supplies to Russia, and the key issue of the Second Front, but few interventions by Cripps are recorded in the minutes, certainly no dissent. For the period during which he was a.member of the War Cabinet eleven volumes of Cabinet memoranda can be consulted, but they contain nothing by Cripps on current relations with Russia. Instead Cripps was obsessed during these months by the fear of Beaverbrook, who had resigned from the war Cabinet on 19 February in order to launch his campaign for a Second Front.

Shortly after entering the War Cabinet, Cripps undertook on behalf of the government a personal mission to solve the constitutional deadlock in India, where the Congress Party was demanding immediate independence as the price of co-operation in the war effort. The mission failed, and Cripps's stock took a tumble, especially among socialists. It was often suggested at the time that he had fallen into a trap prepared for him by Churchill, who, it was said, wanted the mission to fail and imposed on Cripps terms of reference which would ensure that it did. The full details of the Cripps mission are now available.[27] They show that Cripps drew up, in all essentials, the declaration which he carried with him to India; that he put himself forward to undertake the mission; that he stretched the terms of reference further than the Viceroy or the Cabinet could tolerate; and that even the most he could devise was too little for Congress, which flatly turned down his version of the proposals. He fell between two stools: he was more progressive than the War Cabinet but too reactionary for Gandhi and the majority wing of Congress.

In August 1940, in an effort to enlist the co-operation of the Indian peoples in the war, the Viceroy, Lord Linlithgow, had issued a declaration promising India Dominion status after the war, under a constitution to be determined by Indians themselves. But the two main parties, the Congress and the Moslem League, remained dissatisfied. Congress wanted practical independence for India during the war, while recognizing that the British Commander-in-Chief in India must remain in charge of military operations. The Moslem League demanded the right of predominantly Moslem states to secede from the post-war Dominion. There remained also the problem of the princely states, covering two-

fifths of India: a multitude of independent states related by treaty to the
paramount power in Delhi; and the problem of guaranteeing the rights
of religious minorities.

In January 1942 the problem of discontent became acute. The
Japanese were overrunning South-East Asia, including Burma. Pressure
suddenly built up on the British government to make concessions to
the independence movement. Roosevelt and United States opinion
objected to the idea of fighting a war to preserve the British Raj, and
called for changes: Roosevelt sent out to India a personal envoy,
Colonel Louis Johnson, in theory to deal with supply problems, in fact
as a political emissary. The Labour Party, too, roused itself. At first
both Linlithgow, and L. S. Amery, the Secretary for India, stood pat on
the line of doing nothing. Nor did Churchill believe that the co-operation of the predominantly Hindu Congress was worth buying. Linlithgow put the case very brutally:

> Cabinet will I think agree with me that India and Burma have no
> natural association with the Empire, from which they are alien
> by race, history and religion, and for which as such neither of them
> have any natural affection, and both are in the Empire because they
> are conquered countries which had been brought here by force,
> kept there by our controls, and which hitherto it has suited to
> remain under our protection.[28]

The Cabinet did not agree. Attlee, at least, wrote:

> This is an astonishing statement to be made by a Viceroy. It sounds
> more like an anti-imperialist propaganda speech. If it were true it
> would form the greatest possible condemnation of our rule in
> India and would amply justify the action of every extremist in
> India ...
>
> It is one of the great achievements of our rule in India that, even
> if they do not entirely carry them out, educated Indians do accept
> British principles of justice and liberty. We are condemned by
> Indians not by the measure of Indian ethical conceptions but by
> our own, which we have taught them to accept.
>
> It is precisely this acceptance by politically conscious Indians
> of the principles of democracy and liberty which puts us in the
> position of being able to appeal to them to take part with us in the
> common struggle; but the success of this appeal and India's
> response does put upon us the obligation of seeing that we, as far

as we may, make them sharers in the things for which we and they are fighting ...[29]

Churchill, while innocent of such beliefs himself, saw that he had to bow to domestic and American pressure, and a Cabinet Committee was set up under Attlee, with Amery, Cripps, Simon, Anderson and P. J. Grigg. Amery's draft declaration was laid aside, and although the draft submitted by Cripps subsequently disappeared, the new text which emerged owed very little to Amery's version. It was the most explicit promise yet of complete independence for India after the war. To the chagrin of the Viceroy and Amery it referred specifically to the right of India as a Dominion to secede from the Commonwealth. But it also included, for the first time, the right of individual provinces to remain outside the new Indian state, thus conceding in principle the Moslem League's argument in favour of a separate nation of Pakistan. The princely states too were to be allowed to remain outside. The declaration also laid down the procedure for constitution-making after the war. For the present it offered very little except a vague undertaking that

> the task of organizing to the full the military, moral and material resources of India must be the responsibility of the Government of India with the co-operation of the peoples of India. His Majesty's Government desire and invite the immediate and effective participation of the leaders of the principal sections of the Indian people in the counsels of their country ...[30]

The original plan was for the declaration to be issued to the world without any preliminary soundings in India. But after a series of expostulatory telegrams from the Viceroy, who argued that it would stir up divisions while Congress rejected it out of hand, the War Cabinet decided on 9 March to accept an offer from Cripps to fly out to India. He was to test the acceptability of the declaration, and produce it if there seemed a chance of success.[31]

In theory the promise of post-war independence was a radical gesture. But much the same promise had been made in August 1940. It is hard to recall that there was still a great deal of scepticism in Conservative circles about the prospect of any agreed division of power in India between the communities: the very diversity of India seemed to guarantee a role for Britain as arbitrator for many years to come. As for the immediate future, Britain would remain in control through the Viceroy and his Executive Council. L. S. Amery wrote to Linlithgow:

From the point of view of putting across what is essentially a Con-servative policy, both as regards the future and as regards the immediate refusal to transfer control of the Executive, there is much to be said for sending out someone who has always been an extreme Left Winger and in close touch with Nehru and the Congress. The immediate effect on your Muslims, as with my Tory friends here, may be alarming, but the 'result in the end should be both to increase the chances of success, slight as they are, and to mitigate any blame thrown upon the Government as a whole for failure.[32]

As Amery wrote, he was convinced that Cripps would really 'play the game' by the government's policy. But he reckoned without a crucial misunderstanding about the terms of reference. Cripps left for India in the belief that he had a mandate to Indianize the Viceroy's Executive Council, the effective government of India. At first he appeared to be respecting the Viceroy's power to determine the composition of the Executive, and Linlithgow was loud in his praise.[33] But in the first week of April Cripps and Roosevelt's emissary, Colonel Johnson, began to negotiate with Congress behind Linlithgow's back, on the subject of the appointment of an Indian Minister of Defence to the Executive. The powers of Wavell as Commander-in-Chief were to be reserved, and the plan might have been acceptable to both the Viceroy and the War Cabinet. However, Cripps went further, and spoke of 'the new arrangement whereby the Executive Council will approximate to a Cabinet.'[34] It emerged that Cripps was on the one hand declaring that the Viceroy's powers would remain unaffected, according to the 1935 constitution, while on the other promising the Congress politicians effective responsibility. He squared the circle by promising Congress that although the *legal* powers of the Viceroy would remain intact, he would doubtless accept a convention in which he behaved as the head of a Cabinet of responsible ministers. This sleight of hand was too clever by half for the Cabinet in London, which sent a strong telegram telling him to stick to his instructions.[35] On the very day that Cripps replied, stubbornly reserving his position, the President of Congress wrote to him announcing the rejection of all his proposals. Congress demanded outright constitutional change at once. This was an impos-sible demand, raised by Congress for the first time, and with it the mission collapsed. In August Congress began a civil disobedience movement to force the British to quit India, and Cripps announced that law and order must be preserved. Gandhi and other Congress leaders were arrested, and a rebellion followed in which nearly a thousand people had been killed by November 1942.

Cripps's failure in India did little to damage his popular standing. On his return he broadcast again, and this time spoke very strongly on the need for post-war reconstruction. There was a good response to his talk,[36] but he himself continued to be dazzled by the prospect of taking over from Churchill and applying scientific methods to the war effort. The fall of Tobruk on 20 June created another wave of shock and much lobby speculation about Churchill's future. Malcolm MacDonald, on leave from Canada where he was High Commissioner, was astounded to be approached by Cripps and asked whether he would sound out other Cabinet ministers about the acceptability of his succession to the premiership. MacDonald declined to become involved.[37]

No one would be able to usurp Churchill's authority without powerful Conservative endorsement, and it is a startling reminder of how far Cripps had travelled since the days of the United Front, that Cripps expected it. Addressing the Fabians after his return from India, Cripps bade them look forward at the end of the war to the creation by leading men of a Centre party, with the aim of bringing about planned production and consumption. He insisted that there were more Conservative than Labour M.P.s ready to act on these lines.[38] He spoke privately of his faith in Beveridge and Keynes, both of whom, he believed, were 'going Left'.[39] Orwell was taken aback, on meeting him, to discover his indifference to the question of whether the great powers were capitalist or socialist: 'I saw that I was up against the official mind, which sees everything as a problem in administration and does not grasp that at a certain point, i.e. when certain economic interests are threatened, public spirit ceases to function.'[40]

Cripps looked to the Church of England, rather than to any political party, to provide, as he put it, 'the moral force and the driving power for social and economic development. Christian principles must be made so to permeate public opinion that no Government could act against them ... ' In the course of one day in September 1942 he appeared on the platform at an Albert Hall Rally with the Archbishop of Canterbury, William Temple, and broadcast from a pulpit in the evening on the need to make the Church the champion of the poor and oppressed.[41]

The idealist fails through believing too much in the inherent decency and fairness of men with interests and advantages to pursue, and Cripps's principles marked him out as a radical too credulous to be a danger to vested interests. Harold Laski was inevitably dismayed by the new Cripps. Cripps, he wrote, had accepted the terms for national unity laid down by the 1922 Committee, and believed that the Conservatives had undergone a change of heart. Had he been firm and courageous, he might have been a pivotal figure: instead 'he is going to be only the most attractive of those who become the unconscious instruments of the enemy.'[42]

Cripps's sense of destiny seemed to arise from the belief, fortified by ambition, that he represented the new wave of moral and technical progress, while Churchill, for all his talents, belonged to an older generation whose ideas were becoming obsolete. It was fitting that Cripps should have as his aide the young Welsh socialist David Owen, secretary of Political and Economic Planning, and since February 1942 a part-time leader writer for *The Times* on social policy. Owen was a good friend of Basil Liddell Hart, and thus Cripps came into contact with the leading military theorist of his time. Liddell Hart was renowned as the prophet of mobile mechanized warfare, and as a military correspondent. He had enjoyed, however, only a brief period of inside influence as adviser to Hore-Belisha, the Secretary for War, in 1937–8. His ruthlessly logical approach to problems and deep originality made him a difficult figure to integrate into a world of fallible political influences, and he undoubtedly felt highly frustrated. He was also a severe critic of Churchill, believing him too emotional and impulsive a creature to make a wise or consistent strategist. Moreover Churchill blocked the way against Liddell Hart's own demands for the promotion of commanders experienced in mechanized warfare, and the creation of a high-level strategic planning organization. When he met Cripps, he wrote that he had been more impressed by him than by any other political leader.[43] Cripps too was impressed, and felt that Liddell Hart's advice was vital in military affairs. Since he was not a member of the Defence Committee of the War Cabinet, he needed all the advice and information he could find, and he obviously felt that Liddell Hart's opinions were indispensable.

After the fall of Tobruk on 20 June – an unexpected and devastating blow – the malcontents in the House of Commons began to organize under the leadership of Sir John Wardlaw-Milne, chairman of the Select Committee on National Expenditure. He put down a motion, due for debate on 1 July, censuring the central conduct of the war. On 25 June the government lost the Maldon by-election to a left-wing

Beaverbrook journalist, Tom Driberg. The usual gusts of alarmism sprang up in the House, with much talk of the challenge to Churchill's position. There was a whisper, despite the fact that Driberg had stood quite independently for the Left, that his candidature was part and parcel of an obscure intrigue by Beaverbrook. Such talk was all beside the mark, for the challenge was developing slowly from inside the War Cabinet in the person of Cripps. Beaverbrook had no more chance of succeeding Churchill than of succeeding Stalin or de Gaulle, and the parliamentary mavericks were small beer.

Cripps was dabbling enthusiastically in the question of the reform of the military command, and sent Owen to see Liddell Hart to pick his brains. Liddell Hart wanted two mechanized experts, Pile and Hobart, to take over as C.I.G.S. and Commander of the Eighth Army. On 2 July, the opening of the censure debate, Cripps presented to Churchill a guide to current discontents. One of these, he argued, was the belief that commanders were out of date and had insufficient understanding of mechanized warfare. Additionally, Britain seemed to be inferior in many branches of weaponry, notably in aircraft design: there was a feeling that not enough use was being made of research workers, scientists and inventors in the 'race for efficient equipment'.[44]

On 1 and 2 July Churchill survived the vote of censure by the handsome margin of 476 to 25. The two main protagonists of the motion, Sir Roger Keyes and Wardlaw-Milne, had put forward opposite solutions, Keyes wanting Churchill to take all the decisions in defence, Wardlaw-Milne arguing that he delegate them to a Minister of Defence. And such was Churchill's luck that Wardlaw-Milne destroyed the effect of his speech by the extraordinary proposal that the King's brother, the Duke of Gloucester, be made commander-in-chief—at which the House broke into prolonged guffaws. However, apart from the twenty-five M.P.s who voted against the government, it was possible to list by name twenty-seven who had abstained, so that fifty-two M.P.s in all had shown their lack of confidence.[45] The challenge from Cripps remained.

On the day after the debate Cripps handed Churchill another paper. this time concocted with Lyttelton, the Minister of Production; David Owen showed a copy to E. H. Carr who recorded that it included demands for a General Planning Staff in charge of strategy, unspecified changes in army commands, greater powers for the Minister of Production, and a 'Scientific Planning Staff' attached to his Ministry. Andrew Duncan, the Minister of Supply, was to be sacked.[46] These proposals came to nothing, although it is interesting to note that in line with Liddell Hart's advice Cripps did press specifically for Hobart to be given the Eighth Army.[47]

Would another defeat make Cripps Prime Minister? It was a moment when E. H. Carr could argue that the political situation was graver than at any previous time in the war. 'The catchword, "We want the P.M., but we want him to change his Government and methods" rings hollower and hollower.' The government was likely to fall and there must be an alternative. The only solution would be for a leading member of the Cabinet to pluck up the courage to resign and establish himself as a constructive critic on strategic and economic policy, and reconstruction: 'An "After the War" programme, though in form subsidiary, is essential in order to put an adequate sense of purpose behind the war effort.' Surely Carr was thinking of Cripps, with whom *The Times* had close links through David Owen.[48]

A sensitive and balanced estimate of the fortunes of Churchill and Cripps was conveyed to that old *eminence grise* Tom Jones by the Labour M.P. Ivor Thomas, in a letter of such insight and interest as to merit lengthy quotation:

> If Alexandria had fallen, Winston would have fallen also. As it is, he will hold his position until we get another major reverse ... As far as sheer competence in waging war is concerned, there is no one in the country who can hold a candle to Winston, and, if we open a second front in the near future, I cannot think of anyone better fitted to direct it. My complaint against him is not the one commonly made, that he overrules his service chiefs ... We have not, in fact, had any of the typically Churchillian strokes in this war. I wish he would use more forcefully his martial experience ... In a democratic country, however, a Prime Minister needs more than merit: he must also command general approval. It must be confessed that Winston's stock has been falling badly. This ought to be a 'People's War', but Winston has never, owing to his background and record, been able to capture the affections of the working classes as L.G. did ... there will be a change in time, and inevitably (though possibly after a short interlude) Cripps will be PM ... Whatever the Gallup Poll may reveal ... a large number in both the Labour Party and the Conservative Party regard Eden as a weak figure who has got his present position only by birth, the right school, good looks and luck. The Conservatives, anxious to

avoid Eden, are at present canvassing R. A. Butler as PM! ... The bulk of the Labour Party would prefer Cripps to Attlee, and, combined with the Tory feeling I have mentioned, this will bring Cripps to the top. I repeat this conviction even though Cripps' stock in Left circles has fallen heavily, both in the House and outside, since he joined the Cabinet.[49]

This did not so much underestimate Churchill as exaggerate the credibility of Cripps. He was no Lloyd George, and it would have taken someone of that calibre to beat Churchill, who could always threaten to appeal to the public, for whom he remained virtually a sacrosanct figure, despite many military defeats.

Cripps kept up the pressure over matters which other members of the War Cabinet were content to leave to Churchill. He wanted to remove the First Sea Lord, the deaf but wily Admiral Pound; he talked at length to the Director of Political Warfare, R. H. Bruce Lockhart, criticizing propaganda policy. His major priority, according to Owen, was the creation of a genuine War Cabinet on the Lloyd George model: social reconstruction was at the bottom of his list.[50] He brooded still on the unscientific character of the defence machinery. He devised a new plan which he put to Churchill early in September 1942. Under the new dispensation the Chiefs of Staff were to be flanked by an independent War Planning Directorate, which would take over the planning of strategy and future operations. Churchill was badly worried by Cripps's blueprint. In his own mind he was sure it made no sense. It would have created, he wrote later, two rival bodies each trying to direct the armed forces, and the War Planning Directorate would amount to 'a disembodied Brains Trust'. The Minister of Defence must be able to work directly through the responsible heads of the services who could give orders.[51]

By the autumn, Cripps had lost a great deal of ground with public opinion. The Indian mission had at least shown that he was doing something: since then nothing much had been heard of him, and yet the government muddled on much as before. He was in danger of fading into the background. Resignation on a major issue, above all on the question of the machinery for the conduct of the war, would have created a sensation. The military history of the war to date had been a record of defeats. At first they could be blamed on the incompetence of the pre-war government. Increasingly this argument wore thin, and the responsibility for setbacks weighed heavily on Churchill. It appeared to

the Minister of Information, Brendan Bracken, that he was coming to
the end of the road: 'The Prime Minister must win his battle in the
desert or get out,' he told Moran.[52]

By his proposals for a drastic overhaul of the defence machinery,
Cripps had provoked a crisis which, no matter how he handled it,
would boomerang against him. Unbeknown to him the military fortunes of the country were about to mend. On 3 October he wrote to
Churchill to put it on record that he was in fundamental disagreement
over defence, and would have resigned but for the pressure brought to
bear on him not to do so at the critical moment before the battle.[53] No
doubt Cripps wanted the letter to be on the record because he believed
that he would be proved right. Beatrice Webb, meeting her nephew
for the last time on 26 October, noted that he was still confident about
the future:

> Churchill would not last out the war: he was old and had no plan
> for the future, whether within our own country or for the
> international situation when we had won the war. He intimated
> that there were only two possible Prime Ministers: Anthony
> Eden and himself. Eden had all the right instincts, but was an
> aristocratic country squire, and had no control over the Foreign
> Office and still less over the governing group of the Civil Servants
> who dominated Whitehall. In short Stafford expects that *he* would
> succeed Churchill as Prime Minister.[54]

This was no longer the public's view: 'more people now are completely
disillusioned, tending to place Cripps in with the general run of
ineffectuals or yes men.'[55]

In November 1942 the Anglo-American landings in North Africa
and Montgomery's victory at Alamein marked, at last, the turn of the
tide. Churchill quickly capitalized on Cripps's letter of 3 October, and
insisted on his resignation. He accepted the technical non-political
office of Minister of Aircraft Production, outside the War Cabinet. One
of his last acts as Lord Privy Seal was to announce the publication date
of the Beveridge Report. There was the kind of issue on which he
might have been effective; instead he had tried to take over the war
from Churchill.

VIII The People's William

In the year 1903 the celebrated Fabian couple, Sidney and Beatrice Webb, were approaching the zenith of their influence. Beatrice wrote in her diary for 25 July: 'Our general social policy is to construct a base to society in the form of a legally enforced minimum ...'[1] In 1908, the young Liberal President of the Board of Trade, Winston Churchill, took up the slogan of the 'national minimum'. But a third of a century was to pass before the slogan was translated into practical proposals by the Beveridge Report, published as a White Paper on 1 December 1942. The Report was a plan to establish full social security for all from the cradle to the grave, and Beveridge attached to it three 'assumptions' which he declared were necessary for the success of comprehensive social insurance: children's allowances, health and rehabilitation services available to all, and the maintenance of employment. The Report declared: 'Want is only one of five giants on the road of reconstruction and in some ways the easiest to attack. The others are Disease, Ignorance, Squalor and Idleness.'[2] The historian of social administration finds in the Beveridge Report the blueprint of the postwar welfare state in Britain. The political historian sees it also as a brilliant coup by one man, which at once synthesized the pressures for a more progressive capitalism, and jolted all three parties into accepting the resulting formula as the basis of a new post-war consensus. For Beveridge, the report was the outcome of a lifetime's experience, and the pinnacle of an already famous career. In 1905, when Beveridge was a young social worker at Toynbee Hall, Beatrice Webb described him as 'an ugly-mannered but honest, self-devoted, hard-headed young reformer of the practical type.'[3] When Churchill was President of the Board of Trade, he introduced Beveridge into the department as a civil servant, responsible for setting up the new labour exchanges.

Thereafter Beveridge enjoyed a distinguished career in Whitehall, ending as Permanent Secretary at the Ministry of Food in 1919. From 1919 to 1937 he was Director of the London School of Economics, and from 1937 to 1945 Master of University College, Oxford. Between the wars, although no longer a civil servant, he was a natural member of the army of the Great and the Good, the men and women whom governments call upon to chair inquiries or sit on royal commissions; and in 1934 he was appointed chairman of the Unemployment Insurance Statutory Committee, whose job it was to keep the insurance fund solvent.

Beveridge was a conceited man whose egotism often gave offence. He tried to run the London School of Economics as an autocracy, and only gave way when the staff mutinied in favour of a constitution. One of his young lecturers, Lionel Robbins, wrote of him in later years: 'I doubt if it ever occurred to him to regard the great men of those days as his equals, let alone, what some of them certainly were from the academic point of view, his superiors.'[4] He was just as maladroit in his dealings with the politicians in 1942, for it is a rash man who tries to steal the limelight from Cabinet ministers: they responded by adopting his ideas and dispensing with his services. 'Always a mistake', Attlee once commented, 'to think yourself larger than you are.'[5]

Beveridge believed that social policy had to be founded on exhaustive research and analysis, and administered by powerful experts like himself. His emotional sympathy for the underdog was qualified by intellectual contempt, and he once commented to his brother-in-law, R. H. Tawney: 'The well-to-do represent on the whole a higher level of character and ability than the working classes, because in the course of time the better stocks have come to the top. A good stock is not permanently kept down: it forces its way up in the course of generations of social change, and so the upper classes are on the whole the better classes.'[6]

Beveridge's major work as a social researcher was in the field of unemployment. In 1909 he published *Unemployment: A Problem of Industry*, and in the late 1930s at University College he was still compiling a study of the trade cycle. At this period he was pessimistic about the chances of curing unemployment, and seemed to have lost interest in social reform. Beatrice Webb, after two earnest three-mile walks with him in the summer of 1938, confided to her diary:

His conclusion is that the major, if not the only remedy for chronic unemployment is lower wages ... He admitted almost defiantly that he was not personally concerned with the condition of the common people. His human sympathies were satisfied by the family group at the College and his pleasant relations with his fellow dons and his college undergraduates ...

If men were fools in not accepting sound economics—and the common people represented by the Labour party might be fools—there would be universal poverty and war. Possibly there might be an attraction in Communism or in a socialist middle way; but, he repeated, there was, as yet, no proof of that and he was not going to think about it.[7]

As we have seen, the experience of 1940 shook Beveridge into a far bolder frame of mind, and thus led on to the famous report.

The pre-war system of compulsory state insurance had consisted of a number of separate schemes—health, unemployment, pensions and so on—for the working class as defined by a ceiling of income levels. The Beveridge scheme provided for the unification of all the existing schemes, and the inclusion of everyone. It proposed that in return for a single weekly flat rate contribution, every contributor would receive benefits calculated to provide a minimum standard of living whenever his or her earnings were interrupted. The great lacuna in this design was old age pensions. They were so costly to the taxpayer that they were to be raised gradually to subsistence level over twenty years. The report declared proudly that 'a revolutionary moment in the world's history is a time for revolutions, not for patching.'[8] But in many respects it was a fundamentally conservative method of advance, especially in its insistence on the insurance principle, whereby everyone paid his own way, its emphasis on the need for individual thrift, and its reference to the possibility that 8·5 per cent of the population might be unemployed after the war. It implied only a mild redistribution of income between classes. Its accompanying assumptions were, in fact, far more sweeping than the social insurance scheme itself—notably the assumption of a National Health Service.

The report was a major exercise in consensus politics. In the first nine months of 1942 the committee took written or verbal evidence from 127 individuals, pressure-groups, and interests. As Beveridge pointed out, they tended to be in fundamental agreement about the need for reform and the goals to be set. But if the T.U.C., the Liberal Party, and

P.E.P., all gave evidence which fitted in with Beveridge's aims, the Conservative Party did not make proposals. At the annual Labour Party conference in May there was a significant debate on social security, and a resolution was passed calling for one comprehensive system to provide adequate cash payments for security whatever the emergency, the provision of family allowances, and the right to all forms of medical attention through a National Health Service.[9] But the previous week a delegation from the Confederation of British. Employers had gone before the Beveridge committee and attacked his ideas root and branch.

Their main contention was that social security contributions would push up production costs and price Britain out of export markets. The Director of the Confederation Sir John Forbes Watson, strongly urged Beveridge to give up the whole idea of making a report: 'I want to say here — it will go on the shorthand note, but I do not know that I want to say it publicly — we did not start this war with Germany in order to improve our social services; the war was forced upon us by Germany and we entered it to preserve our freedom and to keep the Gestapo outside our houses, and that is what the war means.' The Vice-President of the Shipbuilding Employers' Federation, J. S. Boyd, was equally candid:

> I am saying something I would not like printed — there may have been excellent reasons in the last war for talking about homes fit for heroes and there may be excellent reasons today for talking about improving the social services, but at the same time any of us who are trying to think at all do realize and do appreciate that the problems after the war are not problems that the man in the street concerns himself about, and you may be causing a much greater degree of danger by telling him something which in fact even the most optimistic of us may fear will be impossible after the war.

Beveridge was plainly irritated by the refusal of the employers to accept the assumptions he had in mind, and confine themselves to providing him with the evidence he required. When he argued that there was considerable popular interest in the question of reconstruction, the director of the Mining Association, W. A. Lee, flatly contradicted him. But he then went on to contradict himself by adding that statements about post-war reform had created 'a feeling of restlessness which would otherwise not exist'.[10]

Fortunately for Beveridge, the business community was in two minds about the expansion of social services. In November 1942, 120 industrialists, including Lords Melchett and McGowan of I.C.I., set out 'A National Policy for Industry'. Besides endorsing the improved industrial relations and welfare introduced since 1940, the document envisaged a dramatic expansion of corporate paternalism. For example, industrialists would be responsible for the proper housing of their employees, for supplementing the state pension system, and for subsidies to prevent unemployment. The state meanwhile would provide family allowances and raise the school-leaving age to sixteen.[11] This approach, in spite of its emphasis on corporate rather than state action, was obviously more sympathetic to Beveridge's plans.

In theory, Beveridge's task was simply to present advice to the government. In practice, he lobbied and campaigned in advance with the aim of obliging the War Cabinet to accept his proposals. There was so much inspired comment in the press that as early as April 1942 a Home Intelligence report observed: 'Sir William Beveridge's proposals for an 'all-in' social security scheme are said to be popular.'[12] In July, while appearing to give nothing away about the contents of his report, he unveiled his 'five giants' in an address to the Engineering Industries Association. 'I am not without hope', he wrote of his report in August, 'that it may make sufficient popular appeal to compel the Government to take it up, provided I can satisfy the Treasury that it is financially possible.' Beveridge tackled the Treasury by arranging a 'deal' with Keynes, whereby the cost of the proposals was to be kept down to £100 million for the first five years. However, Keynes had no power to commit the Chancellor of the Exchequer. When the report was in draft, Keynes wrote to Beveridge giving his general blessing, but adding that Beveridge could scarcely expect to see it adopted just as it stood.[13]

In June 1942 the minister responsible for reconstruction, William Jowitt, asked the Ministry of Information to prepare a report on public feeling over post-war issues. Once again, the Home Intelligence department drew on the inquiries of its thirteen regional offices, and noted the high degree of agreement between their reports. The report concluded that the majority were not thinking about the future at all. But there was a 'thinking minority' of between 5 per cent and 20 per cent of the population which had definite views:

    i There must be work at a living wage for everyone who is capable of doing it.

  ii Private profit must cease to be the major incentive to
      work; everyone must work primarily for the good of the
      community.
  iii There must be financial security for everyone who is unable to
      work.
  iv There must be decent homes for everyone at a cost which will
      not reduce people to poverty.
  v The same education must be available to everyone so that all
      will have an equal chance.

There is no evidence that Beveridge knew of this report, but it obviously augured a fair wind of articulate opinion in his favour, especially as it went on to say: 'Three years ago, the term social security was almost unknown to the public as a whole. It now appears to be generally accepted as an urgent post-war need. It is commonly defined as "a decent minimum standard of living for all".' The level of war expenditure had led the majority to believe that finance could not in future be regarded as a barrier to its achievement.

It is sometimes suggested that there was very little interest in reconstruction before the 'turn of the tide' in November 1942, but the Home Intelligence report was based on inquiries carried out between August and October. When Hugh Dalton read it, he was inspired to write to Jowitt: 'This is a most interesting and encouraging document, which should stimulate us all, Ministers and officials alike, to quicken our steps and leap over obstacles placed in our path by timid, short-sighted, or sinister persons.'[14] Would the Beveridge plan receive a fanfare of publicity, or be played down? Obviously the decision would affect its fate. The bigger the splash of publicity, the greater the moral commitment of the War Cabinet. On 27 October the Minister of Information, Brendan Bracken, wrote to Churchill: 'I have good reason to believe that some of Beveridge's friends are playing politics and that when the report appears there will be an immense amount of ballyhoo about the importance of implementing the recommendations without delay.' Beveridge, he urged, should be prevented from leaking details of the report.[15]

Early in November came the news, from North Africa, that the allies had for the first time taken the offensive, and were winning — intelligence whose impact on morale can be compared with that of the news that Mafeking had been relieved. Victory was in sight, and with it demobilization and a return to peacetime life. It was Beveridge's good fortune that his report was timed to catch the high tide of euphoria.

On 16 November the War Cabinet discussed a request from Beveridge that he should be given facilities to expound the report, on its publication, at a Ministry of Information press conference. Beveridge also wanted to address the lobby correspondents. 'It appeared', Bracken told the War Cabinet, 'that he intended to disclose not only the recommendations made in the Report, but his own views on those recommendations, and there were indications that he was already working up a political campaign on this question.' On Bracken's recommendation, Beveridge was to be given no official facilities: explanation of the report was to be entirely a matter for the government.[16] That very day, Beveridge spoke to a reporter from the *Daily Telegraph*, which published a report quoting Beveridge to the effect that his proposals would take the country 'half-way to Moscow', a phrase which Beveridge at once disowned.[17] This new delinquency put him in worse odour with the government, and Jowitt wrote him a stern letter of rebuke. But Jowitt thought it would be unwise to try to restrain Beveridge from publicizing the report after it appeared, and Churchill agreed with him, minuting on 25 November 1942: 'Once it is out he can bark to his heart's content.'[18] Bracken rang Beveridge two days before the report was due to be published and told him that the official line had changed: there would be maximum publicity, including a press conference and a broadcast postscript by Beveridge. Perhaps Bracken realized late in the day that the report would serve as a brilliant propaganda weapon against his opposite number, Goebbels. From dawn on 1 December the B.B.C. broadcast details of the report in twenty-two languages. Not long afterwards, however, there was another change of heart. The Director-General of the Ministry of Information, Cyril Radcliffe, visited the offices of Political Warfare and instructed them not to publicize it.[19] And a War Office Army Bureau of Current Affairs pamphlet containing an account of the report by Beveridge himself was withdrawn on 21 December two days after publication. The government was to remain silent for two months.

The public welcome given to the report was well-nigh universal. The national press, with the exception of the *Daily Telegraph*, behaved as though it fell only slightly short of the millenium. A total of 635,000 copies were sold.[20] A survey of opinion by BIPO showed that 86 per cent believed that the report should be adopted, as against 6 per cent who thought it should be dropped. Especially important was the overwhelmingly favourable reaction of the upper income groups. Although they felt they had little or nothing to gain personally, they declared themselves in favour:

Sub-group	per cent of sub-group believing it would gain	per cent of sub-group in favour of adoption
Employers	16	73
Upper Income (A)	29	76
Professions	48	91
Civil service, police, railways and other groups outside present National Health Insurance	58	92

Public response was not entirely uncritical. Nearly three out of five people thought the proposed pension rates too low. But the overall popularity of the report was established beyond a doubt, and the idea of free doctors' and hospital services for all was approved by 88 per cent, including 81 per cent of the wealthier.[21]

While Home Intelligence registered the nationwide acclaim for the report, it also monitored a hostile minority and, within a week of the report's publication, the extraordinary anxiety among the public that somehow the report would be watered down or shelved. Analysis made by the Ministry of Information indicated five categories of opposition to Beveridge:

(1) Some businessmen – those 'in cotton' are specially mentioned – who fear that the tax on industry will be too great, that prices of goods will have to be raised, and that we shall therefore be in no position to compete in post-war export trade ... (Four Regions).

(2) People who think 'the time is not yet ripe for talking reconstruction'; however, even some of these are pleased with the Report (Two Regions).

(3) 'The more extreme elements' who feel that 'the plan is a palliative and that what is really wanted is the socialization of industry' (Two Regions).

(4) Those who think there is too much 'Soviet flavour' about it. Farmers in Scotland feel that 'this daft socialism will lead to the nationalization of the land next' (Two Regions).

(5) 'The man with shares in the Prudential' (One Region).

In every case the grumblers against the report were a minority, a faint chorus drowned by an orchestra of praise. But with the praise went doubt: the report seemed too good to be true:

There is, according to reports from eleven Regions, 'very real anxiety that the plan will not materialize because of the following: (a) 'Vested interests' (Ten Regions). Particularly mentioned are Insurance Companies, the B.M.A. and big business. It is felt 'amongst the rank and file that even if these powerful interests do not jointly succeed in completely wrecking it, they will hotly contest every inch of the ground, the final plan will therefore be so mutilated that the benefits ultimately received by working people will be small.'

(b) The Government (Six Regions). There is some doubt as to whether the Government is wholeheartedly behind the scheme. A minority of working class people in Wales and Scotland, 'who remember promises made in the last war' are saying: 'This is merely propaganda to keep us at it till the war is over.' On the other hand, the Report is regarded as the first real sign that the Government does in fact mean to tackle post-war problems seriously ...

(c) Party politics (Two Regions). It is felt that 'unless the Beveridge Report is passed before the end of the war, little or nothing will be done to ensure social security because it will become the subject of wrangling between the political parties.'

(d) The cost will be too high (Two regions). 'At the same time, the public are reported to be determined that the plan must go through: 'If not, things will be damned unpleasant for whatever government is in power; if it's mucked up, there will be hell to pay' (Five Regions).[22]

There was not a mention here of anxiety that the Conservative Party would play the villain of the piece; but 'Vested Interests' were associated in people's minds with the Tories. The report was indeed a powder-keg.

The struggle over the Beveridge Report intensified the forces for change which had been gathering strength since 1940. Among the public — a phrase which includes more than three million men serving in the armed forces — the desire for a square deal was outgrowing the stern logic of Conservative pessimism, which insisted that people prepare themselves for hard times, and maybe another slump, after the war. Although the Second World War had turned out to be utterly different from the first, the expectation remained that the aftermath at home would be identical.

The first to draw the sword against Beveridge was the Chancellor of the Exchequer, Kingsley Wood, the last powerful Chamberlainite in the government. In a memorandum for Churchill of 17 November 1942 he declared that the plan involved 'an impracticable financial commitment'. It would not abolish want, but it would give benefits to people with savings, who did not need them: 'The weekly progress of the millionaire to the post office for his old age pension would have an element of farce but for the fact that it is to be provided in large measure by the general taxpayer.' Kingsley Wood listed nine features of the report which he argued would involve public or political controversy, including a state medical service, the abolition of approved societies for health insurance, and the right of strikers to unemployment pay. The financial obstacles were formidable. The scheme would be paid for partly by compulsory contributions, partly by personal taxation, and partly by an increased levy on industry. By increasing the tax burden the proposals would impair the capacity of the nation to pay for other objectives. If the overall level of taxation had represented 3s 5d in the pound in 1938, it would stand at 4s 8d in the pound after Beveridge, an almost intolerable burden: 'Many in this country have persuaded themselves that the cessation of hostilities will mark the opening of the Golden Age (many were so persuaded last time also). However this may be, the time for declaring a dividend on the profits of the Golden Age is the time when those profits have been realized in fact, not merely in imagination.'[23]

Cherwell, Churchill's scientific and economic acolyte, advised him that he faced a dilemma. Britain would need much aid from the United States after the war. If the Beveridge Report were adopted, the Americans might become difficult, arguing that they were being asked to pay for British social services. 'On the other hand there has unfortunately been so much carefully engineered advanced publicity that the Government's hand may have been forced.'[24]

Churchill deployed two main arguments against the Beveridge proposals. Firstly, they must be related to the other post-war demands on national resources, especially the cost of the armed forces, and the necessity of restoring the export trade. Secondly, the mood of optimism developing in the country about the post-war future was potentially dangerous. 'The broad masses of the people face the hardships of life undaunted, but they are liable to get very angry if they feel they have been gulled or cheated.'[25]

The Cabinet first considered the report on 14 January, in the absence of Churchill, who was attending the Casablanca Conference. Kingsley Wood had produced another wrecking paper, hammering home all the alternative claims on resources and calling for an agreed system of priorities. While Wood placed the objective of full employment above the fulfilment of the Beveridge proposals, one of the spanners he threw into the works was the possibility that after the war unemployment might exceed the level of 8½ per cent allowed for in the report.[26]

Churchill had appointed a secret committee of Conservative M.P.s, under the chairmanship of Ralph Assheton, to report the party's view. Their comments, delivered on 19 January, were also severe. They accepted the proposal for children's allowances, and the principle of universal contributions towards old age pensions. But there they drew the line. They emphasized that unemployment insurance should be kept substantially lower than wage rates, should not represent a subsistence level, and should cease to be payable after six months unless the unemployed man placed his services at the disposal of the state and accepted any work that was offered him at a fair wage, whether in his trade or not. They wanted a scheme of compulsory health insurance restricted to those with incomes below £420 a year, in order to preserve private medical practice. And they reiterated that everything depended upon the post-war economy. The plan assumed an ever-increasing national income, but 'there must be certain elements of doubt in this regard.' There was a risk that increased social expenditure would cut into the taxable capacity of the nation, which must be directed first of all to the cost of defence and the National Debt.[27]

The minister in charge of reconstruction was still nominally Jowitt, as chairman of the Reconstruction Problems Committee. But the Beveridge Report was such explosive material that the War Cabinet diverted it to a new and more high-powered body, the Reconstruction Priorities Committee. The chairman was the Lord President, Sir John Anderson, and the other members were Bevin, Morrison and Jowitt from the Labour side, and Kingsley Wood, Oliver Lyttelton, and Cranborne from the Conservatives. The Liberals were conspicuous by their absence from this and every other reconstruction committee. For the first time, reconstruction was being treated as a matter of first-rate importance in Whitehall, worthy of the energies of some of the most powerful politicians and civil servants.

Herbert Morrison swiftly emerged as a formidable champion of Beveridge's ideas. No doubt he saw political capital in this for Labour, who could claim to have got the report implemented. But the occasion also revealed in him that strain of fervent passion for modest progress which so characterized the Labour leaders of the day. When the Priorities Committee met for the first time, it had before it a paper from Morrison which challenged the pessimistic forecasts on which Kingsley Wood's opposition rested. Morrison produced his own more sanguine estimate of the post-war national income, and stressed the bankruptcy of defeatist attitudes:

> Suppose we assume a heavy and permanent burden of armaments, a rise in the unemployment rate and a stagnant national income or worse. We are then, in fact, assuming a bankruptcy of world statesmanship and a prospect of misery and reaction for the whole world, leading inevitably to another war more bitter and deadly than this. It is only if we and our fellows in the United Nations turn our backs upon every major lesson of this past generation, and fall again into the paths of mutual suspicion and cut-throat-competition that we need look forward to so black a picture.

Finally, Morrison pointed out the risk the government ran of alienating popular opinion:

> The public is aware that the problem of deciding upon a scheme like the Beveridge Plan is not merely one of simple arithmetic. It is one of balancing risks and conjectures one against another. As we know, and as the people instinctively feels, finance is within very wide limits a handmaid of policy.
>
> The social benefits of the Beveridge Plan are very great. And to remove the plague spots of extreme poverty, undernourishment and its accompanying diseases, from the body politic is a measure that will react most favourably and in many different ways upon the economic health and soundness of our society ...
>
> I have not argued the matter on that line, though I have felt strongly inclined to do so. I have simply sought to show that this boon of social security which has good claims to be an absolute priority among all the aims of home policy, represents a financial burden which we should be able to bear, except on a number of very gloomy assumptions.

I can see no need to make or act upon such assumptions. I should certainly not like to have to expound and defend them to a nation bearing the full burden of total war.[28]

But Morrison lost this round of the argument. The committee accepted the Treasury estimates, declared that the first claim on resources must be defence, listed the other claims on the Exchequer including social services, and concluded that it was impossible to establish any sort of priority among them or to enter into definite commitments.[29]

No government could have afforded to take such a line of absolute negativism. Cherwell, who was deeply conscious of the popularity of the Beveridge proposals, suggested that the government explain to the people that they could have Beveridge at the price of everything else: 'If the Beveridge Report is adopted out of hand we must on our present information make it plain that other proposals such as higher wages, housing, agriculture, education etc. will have to be postponed.'[30] Cherwell spoke up for this tactic when the War Cabinet met, in the continued absence of Churchill, on 12 February. But a more evasive strategy emerged: to welcome as much as possible of the report in principle, while affirming that no commitments could be entered into. In case his colleagues began to wobble or weaken on this crucial point Churchill underlined it in a directive to the Cabinet on 14 February. The government should undertake to prepare the necessary legislation but only a renewed House of Commons could commit itself to the expenditure involved.[31] Churchill was to get his own way, and legislation (except on children's allowances) be deferred into the post-war period. But his doctrine upset Attlee. If, he wrote, the government was to be prevented from taking policy decisions for the post-war period, the result would be disaster:

I doubt whether in your inevitable and proper preoccupation with military problems you are fully cognisant of the extent to which decisions must be taken and implemented in the field of post war reconstruction *before* the end of the war. It is not that persons of particular political views are seeking to make vast changes. These changes have already taken place. The changes from peacetime to wartime industry, the concentration of industry, the alterations in trade relations with foreign countries and with the Empire, to mention only a few factors, necessitate great readjustments and new departures in the economic and industrial life of the nation.[32]

The Cabinet agreed to plan but not legislate. When Sir John Anderson rose on 16 February to state the government's case he had to adopt a paradoxical stance: 'It has been my duty to point out that there can be at present no binding commitment. Subject only to that, and what I have said about the views of the House, I have made it clear that the Government adopt the scheme in principle.'[33] They also accepted the introduction of a comprehensive state medical service and the institution of a system of children's allowances.

On the first day of the debate, Arthur Greenwood, the Leader of the Opposition since his dismissal from the War Cabinet in February 1942, introduced an anodyne motion, pre-arranged with the government side, welcoming the report in general terms and expressing the hope that it would be implemented. Sir Arnold Gridley, a backbench Conservative industrialist, 'seconded' Greenwood's motion, making it apparent that he would welcome the full implementation of the report at some date close to Doomsday. The chairman of the 1922 Committee of Conservative backbenchers, Alec Erskine-Hill, argued that each of the report's propositions should be considered on its merits: reforms could not necessarily be afforded, and the issue was 'essentially controversial'.

The majority of Conservative backbenchers thought that the government had gone far enough in yielding to the Beveridge clamour. However, a group of forty-five Conservative M.P.s of the newly-formed Tory Reform Committee, led by Quintin Hogg and Lord Hinchingbrooke, put down an amendment calling for the immediate setting up of a Ministry of Social Security. On the Labour benches the demand was for 'Beveridge now'. As rebellion grew, the Labour M.P. James Griffiths took the lead, and put down an even stronger amendment calling for prompt legislation. The government spokesman on the second day of the debate, Kingsley Wood, fanned the flames with an inept speech which emphasized once more the government's reservations and lack of commitment. After this, Labour backbenchers felt they had no option but to vote against the government. Nor could they be deterred by a fine speech on the last day from Herbert Morrison, who skilfully emphasized that the government had accepted the majority of Beveridge's principles, and would do its best to carry them through. In the division on 18 February, 121 votes were cast against the government: ninety-seven Labour, three I.L.P., one Communist, eleven Independent, and nine Liberal, including David Lloyd George, casting his last vote in the House in support of the welfare state which he had helped to found. Only two Labour backbenchers voted with the government.[34]

The Labour Party was faced with a serious rift between its ministers and its backbenchers. At a Parliamentary Party meeting before the division, Bevin lectured M.P.s on the shortcomings of the report. He expressed his dislike of the provisions for children's allowances and workmen's compensation, and said that he saw no reason for disturbing the private practices of doctors. Dalton noted in his diary: ' ... he then begins to shout, protest and threaten, which he is always too much apt to do, and which undoes it all. He says the Party amendment is a vote of censure on him, that they never gave him the chance of speaking before it was put down, that this is not the kind of treatment he has been accustomed to, that this is not the way they do things in the Unions, and that, if this is the way things are to be done, he will refuse to go on.'[35] Although the Parliamentary Party managed to patch up most of its differences, Bevin was as good as his word. From February 1943 to May 1944 Bevin ceased to attend party meetings, behaving as though he were in the War Cabinet as a representative not of the Labour Party, but of the trade unions.[36]

In the month of the Beveridge debate there were six by-elections in England and Scotland (with two other contests in Northern Ireland). Common Wealth fielded its first four candidates, and two left-wing Independent Labour candidates put up, all in Conservative-held seats. Here was a general election in miniature. Unlike the hybrid Independents of the spring of 1942, the new contenders were clearly socialist and/or Labour. At Midlothian North, where Tom Wintringham stood for Common Wealth, the local Labour parties were the backbone of his organization. At King's Lynn the Independent Labour candidate, Major Fred Wise, was the former Labour candidate sailing under a flag of convenience. Aneurin Bevan's wife, Jennie Lee, stood at Bristol Central as 'Independent Labour' and split the borough Labour party, the Crippsite faction springing into action on her behalf and suffering the penalty of expulsion. Even where the local Labour party held its peace, there was still the sense that politics were returning to the normal pattern of Tory versus Socialist. When the result was declared at Watford, the unsuccessful Common Wealth candidate, Raymond Blackburn, advised his supporters to go away and work for the Labour Party.

In the medley of by-election speeches the Beveridge Report loomed up as the principal issue. Four of the constituencies polled before the debate, one on its final day, and one after. The Common Wealth and Independent Labour candidates put the report in the shop window and called for 'Beveridge in full now'. The Conservatives expressed vague or qualified enthusiasm. Thus Jennie Lee began her campaign at Bristol by proclaiming: 'I stand for every word, every letter and comma in the Beveridge Report.' Lord Fermoy, the Conservative candidate at King's Lynn was quoted as saying that with regard to Beveridge, 'he supported the wider issues. It was difficult to say anything about it now because who could say what the value of the pound would be after the war?'[37]

The party leaders in the Coalition, in an effort to damp down enthusiasm for the Independents, had now evolved a standard letter which they addressed to the constituents in each contest, varying only by the name of the constituency involved. The voters in Central Bristol, for example, were exhorted as follows by Churchill, Ernest Brown (for the National Liberals), Attlee and Sinclair: 'The verdict recorded by a single constituency is flashed around the world as though it were the voice of Britain that had spoken, and Bristol will realize that it has the responsibility at this moment of indicating to the United Nations, and to neutral countries, that we are united among ourselves in our un-flinching determination to organize our total resources for victory.' This tactic had some success, judging by the number of working-class voters in Bristol who volunteered to a Mass-Observer: 'Yes, I voted for Churchill's candidate. If he chose her she must be good!'[38] But the electorate contained far more of the knowing type of voter, who realized full well that by voting for an Independent he was neither endangering the Government nor giving Hitler cause for congratula-tion. Hence, even with the patriotic factor working against candidates who rocked the boat, the Conservatives clearly did badly in the little general election of February 1943. At Ashford their vote was 10 per cent up on 1935, at Bristol Central down insignificantly by a fraction of a percent. In the other four seats it was down on average by 8 per cent.

Analysing the popular response to the debate on the Beveridge Report, Home Intelligence then and for weeks afterwards distinguished a 'disappointed majority' and an 'approving minority'. The speeches of Anderson and Morrison, committing the Government in principle to social security, a National Health Service and an employment policy, may be seen now as marking a decisive advance in social and economic policy. At the time, most people simply drew the conclusion that the Beveridge Report had been shelved. In its survey of the week of 16–23 February, Home Intelligence wrote of:

The disappointed majority: Though reports vary, the majority seems to include 'the working classes', Liberals, Labour and the Left, a proportion of the middle classes and, according to three reports, a number of the rank and file of the Conservative Party. The majority are said to be cynical, disappointed or angry because:.
(1) The Government is thought to be trying to kill or shelve the Report, and is thought to have 'whittled down the expected benefits and to have promised little or nothing' (Ten Regions).
(2) This is 'a forecast of what we may expect when the war is over.' The Government's attitude 'augurs ill for the future of social security,' and has 'crystallized people's worst fears of the post-war period' ... (Nine Regions).
(3) 'Vested interests have won again' and are 'at work to ensure that things will remain as they did after the last war' (Six Regions).[39]

In an effort to reassure the public that the government were pressing on with schemes of social improvement, Churchill himself broadcast on 21 March 1943. His speech was the first popular proclamation of the new consensus, and through it Churchill assumed once more the mantle of his youthful days as a Liberal reformer in Mr Asquith's government. Churchill began in his familiar wartime style, urging the public 'to concentrate even more zealously upon the war effort'. But, recognizing a duty to 'peer through the mists of the future', he envisaged the establishment of a new peace-keeping organization by the United Nations, and at home the preparation of a four-year plan 'to cover five or six large measures of a practical character'. When the war with Germany was over, the plan would be put to the country at a general election either by a coalition of the three parties, 'or by a National Government comprising the best men in all parties who are willing to serve'. On the subject of social insurance, Churchill avoided all reference to the Beveridge Report, but declared that he and his colleagues must be ranked 'as strong partisans of national compulsory insurance for all classes for all purposes from the cradle to the grave'. There must be no unemployed after the war, for 'we cannot have a band of drones in our midst, whether they come from the ancient aristocracy or the modern plutocracy or the ordinary type of pub-crawler.' To prevent unemployment, the state must work in partner-ship with private industry, and prepare measures 'which will enable the Government to exercise a balancing influence upon development which can be turned on or off as circumstances require'. He added: 'There is a broadening field for State ownership and enterprise, especially in relation to monopolies of all kinds.' Churchill also spoke of housing, education, and the expansion of the health services. 'There is no finer investment for any community', he declared, 'than putting milk into babies.'[40]

To most people in Britain, Churchill was the great war leader, difficult to associate with domestic issues. His broadcast aroused a mixed response and much bewilderment. Nor did it stem the popular tide of pessimism about post-war conditions, which Home Intelligence continued to monitor. When the Gallup poll resumed its inquiries into voting intentions in the summer of 1943, it estimated that Labour was ahead of the Conservatives by 7, and subsequently 11, per cent.[41]

IX Conservatism in Eclipse 1943–1945

'Crisis' is too strong a term to apply to the affairs of the Conservative Party in the 1940s. Although the 1945 defeat came as a great shock to Conservatives, the 'swing of the pendulum' had to be faced eventually, and very soon the pendulum was to swing back, giving the Conservatives another thirteen years of office from 1951. Even in 1945, when nearly twelve million voted Labour, nearly ten million voted Conservative. The most the Conservatives suffered from was a period of chronic indisposition, originating with the formation of the Coalition in May 1940, and ending with the revision of Conservative ideas by Woolton and Butler in the late 1940s.

When a party loses an election, its members frequently blame the leadership or the state of the party organization: only with difficulty do they blame the character of its ideas. But the root explanation of the eclipse of Conservatism in the war years was the obsolescence of its outlook. The rank-and-file of the party, notably the backbench M.P.s elected under very different circumstances in 1935, lost touch both with the progressive trend of government policy, and with the movement of popular opinion. It is a mistake to try to single out any particular individual as responsible for the malady of a party. Suppose that the party organization had been maintained in a higher gear of efficiency, or the Parliamentary Party led more effectively. Would the social and economic pessimism of the party have had a greater appeal? Perhaps the reverse would have happened, for what could be more deadly to a party than first-rate effectiveness in communicating unpopular attitudes? With the notable exception of the Tory Reform Committee, a minority group, most of the wartime demands for a revival of Conservatism came from the Right, and threatened to plunge the party into still greater irrelevance. The Conservatives were suffering from the consequences of taking power for granted. Only defeat could cure them.

As leader of the Conservative Party, Churchill failed to lead in any consistent direction. At times, as in his Four-Year Plan broadcast, he stood for a progressive Toryism sharing a great deal of common ground with Labour, and possibly allied with Labour in a post-war coalition. At other times. he was amenable to right-wing advocates of a militant party line, notably Lord Beaverbrook. Churchill regarded the party system as the essential base of his role in history as a world statesman, but he resented the claims it made on his time. As a young man, he had turned against the Conservatives in spite of his attachment to the memory of his father, Lord Randolph; he was lukewarm towards the Conservatives of the 1940s. Churchill realized that he must discover the best formula for the prolongation of his leadership after the war, but he was largely indifferent to the content of the formula, so long as it assured him the right to go on making history. Urging his party occasionally to the right, and occasionally to the left, he refused most of the time to lead them either way. Perhaps if he had led them firmly to the left, they might have done better in 1945; but then he would not have been Churchill.

The backbench Conservatives in the House of Commons very much resented the influence wielded by Labour in the Coalition, and the apparent indifference of Churchill to the matter. The first significant explosion occurred in the spring of 1942. Dalton, the President of the Board of Trade, commissioned an inquiry by Beveridge into the level of coal stocks. Beveridge recommended coal rationing, and Dalton announced that it was to be introduced. Here was egalitarian planning, inspired by the Left—or so it seemed to the Conservative backbench 1922 Committee, which mounted a successful public campaign to prevent the introduction of rationing.[1]

In October 1942 there was a particularly gloomy meeting of the 1922 Committee after which one M.P., Lord William Scott, wrote to the Chief Whip:

> Throughout the country the Conservative Party has become a cheap joke: the press and the B.B.C. treat us with the contempt that we have earned and deserve.
>
> You yourself are well aware of what the P.M. thinks of the Tory Rump: he may not say so himself, but R.C., B.B. [Randolph

Churchill, Brendan Bracken] and his other satellites are not so careful of their tongues.

You must agree with the fact that as an effective body of opinion either in the House or the Country, the Conservative Party have ceased to exist.[2]

The editor of the right-wing weekly, *Truth*, Collin Brooks, happened to lunch one day with both the outgoing chairman of the party, Douglas Hacking, and his successor Thomas Dugdale. Later he recorded: 'Both agreed that Winston is a difficult leader, and is not a Conservative at all, or even, perhaps, by normal standards a statesman – being a creature of 'Palace' favourites, of moods and whims and over-riding egotism under his charm and geniality. Dugdale is fearful of what Max Beaverbrook may do. Him he described as a man utterly and completely untrustworthy ... '[3]

Who would capture Churchill? This was a question which greatly exercised Conservative politicians. The 1922 Committee succeeded in revising its constitution during the winter of 1942–3 for the purpose of establishing closer links with Conservative ministers in the government. Churchill, however, remained an aloof and olympian figure. Douglas Hacking speculated on 'the chance of Winston's coming out strongly against the Planners in the spring'. On balance, however, Churchill came out in favour of planning in his broadcast of March 1943.[4]

The drive to reinvigorate Conservatism was mainly inspired by right-wing ideology. A considerable reaction was under way in the party against the wartime direction of industry, which it was feared might be continued in some form into the peace, and the general prejudice against the expansion of state power also coloured attitudes to the social services. Aims of Industry, a pressure-group committed to publicity on behalf of 'free enterprise', was founded in the autumn of 1942 with Collin Brooks as its secretary. A number of big industrialists, including Lord Leverhulme, and Lord Perry of Ford Motors, joined forces with a group of laissez-faire ideologues led by the publisher Ernest Benn to form the Society of Individualists. In April 1943 another anti-state pressure-group, the National League for Freedom, was set on foot with the aid of a number of Conservative M.P.s including Douglas Hacking, Patrick Hannon, Waldron Smithers, Leonard Lyle and A. M. Lyons. In its manifesto, the League declared that its aim was to 'fight the strong movement now on foot to continue unnecessary official control of trade, industry, business and private lives after the war.'[5]

The constraints on party warfare in the House of Commons were greatly eased by the profound change in the military fortunes of the allies at the end of 1942. There was no longer such an intense fear that controversy would disrupt the Coalition and harm the war effort. In the New Year, Bevin as Minister of Labour introduced a Catering Wages Bill to enforce, if necessary, minimum wages and conditions for employees in hotels, bars, restaurants and cafés. Two hundred Conservative M.P.s, led by Douglas Hacking as chairman of a specially formed Parliamentary Catering Trades Committee, signified their opposition. In a division on 9 February 1943, the bill was passed, but with 116 Conservative votes against.[6]

The controversy revealed a remarkable new split in the Conservative ranks. In January 1943 a number of Tory army officers, including Lord Hinchingbrooke, Peter Thorneycroft, Hugh Molson and Quintin Hogg, had demobilized themselves to return to political work. Hartmut Kopsch, in his thesis on wartime Conservative thought, describes how each of them 'on the basis of impressions gained from discussions with the troops, independently reached the conclusion that it was politically necessary for the Conservative Party to change its public image'.[7]

The 'Tory reformers' championed Bevin in the catering wages debate, and in the Beveridge Report they believed they had found a cause through which Conservatism could be revitalized. 'If you do not give the people social reform', said Quintin Hogg in the House of Commons, 'they are going to give you social revolution.' The key to economic recovery, he contended, was social progress. On 17 March 1943, thirty-six Conservative M.P.s formally constituted themselves as the Tory Reform Committee under the chairmanship of Lord Hinchingbrooke. They included, it is interesting to note, the much-maligned Lady Astor, and her son William Waldorf Astor.[8]

The Tory reformers were anxious to repudiate much of inter-war Conservatism, and identify the party wholeheartedly with wartime reforms. Lord Hinchingbrooke wrote:

True Conservative opinion is horrified at the damage done to this country since the last war by 'individualist' business-men, financiers, and speculators ranging freely in a laissez-faire economy and creeping unnoticed into the fold of Conservatism to insult the

Party with their vote at elections, to cast a slur over responsible Government through influence exerted on Parliament, and to injure the character of our people. It would wish nothing better than that these men should collect their baggage and depart.[9]

The activities of the Tory Reformers threw into relief the general condition of Conservatism. The Churchill government was elaborating a major programme of social and economic reform. In theory the Conservatives, as the majority shareholders in the Coalition, were to be identified with its policies. But, as the Beveridge affair disclosed, Conservative ministers were sometimes reluctant converts to the gospel of reconstruction. Conservatives outside the government looked upon much of the reconstruction programme as the work of the Left and the Planners. They accepted it reluctantly, from loyalty rather than conviction, and perhaps believed that it could be whittled down when the Conservatives escaped from the Coalition. Thus Conservatives both high and low were, to some degree, alienated from the principles to which they were formally committed. Even Harold Macmillan, as a junior minister in the Churchill government, held forth in private about the extravagance of the Beveridge Report, and 'the folly of trying for better conditions after this ruinous war' —an unexpected line from the author of *The Middle Way*.[10] The Tory Reform Committee were partly concerned with accelerating the government's reconstruction programme. But their main effort lay in trying to persuade the bulk of the party to adopt the doctrines of the Coalition as battle-cries of a reformed Conservatism. Generally speaking, the effort failed, at least up to the 1945 election. Indeed, Sir Spencer Summers and others founded in November 1943 a highly secret conclave of some thirty Tory M.P.s, the Progress Trust, with the primary aim of countering the influence of the Tory Reformers in the party.[11]

The general rule for post-war planning, successfully imposed by Kingsley Wood and the Treasury, was that no particular commitments should be entered into until it was possible to forecast the financial burden of post-war policy as a whole. In a Cabinet paper of 26 June 1943, Attlee, Bevin and Morrison protested against the delays caused by this rule: 'Without a firm decision by the War Cabinet on the subjects which must be dealt with as matters of urgency for the reconstruction period, our plans must remain uncertain and nothing can be brought to the point of legislative enactment.' They suggested that the only sensible course would be to make the best possible forecast of the post-war position, and on that basis take the necessary decisions on the Uthwatt Report, finance of the building programme, reorganization of transport, energy and power, health and colonial policy. Wood replied that for his part he was ready to let financial discussions proceed on the assumption that in the third year after the war (assumed to be 1948) the aggregate taxable national in-come would be £7,825 million.[12] More than three months later, after the death of Wood and his replacement at the Exchequer by Sir John Anderson, the argument was still going strong. Attlee said the time for preparing plans was coming to an end, and there must be decisions. Churchill introduced a new argument: the Labour Party conference had indicated that after the war Labour ministers would resign: 'There were obvious objections to formulating post-war policies and still more to giving effect to them in legislation, if there were no assurance of the continued co-operation of the Labour Ministers after the war.'

Bevin argued for compromise. He declared that he would accept a programme for agriculture worked out by the Ministry of Agriculture, if a proper place was also made for dealing with basic industries like coal, electricity and water supply. For his part, he said, he was trying to get the trade unions to agree to the continuation of certain controls over labour for a period after the war. He would do his best to get the T.U.C. to agree in the national interest, but other parties would also have to make sacrifices. He mentioned the trade union demand for the amendment of the Trade Disputes Act, which the Conservatives had passed after the General Strike in 1927. Churchill said this might be included in a concerted programme of measures which the government would carry through after the war.[13]

As these exchanges reveal, Churchill and Bevin at least were thinking of the possibility of carrying on in partnership after the war. At this stage, some of the Labour leaders were so convinced that Churchill would win the next election for the Conservatives that they found the idea of a post-war coalition positively alluring. When Churchill mooted the subject in his broadcast of March 1943, Dalton, Morrison and Bevin were all favourably disposed. Morrison devised an ingenious proposal: the three main parties would go to the country with an agreed minimum programme, and pledged to re-form the Coalition afterwards. But there would be normal party contests in the constituencies, with each party advocating a different emphasis to the programme. The party composition of the new House would determine whether the coalition shifted its policies to the right or to the left. Dalton communicated Morrison's scheme to Churchill through the latter's Parliamentary Private Secretary, Harvie Watt; and Bevin broached the subject with Lord Halifax.[14] Morrison told W. P. Crozier, the editor of the *Manchester Guardian*, in July 1943:

> ... the bulk of our fellows don't in the least understand the political position. They have the idea that the country is waiting to hand them the reins of Government on a platter and that eventually they will do the country the kindness of taking office. Some day they will wake up to realize that the position is quite different and that the Tories have got the whole political position nicely in their hands.[15]

Morrison must have taken encouragement from the fact that the Tory Reform Committee and *The Times* were also in favour of a post-war coalition. When the Labour Party National Executive met at the end of February 1944 to discuss the political situation with Morrison, the meeting agreed only that 'the question of any future Coalition Government, its nature and terms, should be left over for future discussion.' A conclusion that there should be a general election 'at the earliest possible moment' after the end of the war in Europe was later corrected and struck from the minutes.[16] In September 1944 Dalton was again talking to Churchill's Parliamentary Private Secretary, and urging that if either of the two main parties obtained a clear working majority at the election, then that party should form the government, but 'if we were very close together there would be a case for a new Coalition.' Harvie Watt, perhaps reflecting Churchill's view, said that it would be 'political damnation for either Party to run the Government alone in the post-war years.'[17] Not until October 1944 did the National Executive put out a statement saying that Labour would fight the next general election as an independent party. The questions of when the election should be, and of whether a coalition might be formed afterwards, were left open.

Such was the atmosphere in which most of the reconstruction programme was devised. Just as the rank and file of the Conservatives longed to be free of the ties with Labour, so the rank-and-file of the Labour Party looked forward to the day when they could march into battle against the Conservatives. But neither Churchill nor the Labour leaders shared these emotions. In September 1943 Churchill was obliged to reshuffle the government on the death of Kingsley Wood, to whom he had always looked as a barometer of Conservative Party

feeling. 'That is why I miss Kingsley Wood so much,' he told Barrington-Ward.[18] The Treasury was such a powerful department, even in
wartime, that Churchill might have been expected to appoint another
Conservative, and in fact he suggested to Oliver Lyttelton that he
should take the job. But the next day he rang Lyttelton and told him
that Sir John Anderson, that dour non-party ex-civil servant, would be
much distressed if he did not become Chancellor: 'Having started life
as a civil servant, it would crown his career to be head of the Treasury.'[19]
Attlee was given the most powerful post on the home front, that of
Lord President, while Beaverbrook, the Conservative who was still
anathema to the Conservatives, was reintroduced to office as Lord
Privy Seal. For a time, Churchill toyed with the idea of making
Beaverbrook Minister of Reconstruction, but after strong resistance
from Attlee and the other Labour ministers, he gave way.[20] In Novem-
ber Lord Woolton, who was still at that time a non-party businessman
brought in solely to organize the Ministry of Food, agreed to become
Minister of Reconstruction. He also took the chair of a new Cabinet
committee on reconstruction, whose members were Attlee, Bevin,
Morrison and Jowitt on the Labour side, Butler, Lyttelton, Cranborne,
H. F. Crookshank·from the Conservatives, and of course Anderson as
Chancellor of the Exchequer.

On the new Reconstruction Committee, the Labour members (in
spite of the personal quarrel between Bevin and Morrison) formed a
powerful combine. Butler was the only seasoned politician in home
affairs among the Conservatives. When Attlee wrote to Churchill in
November 1944 asking that a Labour peer, Lord Listowel, should
attend meetings, Churchill drafted a reply as follows:

> A solid mass of four Socialist politicians of the highest quality and
> authority, three of whom are in the War Cabinet, all working to-
> gether as a team, very much dominates this Committee ...
>
> I feel very much the domination of these Committees by the
> force and power of your representatives, when those members
> who come out of the Conservative quota are largely non-Party or
> have little political experience or Party views.[21]

Attlee has described how Churchill became increasingly suspicious of
the Labour ministers and the plans they were evolving: 'So whenever
he got wind that a report or a memorandum on something outside
his ken was coming up, he would get somebody to spy out the land so
that he could prepare an onslaught on our "machinations". Winston

used to describe this artlessly, as "getting a second, highly qualified and objective opinion on the issue". In fact what he wanted was a hatchet job.'[22] At first the task of hatchet-man was carried out by Cherwell, until Attlee persuaded Churchill to put him on the Reconstruction Committee, after which he began to share the views of the committee. Churchill then turned to Beaverbrook and Bracken, as can be seen from a letter of protest which Attlee addressed to Churchill, probably at the beginning of 1945:

> The conclusions agreed upon by a Committee on which have sat five or six members of the Cabinet and other experienced ministers are then submitted with great deference to the Lord Privy Seal [Beaverbrook] and the Minister of Information [Bracken], two ministers without Cabinet responsibility neither of whom has given any serious attention to the subject. When they state their views it is obvious that they do not know anything about it. Nevertheless an hour is consumed in listening to their opinions. Time and again important matters are delayed or passed in accordance with the decision of the Lord Privy Seal. The excuse is given that in him you have the mind of the Conservative Party. With some knowledge of opinion in the Conservative Party in the House as expressed to me on the retirement from and re-entry into the Government of Lord Beaverbrook I suggest that this view would be indignantly repudiated by the vast majority.

Churchill replied: 'You may be sure I shall always endeavour to profit by your counsels.'[23]

The one sphere of reconstruction in which the Conservatives can be said to have been, in some degree, the driving force, was education, and it is interesting to reflect why it was the exception. The Board of Education had got down to detailed planning well before the publication of the Beveridge Report, and R. A. Butler had skilfully defused the politically controversial aspects. The White Paper on education, published in July 1943, provided a diversion from the Beveridge Report, which Conservatives felt had received too much attention. Moreover, Hartmut Kopsch writes:

> Conservative M.P.s did not perfunctorily acquiesce in Butler's proposals for educational reform; they applauded the White Paper on Educational Reconstruction and the Education Bill, since those measures incorporated many key Conservative beliefs,

notably the belief in the relevance of traditional religious values,
the belief in variety and quality rather than 'gross volume', the
belief in the desirability of preserving educational privileges and
the belief in hierarchy.[24]

Butler very typically commissioned the Ministry of Information to
find out how keen the public were on educational reform during rather
than after the war, and how it ranked in their minds compared with
other problems. The ministry reported that public interest and approval
centred on the White Paper's proposals to raise the school-leaving age
to sixteen, and to abolish fees in the state sector. The majority appeared
to favour the working out of plans now, but employment, housing
and health had the priority.[25] Public opinion was not, in the event, the
decisive factor. One important consideration was economy: Butler
was able to reassure the two Chancellors with whom he dealt, Kingsley
Wood and Anderson, that it would be a generation before the Exchequer had to bear the full cost of the proposals.[26] There was also a
direct party motive in promoting education: the eclipse of Beveridge
by a Tory project. When Butler met Kingsley Wood in June 1943 to
discuss the progress of educational reform, he recorded that Wood was
'definitely desirous of helping me, that Sir William Beveridge was
receding rather than coming forward in the minds of the Treasury ... '
There was also a meeting of Anderson, Wood and Churchill, 'they
having decided that educational reform was the lesser evil than the
Beveridge scheme ... ' When the bill was published in December 1943
it was welcomed by the Chief Whip, James Stuart, as a means of
keeping M.P.s occupied without provoking party strife.[27]

The debate on the second reading, in March 1944, proved more
eventful than was expected. There was discontent on the Labour backbenches, and the Tory Reform Committee led by Quintin Hogg
decided to challenge the government. A member of the Committee,
Thelma Cazalet Keir, moved two amendments, the first calling
for a promise to raise the school-leaving age to sixteen by 1951 (the
Bill set no definite date), the second demanding equal pay for women
teachers. On each occasion a number of Conservatives, mostly Tory
reformers, voted against the government: twenty-five over the school-
leaving age, thirty-seven over equal pay. Over the equal pay issue, the
Labour and Tory rebels together defeated the government by 117
votes to 116—the only significant point on which the Coalition was
beaten in a division. The next day Churchill went to the House and

demanded a reversal of the vote. The government secured a big majority, and in August 1944 the Education Bill became law.[28] After all the apprehension expressed in 1940, the fee-paying public schools were untouched by the Act. The Fleming Report of July 1944, the work of a Scottish judge commissioned by Butler to consider the future of the public schools, recommended that in return for local authority subsidies, they should make a quarter of their places available to scholarship pupils from the state sector. By failing to find a solution which satisfied anybody, Fleming had none the less performed the valuable task, from Butler's point of view, of throwing up a smoke-screen of confusion which protected the public schools from Labour attack.[29]

Outside the realm of education, it was Beveridge who gave the decisive impetus to reconstruction plans in most areas of policy. The National Health Service, although rightly regarded as a great legislative memorial to Aneurin Bevan, the post-war Labour Minister of Health, first became a definite prospect with the acceptance by the government in February 1943 of the main principle as embodied in the Beveridge Report. For two and a half years before Bevan took office, the planning of a National Health Service had been in progress under the Labour Secretary of State for Scotland, Tom Johnston, who was responsible for the Scottish health services, and two Ministers of Health, Ernest Brown, a National Liberal, and the Conservative Henry Willink, who succeeded him in November 1943. Nor was Bevan alone in encountering the opposition of the medical profession: this was very evident, although less shrill, in the last two years of the war.

Early in 1943 the Reconstruction Priorities Committee, set up to pursue Beveridge's many proposals, invited Tom Johnston and Ernest Brown to submit their ideas about a National Health Service. Under the Labour government, Bevan was to take the bold stroke of nationalizing the private voluntary hospitals, but this was never on the agenda under the Coalition. However, the Coalition ministers did make two assumptions which were highly controversial among doctors. They assumed that, at least in the towns, most doctors would no longer work in individual private practice, but would be grouped together in health centres, and paid a salary in place of the traditional fee per individual patient, the capitation fee. They also assumed that both the hospitals and the general practitioners would be run by local government authorities, which for this purpose would be grouped together into larger units. On the issue of payment by salary rather than fee, the two ministers were especially adamant: ' ... it is notorious that a doctor who is most successful in securing patients is not necessarily more competent than his colleagues ... The general principle applicable to public service, civil and military, that exceptional competence or zeal should expect to find its reward in the shape of promotion in the service must, in our view, apply to the present case.'[30] Of course the principle of the health centre was linked to the salary issue: if doctors were in group practice at a centre, it made no sense for them to compete against one another for patients; and as the health centre could only be equipped from public funds it was logical to regard the doctors who worked there as salaried employees of the state, like teachers.

All parties were committed to the goal of a service available to all, and the critical question from a party point of view was the method of achievement. In the Labour Party, much thought had been given to the problem since 1931 by the Socialist Medical Association, a group of Labour doctors who used to meet regularly at the home of Dr Somerville Hastings, an ear, nose and throat surgeon attached to the Middlesex Hospital. Somerville Hastings was the chairman of the Labour Party's wartime reconstruction committee on the health services, whose report, *National Service for Health*, appeared in April 1943.[31] Generally, Labour policy was clear. Doctors were to be salaried employees of the state practising, so far as possible, through health centres. Both the general practitioner service and the hospital service would be run by regional local government authorites, which would have to be created in a sweeping reform of local government. Private practice outside the state scheme was not to be prevented, and the Labour document was unclear about the future of the voluntary hospitals.[32]

The Coalition Health Ministers, judging opinion in the medical profession by the remarkably advanced report of the Medical Planning Commission in 1942, began by trying to impose essentially Labour principles. They discovered, however, that the profession was either divided or definitely hostile. Indeed, the B.M.A. shifted its ground and began to oppose ideas which at first it had advocated. At the annual representative meeting of the B.MA. in September 1943, a new statement of principles was adopted which reverted to the plan of extending health insurance, and rejected any idea of control by local authorities, as then constituted.[33] In November 1943 the task of preparing a White Paper which the profession might be persuaded to accept fell to the new Minister of Health, Henry Willink.

A draft of the White Paper went to one of the first meetings of the Reconstruction Committee in January 1944, and it is interesting to discover what a prominent part the Labour ministers took in the discussion. Attlee regretted that the scheme would permit doctors in state practice to have private patients, because this would lead them into maintaining their private practice at the expense of their public patients. Bevin thought the draft White Paper 'did not sufficiently emphasize the need for a vigorous development of health centres, served by a salaried medical staff'. Morrison thought it should be made clear in the White Paper that the government intended to develop these centres to the fullest practicable extent. Similarly, although it would be impossible to put all public practice on a salaried basis immediately, this should be the declared objective of the government in the long run. The Chancellor of the Exchequer, Sir John Anderson, supported Bevin and Morrison; Cranborne and Butler, for the Conservatives, warned that if the salaried service expanded too far, 'there was a great risk that the standard of the profession would be lowered'.[34] Bevin and Morrison were in a particularly savage state of mutual animosity at this time, owing to Morrison's decision as Home Secretary to release from internment Sir Oswald Mosley, the fascist leader. But between them they were successful in ensuring a prominent place in the White Paper for the future of the health centre.

The War Cabinet approved the White Paper on 9 February; but at once there was a revealing storm in a teacup when Beaverbrook and Bracken attacked the proposals, and persuaded Churchill to order a reappraisal of them at a second Cabinet meeting. Beaverbrook was a strong opponent of maintaining the Coalition after the war. He wanted the Conservatives to pursue a right-wing policy of free enterprise in a militant fashion. 'The Tory Party', he had written, 'has need, not of a Maginot Line, but of a Second Front,' and having rejoined the government as Lord Privy Seal in September 1943, he was increasingly influential on Churchill. Quintin Hogg, as a prominent member of the Tory Reform Committee, viewed the return of Beaverbrook with alarm. On hearing the rumour that Beaverbrook was urging Bracken to resign in protest against the White Paper, he at once called at Printing House Square, the headquarters of progressive Conservatism, to warn the editor of *The Times* what was afoot. At first Barrington-Ward found it hard to believe, but Willink himself confirmed the truth of the story, adding that he himself might have to resign.

Barrington-Ward also found Churchill in a particularly pugnacious mood, tired of all the talk of post-war plans, and strongly opposed to the continuation of the Coalition after the war.[35] However, the 'crisis' passed, and the reconvened Cabinet approved the White Paper for publication.

The details of the White Paper no longer have much interest, but they remained politically significant because of the growing opposition of the B.M.A. In the summer of 1944 the Gallup poll announced the results of a survey based on answers to a questionnaire received from more than 25,000 doctors. The majority declared that they were in general unfavourable to the White Paper, believing that it made medicine less attractive as a profession, and would result in a deterioration of the quality of the health services. The General Council of the B.M.A., dominated by the affluent upper crust of the profession, even came out in opposition to the principle that the service should be available to all, the fundamental principle of the White Paper.[36] Between February 1944 and the end of the Coalition in May 1945, Willink was engaged in modifying his proposals with the aim of appeasing the doctors, and enlisting their co-operation.

On 4 June 1944, two days before the D-Day landings, Churchill invited Bevin to accompany him to Portsmouth to say farewell to some of the troops as they embarked. 'They were going off to face this terrific battle', Bevin recounted, 'with great hearts and great courage. The one question they put to me when I went through their ranks was: "Ernie, when we have done this job for you are we going back on the dole?" ... Both the Prime Minister and I answered: "No, you are not."'[37] Apart from housing, the employment issue was the one that mattered most to ordinary people.

Since 1940 there had been much talk of full employment policies, but so long as the War Cabinet were preoccupied with the war effort, inspiration could not be translated into decision. The Beveridge Report, with its 'Assumption C' of a policy for the maintenance of employment, at once made the subject a priority. Moreover, Beveridge, having tasted as he thought the hors-d'œuvre of supreme power, was anxious to press on to the main course of the feast. He lent his name to a Social Security League set up to champion his report, and in March 1943 announced the establishment of his own personal inquiry into the maintenance of employment. Funds were provided by David Astor of the *Observer*, Edward Hulton, the proprietor of *Picture Post*, and Sir Kenneth Lee, Director-General of Raw Materials at the Ministry of

Supply. To assist him, Beveridge recruited a team of young economists: Joan Robinson, Barbara Wootton, Nicholas Kaldor, E. F. Schumacher, and Frank Pakenham. He entered into detailed discussions with the T.U.C. Seldom had the chairman of a government inquiry, having presented his report, behaved so much like a prime minister who was about to accept his own recommendations. When, however, Beveridge began to seek the advice of civil servants, he found that he had definitely overstepped the proper limits. Late in October 1943, when the editor of the *Manchester Guardian* asked Churchill whether Beveridge's new inquiry would be included in the government's postwar plans, Churchill replied: 'Beveridge! He puts his nose into too many things!' The following month it was officially announced that Beveridge had been banned from talking to civil servants on the subject of employment policy.[38]

Beveridge's initiative spurred the government not only to reflect upon employment policy, but to publish its conclusions. 'It seems most desirable', wrote Churchill's adviser Lord Cherwell on 20 October 1943, 'that the government should make proposals about this [employment policy] at an early date, in any event before Sir William Beveridge brings out his plan which will no doubt be boosted in the press like his social insurance scheme.'[39]

The evolution of the Coalition's employment policy took place in three stages. Immediately after the publication of the Beveridge Report, the temporary civil servants in the Economic Section of the War Cabinet set to work on a full analysis of Keynesian techniques of maintaining demand. In July, the Reconstruction Priorities Committee remitted this paper to a committee of officials chaired by the head of the Treasury, Sir Richard Hopkins, and invited them to frame a report. Finally this report was sent up to the politicians of the War Cabinet Reconstruction Committee in January 1944, and debated in two lengthy meetings.

The discussions took the form of an argument between divergent schools of thought, the result being a masterpiece of compromise. The Economic Section of the War Cabinet consisted of academics who had been drawn into government service by the war. They still preserved a fresh and unorthodox approach, and, led by Lionel Robbins, strongly pressed the Keynesian case for tackling unemployment by financial and fiscal devices designed to 'prime the pump' of aggregate demand. They argued for the conscious use of deficit budgeting in a period of depression. At the political stage of the debate, the Keynesian view was warmly supported by the Labour leaders on the Reconstruction Committee. But the Treasury officials, led by Sir Wilfrid Eady, were still sceptical of Keynesianism. They were inclined to blame structural problems in British industry for the unemployment of the 1930s, and place the emphasis upon the need to restore Britain's export markets. They disliked the principle of the budget deficit, and regarded the apparatus of demand management as something to be kept in reserve for use in abnormal times. The economist Hubert Henderson, who was attached to the Treasury, wrote a severe denunciation of the Keynesian approach in the course of which he commented: 'In my opinion, these doctrines are unhistorical, unimaginative, and unscientific ... '[40] The Treasury view found its advocates chiefly among Conservatives, including members of the Reconstruction Committee.

The radicalism of yesterday is often the conservatism of today, and Keynesianism may seem a reasonably uncontroversial doctrine, easily absorbed by the wartime Establishment—all the more so, since Keynes himself was at the Treasury. The minutes of the official committee on employment policy show otherwise. By October 1943, the members of the Economic Section were so frustrated by Treasury resistance to their ideas that they drew up a reply which read, in part:

> In various papers put forward to the Steering Committee the Treasury has rejected almost all the proposals advanced by the Economic Section in P.R.(43)36 with a view to stabilizing demand at a high level. The rate of interest, they say, cannot be allowed to rise in the immediate post-war period, and it may well be some time before rates can be permitted to vary according to the state of trade. Nor can fiscal incentives be given—or, at least, not through the Income Tax—to encourage capital development at particular times. It would seem to follow that little can be done to control the fluctuations of private investment. Elsewhere, they maintain that it is impracticable to vary public investment, and that the best that can be hoped for in this field is to stabilize it. As for consumption, variations in social security contributions are also regarded as impracticable because they would endanger the finance of the Social Security Fund; while political considerations prevent the manipulation of rates of taxation according to the state of trade ... If this view were to prevail the role of the state in respect of cyclical unemployment would be essentially passive. The state would refrain from aggravating the depression by mistimed

campaigns for economy, but could take no positive steps to relieve it. This conclusion seems to us unduly pessimistic.[41]

Gradually a compromise formula was developed, and after more argument in the Reconstruction Committee, the draft White Paper on Employment Policy reached the War Cabinet on 19 May 1944.

Churchill had been so absorbed in the final preparations for the Normandy landings that he had been unable to read the draft White Paper, or the memorandum which Cherwell had prepared to guide him. But he had read Cherwell's first sentence, he informed the War Cabinet, and this commended the White Paper as bold, able, and worthy of full support. He gathered that what was proposed for public authorities was the reverse of what private citizens would do: when things looked bad, they would launch into all sorts of new expenditure. 'I suppose', he continued, 'that, at such times, it would be helpful to have a series of Cabinet banquets, a sort of Salute the Stomach Week.' The White Paper was finally approved, subject to the inclusion of a sentence to meet Beaverbrook's view that more should be said on the need to stimulate private investment when a recession was in the offing.[42]

The White Paper examined both the short- and the long-term prospects for employment. For the first few years after the war there would be a shortage of manpower. The main source of unemployment would be the switch from wartime to peacetime production, and during this stage it would be vital to retain certain of the wartime physical controls over the economy. In the long run the maintenance of demand would be ensured by the encouragement of exports, action to influence the level of private investment, the careful timing of public investment, including public works, and the regulation of consumption by variations in the level of social insurance contributions, the ingenious idea of James Meade. The economist John Jewkes, a strong opponent of economic planning, pointed out in 1948 how little planning the White Paper envisaged:

> The essence of the programme ... was that of allowing the market economy to run without hindrance or interference unless private and normal Government expenditure seemed to be inadequate ... There is nothing here of programmes for individual firms or industries, nothing of the establishment of social priorities which would bind the consumer or producer, nothing, in fact, of what is normally understood as comprehensive planning by the modern socialist.[43]

The White Paper specifically ruled out the deliberate use of a budgetary deficit to stimulate demand in a period of recession. From the Keynesian, as well as from the socialist point of view, it was a feeble document, and Keynes's reaction was inevitably mixed: 'He recognizes a praiseworthy groping towards the light, but deplores the undue timidity attributable to muddled thinking and the tenacity of error.'[44] More important, from the political point of view, than the techniques proposed for employment policy, was the opening pledge of the White Paper: 'The Government accept as one of their primary aims and responsibilities the maintenance of a high and stable level of employment after the war.'

The White Paper was commended to the House of Commons by Bevin himself. The Conservative spokesman on industry, Henry Brooke, declared: 'My aim is that no man, except through his own fault, should ever have to be many days without the prospect of a job.'[54] For the Tory Reform Committee, Hugh Molson gave the White Paper a glowing welcome. More surprisingly, the right-wing industrialist Sir Arnold Gridley declared that it was the best of all the White Papers, and would have widespread support in industry. But without imposing too neat a verdict, it can be argued that the consensus on employment policy was far more an affair of the front benches than of the backbenches. In the Labour Party, Dalton had recently pushed through the National Executive a paper committing the party to a largely Keynesian policy. But most of the Labour backbenchers who spoke in the debate on employment policy contended that unemployment was inseparable from capitalism. Aneurin Bevan regarded the White Paper as a sham designed to discredit socialism, for, he argued, 'If a progressive society and an expanding standard of life can be achieved by this document and unemployment can be avoided, then there is no justification for public ownership and there is no argument for it. Nobody believes in public ownership for its own sake.'[46]

Several Conservatives also made it plain that in their view there was no cure for unemployment except a revival of trade. In January 1945 the editor of *The Times*, talking to the new chairman of the Conservative party, Ralph Assheton, found him 'scathing about the White Paper on employment, which he thinks no better than a series of empty shams. Fears the public has been promised more than can possibly be performed.'[47]

*

Churchill complained, in a world broadcast of March 1944, that the Coalition was receiving very few bouquets for the bold progress it was making in social and economic affairs. Turning his attention to the housing problem, he announced that as an emergency measure, half a million prefabricated steel houses, devised at the Ministry of Works under Wyndham Portal, would be produced immediately after the war, and two to three hundred thousand permanent houses within two years of the defeat of Germany.[48] (Later it was discovered that because of the shortage of steel the 'prefabs' would have to be made of alternative materials, and the target was scaled down.) By comparison with, say, the actions of the National government in the aftermath of the 1931 crisis, the Coalition was a truly dynamic force: the National Health Service White Paper of February was followed by the Employment Policy proposals in May, the passing of the Butler Education Act in August, and in September the publication at last of the government's own proposals for social insurance, which largely embodied those of the Beveridge Report.

Popular opinion was apparently unimpressed. The White Paper on Employment Policy, which *The Economist* welcomed as revolutionary, brought hardly a ripple of reaction, and the health proposals were the subject of very little comment. Not even the government's acceptance of the Beveridge social insurance scheme, which evoked widespread approval, could dispel the pessimistic expectations which many people had formed of the peace. Home Intelligence, in one of its last reports before it was wound up as superfluous to the war effort, commented on the subject of the social insurance White Paper:

> Once again many people, especially workers, while approving the plan, are sceptical as to its ever becoming law in anything like its present shape; a smaller number think that even if it is implemented, this will not be for many years. Most people base their fears on a belief that 'big vested interests', especially insurance companies, will see that the proposals are whittled away; others say 'there will be a catch' – 'they'll give us a family allowance for children and then take it away again by reducing the income tax allowance for children.' (Nine Regions)[49]

In fact one of the last achievements of the Coalition government was the Family Allowances Act of 1945, which gave every family an allowance of five shillings a week, without a means test, for the second and each subsequent child under school-leaving age.

According to Home Intelligence, the greatest anxieties related to housing and jobs. The housing shortage was obvious in every bombed city, but the 'prefabs' promised by Churchill were unpopular because of their appearance, their price, and the fear that they would remain permanent homes. 'Gloom and despair are widespread,' Home Intelligence commented, as though beginning to extract some masochistic satisfaction from affairs. The imminence of demobilization from the services, and the contraction of the munitions industry, raised the spectre of unemployment:

> Widespread apprehension is reported: people dread and expect mass unemployment, of which present unemployment and rumours of impending discharges are regarded as a foretaste. Particular anxiety is expressed by, or on behalf of, people in war industries (Twelve Regions) who see their jobs coming to an end; demobilized men (Seven Regions); miners, Bevin Boys, Civil Defence workers, land girls, seamen ...[50]

Mass-Observation's study of attitudes towards demobilization, *The Journey Home*, confirms the picture of anxiety. Most people remembered the aftermath of World War I, and expected the same heavy unemployment to recur; many recalled Lloyd George's celebrated election pledge of November 1918 to build 'a fit country for heroes to live in', and the disillusion which followed. One man in ten, and one woman in five, expected that he or she would have difficulty in finding a job.[51] The demand for jobs, homes, and social security was the very reverse of revolutionary, but it was none the less radical: for these modest needs had never been satisfactorily met by the system of parliamentary capitalism. The Labour Party reaped the benefit.

The general election forecasts made by B.I.P.O. from 1943 up to the break up of the Coalition were unequivocal:

	% Voting Intention		
	Con	Lab	Lib
1943 June	31	38	9
July	27	39	9
December	27	40	10
1944 February	23	37	10
1945 February	24	42	11
April	24	40	12

Churchill was unaware of these figures until at least 1946, when his doctor Lord Moran told him of them.[52] The Gallup polls were either ignored or dismissed as unreliable. Political commentators could not believe that a small sample could indicate the preference of millions or that voting behaviour had a strong uniform pattern despite differences of region, candidate, safety of seat and so forth.

Between 1943 and 1945 four Conservatives loyal to the government were defeated at by-elections by Common Wealth or Independent Socialist candidates, and there was a general tendency for the Conservative share of the vote to fall. Examining contests where Labour had come second in 1935, and the wartime interloper was definitely on the left, we can compare the percentage won by Labour in 1935 with the percentage won by the 'Labour substitute' in 1943–5, and by Labour in 1945:

Swings to Labour substitutes 1943 to 1945, and to Labour at the general election of 1945:

		By-Election	Candidate	Swing at By-Election	Swing at General Election
11 Feb	43	Midlothian and North Peebles	Common Wealth	+11·0	+11·8
12 Feb	43	King's Lynn	Ind. Labour	+ 3·6	+12·2
16 Feb	43	Portsmouth North	Common Wealth	+ 6·9	+18·4
18 Feb	43	Bristol Central	Ind. Labour	− 4·5	+16·5
23 Feb	43	Watford	Common Wealth	+11·5	+17·0
20 Apr	43	Daventry	Common Wealth	+ 7·5	+12·0
9 June	43	Birmingham Aston	Common Wealth	− 6·7	+30·7
15 Oct	43	Peterborough	Ind. Labour	+ 4·2	+ 5·9
7 Jan	44	Skipton	Common Wealth	+ 6·7	+ 3·6
17 Feb	44	West Derbyshire*	Ind. Labour	+16·2	+ 8·3
8 July	44	Manchester, Rusholme	Common Wealth	+11·0	+16·6
20 Sep	44	Bilston	I.L.P.	+ 0·3	+19·2
26 Apr	45	Chelmsford	Common Wealth	+28·3	+22·6
17 May	45	Newport	I.L.P.	+ 4·6	+12·0

* Comparing the 1945 result with the 1938 by-election, there being no contest in 1935.

Until Chelmsford, all by-elections were fought on the out-of-date register of March 1939. If we assume that the younger voters were more likely to be anti-Tory, then the Conservative wartime candidates were still more unpopular than the by-election results indicate. Of the four seats which Conservative candidates lost, Eddisbury, won by Warrant-Officer John Loverseed for Common Wealth in April 1943, and Derbyshire West, won by the Independent Labour candidate Charles White (not an I.L.P. candidate, but a member of the Labour Party standing as an Independent), had been so safe in 1935 that neither had been contested by Labour. Chelmsford, won for Common Wealth by Wing-Commander Ernest Millington, had been won by the Conservatives in 1935 with more than 70 per cent of the vote.

Could there have been a clearer warning of what was to come than the result at Derbyshire West? The seat and its neighbourhood had been virtually a family heirloom of the Cavendishes since 1572. Following the drawing of the Derbyshire West boundaries in 1885, the seat had passed from the family's hands only twice, when the Liberal candidate C. F. White won it in 1918 and 1922. The sitting member in the New Year of 1944 was the Duke of Devonshire's brother-in-law, Lieutenant-Colonel Henry Hunloke. On 24 January the Duke told the local party association that Hunloke had decided to retire. The Duke's heir, Lord Hartington, was by no mere chance on leave at that moment, and indeed was waiting outside the door. He was at once adopted as the candidate, and two days later another brother-in-law of the Duke, the Government Chief Whip James Stuart, arranged in the House for the moving of the writ. This cosy little arrangement was disturbed by the decision of C. F. White's son, who had contested the by-election of 1938, to stand again as Independent Labour. Common Wealth sent in a team of half a dozen organizers to help him, while Reakes, Horabin, Clement Davies and even Kendall came down to speak on his behalf. The local Liberal association broke the truce by advising Liberals to vote according to their judgment. Gilbert and Sullivan could hardly have improved on the story of the campaign, which has been recorded in glorious detail by Angus Calder.[53] Charlie White romped home to victory. The Marquess of Hartington went off to serve his country — and was later killed.

But the result was lost on the pundits. 'No Tory agent need yet be seriously alarmed,' said the *Observer*. 'It is certainly true', added *The Economist*, 'that there are no signs of any enthusiasm for Labour.' In the autumn 'Chips' Channon was delighted to hear from Barrington-Ward, the editor of *The Times*, that there was no serious swing to the left. 'So much for the foolish prophecy of that very nice ass Harold Macmillan who goes about saying that the Conservatives will be lucky to retain a hundred seats at the election.'[54] At Conservative Central Office the Derbyshire West result was statistically refuted by averaging out the pro- and anti-government votes at by-elections since the outbreak of war. The average government vote in sixty-four contests was 12,361, the average anti-government vote 4,116.[55] While Attlee, as Labour leader, felt there was a leftward swing going on in the country, his own interpretation of the by-election results just after Derbyshire West emphasized:

(1) The inevitable accumulation of individual irritations against particular actions of the Government which find a natural ventilation at the polls.

(2) The fact that an adverse vote will not effect a change in the Government, thus adding a sense of security to the gratification of an impulse.

(3) The attraction to people, who have to submit to many Government regulations, of being able to act contrary to the wish of the Government with impunity. The more the Government expresses its support of a particular candidate, the greater the attraction.

(4) The fact that a vote for a splinter candidate does not carry with it support for an alternative Government which, if in being, might well be less attractive than the present one. The insignificance of Acland is thus a positive advantage.

(5) The reluctance of regular supporters of particular parties to vote for their natural enemies.

(6) In many instances the poor quality of the official candidates.[56]

This was tantamount to explaining the results away as the product of freak circumstances.

The major blind spot in most calculations was the assumption that Churchill would inevitably take the country by storm as Lloyd George had in 1918, as 'the man who won the war'. In the files of Mass-Observation were inquiries which indicated that as the church bells rang out to celebrate victory at Alamein, a majority of people already thought it would be a bad thing for Churchill to be post-war Prime Minister: by February 1944, 62 per cent were said to be against. 'Supremely popular as he is today', wrote Tom Harrisson in 1944, 'this is closely connected with the idea of Winston the war leader, Bulldog of Battle, etc. Ordinary people widely assume that after the war he'll rest on his magnificent laurels. If he doesn't, many say they will withdraw support, believing him no man of peace, domestic policy, or human detail.'[57]

Another sharp observer was Common Wealth's election agent at Skipton and Derbyshire West, Kay Allsop:

In West Derbyshire speakers in support of White would make reference to Churchill's war record and debt owed him by the people of this country. Great and enthusiastic applause always greeted this. Then they would go on to say that despite his services to the nation no man, Churchill nor any other, had the right to dictate to the people of this country how they should vote. Invariably this brought even louder applause.[58]

Why did the Coalition government break up? The records of the War Cabinet show that Labour and Conservative ministers gradually exhausted the subjects on which they could agree, and were left with those on which they differed. But it is difficult to tell, especially with Attlee and the Labour leaders, whether they differed in their heart of hearts or only because they were compelled to do so by the revival of party feeling on the backbenches and at the grassroots.

'The question of the ownership of land', writes Michael Foot, 'was the real rock on which the Coalition was broken.'[59] In June 1943 the Labour Party's annual conference had reaffirmed the party's traditional policy of the nationalization of land. In September, however, the party's policy committee, under the chairmanship of Dalton, decided that for the time being it was better to plump for what could be had — namely the proposals of the Uthwatt Committee — on the grounds that outright nationalization would cause political controversy. Thus the main principles of the Uthwatt Report were adopted, lock, stock and barrel, as Labour policy.[60] However, Conservative opposition to the Uthwatt proposals, especially from landed pressure-groups, had always been intense. So it was not surprising that a Conservative Party reconstruction committee, including the Duke of Devonshire, who spoke of 'this fellow Youthat', concluded that the Uthwatt Report was unacceptable.[61]

Although the main principles of town and country planning were agreed between the two main parties, nothing could be settled by the local authorities until there was a solution to the problem of compensation and betterment. As an interim measure, a town and country planning Bill was introduced in June 1944 to empower local authorities to deal with blitzed or slum areas urgently in need of development. An accompanying White Paper on the control of land use suggested an 80 per cent levy on the profit from development — but this was allowed to gather dust, and the shape of town and country planning legislation was left to be decided by the next government. When Labour came to power, the Uthwatt proposals were to form the basis of Lewis Silkin's 1947 Town and Country Planning Act.

The Coalition partners were able to work together on the finance of post-war industry, and to some degree over its control, but the sticking-point was always reached when the question of nationalization was raised. In the autumn of 1944 the Governor of the Bank of England put forward proposals for the formation of two separate companies, one to provide long-term finance for small businesses, and the other finance for larger businesses and industrial reorganization. The Labour ministers agreed, and the government set up the Industrial and Commercial Finance Corporation, and the Finance Corporation for Industry.[62]

There was a new measure of agreement between the parties during the war over the coal industry. The Conservatives were under no circumstances prepared to nationalize it. Indeed, in October 1943, when Gwilym Lloyd George, the Minister of Fuel and Power, himself recommended that the state should requisition the pits for the duration of the war, Churchill imposed a veto. Defending himself against the clamour of Labour backbenchers for nationalization, he defined the principle of the Coalition in a striking phrase: 'Everything for the war, whether controversial or not, and nothing controversial that is not *bona fide* needed for the war.'[63] When, however, the question was the technique of control in the mines, there was broad agreement. The mines were notoriously organized into a multitude of small and inefficient companies under unimaginative owners. The industry had already been reorganized in the summer of 1942, following a coal shortage. The state had taken over the management of the pits and established a National Coal Board responsible for regional and district production targets, new plant and equipment, overall efficiency, and industrial relations. Later on, Lloyd George appointed a committee of mining engineers under Sir Charles Reid to make recommendations about the best technical structure for the industry. The Reid Committee naturally advocated centralized management, leaving open the question of ownership. In vain did the mine owners appoint their own committee under Robert Foot, a former Director-General of the B.B.C., to champion self-government by the owners. The government, and with it the Conservative Party, committed itself to the continuation of state authority in management, with reserve powers to carry through the compulsory amalgamation of pits. The Tory Reform Committee went a step further in seeking a 'miners' charter' with a guaranteed minimum

wage and various other improvements in conditions. The Labour Party, of course, believed that the structural changes advocated by Reid could best be implemented through nationalization.[64]

On 7 October 1944 the Labour Party N.E.C. issued a statement proclaiming that Labour would fight the next election as an independent party. Without setting a date for withdrawal from the Coalition, the statement placed the decision in the hands of a party conference and declared: 'Despite malicious whisperings to the contrary, no responsible leader of Labour has ever toyed with the idea of "a coupon Election".'[65] Any doubt on the score seemed to dissolve with the events in Greece at the end of the year. In October, the Germans had withdrawn from Greece. Churchill sent in the British army to fill the vacuum and prevent a take-over by the Communist-dominated resistance movement E.A.M. Early in December tensions between E.A.M. and the British-backed government of Papandreou escalated into civil war, and Churchill ordered the ruthless suppression of the E.A.M. rebellion. Within a month, the military wing of E.A.M., known as E.L.A.S., was defeated. The Communists had borne the main burden of the struggle against the Nazis in Greece, and British opinion was quite unprepared for this breathtaking transition to a Cold War strategy, and the use of British troops against former leaders of the resistance. Sympathy for E.A.M. and anger against Churchill extended from the *Tribune* M.P.s on the Left to E. H. Carr and Barrington-Ward at *The Times*, which publicly lectured the government. In the House of Commons a motion of censure was moved by Seymour Cocks of the *Tribune* group, and supported amongst others by Sir Richard Acland, the leader of the Common Wealth party. The motion was defeated by 279 votes to 30, with the official Labour Opposition under Greenwood abstaining, and 24 Labour M.P.s voting against the Government.

At the Labour Party conference of 11–15 December, held while fighting was still going on in Greece, Greenwood proposed an N.E.C. resolution calling for a ceasefire, innocuously dissociating the party from Cabinet policy. Ernest Bevin made one of his massive interventions to secure the block votes of the unions for the N.E.C. motion, and took the platform in person to champion the government's actions. 'These steps that have been taken in Greece', he told the conference, 'are not the decisions of Winston Churchill, they are the decisions of the Cabinet.' Later in his speech he declared: 'The British Empire cannot abandon its position in the Mediterranean. On the settlement of these countries much of the peace of the future world depends.'[66] The details of Bevin's arguments belong to the analysis of foreign policy: politically, his speech disclosed the gulf between Labour ministers who had spent nearly five years in office, and the ideals of the Labour rank and file. At the summit of power, Bevin could already see the mist of the Cold War rolling off distant seas. But all this was concealed from the ordinary spectator. As the Labour activist tended to view things, the Left was on the march across Europe: the Red Army was liberating the east, while in Italy and France the Communists were reaping the reward of popularity for their courage as resistance fighters. The Continent was being united by the glow of radicalism, and the old privileged elites were to be consigned like waxworks to the flame. Yet Churchill's policy was to sustain the old order. He was a strong partisan of monarchies in Yugoslavia and Greece. In Italy he had struggled to maintain the rule of Marshal Badoglio, the man who conquered Abyssinia for Mussolini. At the Labour Party conference the Chippenham delegate, A. Tomlinson, warned: 'I ask you to consider the sinister entanglements abroad to which the Party has been committed, the faded, petty royalties of Europe, the squabbles for oil, the compromises that have been made behind the scenes in regard to aviation, and so on.'[67] The candidate for Pudsey and Otley, Major Denis Healey, told the May 1945 party conference that he was just back from service in Italy, and could tell from personal experience who were Labour's friends, and who were Labour's enemies in Europe:

> The upper classes in every country are selfish, depraved, dissolute and decadent. These upper classes in every country look to the British Army and the British people to protect them against the just wrath of the people who have been fighting underground against them for the past four years. There is very great danger, unless we are very careful, that we shall find ourselves running with the Red Flag in front of the armoured car of Tory imperialism and counter-revolution ... '[68]

Difficult though it is to chart the tides within the Labour Party, the Labour Left were in crusading mood towards the end of the war, and on one significant occasion inspired a successful conference revolt against an N.E.C. policy document. Among the N.E.C. reconstruction committees was one on Full Employment and Financial Policy. Hugh Dalton had pushed through the committee a somewhat Keynesian statement, and the N.E.C.'s resolution commending it to the 1944 conference avoided any specific commitment to nationalization by referring to 'the transfer to the State of power to direct the policy of our main industries, services and financial institutions'. Ian Mikardo, a delegate from the Reading Trades Council and Labour Party, moved a resolution for a clear-cut commitment to 'the transfer to public ownership of the land, large-scale building, heavy industry, and all forms of banking, transport and fuel and power ... ' The seconder of the resolution, Mrs E. Denington of the South West St Pancras Labour Party, explained: 'Everybody now can see that anarchic capitalism means unemployment, degradation, malnutrition, and misery, and that any form of capitalism means inevitable war. Sir William Beveridge in trying to put forward a new solution dressed the old wolf in sheep's clothing, but the wolf is still there, and the only way of getting rid of it is to kill it stone dead.'[69] Over the objections of Philip Noel-Baker of the N.E.C., the resolution was carried. The 1945 party manifesto ignored most of the Mikardo formula—no Labour government composed of Attlee and his wartime colleagues would have dreamt of nationalizing all the banks—but the reference to 'heavy industry' probably determined the inclusion in the election programme of the pledge to nationalize iron and steel.[70]

Early in 1945 the Reconstruction Committee began to founder on the banal rock of the electricity industry. Two-thirds of the industry was already in the hands of public authorities. Herbert Morrison and Gwilym Lloyd George (the Minister of Fuel and Power) pressed for its reorganization into a public corporation. The Conservative ministers resisted, and for the first time the committee was unable to reach a conclusion. In April Bevin and Bracken, both Coalition ministers, attacked each other in public speeches. On the last day of the month the Reconstruction Committee considered proposals for the future efficiency of the iron and steel industry. Ironically, as will appear later, it fell to Morrison to declare that 'in the opinion of the Labour Party the industry had reached the stage at which its efficient operation could be assured only by nationalization.' For the Conservatives, R. A. Butler replied that 'there was no case for the nationalization of an industry that had shown itself highly efficient and fully conscious of its national responsibilities.'[71] The politicians were emerging at last into the light of common day. When Germany surrendered on 7 May 1945, a return to full party politics was universally expected.

Churchill at the last minute tried once more to keep the Coalition going. On 12 May he received a long telegram from President Truman, arguing that Britain and the United States should take a strong stand against Tito's occupation of Venezia Giulia —and by implication against Russia, which was backing him up. Increasingly obsessed by the new crisis which he saw opening up between Russia and the West, Churchill wrote to Eden:

> We can hardly ask for the support in so serious a venture of our Labour colleagues and then immediately break up the Government. If there is going to be trouble of this kind, the support of men like Attlee, Bevin, Morrison and George Hall [Labour Under-Secretary at the Foreign Office] is indispensable to the National presentation of the case. In that event, I should on no account agree to an Election in October, but simply say that we must prolong our joint tenure. It is common objectives not fixed dates which should determine the end of such an alliance as ours.[72]

On 18 May Churchill wrote to the leaders of the Labour and Liberal Parties inviting them to continue in coalition until the defeat of Japan, or accept an immediate election. After seeing Attlee he added to his letter —which of course was to be published —a paragraph emphasizing that the renewed coalition would do its utmost to implement the proposals for social security and full employment.[73] Such matters were small beer, Churchill must have felt, beside the new confrontation with Moscow and the need for national unity.

The proposals reached the Labour leaders on the eve of the party conference. At the meeting of the National Executive Committee on 19 May, Attlee, Bevin and Dalton argued for acceptance, but Morrison led the argument against and the proposal was rejected. The National Executive Committee took the only decision which the party conference would have tolerated. Replying to Churchill on 21 May, Attlee argued for an autumn election, in line with the Labour calculation that an early election would favour the Conservatives by cashing in on the euphoria of victory and the gratitude of the public to Churchill. The Liberals under Sinclair, as compliant to Churchill as he had once been to Chamberlain, would have been ready to stay in Coalition —but Labour having refused, the issue was decided.

Churchill resigned as leader of the Coalition on 23 May and was re-appointed at the head of a 'Caretaker' government of Conservatives, National Liberals, and non-party functionaries. The new government

had the air of a light-hearted revue by Noel Coward, with Brendan
Bracken as First Lord of the Admiralty, the Earl of Rosebery as
Secretary for Scotland, and the Duke of Devonshire introduced as
Under-Secretary at the Colonial Office. On the serious side it con-
firmed Churchill's instinctively Whiggish approach: Woolton, who
was still non-party, was to be in charge of reconstruction as Lord
President, while R. A. Butler, the great domestic appeaser, became
Minister of Labour. The great neutral functionary, Anderson, remained Chancellor of the Exchequer, and Macmillan entered the
Cabinet for the first time as Secretary for Air. At the same time as the
new government was formed, it was announced that parliament would
be dissolved on 15 June. Polling day would be 5 July, but it was later
decided that voting in twenty-three constituencies should be postponed
for up to three weeks to avoid interfering with local holidays. The
ballot boxes would not be opened until 25 July.

Churchill wrote in his memoirs that the Conservative Party organization was much less well prepared for an election in 1945 than the
Labour organization. Practically all the agents on Conservative constituency associations had found war work or gone into the services. But
the trade unions were the core of Labour's local organization, and
trade unionists had been obliged to remain at home along with other
members of 'reserved occupations', organizing war production. 'Thus
on the one side there had been complete effacement of party activities,
while on the other they ran forward unresisted.'[74]
   In 1944 Churchill had inquired about the number of political agents
engaged in national service at home or in the forces. There were 246
Conservative agents and 16 Labour agents so employed. But as the
Labour National Agent, Shepherd, pointed out, Labour had possessed
very few full-time agents before the war.[75] In March 1945 Labour
faced the future with only 58 full-time agents: meanwhile the 246
Conservative agents were being released from national service.[76] The
idea that Labour had a large number of agents on the home front,
keeping its associations going, is therefore a myth. The reports of
Labour organizers in the 1945 campaign make it clear that the great
majority of Labour agents were without any previous experience of
the task, and were pressed into service at the last minute.[77] Nor was it
correct to imply that local Conservative associations had ceased to be
active during the war. They were constantly enjoined by headquarters

to keep their organization in being by switching it over to war work. In January 1941, for example, the local associations received a pamphlet entitled 'Wartime Activities in the Constituencies' with a preface by Churchill in which he declared: 'It would be disastrous if the Conservative Party were to disappear or its structure fall into decay.' The Conservatives could count on the loyalty and enthusiasm of the Tory ladies. It was only in a very few constituencies, reported the Executive of the National Union in April 1941, that associations were inactive, 'while in many an efficient organization is being maintained.'[78] In October 1944 the incoming party chairman, Ralph Assheton, found that in the constituencies there was usually an active chairman or vice-chairman, treasurer and committee: although in a number of constituencies activities had ceased, owing to the war.[79] In other respects, too, efforts had been made to keep the machinery turning. The Reconstruction Problems Committee had issued a series of reports which acted as the focus for 'Looking Ahead' discussion circles in the constituencies – although the device was not very successful.[80]

After a fashion, then, the Conservative Party organization was ticking over. Undoubtedly it was in a very poor state by comparison with peacetime: a meeting of area agents at party headquarters, before the dissolution of the Coalition, warned that the party could not win an election in 1945. Only after the beginning of the campaign did their optimism reassert itself.[81] It does not follow that Labour had any great organizational advantage. The membership figures for the constituency parties were beginning to recover at the end of the war, but the 1944 total was 265,763, compared with 304,124 in 1940. The number of trade unionists had increased by two million during the war, but as the principle of 'contracting-in' to the political levy still operated, the trade union membership of the Labour Party had risen only slightly. In the election campaign, Labour's regional organizers noted the relative absence of Conservative activity in the East Midlands and the Home Counties, but the same reports give a vivid picture of the last-minute, makeshift character of Labour organization.[82]

One of the handicaps of the Conservatives was their selection of indifferent candidates, a prominent feature of wartime by-elections. Before the war there had been discontent in the party with the tendency of local associations to select the candidate who offered to pay the largest subscription to the local party, but nothing had been done since to bring about effective reform. Another temptation for constituency associations was to choose the safe, local man. The chairman of the party was complaining privately in 1942 of the strong tendency of local associations to support as a candidate the local party chairman, with too many years of worthy service behind him.[83] Perhaps the Conservatives' long tenure of power in many areas had created exclusive local caucuses which were out of touch with voters. At Newcastle North in May 1940, and again at Brighton in June 1944, the choice of the local association sparked off a rebellion and the adoption of an alternative Conservative candidate. At Newcastle North the 'rebel' won. For the 1945 Chelmsford by-election—the first to be held on the new electoral register, which enfranchised voters who had come of age since 1939— the Tory caucus, according to a private report which Beaverbrook received from the editor of the local paper, had gone out of their way to select a 'safe' man from among the thirty applicants. They had no concept of the art of publicity. The local party chairman could only preach negations—the need for wartime controls to be removed. 'Hundreds of our local houses have been destroyed,' remarked Beaverbrook's correspondent. 'If the Conservatives could get the houses built, then they would have something really good to talk about.' Meanwhile, the Common Wealth candidate, Wing-Commander Millington, had been attracting large crowds through sheer vitality of personality, and could have got away with advocating a policy of trips to the moon.[84]

Churchill himself had first been elected to the House in the 'khaki election' of 1900, when the Conservatives swept to triumph as the patriotic party during the Boer War. The electors of Oldham had given him a hero's welcome after his celebrated escape from a Boer prisoner-of-war camp, and it was natural for Churchill in 1945 to believe that candidates with good war records would carry the day. He persuaded several servicemen to stand as Conservatives, often against their inclination.[85] With the encouragement of Beaverbrook, now frequently at his side, he tried to waive the rule which forbade all candidates, including ex-M.P.s, from wearing uniform during the campaign. On 29 April he gave instructions that all candidates should be entitled to do so. But P. J. Grigg, the Secretary for War, pointed out the dangers of involving the officer class and the services in political controversy. The majority of officer candidates were Conservative. The War Office was afraid of the accusation 'that the wearing of uniform was a device of the upper class to try to stem a drift of public opinion to the left'. Under the Caretaker government, Churchill set up a party committee (Beaverbrook, Butler, Stuart and Assheton) which endorsed his ruling: but Labour protested so strongly that the idea was dropped.[86]

The presence of Lord Beaverbrook at Churchill's elbow appears to have set up a divided command on the Conservative side. In the spring of 1945, A. J. P. Taylor writes, Beaverbrook pushed aside the party chairman, Ralph Assheton, as 'inadequately aggressive', and became virtual party manager himself.[87] Later, Beaverbrook wrote to Churchill to say that there were two groups operating independently in the Conservative campaign, himself and Brendan Bracken on the one hand, and the Chief Whip and party chairman on the other:

> Mr Bracken and I take views opposed to those of this group on almost every occasion when issues arise.
>
> There is not any co-ordination. We have not worked together in making recommendations to you.
>
> Accordingly I have retired from further discussion.

Beaverbrook's influence was extremely unpopular in the Conservative Party. 'I believe there is no man living', said one Conservative M.P. after his defeat, 'more detested throughout the political world than Lord Beaverbrook.'[88]

The Labour Party's strategy in 1945 was essentially a conservative one. Had they gone to the country in 1939 with the programme of 1945, they would have been issuing a strongly radical challenge. But in 1945 they had only to consolidate and extend the consensus achieved under the Coalition, and build upon the new foundations of popular opinion. The leaders of the party approached both these tasks with caution. In a fascinating memorandum, Attlee listed the extensive property rights which, he argued, 'the majority of the people had acquired through pension schemes, Co-op shares, Post Office and savings bank deposits, war savings, post-war credits and social security rights. The 1931 election had shown how strong was the working class fear of losing savings: 'In face of this it is time that the Labour Party ceased to mouth Marxian shibboleths about the proletariat having nothing to lose but their chains. It is just not true.' Labour should defend savings and condemn inflation: 'A silly speech by Aneurin Bevan might easily be used to stampede the electors away from Labour.'[89]

In a message to party workers in March 1945, Morrison recommended the strategy which he had advocated since the 1930s of presenting Labour as the friend of the 'small man', the black-coated worker and the technician. In a no doubt well-calculated acceptance of risk, Morrison gave up his safe seat at South Hackney and proclaimed that he would pursue the lower middle-class vote in East Lewisham, which had been held for the Conservatives since 1918 by Sir Assheton Pownall. Cripps, too, was advising the party to aim for the 'middle ground'. In his first appearance at a Labour Party conference since rejoining the Party, Cripps declared: 'We must not lead the people to believe that this is some easy Utopia into which we are inviting them to step.'[90] Shades, already, of post-war Crippsian austerity.

Labour were able to adopt an especially 'statesmanlike' posture on the question of the future of industry. In the 1930s, capitalism had been largely uncontrolled by the state. To have demanded powers to allocate raw materials between firms, direct labour, or determine the type and quantity of goods produced, would have been revolutionary doctrine in British terms. But as the result of the war the state now possessed all these powers, and even right-wing Conservatives had to admit that it was essential for many of them to be continued for a transition period. Thus Labour could stand for the retention – for how long was not clear – of the system of state planning which already existed. Here, indeed, were fresh grounds of justification for the piecemeal approach to nationalization which Labour leaders already cherished. Through the apparatus of wartime planning, they had been able to control industry without having to nationalize it. Directors and managers of great companies had obeyed the instructions of the state. 'Oh no, my dear Richard,' said Cripps to Acland in October 1944, 'we have learned in the war that we CAN control industry.' After the war, Cripps went on, there would be an export crisis and a fall in the standard of living. 'Now, my dear Richard, you can't nationalize the cotton industry in the middle of *that*.'[91]

Herbert Morrison, the prophet of the public corporation, made a series of wartime speeches in which the theme of state control of industry was advanced side by side with the argument for nationalization. In a preface to a Fabian Society pamphlet on 'Government and Industry' he argued that it was only in a few vital industries that nationalization was essential. The electorate would not agree to anything more, 'and, even if they did, speaking as one with some experience of administration, I do not believe that their wishes would be carried out.' By emphasizing that nationalization was not a general principle, but a device whose application to any particular industry had to be justified on criteria of welfare and efficiency, Morrison was seeking to establish Labour as the pragmatic party, with the Conservatives as the doctrinaires of free enterprise.[92]

It is often said that the Labour leaders entered the election in the expectation of defeat, but if so Bevin must be regarded as one of the more optimistic. Lord Wavell, the Viceroy of India, had a long talk with him on 15 May and noted: 'He said that he thought Labour would get into office very soon and would then hold power for 20 or 30 years. He professed optimism about Labour's attitude, about agreement with employers, about the standard of living, abolition of unemployment etc., which many other knowledgeable people do not share.'[93]

In the approach to the 1945 general election, Morrison was chairman of both the policy committee and the campaign committee. At a campaign committee meeting with Morrison in the chair on 19 March, the decision was reached that 'the main election issue must run firmly as a common theme, with whatever variations of treatment that might be necessary for each service, through all election literature, that theme being the basic, clear cut one of Public versus Private Enterprise.' For once, Morrison was not moderate enough. The National Executive substituted a new campaign theme: 'economic and industrial reconstruction'.[94] In April, Morrison and Greenwood proposed to leave out of the Labour manifesto the commitment to the nationalization of iron and steel. Morrison told Dalton that he had been lunching 'with some friends of ours in the City', who had told him that it was too ambitious to think in terms of a public board owning the steel industry. Dalton forced the commitment through.[95]

The Labour policy document, *Let Us Face the Future*, was published the same month. The Labour Party pledged itself to nationalize the Bank of England, fuel and power, inland transport, and iron and steel. Monopolies and cartels were to be supervised by the state 'with the aim of advancing industrial efficiency'. On physical controls the document declared: 'There must be priorities in the use of raw materials, food prices must be held, homes for the people must come before mansions, necessities for all before luxuries for the few.' Full employment would be maintained through the maintenance of purchasing power, the National Health Service and social security schemes implemented, the Education Act given practical effect, and the location of industry regulated.[96] Whether or not Morrison was aware of the fact, *Let Us Face the Future* harmonized well with popular attitudes as the students of public opinion gauged them. The majority of the public had *welcomed* during the war each new instalment of planned austerity, from the conscription of women in 1941, to the reduction of the cheese ration in 1943. According to opinion polls, a majority approved of the nationalization of land, state control and ownership of the mines and railways, state control of the post-war purchase and distribution of food, and general state direction of the transition from war to peace.[97]

The Liberal Party went into the election with 306 candidates, led by Sir Archibald Sinclair and Sir William Beveridge. Beveridge had joined the Liberals in September 1944. Morrison had tried to interest him in joining Labour — but Beveridge thought he would be unable to tolerate the influence of the trade unionists, notably Bevin, in Labour counsels. Perhaps Beveridge would have been interested in an invitation from the Conservatives, for he had remarked that a Conservative government would be the best instrument for carrying through his policies. But on the assumption that the Conservatives would do a little worse, and Labour a little better, at the next election, the Liberals might well form a significant third party, so it was with high expectations that Beveridge entered parliament as Liberal M.P. for Berwick at a by-election in October 1944. He was reported in the New Year to be confident that he would be, in effect, the new Liberal leader, and optimistic because of an opinion survey which claimed to show the Liberals lying second to Labour in popular estimation. From the Liberals' point of view he was a brilliant catch. Already famous for his social security plan, he published in November 1944 his report *Full Employment in a Free Society*, which advocated a fairly bold measure of central direction of the economy, avoiding nationalization but controlling the pattern of private investment and laying down social priorities in production. The manpower budget was to be the centre-piece of economic planning. At the Liberal assembly in February 1945, Beveridge had only to move the adoption of his plans for employment to see them gleefully snapped up by the party.[98] As in 1929, the Liberal Party went to the country with a coherent philosophy, but this time the carnage was to be even worse, with Beveridge and Sinclair both doomed to defeat in their own constituencies.

The Conservative election manifesto was a twenty-page document, *Mr Churchill's Declaration of Policy to the Electors*. Couched for the most part in the language of Whitehall, with an occasional Churchillian flourish added, it stated unexceptionable goals in foreign and defence policy, and committed the party once more to the full programme of post-war reconstruction agreed by the Coalition: full employment, social security, a National Health Service. While it was naturally silent about the modifications which had been agreed in the health service, it was both forward-looking and constructive. The exceptional vagueness of the passages dealing with the future of wartime controls, and the future organization of industry, revealed the considerable variety of opinion within the party on these subjects. Taken as a whole, however, it was a sober restatement of the new wartime consensus. The Conservative campaign was a different matter. Instead of taking a positive line about what they themselves would do, they concentrated on stampeding the electorate away from Labour. In a message to all candidates, the Party chairman proclaimed that they would not try to outbid the 'appetizing prospects' put forward by their opponents. The two great issues were the choice between an experienced government under Churchill and an Attlee government 'controlled by extremists'; and the question of nationalization and bureaucracy.[99] Assheton himself had foreshadowed the libertarian, anti-planning theme in a speech on 21 April: 'He did not think that most of those who toyed with Socialist theories and doctrines in this country realized sufficiently that socialism, which meant the ownership by the state of all the means of production, distribution, and exchange, inevitably led to a totalitarian state.'[100] Directly or indirectly, Conservative propaganda reflected the arguments of Professor Friedrich von Hayek of the London School of Economics, whose book *The Road to Serfdom*, published in 1944, argued that economic planning necessitated the apparatus of tyranny.

In his first election broadcast on 4 June, Churchill declared 'from the bottom of my heart' that the introduction of socialism into Britain would require some form of Gestapo, 'no doubt very humanely directed in the first instance'. For good measure he argued that a Labour government would mean the erosion of the value of the people's savings. After nearly six years of high exhortation from Churchill, many were shocked by his sudden descent to the bottom of the electoral barrel. 'It would be difficult to exaggerate', wrote Mass-Observation, 'the disappointment and genuine distress aroused by this speech.' Attlee retorted the next day: 'The voice we heard last night was that of Mr Churchill, but the mind was that of Lord Beaverbrook.' Beaverbrook denied it, stating in 1946 that he had made no contribution to the broadcast, nor had his advice been asked.[101] The 'Gestapo speech' was Churchill's folly. Beaverbrook's major contribution was probably the Laski scare, which figured for several days on the front page of the *Daily Express*. When Attlee accepted an invitation from Churchill to attend the allied conference at Potsdam, Laski, the Party chairman, foolishly put out a statement declaring that Attlee's presence at Potsdam could not bind the Labour Party to the decisions reached there. The *Express* discovered that the chairman of a mysterious unparliamentary committee (the National Executive) was dictating to the parliamentary Labour Party: the Left were pulling the strings of their moderate puppet, Mr Attlee. The *Express* followed up with a story that Laski had used revolutionary language in a speech at Newark. On 25 June, when the Laski scare was in full spate, Beaverbrook wrote to Churchill saying that he now proposed to take full editorial control of his papers. Churchill replied that the leaders and lay-out of the *Express* and *Evening Standard* had been 'admirable'. While Churchill made some use of the Laski issue in his broadcasts, he did so sparingly, and he was careful to rebuke his friend Lord Croft for a xenophobic remark: 'I see you used an expression in your speech the other day about Laski that he was "a fine representative of the old British working class", or words to that effect. Pray be careful, whatever the temptation, not to be drawn into any campaign that might be represented as anti-semitism.'[102]

It is tempting to suggest that the 'Gestapo speech' and the Laski bogy did the Conservative Party harm, and that Churchill was chiefly responsible for the style of campaign adopted. To keep the criticisms of Churchill in perspective, it has to be recalled that the opinion polls had been against the Conservatives since 1943, and that after the beginning of June, when Churchill entered the fray, they suggested that voters were swinging back to the Conservatives. The Gallup polls showed a Labour lead of 16 per cent on 28 May (the date of the publication of the poll), 9 per cent on 18 June, and 6 per cent on 4 July.[103] On the assumption that there was a swing, the impact of Churchill is the most likely explanation. Between 4 June and the end of the month he broadcast four times: more people listened to him than to the Labour and Liberal broadcasts. At the end of the month he undertook a triumphal tour through the country, greeted by cheering crowds from Birmingham to Glasgow. On 3 July he was, by contrast, booed by a crowd of 20,000 at Walthamstow: but there was a persistent rumour abroad that whichever party returned to power, Churchill would remain Prime Minister, a story which Churchill several times denied. Churchill was still thought of as a great man rather than a party politician pure and simple, and Mass-Observation found that the most frequently stated reason for voting Conservative was loyalty to Churchill. 'We can't let him down—he didn't let us down', was a typical sentiment, and the Conservative election slogan, 'Help Him finish the Job', was frequently cited.[104] (An extra complication was the possibility that some Labour voters failed to realize that they were voting *against* Churchill. As one witness writes: 'Many Labour men had a shock when they knew that Churchill was OUT—they somehow imagined that he would still be there in a coalition.'[105])

When asked what they thought would be the question most discussed in the election campaign, most people named housing as the biggest issue, with jobs, social security, and nationalization following. The priorities carefully listed by Churchill in each of his broadcasts were markedly different. On 13 June, for example, he spoke of five tasks to come: the completion of the war against Japan, demobilization, the re-starting of industry, the rebuilding of exports, and the four-year plan of 'food, work and homes'. Thus homes came last on Churchill's list, first on the voters'. Meanwhile Labour made much of the housing issue, with Bevin introducing the staggering claim that Labour would build four or five million houses.[106] A simple but vital point about the 1945 election is that Labour put the material needs of the average family above all else in its campaign.

When the election results were declared, during the course of 26 July, it became apparent that Labour had won a massive victory. In the final reckoning, Labour won 393 seats, with 47·8 per cent of the total vote, the Conservatives 213 seats with 39·8 per cent of the total vote, and the Liberals 12 seats (after putting up 306 candidates) with 9 per cent of the total vote. Five members of Churchill's Caretaker Cabinet including Bracken and Macmillan, and thirty-two members of his administration all told, were defeated. Beveridge and Sinclair, sharing the fate of 294 other Liberal candidates, were removed from political life.

More than thirty-three million people had been entitled to vote, including nearly three million servicemen whose officers managed to arrange for their names to be placed on the service register. All told, 1,700,653 service votes, cast either directly, by post, or by proxy, were included in the count. As the service votes were taken from separate boxes to be counted, it was an open secret that they were predominantly Labour. If, however, experience of life in the services turned voters to the left, the Conservatives were fortunate in the fact that more than half the men and women in the services did not vote at all.[107] It has been estimated that 21 per cent of voters were voting for the first time (by-elections apart). Mark Abrams drew up a table to show that if two out of three of the new voters had voted Labour, this in itself would have been sufficient to account for Labour's margin of victory. Several years later, retrospective interviews conducted by Butler and Stokes concluded that Labour won 61 per cent of the new voters in 1945.[108]

Labour had broadened its class appeal very considerably. John Bonham, in his stimulating book *The Middle Class Vote*, sought to chart the growth of Labour support in the higher, middle, and lower-middle income areas of London, which he dubbed 'Westendia', 'Suburbia' and 'Blackcoatia'. While the categories could only be very approximate, they showed a 19·8 per cent improvement in the Labour vote in 'Westendia', 18 per cent in 'Suburbia' and 8·5 per cent only in 'Blackcoatia'. The two working-class areas also showed an important increase in the Labour vote – up 17·1 per cent in 'Artisania', and 14·6 per cent in 'Eastendia'. Butler and Stokes, examining the 'cohort' of electors who first voted between 1935 and 1950, estimated that they included 7 per cent fewer working-class Tories, and 7 per cent more middle-class voters, than the cohort of 1918 to 1935.[109] When we look at the electoral map, the most striking changes between 1935 and 1945 appear to be in the London suburbs, where Labour won many 'white-collar' constituencies; the West Midlands, a traditional home since Joseph Chamberlain's day of the working-class Conservative; and the agricultural counties of East Anglia, where, perhaps, the agricultural labourer had at last emancipated himself. The Labour Party's regional organizer in the Home Counties wrote: 'Not since the field-preaching of the Wesley brothers has such a surge of "revival" swept the hamlets and county towns of Southern England. Villages steeped in century-old Tory tradition bloomed with Labour posters.'[110]

In the general election of 1945 the working classes of the declining areas of heavy industry joined forces through the ballot-box with much of the more prosperous working class in the Midlands and South-East, and a substantial section of the urban middle classes. The new mix was also evident in the House of Commons. Between the wars, trade unionists had always been in the majority on the Labour benches. In the Labour Parliamentary Party of 1945 they were out-numbered for the first time by members of the professions. 'I claim that we are a really national Party,' said Arthur Greenwood. 'We are are a cross-section of the national life, and this is something that has never happened before.'[111] On 2 September 1939, when Chamberlain seemed to be hesitating about whether to declare war, Arthur Greenwood had been rising to speak for the Labour Party when L.S. Amery called out from the Conservative benches: 'Speak for England!'[112] Greenwood and his party had carried out that instruction more fully than Amery had ever intended.

X Attlee's Consensus

Clement Attlee, who became Prime Minister on 26 July 1945, was
from many points of view a recognizable type of upper-middle-class
professional Englishman. 'He came', wrote Francis Williams, 'from
one of those middle-class Conservative Christian homes, more common in Queen Victoria's day than now, all the members of which were
taught that both their religious beliefs, which were held with deep
sincerity, and their social position imposed upon them obligations as
well as privileges.'[1] He was educated at Haileybury College and Oxford
University, and always retained his affection for both. He qualified as a
barrister, and at the outbreak of war in 1914 hastened to volunteer and
get himself a commission. He was posted to Gallipoli, and as a junior
officer formed the impression that Churchill's strategic judgment in
mounting the expedition was sound. Although his army career ended
in 1918, he retained much of the bearing of the more selfless type of
officer, emotionally self-disciplined, ordered and functional in his
thought, and laconic in speech. On one occasion when he was Prime
Minister he rebuked a colleague by saying: 'Don't talk about your
platoon in the bloody mess.' In manners he was notably punctilious. He
rebuked Aneurin Bevan for attending a royal banquet in a lounge suit,
and could be seen to shudder at dinner if the port was passed the wrong
way. Mrs Attlee, the daughter of a Treasury official, was strongly
suspected of Tory leanings. When it was announced in 1937 that the
Leader of the Opposition was in future to have an annual salary, Mrs
Attlee told the press that she would now be able to have enough maids
to run her house properly.[2]

As a young man, Attlee's sense of duty led him to work in his spare
time at a boys' club supported by Haileybury College in the East End
of London. Apart from the interruption of World War I, he lived for

fourteen years in the East End undertaking social work, joining the Fabians and the Independent Labour Party, and becoming in 1920 the first Labour mayor of Stepney. When Attlee first entered the House of Commons in 1922, *The Times* described him as 'a type that would construct a new heaven on earth on violently geometrical principles.' The fragments of Attlee's political thought which remain from the 1920s suggest a strong ethical and abstract commitment to socialism.[3] The world slump and the collapse of the MacDonald government emboldened Attlee to call for an immediate assault on capitalism by the next Labour government. In his book, *The Labour Party in Perspective* (1937), Attlee wrote: 'The evils that Capitalism brings differ in intensity in different countries, but, the root cause of the trouble once discerned, the remedy is seen to be the same by thoughtful men and women. The cause is the private ownership of the means of life; the remedy is public ownership.' Attlee made it clear that in his view the ultimate Labour objective included the state ownership of all major industries, and substantial economic equality. 'The abolition of classes', he wrote, 'is fundamental to the Socialist conception of society.'[4]

Here were aims sincerely stated. Had they been acted upon, consensus would have been impossible, but there was never a serious prospect that they would be. This is not to say that Attlee was a hypocrite: on the contrary. But how did he cross the bridge from socialist principle to consensus politics? Attlee was subject to the common enough human predicament of being compelled to believe in certain aims, and compelled to behave as though he did not. His ethics compelled him to believe that Britain must become a socialist commonwealth. His upbringing, affection for the parliamentary system, and professional commitment as a politician to represent his party and win the consent of the electorate, forced him steadily down the road to reformed capitalism. Like many socialists of his generation, he bridged the gulf by arguing that reform within capitalism would provide the first instalment, and thus the foundation, of a socialist Britain. Westminster was not the terminus of British politics, but a station on the line to the new Jerusalem. Such was Attlee's belief in recommending *Labour's Immediate Programme* in 1937.

For all practical purposes, Attlee stood in 1937 for no more, and probably for less, than the wartime Coalition established as the norm in social and economic policy. The consensus developed in the 1940s represented a dilution of Conservative rather than Labour politics. None the less there was also a change in Attlee's outlook. He had never been a deep theorist. He had rejected capitalism because of the social conditions he found, as a young man, in the East End of London. His affection for the people he met there, and his detailed knowledge of their hardships, was the true impulse which sustained him. When he was active in the East End after the First World War, it was the practical details of poverty which occupied his time. He gave away large sums of money from his income as a lecturer so that mothers could buy shoes for their children, or tenants catch up with the rent. The people of the East End were the touchstone of his political life. In Cabinet when he was Prime Minister he told a civil servant who had drawn up a fuel rationing scheme: 'You seem to assume that *everyone* can store domestic coal in the summer for winter use. The people of the East End haven't anywhere to store it. They can keep a few lumps under the stairs, that's all. When I lived there I kept it under the bed. And at first I bought too big a sack and had to sleep on a mattress with a hump like a camel.'[5]

To a man with Attlee's frame of reference, any substantial increase in the welfare of the working class was in itself a revolution. The Coalition government, besides educating him in the realities and limitations of power, afforded him and his colleagues real scope for the first time to raise standards of welfare. The warm currents of social security and full employment began to melt the icy layers of anti-capitalist principle. When Laski wrote to Attlee in 1944, urging his familiar policy of 'socialism now', Attlee replied:

Although you are a theorist and I am only a working politician I think that I give more and you give less attention to changes of conception than to legislative achievements. For instance I have witnessed now the acceptance by all the leading politicians in this country and all the economists of any account of the conception of the utilization of abundance. From 1931 onwards in the House I and others pressed this. It was rejected with scorn. It is now accepted and important results flow from it. It is the basis of our conversations with the Dominions and our Allies. It colours all our discussions on home economic policy. There follows from this the doctrine of full employment. The acceptance of this again colours our whole conception of the postwar set-up in this country. You will appreciate that in discussions with Cabinet colleagues not of our party the full acceptance of these conceptions concedes much of our case in advance.[6]

The Attlee governments of 1945 to 1951 completed and consolidated the work of the Coalition by establishing a peacetime managed economy, and the expanded welfare state envisaged by Beveridge. To some extent they also exercised the right to go beyond the Coalition framework and implement specifically party ideas. But this was often because the Left of the party, which had strongly opposed many of the Coalition policies, managed to exert itself successfully. Aneurin Bevan, the new Minister of Health, refused to start from the point where the wartime White Paper on the National Health Service had left off, and devised his own approach. After an heroic struggle against the B.M.A., the Conservative press, and Churchill (who dubbed him the 'minister of disease'), Bevan was able to introduce a fully fledged National Health Service on 5 July 1948. Bevan's boldest stroke was to nationalize the voluntary hospitals, but in other respects his policy was no more socialist than his predecessor's had been. The health centre with its salaried staff of doctors remained a distant goal, and it was a Labour M.P., Sir Frederick Messer, who said that Bevan's outstanding success 'was the way he applied the anaesthetic to supporters on his own side, making them believe in things they had opposed almost all their lives.'[7] In a less spectacular fashion James Griffiths piloted into law the National Insurance Act of 1946, which gave effect, with some modification, to the Beveridge plan.

The nationalization programme embraced the Bank of England (May 1946), the coal mines (January 1947), electricity (April 1948), gas (May 1948) and the railways (May 1948). To these measures the Conservatives put up only a token opposition. In each case the argument for state control was as much accepted by businessmen as by Labour politicians, and the industries concerned were either public utilities or ailing concerns of little value to their owners and no interest to other capitalists. Because of the conference resolution passed against the wishes of the National Executive in 1944, Labour were committed to the nationalization of iron and steel, one of the most glittering prizes in the private sector. In vain did Morrison, encouraged by Attlee, try to evade the commitment by devising a system of control which fell short of public ownership. The industry was nationalized in February 1951.

The Town and Country Planning Act of 1947 made all land subject to planning schemes for the first time, and following the spirit if not the letter of the Uthwatt Report, imposed a 100 per cent development levy on the value created by permission to develop land. The Conservatives, who argued that the development levy required cumbrous machinery, and prevented land from coming on to the market, repealed the development charge in 1953. The Labour housing programme, for which Bevan was responsible, was not particularly successful, owing largely to the deliberate decision of the government to cut back the programme in 1947 to aid the balance of payments. But one million new houses were built.[8]

Labour's management of the economy was open to the normal criticisms of the professional economist—bad forecasting, poor timing of decisions, wrong weighting of policies and so forth—and also to the accusation that it progressively abandoned the most distinctive plank of the Labour platform. In 1946 Herbert Morrison, who was responsible for the co-ordination of economic policy, declared: 'Planning as it is now taking shape in this country under our eyes, is something new and constructively revolutionary which will be regarded in times to come as a contribution to civilization as vital and distinctly British as parliamentary democracy and the rule of law.'[9] The *Economic Survey* for 1947 set out production targets for the economy and listed industry by industry the manpower necessary to achieve these goals. But the power to direct manpower had already lapsed, and one by one the other physical controls established in wartime were relinquished when they could no longer be justified because of shortages. In peacetime neither businessmen, trade unionists, nor the people as consumers, were prepared to tolerate indefinitely the physical direction of the economy. On Guy Fawkes Day 1948 the President of the Board of Trade, Harold Wilson, highlighted the change of policy with his 'bonfire of controls', ending restrictions on more than sixty commodities. 'Between 1947 and 1950', writes Samuel Beer, 'the Labour Governments' approach to economic affairs was radically transformed. At the heart of this transformation was the shift from the manpower budget to the financial budget as the principal means of guiding the economy.' Dalton, writes Donald Winch, was the last pre-Keynesian Chancellor of the Exchequer, in the years 1945–7; Cripps, the Chancellor from 1947 to 1950, 'was more at home with Keynesian terminology and methods', while Gaitskell, the Chancellor in 1950–1, 'was perhaps the first entirely self-conscious Keynesian to occupy the chancellorship'.[10] The commitment to centralized economic planning had gradually faded away.

The Conservative Party was not slow, after 1945, to recover its instinct for power. Churchill appointed Lord Woolton, a convert to

Conservatism on the day the election results were announced, as chairman of the Party with a mandate to overhaul the organization. Among the consequences of this was a radical change in the rules by which local constituency associations chose their candidates. A committee under Sir David Maxwell Fyfe imposed strict limitations on the sum which any candidate could pay towards constituency and election funds—an attempt to broaden the social profile of the Conservative Party in the House of Commons. Under the inspiration of R. A. Butler, a number of front-bench Conservatives set out, with the baffled acquiescence of Churchill, to draw up for the party a new Tamworth manifesto. The resulting document, the *Industrial Charter*, was released with a fanfare of publicity in 1947. First and foremost, Butler has written, the Charter was 'an assurance that, in the interests of efficiency, full employment and social security, modern Conservatism would maintain strong central guidance over the operation of the economy.'[11]

Thus the convergence of the two main parties, which had begun in 1940, was largely completed in the late 1940s. When the Conservatives won the election of October 1951, Churchill appointed R. A. Butler as Chancellor of the Exchequer in succession to Hugh Gaitskell. So little break did there seem to be in the continuity of policy that the term 'Butskellism' was coined to describe the phenomenon.

Is it possible, by placing the war in a more long-term perspective, to sum up its impact on British politics? Arthur Marwick, in his work on the relationship between war and social change, has emphasized the various respects in which twentieth-century war has a radical potential, especially in so far as it tests the efficiency of institutions, and leads to the participation in the war effort of relatively underprivileged groups who, as a result, benefit socially and politically.[12] Angus Calder, in his social history of life on the home front from 1939 to 1945, *The People's War*, has described the consequences of the war in sharply pessimistic terms:

> The war was fought with the willing brains and hearts of the most vigorous elements in the community, the educated, the skilled, the bold, the active, the young, who worked more and more consciously towards a transformed post-war world.
>
> Thanks to their energy, the forces of wealth, bureaucracy and privilege survived with little inconvenience, recovered from their shock, and began to proceed with their old business of manœuvre,

concession and studied betrayal. Indeed, this war, which had set off a ferment of participatory democracy, was strengthening meanwhile the forces of tyranny, pressing Britain forward towards *1984*.[13]

From a slightly different angle, Henry Pelling has also argued the case against regarding the war as innovatory. He suggests that, having won the war, the British concluded that their institutions had, in general, been vindicated, and that 'somehow or other, things in their own country were arranged much better than elsewhere in the world — even if, in limited directions only, there might be some room for improvement.'[14]

The problem is, of course, largely a subjective one. The war hastened the introduction of a reformed style of capitalism. If capitalism is regarded as inherently productive of ruthless exploitation and inequality, then by definition the war changed little. But, on the social democratic thesis that parliamentary democracy enables the labour movement to achieve worthwhile benefits within capitalism, the war might be regarded as radical in its effects. If radicalism be measured solely against the British political tradition, then Bevin, Keynes and Beveridge are radical reformers. If comparison is made with revolutionary societies abroad, then all three must figure as notable pillars of the existing social order.

In my own view, one of the most important facts is that the trade union movement, and the Labour Party, were controlled on the eve of the war by a generation of leaders who were essentially moderate social patriots. Working-class politics had suffered numerous defeats. For all the divisions in its social structure, Britain was a small and closely knit community, insular, and bound together by strong patriotic or perhaps nationalistic feelings which no historian has yet fully documented. For five years, an aristocrat steeped in a romantic vision of his nation's role was the undisputed leader of an overwhelmingly working-class nation of whose social conditions and daily concerns he was largely in ignorance. Churchill is a symbol of how little class-feeling counted in the final analysis. The Labour movement's participation in the war effort might have had more radical consequences in a more class-conscious society, but in practice the demands of the leaders were modest, and there is no evidence that the rank-and-file, in the factories or the services, demanded more. The Conservatives were reluctant, from Churchill downwards, to make any changes, but they accepted a range of reforms in the belief that national unity would be strengthened. In general, the reform programme originated in the thought of the upper-middle class of socially concerned professional people, of whom Beveridge and Keynes were the patron saints. To render capitalism more humane and efficient was the principal aim of the professional expert. In World War II the humane technocrat provided a patriotic compromise between Socialism and Conservatism which virtually satisfied the desire of the Labour Party for social amelioration, without in any way attacking the roots of exploitation and injustice. Hence, no doubt, the peculiar character of the post-war Labour Government, with its combination of heroic energies and confident pragmatism. Summing up the work of the Attlee government, Harry Eckstein wrote:

> Whatever aspect of the Labour program one considers, one always returns to the same theme: a similar policy was advocated, perhaps even before Labour advocated it, by nonsocialists. Central economic planning under the post-war Labour Governments — except for a period after the war, especially after the financial crisis of 1947, when conditions made necessary a large volume of physical control — has involved little more than the application of Keynesian nostrums ... one of the most remarkable things about Labour's nationalization measures is that most of them were enacted in response to the reports of Conservative-dominated investigating committees: the Bank of England measure as a result of the Macmillan Report, coal because of the Reid Report, gas because of the Hayworth Report, electricity because of the McGowan report. Moreover, nationalization, as carried out by Labour, made use of an administrative device first worked out by Liberal and Conservative governments — the 'public corporation'.[15]

In similar fashion, Labour Ministers of Education, Ellen Wilkinson and George Tomlinson, were content with the division of secondary schools into grammar and secondary modern, and were reluctant to act on the party's formal commitment, registered at the 1942 party conference, to the multilateral or comprehensive school.[16]

The style of Attlee's government was strongly criticized from the Left, especially in later years. Thus Richard Crossman wrote in 1965:

> How much more humane and imaginative our post-war reconstruction would have proved if government departments had been invigorated by an influx of experts with special knowledge, new

ideas and a sympathy for the Government's domestic and foreign policies. But the Premier dismissed such suggestions as Left-Wing claptrap. Once again, as after 1918, the best of the temporary civil servants returned to their peacetime occupations, and the old establishment ruled unchallenged, over a bureaucratic empire which had been both enormously enlarged and dangerously centralized during the war.[17]

The 1940s were the decade when the Conservatives were obliged to integrate some of Labour's most important demands into their own philosophy. They were able to do so without too much pain because Labour's demands had largely been cast in a mould of thought provided by the non-socialist intelligentsia between the wars and during World War II. In his last years in politics, under the premiership of Churchill, Attlee could argue that Labour had completed a peaceful revolution. When he revisited the boys' club at which he had worked in Stepney, he could observe how much better nourished the boys were than they had been in Edwardian England.[18] Such was Mr Attlee's consensus, the new dispensation which began after Dunkirk in 1940, and until recent years seemed to be the natural order of British politics. We were all —*almost* all —Butskellites then.

Appendix
Labour in the Coalition

The chief Labour office-holders in the Coalition Government were:

A. V. Alexander: First Lord of the Admiralty, 11 May 1940 to 23 May 1945.

C. R. Attlee: Lord Privy Seal, 11 May 1940 to 19 Feb. 1942; Secretary for Dominions; 19 Feb. 1942 to 24 Sep. 1943; Lord President, 24 Sep. 1943 to 23 May 1945; deputy Prime Minister from 19 Feb. 1942; member of the War Cabinet throughout.

Ernest Bevin: Minister of Labour and National Service, 11 May 1940 to 23 May 1945; member of the War Cabinet from 3 Oct. 1940.

Hugh Dalton: Minister for Economic Warfare, 11 May 1940 to 22 Feb. 1942; President of the Board of Trade, 22 Feb. 1942 to 23 May 1945.

Charles Edwards: Joint Chief Whip, 17 May 1940 to 12 Mar. 1942.

Arthur Greenwood: Minister without Portfolio, and member of the War Cabinet, 11 May 1940 to 22 Feb. 1942.

Thomas Johnston: Secretary of State for Scotland, 8 Feb. 1941 to 23 May 1945.

William Jowitt: Solicitor-General, 15 May 1940 to 4 Mar. 1942; Paymaster-General, 4 Mar. 1942 to 30 Dec. 1942; Minister without Portfolio, 30 Dec. 1942 to 8 Oct. 1944; Minister of Social Insurance, 8 Oct. 1944 to 23 May 1945.

Herbert Morrison: Minister of Supply, 12 May 1940 to 3 Oct. 1940; Home Secretary and Minister of Home Security, 3 Oct. 1940 to 23 May 1945; member of the War Cabinet, 22 Nov. 1942 to 23 May 1945.

Ben Smith: Minister resident in Washington for Supply, 11 Nov. 1943 to 23 May 1945.

William Whiteley: Joint Chief Whip, 12 Mar. 1942 to 23 May 1945.

Labour politicians and War Cabinet committees

When Churchill first established his government, it was decided that there would be five key committees to manage the home front. Attlee took the chair of the Food and Home Policy Committees, Greenwood of the Production Council and Economic Policy Committees. To co-ordinate their efforts there was also to be an informal steering committee under the Lord President, Neville Chamberlain. Greenwood failed to cope with his responsibilities and in January 1941 both his committees were abolished. The functions of the Economic Policy Committee passed to the Lord President's Committee, now directed by

Sir John Anderson, who became Lord President on Chamberlain's retirement in September. The work of the Production Council was henceforth to be transacted by a production executive under Bevin. Partly because of rows between Bevin and Beaverbrook and partly because of technical difficulties, the production executive had to be replaced in February 1942 by a Ministry of Production. Beaverbrook himself was Minister for a few days, but on his resignation the job went to Oliver Lyttelton, who held the post for the duration of the war. In the February reshuffle both of Attlee's committees were wound up. Although a punctilious chairman, Attlee had proved to be no heavyweight. Bridges, the Secretary to the Cabinet, informed Churchill in March 1941 that the Food Policy Committee, whose main function was to arbitrate on the quarrels between the Ministries of Food and Agriculture, was failing to do so, since Attlee was incapable of dominating powerful departments (see Bridges to Churchill, 10 March 1941, in PREM 4/6/9). The functions of Attlee's committees passed to the Lord President's Committee. It very much looks as though Attlee's new posts of deputy Prime Minister and Secretary for Dominions were designed to disguise the fact that the leader of the Labour Party had very little influence in the Government. Perhaps there was truth in the comment of the editor of *The Times*, Barrington-Ward, who wrote of Attlee after talking to him in March 1942: 'He is worthy, but limited. Incredible that he should be where he is. Impossible to discuss any matter of policy with him. He would be too unsure of himself, too doubtful about being given away.' (See Barrington-Ward diary, 8 March 1942.)

In a sense, then, Labour failed to rise to the opportunity which Churchill had offered in May 1940. He had hoped to delegate social and economic policy to Attlee and Greenwood: instead, it had passed into the capable hands of Sir John Anderson. Having been one of the most powerful of civil servants himself, Anderson had both the experience and the capacity to co-ordinate the Whitehall machine. But Labour also recovered from their initial setback, largely owing to the rise of Bevin and Morrison. Both men became powerful figures on the Lord President's Committee; and from the time the first important committee on reconstruction was set up in January 1943, they were the most influential voices in post-war planning. Finally, as though the wheel had turned full circle, Attlee himself became Lord President in September 1943. A civil servant who followed the work of the Lord President's Committee at close quarters has described to me how Attlee habitually remained silent when points arose on which he had been briefed to guide his colleagues. One weekend, however, Mrs Attlee complained to her husband that lettuces were becoming very expensive: on the following Monday, Attlee circulated a memorandum to the Committee about the need to stabilize the price of vegetables.

Notes

INTRODUCTION

1. *Report of the 39th annual conference of the Labour Party* 13–16 May 1940, 123.
2. J. E. D. Hall, *Labour's First Year* (Harmondsworth: Penguin, 1947), 1.
3. J. L. Hodson, *Home Front* (London: Gollancz, 1944), 255.
4. Arthur Marwick, 'Middle Opinion in the Thirties', in *English Historical Review* (April 1964), 285.
5. *New Statesman*, 28 January 1939, 123.
6. Francis Meynell, *My Lives* (London: Bodley Head, 1971), 269–70.
7. J. L. Hodson, *The Sea and the Land* (London: Gollancz, 1945), 238.

CHAPTER I. THE SUPREMACY OF 'SAFETY FIRST' 1922–1939

1. Ellen Wilkinson, *The Town that was Murdered* (London: Left Book Club, 1939), 211.
2. David Butler and Donald Stokes, *Political Change in Britain* (London: Macmillan, 1969), 109; G. D. H. and M. I. Cole, *The Condition of Britain* (London: Victor Gollancz, 1937), 394.
3. David Butler, 'Trends in British by-elections', in *Journal of Politics*, XI (1949), 396–407.
4. Patricia Strauss, *Cripps – Advocate and Rebel* (London: Gollancz, 1943), 196–203.
5. Percy Cohen, 'Disraeli's Child: A History of the Conservative and Unionist Party Organisation', Vol. II, 1924–1961, Unpublished MS, 570.
6. Derek H. Aldcroft, *The Inter-War Economy* (London: Batsford, 1970), 20. See also H. W. Richardson, *Economic Recovery in Britain 1932–1939* (London: Macmillan, 1967).
7. *The Elector*, October 1937, 4.
8. Quoted in Keith Middlemas and John Barnes, *Baldwin* (London: Weidenfeld & Nicolson, 1969), 506.

9. See, for example, Stanley Baldwin, *This Torch of Freedom* (London: Hodder and Stoughton 1935).

10. Middlemas and Barnes, *Baldwin*, 502–3.

11. *The Collected Writings of John Maynard Keynes: Vol. IX, Essays in Persuasion* (London: Macmillan, 1972), 299; *Time* Magazine, 13 November 1933. I am grateful to Mr Owen Dudley Edwards for the latter reference.

12. Keith Feiling, *The Life of Neville Chamberlain* (London: Macmillan, 1946), 132.

13. Bentley B. Gilbert, *British Social Policy 1918–1939* (London: Batsford, 1970), 196.

14. Sir Arthur Salter, *Personality in Politics* (London: The Right Book Club, 1947), 72.

15. The statistics are usefully set out in Gilbert, *British Social Policy*, 312–16.

16. Aldcroft, *The Inter-War Economy*, 85, 147.

17. See the illuminating study by Nigel Harris, *Competition and the Corporate Society*, (London: Methuen, 1972), 39–45.

18. Aldcroft, *The Inter-War Economy*, 102–3.

19. Cabinet 6 (38), 19 February 1938.

20. ED 136/131, Deliberations of the Board of Education on the Spens Report.

21. Quoted in Sidney Pollard, *The Gold Standard and Employment Policies* (London: Methuen, 1970), 23.

22. Quoted in Donald Winch, *Economics and Policy* (London: Fontana, 1972), 118.

23. Feiling, *Chamberlain*, 220.

24. *The Times*, 22 July 1935.

25. Kurt Samuelson, *From Great Power to Welfare State* (London: Allen & Unwin, 1968), 234–48; William Beveridge, *Full Employment in a Full Society* (London: Allen & Unwin 1960), 107.

26. Chamberlain to Simon, 6 October 1940, Simon Papers.

27. A. T. Peacock and J. Wiseman, *The Growth of Public Expenditure in the United Kingdom* (London: Allen & Unwin 1967), 184–5.

28. Brian Simon, *The Politics of Educational Reform 1920–1940* (London: Lawrence & Wishart, 1974), 288–9, 294.

29. James Stirling Ross, *The National Health Service in Great Britain* (London: Geoffrey Cumberledge and Oxford University Press, 1952), 53.

30. *New Statesman*, 28 January 1939, 122.

31. I derive this picture from the opening chapter of R. F. Harrod, *The Life of John Maynard Keynes* (London: Macmillan, 1951).

32. *The Collected Writings of John Maynard Keynes*, Vol IX, 258.

33. Ibid., 297.

34. Harrod, *Keynes*, 392–3.

35. J. M. Keynes, *The General Theory of Employment Interest and Money* (London: Macmillan, 1936), 379–80.

36. Arthur Marwick, 'Middle Opinion in the Thirties', *English Historical Review*, April 1964, 285–98.

37. Ibid., 297.

38. Kenneth Lindsay, 'Early Days of P.E.P.' in *Contemporary Review*, February 1973, 57–61; Israel Sieff, *Memoirs* (London: Weidenfeld & Nicolson, 1970), 164–75; P.E.P. circular June 1942, in the P.E.P. archive.

39. *The Next Five Years: An Essay in Political Agreement* (London: Macmillan, 1935).

40. Mary Stocks, *Eleanor Rathbone* (London: Gollancz, 1949), ch. 8; and see the introduction by Eva Hubback, and epilogue by William Beveridge, to Eleanor Rathbone, *Family Allowances* (London: Allen & Unwin, 1949).

41. Sir John Boyd Orr, *Food, Health and Income* (London: Macmillan, 1937).

42. Simon, *The Politics of Educational Reform*, 125–37.

43. Ibid., 217–24, 257–70.

44. The B.M.A. produced two major policy statements, in 1930 and 1938. See Harry Eckstein, *The English Health Service* (Harvard University Press, 1964), 116–17.

45. Gladys Keable, *Tomorrow Slowly Comes* (Town and Country Planning Association, 1963), 6; J. B. Cullingworth, *Town and Country Planning in Britain* (London: Allen & Unwin, 1972), 25–8.

46. Osborn to Mumford 17 Oct 1941 in *The Letters of Lewis Mumford and Frederic J. Osborn* (Bath: Adams & Dart, 1971), 17.

47. Gladys Keable, *Tomorrow Slowly Comes*, 6; Cullingworth, *Town and Country Planning in Britain*, 25–8.

48. The best account of Macmillan in the 1930s is in Anthony Sampson *Macmillan* (London: Allen Lane, 1967), ch. 3.

49. Alan Bullock, *The Life and Times of Ernest Bevin* Vol. 1 (London: Heinemann, 1960), 371.

50. Robert Skidelsky, *Politicians and the Slump* (London: Macmillan, 1967), xii.

51. Pollard, *The Gold Standard and Employment Policies*, 147.

52. A. J. P. Taylor, *English History* (Oxford: Clarendon Press, 1965), 142 fn 3.

53. Henry Pelling, *A Short History of the Labour Party* (London: Macmillan, 1968), 77.

54. G. D. H. Cole, *The People's Front* (London: Gollancz, 1937), 293.

55. Quoted in W. Golant, 'The Emergence of C. R. Attlee as leader of the Parliamentary Labour Party in 1935', in *Historical Journal* XIII (1970), 320.

56. Winch, *Economics and Policy*, 350–60; A. L. Rowse, *Mr Keynes and the Labour Movement* (London: Macmillan, 1936).

57. Michael Foot, *Aneurin Bevan, Vol II: 1945–1960* (London: Davis-Poynter, 1973), 288.

58. Bernard Donoughue and G. W. Jones, *Herbert Morrison* (London: Weidenfeld & Nicolson, 1973), 178.

59. Labour Party, *Labour's Immediate Programme*, 1937.

60. Hugh Dalton, *The Fateful Years* (London: Frederick Muller, 1957), 200.

CHAPTER II. LABOUR AT THE GATES 1939–1940

1. I have drawn these figures from an analysis of the division in an unpublished paper, 'Chamberlain and the Conservative Party 1937–1940'; and see pp. 97–8.

2. PREM 1/238, Air Ministry memo of July 1938.

3. PREM 1/251, Memos by Sir Horace Wilson of 21 March, 28 March, 5 May, 30 May 1938.

4. PREM 1/264, Memo of 23 September by C.G.L.S. to Oliver Harvey.

5. Diary of Collin Brooks 5 October 1938.

6. R. S. Sayers, *Financial Policy 1939–1945* (London: H.M.S.O., 1956), 28–30.

7. *Report of the 38th annual conference of the Labour Party* 29 May to 2 June 1939, 243.

8. Mass-Observation, *War Begins at Home* (Harmondsworth: Penguin Book, 1940), 134.

9. Herbert Tracey, *Trade Unions Fight – for What?* (London: Labour Book Service, 1940), 133–7, 153–62.

10. *Agenda for the 39th annual conference of the Labour Party*, 10–19; Middleton to Attlee 15 March 1940, Attlee Papers (University College), Box 7.

11. *Daily Herald*, 10 January, 30 March, 1940.

12. CAB 89/26, Rowntree to Bevin 12 December 1939; Bevin to Rowntree 29 December 1939, Keynes to Stamp 12 January 1940.

13. H. M. D. Parker, *Manpower* (London: H.M.S.O., 1957), 62–3, 67–8; P. Inman, *Labour in the Munitions Industries* (London: H.M.S.O., 1957). 40; Winston S. Churchill, *The Second World War*, Vol. I: *The Gathering Storm* (London: Cassell, 1948), 439–40.

14. Dalton Diary 2,.3, 9 September 1939.

15. *Manchester Guardian*, 21 April 1940.

16. John Harvey (ed.), *The Diplomatic Diaries of Oliver Harvey 1937–1940* (London: Collins, 1970), 340; *Manchester Guardian*, 28 March 1940.

17. Keith Middlemas, *Diplomacy of Illusion* (London: Weidenfeld & Nicolson, 1972), 56; Diary of Sir John Simon 9 May 1940, Simon Papers.

18. Margesson to Baldwin 4 March 1941, Margesson Papers; *Clem Attlee: the Granada Historical Records Interview* (Panther Record, 1967), 17.

19. Bernard Donoughue and G. W. Jones, Herbert *Morrison* (London: Weidenfeld & Nicolson, 1973), 268–9.

20. 'Politicus', 'Labour and the War', in *Political Quarterly* X (1939), 480–83.

21. Sinclair to H. A. L. Fisher (n.d.), Gilbert Murray Papers.

22. Diary of Viscount Crookshank 29 December 1939.

23. Winston S. Churchill, *The End of the Beginning* (London: Cassell, 1943), 86; speech of 26 March 1942 to Central Council of the Conservative Party.

24. For Chamberlain's confidence that the war would peter out, see Paul Addison, 'Political Change in Britain September 1939 to December 1940', Oxford Ph.D. thesis 1971, 86–91, 306–8: Keith Feiling, *The Life of Neville Chamberlain* (London: Macmillan, 1946), 425–6.

25. Anthony Eden, *The Eden Memoirs: The Reckoning* (London: Cassell, 1965), 73.

26. J. C. W. Reith, *Into the Wind* (London: Hodder & Stoughton, 1949), 352–3, 373.

27. I am grateful to Mr Ian MacLaine, of Balliol College, Oxford, for allowing me at this point to draw upon his unpublished paper, 'The Work and Archives of the Ministry of Information'.

28. *K-H Newsletter* No. 173, 3 November 1939, Bordon, Hants.

29. Nancy Astor to Lothian 23 November 1939, Lothian Papers MSS GD/40/17/407.

30. Hoare to Beaverbrook 15 February 1943, Beaverbrook Papers Bbk C/308.

31. Nigel Nicolson (ed.), *Harold Nicolson: Diaries and Letters 1939–1945* (London: Collins, 1967), 38; Dawson Diary 5 February 1940, Dawson Papers.

32. J. W. Wheeler-Bennett, *John Anderson, Viscount Waverley* (London: Macmillan, 1962), 233; *The Times*, 7 December 1939, 5.

33. PREM 1/359, Stanley to Chamberlain 5 December 1939.

34. This account, based partly on the Papers of Eleanor Rathbone at the University of Liverpool, is from Addison, *Political Change*, 384–93.

35. *The Times*, 16 December 1939.

36. James to Simon 5 March 1940, Simon Papers.

37. *News Review*, 25 January 1940, 10.

38. J. Harry Jones, *Josiah Stamp, Public Servant* (London: Pitman & Sons, 1964), 337–8.

39. *The Times*, 6 January 1940.

40. *Manchester Guardian*, 19 January; *The Times*, 2 February; *Daily Telegraph*, 2 February 1940.

41. Hoare to Lothian 13 February 1940, Templewood Papers XI/5.

42. HC Debs. Vol. 356, 1 February 1940, col. 1336.

43. Diary of L. S. Amery 13 December 1939.

44. Nicolson: *Diaries and Letters*, 56; Unpublished Nicolson Diary, 20 December 1939.

45. CAB 39 (40), 12 February 1940; Halifax to Chamberlain 10 February 1940 and Noel-Baker to Halifax 17 February 1940, F.O. 800/310, Halifax Papers.

46. Diary of Viscount Crookshank 2 April 1940.

47. I am grateful to the secretary of the Committee, the late Paul Emrys-Evans, for correspondence on the subject. See also C. R. Attlee, *As It Happened* (London: Heinemann, 1954), III.

48. Nicolson, *Diaries and Letters*, 57.

49. PREM 1/418, Brocket to P.M. 27 January 1940.

50. Neville to Hilda Chamberlain 17 September 1939, Chamberlain Papers. H. C. Dent, *Education in Transition* (London: Kegan Paul, Trench, Trubner, 1944), 1–31, has a remarkable account of evacuation.

51. HC Debs. Vol. 355, 5 December 1939 col. 515.

52. Anthony Eden, *Freedom and Order* (London: Faber, 1946), 48; Barrington-Ward Diary 12 February 1940.

53. Boothby to Lloyd George enclosing a memo on war aims (from which the quotation is taken) 7 November 1939, Lloyd George Papers LG G/3/13.

54. HC Debs. Vol. 355, 5 December 1939, col. 499; 6 December, col. 741.

55. *Labour's Aims in War and Peace* (New York: Lincolns-Praeger, 1940), 144.

56. *Foreign Relations of the United States* 1940 Vol. I, U.S. Government Printing Office, Washington, 1959, 81.

57. R. F. Harrod, *The Life of John Maynard Keynes* (London: Macmillan, 1951), 489–94.

CHAPTER III. CHURCHILL'S BREAKTHROUGH 1939–1940

1. Peter de Mendelssohn, *The Age of Churchill* (London: Thames & Hudson, 1961), 495–7.

2. *The Record*, December 1938, 128; *Report of the 38th annual conference of the Labour Party* 29 May to 2 June 1939, 330; L. S. Amery, *My Political Life, Vol. III*: (London: Hutchinson, 1955), 371.

3. Fraser to Dalton 20 October 1938, Dalton Papers.

4. Lord Citrine, *Two Careers* (London: Hutchinson, 1967), 16.

5. Eugen Spier, *Focus* (London: Oswald Wolff, 1963); *New Statesman*, 7 January 1939.

6. Cartland, quoted in Neville Thompson, *The Anti-Appeasers* (Oxford: Clarendon Press, 1971), 171; Hadley Cantril, *Public Opinion 1939–1946* (Princeton University Press, 1951), 106.

7. Hoare to William Astor 11 July 1939, Templewood Papers X/4.

8. Cantril, *Public Opinion*, 96–7.

9. Nigel Nicolson (ed.), *Harold Nicolson: Diaries and Letters 1939–1945* (London: Collins, 1967), 37.

10. Hamilton Fyfe, *Britain's Wartime Revolution* (London: Gollancz, 1944), 15, 17; *Daily Herald*, 4 October 1939; *Daily Mirror*, 3 October 1939; *Sunday Pictorial*, 1 October 1939.

11. Mass-Observation, *Us* No. 6, 9 March 1940, 44.

12. 'The Naval Memoirs of Admiral J. H. Godfrey' (unpublished) GD 1/6 Vol. V, 35–6, 62–4.

13. Donald MacClachlan, *Room 39* (London: Weidenfeld & Nicolson, 1968), 127–33.

14. Barrington-Ward Diary 8 February 1940.

15. *News Chronicle*, 1 January 1940.

16. Mass-Observation, *Us*, 9 March 1940, 48; 3 February, 4; Cecil H.

King, *With Malice Toward None* (London: Sidgwick & Jackson, 1970, 22.

17. *Us*, 9 March 1940, 44.

18. Addison, 'Political Change in Britain September 1939 to December 1940', Oxford Ph.D. thesis 1971, 325.

19. Winston S. Churchill, *The Second World War, Vol. I: The Gathering Storm* (London: Cassell, 1948), 355, 359–60, 361.

20. Addison 'Political Change', 87–9.

21. Boothby to Lloyd George 18 September 1939, Lloyd George Papers G/2/13.

22. Roy Harrod, *The Prof* (London: Macmillan, 1969), 180, 187–8; CAB 86 (39), 17 November 1939.

23. CAB 39 (38), 5 October 1939.

24. Charles Eade (ed.), *The War Speeches of the Rt. Hon. Winston S. Churchill* Vol. I (London: Cassell, 1951), 119; Ivan Maisky, *Memoirs of a Soviet Ambassador: The War 1939–1943* (London: Hutchinson, 1967), 31–4.

25. Eade, *War Speeches of Churchill*, 119.

26. *Documents on German Foreign Policy 1918–1945*, Series D, Vol. VIII, No. 375 (London: H.M.S.O., 1957).

27. HC Debs. Vol. 352, 12 October 1939, col. 568.

28. *Foreign Relations of the United States* 1940, Vol. I. 84.

29. CAB 58 (39), 24 October 1939; John Harvey (ed.), *The Diplomatic Diaries of Oliver Harvey 1937–1940* (London: Collins, 1970), 326.

30. CAB 30 (40), 2 February 1940.

31. Eade, *War Speeches of Churchill*, 137.

32. F.O. 800/322, Churchill to Halifax 26 January 1940

33 The Diary of Sir Thomas Inskip, Churchill College, Cambridge, 10 November 1939; J. R. M. Butler, *Grand Strategy Vol. II* (London: H.M.S.O., 1957), 78.

34. Arthur Marder, 'Winston Is Back' in *English Historical Review* Supplement 5 (London: Longman, 1972), 5.

35. Ibid., 31–7.

36. Basil Liddell Hart, 'Churchill in War', in *Encounter*, April 1966, 17.

37. Paul Reynard, *Mémoires*, Vol. II (Paris: Flammarion, 1963), 316.

38. R. Macleod and D. Kelly (eds.), *The Ironside Diaries 1937–1940* (London: Constable, 1962), 234.

39. Macleod and Kelly, *Ironside Diaries*, 237.

40. Addison, 'Political Change', 307.

41. *Manchester Guardian*, 5 April 1940.

42. Inskip Diary 9 April 1940.
43. *The Times*, 6 October 1939.
44. Lord Chatfield, *It Might Happen Again* (London: Heinemann, 1947), 179–82.
45. Templewood Papers XI/2, under the heading 1 January; Hickleton Papers, Diary of Lord Halifax 18 March 1940.
46. Sir John Wheeler-Bennett (ed.), *Action this Day* (London: Macmillan, 1968), 48.
47. Macleod and Kelly, *Ironside Diaries*, 260.
48. PREM 1/404, Memo by Bridges 25 April 1940; Memo by Wilson 17 April 1940.
49. PREM 1/404, Memo by Wilson 25 April 1940.
50. Churchill, *The Gathering Storm*, 505.
51. John Evelyn Wrench, *Geoffrey Dawson and our Times* (London: Hutchinson, 1955), 409.
52. For the new arrangement, *The Memoirs of General the Lord Ismay* (London: Heinemann, 1960), 113–14.
53. Robert Rhodes James (ed.), *Chips* (London: Weidenfeld & Nicolson, 1967), 244.
54. Wheeler-Bennett, *Action This Day*, 46–7.
55. Simon Diary, 8 May 1940.
56. Note dated April 1940, Templewood Papers XII/3.
57. Interview with Lord Reith 11 July 1968.
58. Rhodes James, *Chips*, 242.
59. Nicolson, *Diaries and Letters*, 74–5; R. H. Bruce Lockhart, *Comes the Reckoning* (New York: Putnam, 1947), 83; Sir Edward Spears, *Assignment to Catastrophe, Vol. I: Prelude to Dunkirk* (London: Heinemann, 1954), 112.
60. Percy Harris, *Forty Years in and out of Parliament* (London: Andrew Melrose, 1947), 149.
61. *The Times*, 4 May 1940; Amery, *My Political Life*, Vol. III, 358; Harold Macmillan, *The Blast of War 1939–1945* (London: Macmillan, 1967), 66.
62. HC Debs. Vol. 360, 7 May 1940, col. 1084.
63. Ibid., cols. 1086–94.
64. Ibid., cols. 1094–1106; Sinclair to Cecil 8 May 1940, Cecil of Chelwood Papers, Bm Add. MSS, 51185 f217.
65. Nicolson, *Diaries and Letters*, 77.
66. HC Debs Vol. 360, 7 May 1940, cols. 1140–50.
67. Amery Diary 7 May 1940.

68. Sinclair to Cecil, Cecil of Chelwood Papers.

69. C. R. Attlee, *As It Happened* (London: Heinemann, 1954), 112; Herbert Morrison, *Autobiography* (London: Odhams, 1960), 172–3; Hugh Dalton, *Memoirs 1931–1945: The Fateful Years* (London: Muller, 1957), 305 (I have checked this against the entry in his diary for 8 May); Francis Williams, *A Prime Minister Remembers* (London: Heinemann, 1961), 30; Bernard Donoughue and G. W. Jones, *Herbert Morrison* (London: Weidenfeld & Nicolson, 1973). 271–2; interview with Lord Attlee 31 January 1967; Ian Angus and Sonia Orwell (eds.), *The Collected Essays, Journalism and Letters of George Orwell* Vol. II (London: Penguin, 1970), 399.

70. Nicolson, *Diaries and Letters*, 77–8.

71. Notes passed to Lloyd George in the debate of 8 May 1940, Lloyd George Papers G/189.

72. For Lloyd George's speech, HC Debs. Vol. 360, 8 May 1940, cols. 1277–85.

73. I am grateful to Lord Boothby, and to the late Paul Emrys-Evans, who was secretary of the Watching Committee, for correspondence which clarifies Harold Nicolson's description of the meeting of the backbench rebels.

74. Addison, 'Political Change', 449–53; Jorgen S. Rasmussen, 'Party Discipline in War-Time: the Downfall of the Chamberlain Government', in *Journal of Politics*, 32 (1970), 385. Mr Rasmussen would even guess the figure for abstentions to be as low as 36.

75. Classification of this kind is arbitrary, but based on considerable checking of the record of the M.P.s concerned. I would classify as the 'anti-appeasement' element: Amery, Boothby, Bower, Duff Cooper, Duggan, Emrys-Evans, Gunston, Kerr, Keyes, King-Hall, Law, Macmillan, Macnamara, Molson, Nicolson, Patrick, Spears, Tree and Wolmer; and as the 'services' element: Anstruther-Gray, De Chair, Hogg, Keeling, Medlicott, Profumo, Russell, Taylor, Wise and Wright.

76. Churchill, *The Gathering Storm*, 522; Simon Diary 9 May 1940.

77. Amery, *My Political Life*, 370–71; Nicolson, *Diaries and Letters*, 81.

78. Hannon to Chamberlain 9 May 1940, Hannon Papers; Laurence Thompson, *1940* (London: Collins, 1966), 86.

79. Williams, *A Prime Minister Remembers*, 32–3, Williams dates 9 May as 10 May and 10 May as 11 May.

80. A. J. P. Taylor, *Beaverbrook* (London: Hamish Hamilton, 1972), 410.

81. Labour Party NEC Minutes, E.C. 16 1939–40, 10 May 1940.

82. Churchill, *The Gathering Storm*, 523.

83. Beaverbrook to Margesson 21 November 1963 and reply of 27 November, Beaverbrook Papers Bbk C/240.

84. Churchill, *The Gathering Storm*, 523–4; Lord Moran, *Winston Churchill: The Struggle for Survival 1940–1965* (London: Constable, 1966), 323.

85. Unclassified file in the Beaverbrook Papers entitled, 'Fall of Chamberlain and rise of Churchill'.

86. Donoughue and Jones, *Herbert Morrison*, 275; *Manchester Guardian*, 7 May 1940; Cripps to Lloyd George 5 May 1940, Lloyd George Papers G/5/6; *Daily Mail*, 6 May 1940.

87. *The Times*, 9 May 1940; Spears, *Assignment*, 125; Macmillan, *Blast of War*, 67; Dalton Diary 2 May 1940; *News Chronicle*, 7 May 1940 (Layton wrote as 'John Bouverie').

88. Moran, *Churchill*, 323; Taylor, *Beaverbrook*, 409.

89. Colin Coote, *Editorial* (London: Eyre & Spottiswoode, 1965), 203–4; Anthony Eden, *The Eden Memoirs: The Reckoning* (London: Cassell, 1965), 96–7.

90. Beaverbrook Papers World War II Box, 'Italy to Reader's Digest'. Wood died in October 1943. Beaverbrook often filed notes for his future historical writing, and this is likely to be the record of a talk he himself had with Wood.

91. Interview with Sir Horace Wilson 4 April 1967.

CHAPTER IV. NEW DEAL AT DUNKIRK

1. David Farrer, *G- For God Almighty* (London: Weidenfeld & Nicolson, 1969), 37. Farrer does not state that Hankey was the author of this letter: he was.

2. Anthony Eden, *The Eden Memoirs: The Reckoning* (London: Cassell, 1965), 107.

3. Ian Angus and Sonia Orwell (eds.), *The Collected Essays, Journals and Letters of George Orwell*, Vol. II (Harmondsworth: Penguin, 1970), 400.

4. Nigel Nicolson (ed.), *Harold Nicolson: Diaries and Letters 1939–1945* (London: Collins, 1967), 106.

5. Lord Robbins, *Autobiography of an Economist* (London: Macmillan, 1971), 173.

6. E. L. Woodward. *British Foreign Policy in the Second World War* Vol. I (London: H.M.S.O., 1970), 197–206.

7. Percy Harris, *Forty Years in and out of Parliament* (London: Andrew Melrose, 1947), 150–52, 12–15.

8. Tom Jones, *Lloyd George* (Oxford: University Press, 1951), 464–5.

9. Unpublished Memoirs of General Mason-MacFarlane.

10. Nicolson, unpublished Diary, 27 May 1940; Angus and Orwell, *Orwell*, Vol. II, 387; information from Mrs MacFarlane Hall.

11. INF 1/264, Report of Home Intelligence 3 June 1940.

12. *Tribune*, 7 June 1940, 12–13.

13. *Daily Mirror*, 6 June 1940; *Daily Herald*, 5 June 1940.

14. Garvin to Simon 10 June 1940, Simon Papers.

15. Earl of Birkenhead, *Halifax* (London: Hamish Hamilton, 1965), 458; Cecil King, *With Malice Toward None* (London: Sidgwick & Jackson, 1970), 47. Churchill promised King that efforts would be made to ease out Chamberlain on grounds of ill-health.

16. Minute by Sylvester 9 June 1940, Lloyd George Papers G/24; Addison, 'Political Change in Britain September 1939 to December 1940', Oxford Ph.D. thesis 1971, 483.

17. Copy of Boothby to Churchill 19 June 1940 in Lloyd George Papers G/3/13. See also R. Boothby, *My Yesterday, Your Tomorrow* (London: Hutchinson, 1962), 74.

18. Diary of L. S. Amery 17 and 18 June 1940, in the possession of the Rt. Hon. Julian Amery M.P.

19. Winston S. Churchill, *Into Battle* (London: Cassell, 1941), 226.

20. Minute by Sylvester 3 July 1940, Lloyd George Papers G/24.

21. A. J. P. Taylor, *Beaverbrook* (London: Hamish Hamilton, 1972), 435; Beaverbrook to Hoare, 6 July 1940, Templewood Papers.

22. Tom Harrisson, 'Should Leaders Lead?' in *New Statesman*, 13 July 1940, 36; *News Chronicle* 8 July 1940.

23. Minutes by Sylvester 8 and 15 July 1940, Lloyd George Papers G/24; *News Chronicle*, 3 July 1940; *Manchester Guardian*, 17 July 1940; Hamilton Fyfe, *Britain's Wartime Revolution* (London: Gollancz, 1944), 83.

24. Waldorf Astor to Carolyn Martin 28 May 1940, Waldorf Astor MSS, Box XI.

25. Headlam Diary 1 July 1940.

26. See below, Ch. 5.

27. Chamberlain to Hoare 15 July 1940, quoted in Henry Pelling, *Britain and the Second World War* (London: Fontana, 1970), 91.

28. Dalton Diary 18 May, 8 June, 9–16 July 1940.

29. Bullock, *The Life and Times of Ernest Bevin*, Vol. II (London: Heinemann, 1967), 12–15.

30. Diary of Viscount Crookshank 22 May 1940, Bodleian Library, Oxford.

31. Ernest Bevin, *The Job to be Done* (London: Heinemann, 1942), 26.

32. Lord Citrine, *Two Careers* (London: Hutchinson, 1967), 50.

33. Diary of Euan Wallace 3 July 1940, Bodleian Library, Oxford.

34. Diary of Sir Cuthbert Headlam 21 July 1940.

35. *New Statesman*, 1 June 1940, 692.

36. R. S. Sayers, *Financial Policy 1939–1945* (London: H.M.S.O., 1956), 46.

37. W. K. Hancock and M. M. Gowing, *British War Economy* (London: H.M.S.O., 1949), 94.

38. R. M. Titmuss. *Problems of Social Policy* (London: H.M.S.O., 1950), 508–11.

39. D. N. Chester, 'The Central Machinery for Economic Policy', in D. N. Chester (ed.), *Lessons of the British War Economy* (Cambridge University Press, 1951), 7; Robbins, *Autobiography*, 170.

40. R. F. Harrod, *The Life of John Maynard Keynes* (London: Macmillan, 1951), 498.

41. Diary of Beatrice Webb 11 August 1940.

42. Asa Briggs, *The History of Broadcasting in the United Kingdom, Vol. III: The War of Words* (Oxford University Press, 1970), 210; R. J. E. Silvey, 'Some Recent Trends in Listening', in *BBC Year Book 1946*, 28.

43. J. B. Priestley, *Postscripts* (London: Heinemann, 1940), 38.

44. Unpublished diaries of Harold Nicolson 9 August and 19 September 1940.

45. *Spectator*, 13 December 1940.

46. *Daily Herald*, 31 May 1940; Dalton Diary 16 August 1940.

47. PRO INF 1/862. I wish to express my gratitude to Dr Ian MacLaine, of Balliol College, Oxford, for drawing my attention to this and certain other material relating to reconstruction in the archives of the Ministry of Information.

48. Barrington-Ward Diary 31 July 1940. I am grateful to Mr Gordon Phillips, archivist of *The Times*, for identifying the authorship of 'The New Europe'. E. H. Carr developed his ideas to their logical conclusion in *Conditions of the Peace* (London: Macmillan, 1942), which argued the classic doctrine of the Left at the time: the idea that the profit motive, the basis of the liberal state, had broken down, and

would have to be replaced by purposive central planning sustained by a new social faith.

49. As I mention below, morale *was* intelligently defined and analysed by Dr Stephen Taylor, the head of Home Intelligence, in a paper of September 1941.

50. INF 1/849, Minutes of the home policy committee 18 June 1940; Nicolson, *Diaries and Letters*, 99–101; INF 1/862, Memo by Nicolson 17 July 1940.

51. INF 1/862 Halifax to Duff Cooper 30 July 1940, 9 August 1940.

52. CAB 233 (40), 23 August 1940.

53. Presumably in pursuance of Keynes's proposal in *How to Pay for the War* (London: Macmillan, 1940).

54. W. A. (40) 6, Memo by Toynbee circulated 22 October 1940.

55. Bullock, *Bevin*, Vol. II, 37.

56. *Manchester Guardian*, 3 October 1940.

57. Londonderry to Halifax 23 November 1940, Hickleton MSS A 4 410 28.

58. Priestley *Postscripts*, 98 (20 October).

59. Michael Foot, *Aneurin Bevan*, Vol. I (London: MacGibbon & Kee, 1962), 322.

60. W. A. (40), Meetings 1 to 4, 4 October to 13 December 1940; INF 1/862, Duff Cooper to Attlee 4 December 1940; PREM 4/100/4.

61. Winston S. Churchill, *The Unrelenting Struggle* (London: Cassell, 1943), 17.

62. *Tribune*, 4 October 1940.

CHAPTER V. TWO CHEERS FOR SOCIALISM 1940–1942

1. Mass-Observation, 'Social Security and Parliament' in *Political Quarterly* (XIV) 1943, 246.

2. Winston S. Churchill, *The End of the Beginning* (London: Cassell, 1943), 86, speech of 26 March 1942.

3. *The Onlooker*, August 1945, 3.

4. Mass-Observation file report No. 2545, 'Penguin World', 43.

5. Pollard, *Development of the British Economy 1914–1950* (London: Edward Arnold, 1962), 344–5.

6. I have taken these figures from Angus Calder, *The People's War*, (London: Jonathan Cape, 1969), 193, 224, 315; and W. K. Hancock and M. M. Gowing, *British War Economy* (London: H.M.S.O., 1949), 351.

7. Quoted in Nicholas Davenport, *Vested Interests or Common Pool?* London: Gollancz, 1942), 30.

8. Ibid., 26.

9. I derive this interpretation from W. G. Runciman, *Relative Deprivation and Social Justice* (London: Routledge & Kegan Paul, 1966), ch. 4.

10. Hancock and Gowing, *British War Economy*, 506.

11. *Low's Autobiography* (London: Michael Joseph, 1956), 265–75; PREM 4/14/5, Minute by Churchill of 10 September 1942, and accompanying items; Jeffrey Richards, *Visions of Yesterday* (London: Routledge & Kegan Paul, 1973), 165.

12. Viscount Astor Papers, Box II, *Picture Post* correspondence; Nancy Astor Papers, Box labelled 'Political Files 1938–1945' for this and related matter.

13. *The Onlooker*, February 1942, 3; September 1943, 7.

14. INF 1/292, Home Intelligence weekly report No. 70 for 26 January to 2 February 1942.

15. Briggs, *History of Broadcasting in the United Kingdom Vol. III*, 389–91.

16. F.O. 371/29602, Minute by Harvey of 11 July 1941: F.O. 371/32960, Note from Eden to Churchill 20 January 1942 and Note from Martin to Harvey 21 January 1942; Asa Briggs *History of Broadcasting in the United Kingdom, Vol. III*, 393–4.

17. INF 1/849, Home Policy Committee 4 September 1941; I am extremely grateful to Mr Ian MacLaine of Balliol College Oxford for allowing me to quote the minute by R. H. Parker from Mr MacLaine's unpublished paper 'The Work and Archives of the Ministry of Information'.

18. F.O. 371/29523, Ministry of Information home division directive of October 1941.

19. MacLaine, unpublished paper.

20. PREM 4/21/3, Sargent to Bridges 20 November 1941.

21. PREM 42/1/3, Eden to Churchill 22 August 1941.

22. Lord Citrine, *Two Careers* (London: Hutchinson, 1967), 116–24; INF 1/292, Home Intelligence weekly report No. 70 for 26 January to 2 February 1942, Appendix I.

23. PREM 4/14/13, Sinclair to Churchill 13 January 1943; T. S. Eliot, quoted in Henry Pelling, *Britain and the Second World War* (London: Fontana, 1970), 306.

24. A. J. P. Taylor, *Beaverbrook* (London: Hamish Hamilton, 1972), 528.

25. Leonard Barnes, *Soviet Light on the Colonies* (Harmondsworth: Penguin, 1944),

26. Victor Gollancz (ed.), *The Betrayal of the Left* (London: Gollancz, 1941). This included essays by Laski, Strachey, and Orwell; *Left News*, October 1941, 1874.

27. Details of the meeting found in a Mass-Observation box of unpublished materials entitled 'Public Meetings'.

28. Ibid.

29. Ibid.

30. F.O. 371/29634.

31. Calder, *The People's War*, 297–302; Taylor, *Beaverbrook*, 535–6.

32. F.O. 371/36973, Bracken to Eden 6 January 1943, and accompanying material.

33. W. P. (44) 80, Memo by Bracken of 4 February 1944.

34. *Public Opinion Quarterly*, iv (1940), 79; Ian Angus and Sonia Orwell (eds.), *The Collected Essays, Journalism and Letters of George Orwell*, Vol. II (Harmondsworth: Penguin, 1970), 174.

35. Henry Pelling, *The British Communist Party* (London: Adam & Charles Black, 1958), 104, 120–29.

36. INF 1/292, Home Intelligence weekly report No. 58, 3–10 November 1941.

37. Beaverbrook Papers. Report of conference of Conservative candidates found in 'Bretton Woods to Czechoslovakia' box in World War II series.

38. NEC Memoranda on 'Platform Propaganda', 28 January 1942, and 'Condition of the Party', 25 March 1942.

39. NEC Minutes 9 April 1942; and 'Report on Women in the Labour Party May 1942 to April 1943' in NEC Minutes Vol 88.

40. G. D. H. Cole, *History of the Labour Party since 1914* (London: Routledge & Kegan Paul, 1948), 480.

41. Bullock, *The Life and Times of Ernest Bevin*, Vol. II (London: Heinemann, 1967), 276.

42. NEC Memo on 'Platform Propaganda'; NEC Minutes 9 April 1942.

43. NEC Minutes 28 July 1943.

44. Angus and Orwell, *Orwell*, Vol. II, 381.

45. Roger Manvell, *Film* (Harmondsworth: Penguin 1946), 114–18.

46. *Daily Herald*, 13 March 1941.

47. Asa Briggs, *History of Broadcasting in the United Kingdom*, Vol. III, 321–2.

48. Ibid., 318, 560–64. The first edition of the 'Brains Trust' was broadcast under the title 'Any Questions?' on 1 January 1941.

49. Croft to Stuart 13 April 1942, Croft Papers 1/19, Churchill College, Cambridge.

50. A. T. C. White. *The Story of Army Education* (London: Harrap, 1963), 85–90.

51. Memo by Croft of 12 August 1940, Croft Papers 2/6.

52. White, *Army Education*, 101.

53. Kingsley Martin, *Harold Laski* (London: Jonathan Cape, 1969), 124–5.

54. Petherick to Watt 23 December 1942, PREM 4/14/13.

55. PREM 4/14/13.

56. In 1943 both Wigg and Hall joined Common Wealth. At the Aston by-election of June 1943 Wigg was to be candidate but stood down in favour of Hall.

57. Memo by Croft 8 January 1943, Croft Papers.

58. Winston S. Churchill, *The Grand Alliance* (London: Cassell, 1950), 739; Margesson to Churchill 8 October 1941; Bracken to Churchill 15 October 1941, PREM 4/6/2.

59. ABCA Report found in PREM 4/6/2.

60. Duff Cooper, *Old Men Forget* (London: Rupert Hart-Davies, 1953), 359.

61. Undated memo by Page Croft, Page Croft papers.

62. *The Times*, 22 September 1942.

63. *News Chronicle*, 23 June 1942.

64. Churchill to Grigg 30 April 1943; Anderson to Churchill 30 July 1943, PREM 4/6/2.

65. J. L. Hodson, *The Sea and the Land* (London: Gollancz, 1945), 349.

66. Cmd 7700 *Royal Commission on the Press 1947–9: Report*, 190.

67. The *Mirror* changed sides. I have classified *The Times, Telegraph, Daily Express, Daily Mail* and *Daily Sketch* as 'Right', and the *Daily Herald,* and *News Chronicle* as 'Left.' In fact *The Times*, with its 2 per cent of readers, became leftish during the war. I have taken the percentages from the Royal Commission *Report*, page 190. Even there, they do not quite add up to 100 per cent.

68. *News Chronicle*, 4 April 1934.

69. I am grateful to Mr John Grigg for showing me the relevant papers

of his father, Sir Edward Grigg, one of the members of the tribunal which arbitrated between the editor and proprietor of the *Observer*; and for discussing the point with me.

70. Interview with Sir Allen Lane 26 July 1965.

71. On Billing, Mass-Observation file report No. 725 (Hornsey) and 905 (the Wrekin).

72. On Hipwell and Henney, *Scarborough Evening News*, 23 September 1941, 3; Mass-Observation file reports numbers 725 (Scarborough), and 1014 (Harrow).

73. For Kendall see *The Times*, 4, 23, 24 March 1942; *Picture Post*, 18 April 1942, 6; *Lincolnshire Echo*; and Mass-Observation's boxed material. I am very grateful to Dr Owen Hartley for a mass of useful information about the constituency.

74. For Brown, W. J. Brown, *So Far* (London: Allen & Unwin, 1943); *Birmingham Post*, 15 April 1942, 4.

75. G. L. Reakes, *Man of the Mersey* (London: Christopher Johnson, 1956), 83; apart from Reakes, see on Wallasey, *The Times*, and *Wallasey News* of 4 to 25 April 1942.

76. Bernard Dixon (ed.), *Journeys in Belief* (London: Allen & Unwin, 1968), 15–17; Angus Calder, 'The Common Wealth Party 1942–1945', unpublished Ph.D. thesis, Sussex University 1968, Vol. I, 80–88.

77. Calder, 'The Common Wealth Party', Vol. I, 90–91.

78. Information from Mr A. J. P. Taylor; Tom Driberg, *The Best of Both Worlds* (London: Phoenix House, 1958), 181–5.

79. My understanding of Common Wealth derives entirely from Dr Calder's dissertation, already cited. For Moeran's slogan, see Calder 'The Common Wealth Party', Vol. I, 166. I am grateful also to the present secretary of Common Wealth for permission to read through the wartime minutes and papers of the party.

80. Winston S. Churchill, *The Second World War Vol. IV: The Hinge of Fate* (London: Cassell, 1951), 756, Minute to Cherwell of 10 March 1942.

81. INF 1/292, Home Intelligence weekly report No. 77, 16–23 March 1942.

82. Ibid.

83. Wartime Social Survey Report on Food Schemes, 1942. I am grateful to the Director of the Government Social Survey, Mr Louis Moss, for giving me access to wartime reports and for discussing the role of the Social Survey with me.

84. INF 1/292, Home Intelligence weekly report No. 15, 8–15 January 1941.
85. J. B. Priestley, *Here are your Answers* (London: Common Wealth, 1943), 1.
86. Tom Harrisson, 'Who'll Win?', in *Political Quarterly*, XV (1944), 27.
87. INF 1/292, Appendix to the Home Intelligence weekly report for 24 March 1942.

CHAPTER VI. BLUEPRINTS FROM ABOVE 1940–1942

1. Winston S. Churchill, *The Unrelenting Struggle* (London: Cassell, 1943), 85.
2. *News Chronicle*, 23 June 1941.
3. William Beveridge, *Why I Am A Liberal* (London: Herbert Jenkins, 1945), 1.
4. Churchill, *The Unrelenting Struggle*, 45–6, speech of 22 January 1941.
5. R.P. (41) 3, 27 February 1941.
6. INF 1/177 contains considerable correspondence on this subject for the first half of 1941.
7. Kingsley Martin, *Editor* (London: Hutchinson, 1968), 305.
8. PREM 4/100/5, Professor Keynes's Memo on War Aims.
9. Anthony Eden, *Freedom and Order* (London: Faber, 1947), 154; Winston S. Churchill, *The Grand Alliance* (London: Cassell, 1950), 392.
10. S.I.C. (42)2, T.U.C. Memo circulated 3 January 1942.
11. Lord Beveridge, *Power and Influence* (London: Hodder & Stoughton, 1953), 298; Janet Beveridge, *Beveridge and his Plan* (London: Hodder & Stoughton, 1954), 106, 111.
12. I am grateful to Sir Norman Chester, who was the secretary of the Beveridge committee, for discussing Beveridge and his report with me in an interview on 9 July 1974.
13. W. K. Hancock and M. M. Gowing, *British War Economy* (London: H.M.S.O., 1949), 452 and see ch. XV.
14. Richard Stone, 'The Use and Development of National Income and Expenditure Estimates', in Chester, *Lessons of the British War Economy* (Cambridge University Press, 1951), 85; and see R. S. Sayers, *Financial Policy 1939–1945* (London: H.M.S.O., 1956), ch. 3.
15. I.E.P. (41) 3, 'Internal Measures for the Prevention of General Unemployment', circulated 3 November 1941; Lord Robbins, *Autobiography of an Economist* (London: Macmillan, 1971), 186–7.

16. R. S. Sayers, *Financial Policy 1939–1945* (London: H.M.S.O., 1956), 97–8.

17. For the origins of reconstruction see ED 136/22 and 136/212. Note by R. S. Wood 17 January 1941, ED 136/217.

18. Lord Butler, *The Art of the Possible* (London: Hamish Hamilton, 1971), 93–4.

19. Note of a talk with H. G. Wells 3 October 1941, ED 136/215.

20. Butler to Churchill 12 September 1941, ED 138/21.

21. Butler to Churchill 12 September 1941, ED 138/21; Butler, *The Art of the Possible*, 95.

22. Marjorie Cruikshank, *Church and State in English Education* (London: Macmillan, 1963), 135 *et seq.*

23. ED 136/378.

24. G. M. Young, *Country and Town* (Harmondsworth: Penguin, 1943), 88–90. This provides a convenient summary of the Scott and Uthwatt Reports, referred to below. See also William Ashworth, *The Genesis of Modern British Town Planning* (London: Routledge & Kegan Paul, 1954), ch. 8.

25. Bernard Donoughue and G. W. Jones *Herbert Morrison* (London: Weidenfeld & Nicolson, 1973), 202.

26. *Dictionary of National Biography* 1951–1960, 'Sir Leslie Patrick Abercrombie' by Lord Holford, 2–3.

27. Cmd 6153, *Report of the Royal Commission on the Distribution of the Industrial Population* (London: H.M.S.O., 1940), 218–26.

28. *News Chronicle*, 27 September 1940 (Jordan); 17 February 1941 (Lloyd Wright).

29. *The Times*, 25 October 1940.

30. Collin Brooks, 'Churchill the Conversationalist', in Charles Eade (ed.), *Churchill, by his Contemporaries* (London: Hutchinson, 1953), 362.

31. I am grateful to the late Lord Reith for allowing me to read his wartime diaries as background information, and for interviews of 11 July and 9 September 1968.

32. Gladys Keable, *Tomorrow Slowly Comes* (Town and Country Planning Association, 1963), 24; J. C. W. Reith, *Into the Wind*, (London: Hodder & Stoughton, 1949), 422, 426.

33. Reith, *Into the Wind*, 442–6.

34. *The Memoirs of Lord Chandos* (London: Bodley Head, 1962), 342; Sir Oswald Mosley, *My Life* (London: Nelson, 1970), 344–5. I am

grateful to Lord Conesford, who as Mr H. Strauss was parliamentary secretary at the Ministry of Works and Planning, and subsequently at the Ministry of Town and Country Planning, for discussing Portal with me in an interview of 13 September 1973.

35. G. M. Young, *Country and Town*, 84–139; J. B. Cullingworth, *Town and Country Planning* (London: Allen & Unwin, 1972), 40–41.

36. MH 77/25, 'The Emergency Hospital Service as a Starting Point for Future Developments', Memo by A. W. Neville, 2 September 1941.

37. MH 77/25, Memo by A. N. Rucker of 6 February 1941.

38. MH 77/25, 'Suggestions for a Post-War Hospital Policy', unsigned Memo by Maude, August 1941; and Maude to Sir Laurence Brock 25 August 1941.

39. Lord Hill of Luton, *Both Sides of the Hill* (London: Heinemann, 1964), 81.

40. J. S. Ross, *The National Health Service in Great Britain* (London: Geoffrey. Cumberledge and OUP, 1952), 75–80; Hill, *Both Sides of the Hill*, 82–3.

41. For the origins of the Nuffield survey, Margaret Cole, *The Life of G.D.H. Cole,* (London: Macmillan, 1971), 237–8; the work of academics on economic reconstruction was noted in a memo of the official committee on post-war internal economic problems, I.E.P. (41) 2; for a list of town and country planners see, for example, Waldorf Astor to Lord Balfour of Burleigh 4 February 1942, in Waldorf Astor papers file 206.

42. Percy Harris, *Forty Years in and out of Parliament* (London: Andrew Melrose, 1947), 158.

43. *The Onlooker*, August 1941, 5.

44. *Report of the 41st annual conference of the Labour party*, 25–8 May 1942, 23.

45. Labour Party NEC minutes, 9 April 1942.

46. Harold Laski, *Where do we go from here?* (Harmondsworth: Penguin 1940), 88.

47. Copy of Barrington-Ward to Churchill 14 April 1942. *The Times* archive.

48. William Beveridge, *Pillars of Security* (London: Allen & Unwin, 1943), 32. Broadcast of 22 March 1942.

49. Harold Laski, *Reflections on the Revolution of our Time* (London: Allen & Unwin, 1943), 7.

50. Hancock and Gowing, *British War Economy*, 541.
51. INF 1/292, 'Home Morale and Public Opinion' by Stephen Taylor, appendix to weekly report for 22–9 September 1941.
52. See below, ch. 9.
53. Labour Party, *The Old World and the New Society* 1942, 4.
54. Angus Calder, *The People's War* (London: Jonathan Cape, 1969), 482–4; F. A. Iremonger, *William Temple* (Oxford University Press, 1948).
55. Headlam Diary 31 January 1942..
56. Iremonger, *Temple*, 436–9; Sidney Dark, *The People's Archbishop* (Cambridge: James Clarke, 1942); Calder, *The People's War*, 484–6.
57. H. G. Wells, *'42 to '44* (London: Secker & Warburg, 1944), 163–4. I have taken my list of 1941 Committee members from Mass-Observation's records of the Bedales conference of the committee, and from the Committee's 'Open Letter to the New War Cabinet', a copy of which can be found in M-O's material relating to the Maldon by-election.

CHAPTER VII. STAFFORD CRIPPS'S PROGRESS

1. Winston S. Churchill, *The Hinge of Fate* (London: Cassell, 1951), 56.
2. Eric Estorick, *Stafford Cripps* (London: Heinemann, 1949), 166.
3. Diary of Beatrice Webb 9 July 1939.
4. Cripps to Beatrice Webb 23 June 1939.
5. Diary of Beatrice Webb 9 July 1939.
6. Colin Cooke, *The Life of Richard Stafford Cripps* (London: Hodder & Stoughton, 1957), 249.
7. E. L. Woodward, *British Foreign Policy in the Second World War*, Vol I, (London: H.M.S.O., 1970), 498–501.
8. Estorick, *Stafford Cripps*, 259.
9. *Foreign Relations of the United States* 1940, Vol. I, 629, Steinhardt to Secretary of State 17 November 1940.
10. Winston S. Churchill, *The Grand Alliance* (London: Cassell, 1950), 320–23.
11. INF 1/192, Home Intelligence weekly report No. 119, 5–12 June 1943.
12. *Tribune*, 4 October 1940, 11–12.
13. Hugh Thomas, *John Strachey* (London: Eyre Methuen, 1973), 207.
14. *Left News*, March 1941, 1645.
15. Viscount Astor Papers Box 65

16. A. J. P. Taylor, *Beaverbrook* (London: Hamish Hamilton, 1972), 494–5.

17. I am grateful to Tom Harrisson for recalling this incident.

18. INF 1/292, Home Intelligence Weekly Report No 73, 16–23 February 1942.

19. Victor Gollancz, for example, told me (28 February 1966) that Cripps believed in June 1941 that Russia would not last a fortnight, since the Germans would take control of their oil. See also Taylor, *Beaverbrook*, 474–5.

20. Woodward, *British Foreign Policy* Vol. II, 31.

21. Taylor, *Beaverbrook*, 491, Beaverbrook Papers, Box on Russia 1941–2, copy of Cripps to Foreign Office 30 October 1941.

22. Woodward, *British Foreign Policy*, Vol. II, 31, 42–5, 51; Beaverbrook Papers, loc. cit., Cripps to Foreign Office 13 November 1941, Churchill to Eden 1 December 1941.

23. Churchill, *The Hinge of Fate*, 56–7.

24. Estorick, *Stafford Cripps*, 291.

25. Estorick, *Stafford Cripps*, 291.

26. Mass-Observation file report No. 1166; Hadley Cantril, *Public Opinion 1939–1946* (Princeton University Press, 1951), 279–80.

27. Nicholas Mansergh (ed.), *Constitutional Relations between Britain and India. The Transfer of Power 1942–1947, Vol. I: The Cripps Mission* (London: H.M.S.O., 1970).

28. Ibid., Doct. 43.

29. Ibid., Doct. 60.

30. Ibid., Doct. 456.

31. Ibid., Doct. 282.

32. Ibid., Doct. 304, Amery to Linlithgow 10 March 1942.

33. Ibid., Doct. 474, Linlithgow to Amery 31 March 1942.

34. Ibid., Doct. 519, Cripps to Churchill 4 April 1942.

35. Ibid., Doct. 578, Linlithgow to Amery 10 April 1942; Doct. 556, War Cabinet 42 (45), 9 April 1942.

36. M-O file report No. 1361, 27 July 1942, 'Who likes and dislikes Sir Stafford Cripps'.

37. Malcolm MacDonald, *Titans and Others* (London: Collins, 1972), 109–10.

38. Diary of Beatrice Webb 23 July 1942.

39. Ibid., 26 October 1942.

40. Ian Angus and Sonia Orwell (eds.), *The Collected Essays, Journalism*

and Letters of George Orwell, Vol. II (Harmondsworth: Penguin, 1970), 485–6.

41. *The Times*, 28 September 1942.
42. Laski to Beatrice Webb 5 July 1942, Passfield Papers.
43. Liddell Hart to Owen 20 June 1942, Liddell Hart Papers.
44. Churchill, *The Hinge of Fate*, 354–6.
45. *News Chronicle*, 3 July 1942.
46. E. H. Carr to Barrington-Ward 3 July 1942, *The Times* archive.
47. Note of talk with David Owen 28–9 August 1942, Liddell Hart papers.
48. Memorandum by Carr (undated but plainly summer 1942), *The Times* archive.
49. Ivor Thomas to Tom Jones 14 August 1942, Viscount Astor Papers Box 43, file 823.
50. R. H. Bruce Lockhart, *Comes the Reckoning* (New York: Putnam, 1947), 184–5; Liddell Hart, 'Notes for History', talk with Owen 28–9 August.
51. Churchill, *The Hinge of Fate*, 497–500.
52. Lord Moran, *Winston Churchill: The Struggle for Survival 1940–1965* (London: Constable, 1966), 72.
53. Churchill, *The Hinge of Fate*, 501–2.
54. Diary of Beatrice Webb 26 October 1942.
55. Mass-Observation file report No. 1484, 13 November 1942.

CHAPTER VIII. THE PEOPLE'S WILLIAM

1. Beatrice Webb, *Our Partnership* (London: Longmans, Green, 1948), 272.
2. P. P. 1942–3, VI, Cmd 6404, *Social Insurance and Allied Services*, para 8.
3. Beatrice Webb, *Our Partnership*, 309.
4. Lord Robbins, *Autobiography of an Economist* (London: Macmillan, 1971), 137.
5. Francis Williams, *A Prime Minister Remembers* (London: Heinemann, 1961), 57; Interview with Sir Norman Chester.
6. J. M. Winter and D. M. Joslin (eds.), *R. H. Tawney's Commonplace Book,* (Cambridge University Press, 1972), 26–7. I am grateful to Dr John Brown of Edinburgh University for this reference.
7. Beatrice Webb Diary 10 August 1938.
8. Cmd 6404, para 7.
9. *Report of the 41st annual conference of the Labour Party 25–8 May 1942*, 132. The resolution was introduced by James Griffiths.

10. S.I.C. (42), 20 May 1942.
11. Charles Madge, *Industry after the War* (London: Pilot Press, 1943), 32–4.
12. Home Intelligence weekly report No. 80, 15 April 1942.
13. Beveridge, *Pillars of Security* (London: Allen & Unwin, 1943), 42–4; Lord Beveridge, *Power and Influence* (London: Hodder & Stoughton, 1953), 309–10.
14. CAB 117/209 'Public Feeling on Post-War Reconstruction'; Dalton to Jowitt 6 December 1942.
15. PREM 4/89/2, Bracken to Churchill 27 October 1942.
16. CAB 153 (42), 16 November 1942.
17. Beveridge, *Power and Influence*, 315.
18. PREM 4/89/2, Jowitt to Churchill 23 November 1942.
19. Private information.
20. For a thorough and rewarding account of reactions to Beveridge, see Arthur Marwick, *Britain in the Century of Total War* (London: Bodley Head, 1968), 309–14.
21. B.I.P.O., *The Beveridge Report and the Public*, 1943.
22. INF 1/292, Home Intelligence weekly report No. 114, 1–8 December 1942.
23. PREM 4/89/2, Memo by Kingsley Wood 17 November 1942.
24. PREM 4/89/2, Memo by Cherwell 25 November 1942.
25. Note by Churchill for the Cabinet 12 January 1943, Winston S. Churchill, *The Hinge of Fate* (London: Cassell, 1951), 861–2.
26. CAB 8 (43), Memo by the Chancellor of the Exchequer and the Treasury, 14 January 1943.
27. 'Report on the Beveridge proposals'. A copy of this document was made available to me by the kindness of Lord Clitheroe, the former Ralph Assheton, and the Conservative Research Department.
28. P.R. (43) 2, Memo by the Home Secretary 20 January 1943.
29. P.R. (43) 13, 11 February 1943. Interim report of the Committee on Reconstruction Priorities on the Beveridge Plan.
30. PREM 4/89/2, Memo by Cherwell 11 February 1943.
31. Ibid., Memo by Cherwell of 12 February 1943; Winston S. Churchill, *The Hinge of Fate* (London: Cassell, 1951), 862.
32. Undated memo by Attlee, Attlee Papers (Churchill College) 2/2.
33. HC Debs. Vol. 386, 16 February 1943, col. 1678.
34. HC Debs., Vol. 386, 16–18 February 1943; Nigel Nicolson (ed.), *Harold Nicolson: Diaries and Letters 1939–1945* (London: Collins, 1967), 281–2; *The Times*, 20 February 1943.

35. Cecil King, *With Malice Toward None* (London: Sidgwick & Jackson, 1970), 211; Dalton Diary 18 February 1943.

36. Alan Bullock, *The Life and Times of Ernest Bevin*, Vol. II (London: Heinemann, 1967), 233–4.

37. On all these contests see Angus Calder, 'The Common Wealth Party', and also for Midlothian North, *Picture Post*, 6 February 1943, 16–17, 26; for King's Lynn, *Norfolk News and Weekly Press*, 23 January, 6 February 1943; for Bristol Central, *Bristol Evening Post*, 1 January to 19 February 1943; for Watford, Raymond Blackburn, *I Am An Alcoholic* (London: Allan Wingate, 1959), 48–50.

38. Mass-Observation file report No. 1649, 18 February 1943.

39. INF 1/292, Home Intelligence weekly report No. 125, 16–23 February 1943.

40. Winston S. Churchill, *Onwards To Victory* (London: Cassell, 1944), 33–45. World broadcast of 21 March 1943.

41. INF 1/292, Home Intelligence weekly report No. 129, 16 to 23 March 1943, and subsequent reports up to the autumn of 1944; David Butler and Jennie Freeman, *British Political Facts 1900–1967* (London: Macmillan, 1968), 159. The first poll results were dated June and July 1943.

CHAPTER IX CONSERVATISM IN ECLIPSE 1943–1945

1. Philip Goodhart, *The 1922* (London: Macmillan, 1973), 114–19.

2. Goodhart, *The 1922*, 124.

3. Diary of Collin Brooks 12 March 1942.

4. Goodhart, *The 1922*, 126–30; Diary of Collin Brooks 29 September 1942.

5. *Daily Herald*, 17 April 1943.

6. Alan Bullock, *The Life and Times of Ernest Bevin*, Vol. II (London: Heinemann, 1967), 220–24.

7. Hartmut Kopsch, 'The Approach of the Conservative Party to Social Policy during World War II', unpublished University of London Ph.D. thesis 1974, 44.

8. Hugh Molson, 'Ourselves and Churchill', *Evening Standard* 31 May 1945; HC Debs., Vol. 386, 17 February 1943, col. 1818; *The Times*, 18 March 1943.

9. Viscount Hinchingbrooke, *Full Speed Ahead!* (London: Simpkin Marshall, 1944), 21; article of 8 February 1943 in the *Evening Standard*.

10. Barrington-Ward Diary of 9 November 1942.

11. Kopsch, 'The Approach of the Conservative Party', 70–72.

12. W.P. (43) 255; W.P. (43) 308.

13. W. M. (43) 140, Meeting of ministers of 14 October 1943 recorded in a confidential annexe to the War Cabinet minutes.

14. Dalton Diary 22 March, 26 March, 24 May, 6 September, 16 September 1943; Halifax Diary 18 August, 3 September 1944, Hickleton Papers.

15. A. J. P. Taylor (ed.), W. P. Crozier: *Off The Record. Political Interviews 1933–1943* (London: Hutchinson, 1973), 371.

16. Labour Party NEC Minutes, 26–7 February 1944.

17. Dalton Diary 26 September 1944.

18. Barrington-Ward Diary 14 February 1944.

19. Samuel Brittan, *Steering the Economy* (Harmondsworth: Penguin, 1971), 189.

20. Dalton Diary 10 November 1943.

21. PREM 4/88/1, Unsent note of Churchill to Attlee 20 November 1944.

22. Lord Attlee, 'The Churchill I Knew', in *Churchill by his Contemporaries: An 'Observer' Appreciation* (London: Hodder & Stoughton, 1965), 19–20.

23. Attlee to Churchill undated: Churchill to Attlee 19 January 1945, Attlee Papers (Churchill College).

24. Kopsch, 'The Approach of the Conservative Party', 385–6.

25. INF 1/293, Special Report no. 49, 'Public feeling about education and educational reform'.

26. Lord Butler, *The Art of the Possible* (London: Hamish Hamilton, 1972), 117.

27. ED 136/278, Memo by Butler; ED 138/20, Dr Sophie Weizman's interview with Butler May 1945. I am grateful to Mr Graham Rimmer for bringing this evidence to my notice. Butler, *The Art of the Possible*, 117.

28. *The Times*, 28 and 30 March 1944; Butler, *The Art of the Possible*, 120–22.

29. Butler, *The Art of the Possible*, 119–20.

30. P.R. (43) 3, Memorandum by Ernest Brown and T. Johnston, 'Comprehensive Medical Service'.

31. Edith Summerskill, *A Woman's World* (London: Heinemann, 1967), 215; Labour Party National Executive Central Committee on Reconstruction Problems, minutes of meetings of 19 and 20 December 1942.

32. Labour Party, *National Service for Health* (1943).

33. J. M. Mackintosh, *The Nation's Health* (London: Pilot Press, 1944), 49.

34. R (44), 3rd meeting 10 January 1944; 4th meeting 11 January 1944.

35. Barrington-Ward Diary 11 and 14 February 1944; PREM 4/36/3, Churchill to Eden 10 February 1944.

36. *The Times*, 4 August 1944; *The Economist*, 20 May 1944, 675.

37. HC Debs. Vol. 401, 21 June 1944, cols. 212–13.

38. Lord Beveridge, *Power and Influence* (London: Hodder & Stoughton, 1953), 228–9; Donald Winch, *Economics and Policy* (London: Fontana, 1972), 391; Lord Citrine, *Two Careers* (London: Hutchinson, 1967), 239–40; Taylor, W. P. Crozier: *Off The Record*, p. 380.

39. W.P. (43) 465, Memo by the Paymaster-General of 20 October 1943.

40. I derive my account of the debate on employment policy from the minutes and papers of the Committee on Post War Employment, E.C. (43). For Henderson's paper see Henry Clay (ed.), *The Inter-War Years and other Papers* (Oxford: Clarendon Press, 1955), 316–17 and 316–25.

41. E.C. (43), 'Maintenance of Employment', Note by the Economic Section 18 October 1943.

42. Dalton Diary 19 May 1944; Hugh Dalton, *Memoirs 1931–1945: The Fateful Years* (London: Muller, 1957), 428.

43. John Jewkes, *Ordeal by Planning* (London: Macmillan, 1948), 64; 'Employment Policy', Cmd 6527 (London: H.M.S.O., 1944).

44. Clay, *The Inter-War Years*, 316.

45. HC Debs., Vol. 401, 21 June 1944, col, 232.

46. Ibid., col. 527.

47. Barrington-Ward Diary 8 January 1945.

48. Winston S. Churchill, *The Dawn of Liberation* (London: Cassell, 1945), 43–5, world broadcast of 26 March 1944.

49. INF 1/292, Home Intelligence weekly report No. 210, 3–10 October 1944.

50. INF 1/292, Home Intelligence weekly report No. 210, 3–10 October 1944, monthly review of post-war reconstruction.

51. Mass-Observation, *The Journey Home* (London: John Murray, 1944), 116.

52. Hadley Cantril, *Public Opinion 1939–1946* (Princeton University Press, 1951), 195; Lord Moran, *Winston Churchill: The Struggle for Survival 1940–1965* (London: Constable, 1966), 309.

53. Angus Calder, *The People's War* (London: Jonathan Cape, 1969), 552–4.

54. *Observer*, 12 March 1944; *The Economist*, 4 March 1944; Robert Rhodes James (ed.), *Chips* (London: Weidenfeld & Nicolson, 1967), 393.

55. *Notes on Current Politics*, March 1944, 2.

56. Attlee to Bevin 1 March 1944, Attlee Papers (University College) Box 7.

57. Tom Harrisson, 'Who'll Win?', in *Political Quarterly*, Vol. XV, 1944, 23; Mass-Observation file report No. 2084, 8 February 1944.

58. *Common Wealth Review*, March 1944, 9.

59. Michael Foot, *Aneurin Bevan*, Vol. 1 (London: MacGibbon & Kee, 1962), 474.

60. Labour Party NEC Policy Committee minutes, 21 September 1943.

61. Earl of Kilmuir, *Political Adventure* (London: Weidenfeld & Nicolson, 1957), 75–6.

62. R(44), 68th meeting 23 October 1944; R(44), 72nd meeting 16 November 1944; C. N. Ward-Perkins, 'Banking Developments', in G. D. N. Worswick and P. H. Ady (eds.), *The British Economy 1945–50* (Oxford University Press, 1952), 223.

63. Churchill, *Onwards to Victory* (London: Cassell, 1944), 238, speech of 13 October 1943; W. H. B. Court, *Coal* (London: H.M.S.O., 1951), 237–48.

64. Robert A. Brady, *Crisis in Britain* (University of California Press, 1950), 78–106.

65. *Report of the 43rd annual conference of the Labour Party 11–15 December 1944*, 37.

66. *43rd Annual Conference Report*, 145; Bullock, *Bevin*, Vol. II, 343.

67. *43rd Annual Conference Report*, 114.

68. *44th Annual Conference Report*, 114.

69. *43rd Annual Conference Report*, 163.

70. Foot *Bevan*, Vol. 1, 490–2; Samuel H. Beer, *Modern British Politics* (London: Faber, 1965), 174–8.

71. R(45) 14th meeting 9 April 1945; R(45) 17th meeting 30 April 1945.

72. PREM 4/65/4, Churchill to Eden 12 May 1945.

73. Ibid., Memo by Churchill to the Chief Whip 18 May 1945.

74. Winston S. Churchill, *The Second World War Vol. VI: Triumph and Tragedy* (London: Cassell, 1954), 509.

75. PREM 4/64/2.

76. *Labour Organiser*, 1 March 1945, 4.

77. See the vivid reports from regional organizers, made before the result was known, in *Labour Organiser*, August 1945. In the West Midlands, 80 per cent of the agents were doing the job for the first time.

78. *Onlooker*, April 1941, 8.

79. Interview with Lord Clitheroe, chairman of the party from 1944–6, 4 July 1973.

80. See the *Onlooker*, and Butler, *The Art of the Possible*, 127.

81. J. D. Hoffman, *The Conservative Party in Opposition 1945–1951* (London: MacGibbon & Kee, 1964), 22.

82. G. D. H. Cole, *History of the Labour Party since 1914* (London: Routledge & Kegan Paul, 1948), 480–81; *Labour Organiser*, August 1945, 11.

83. Barrington-Ward Diary 1 May 1942.

84. R. J. Thompson to Beaverbrook 30 May 1945, General Election Box B, Beaverbrook Papers.

85. Randolph S. Churchill, *Winston S. Churchill, Vol. I: Youth* (London: Heinemann, 1966), 361.

86. Churchill to Grigg 29 April, Grigg to Churchill 4 May, Beaverbrook to Churchill 24 May, Beaverbrook Papers.

87. A. J. P. Taylor, *Beaverbrook* (London: Hamish Hamilton, 1972), 564.

88. Unfortunately the letter from Beaverbrook is undated. For Sir Derrick Gunston's comment on Beaverbrook see the summary of the October 1945 Conservative candidates' conference in the 'Bretton Woods to Czechoslovakia' Box, Beaverbrook Papers.

89. Undated memo, Attlee Papers (Churchill College) 1/24.

90. *Report of the 44th annual conference of the Labour Party 21–25 May 1945*, 95.

91. Acland Diary 12 October 1944.

92. Herbert Morrison, *Looking Ahead* (London: Hodder & Stoughton, 1943); Bernard Donoughue and G. W. Jones, *Herbert Morrison* (London: Weidenfeld & Nicolson, 1973), 332; *The Economist*, 22 July 1944, 103.

93. Penderel Moon (ed.), *Wavell: The Viceroy's Journal* (Oxford University Press, 1973), 131.

94. NEC minutes Campaign sub-committee, 19 March 1945, 11 April 1945.

95. Dalton, *The Fateful Years*, 432–3.

96. Labour Party, *Let Us Face The Future* (1945).

97. Mass-Observation, *The Journey Home*, 103; Frank V. Cantwell, 'The Meaning of the British Election', in *Public Opinion Quarterly*, IX (1945), 156.

98. Lord Beveridge, *Power and Influence* (London: Hodder & Stoughton 1953), 336–7; Donald McLachlan, *In the Chair: Barrington-Ward of 'The Times' 1927–1948* (London: Weidenfeld & Nicolson, 1971), 208; King, *With Malice Toward None*, 287; Beveridge, *Why I am a Liberal* (London: Herbert Jenkins, 1945); interview with Sir Norman Chester.

99. *Onlooker*, June 1945, 1.

100. *The Times*, 23 April 1945.

101. Winston S. Churchill, *Victory* (London: Cassell, 1946), 186–92; Mass-Observation file report No. 2268, 'Report on the General Election', October 1945, 10; *Daily Express*, 17 January 1946.

102. Churchill to Beaverbrook 28 June 1945, Beaverbrook Papers Bbk C/56; Churchill to Page Croft 20 June 1945, Croft Papers 1/8.

103. *News Chronicle*, dates as given.

104. The best account of the election campaign is to be found in R. B. McCallum and Alison Readman, *The British General Election of 1945* (Oxford University Press, 1947). On feeling for Churchill, Mass-Observation file report No. 2268, 95; and No. 2265, July 1945.

105. I am quoting Mrs E. W. Walker, my grandmother, from her memory of the election in the Staffordshire village of Whittington.

106. Churchill, *Victory*, 184, speech of 13 June; *The Times*, 18 June 1945.

107. McCallum and Readman, *British General Election*, 43; Calder, *The People's War*, 581–2.

108. David Butler, 'Trends in British by-elections', in *Journal of Politics*, XI (1949), 403; Mark Abrams, 'The Labour vote in the General Election', in *Pilot Papers*, Vol. I, No. 1 (1946), 7: David Butler and Donald Stokes, *Political Change in Britain* (London: Macmillan, 1969), 54.

109. John Bonham, *The Middle Class Vote* (London: Faber, 1954), 154; Butler and Stokes, *Political Chance*, 109.

110. *Labour Organiser*, August 1945, 11.

111. Quoted in J. E. D. Hall, *Labour's First Year* (Harmondsworth: Penguin, 1947), 1.

112. *The Times*, 4 September 1939.

CHAPTER 10 ATTLEE'S CONSENSUS

1. Francis Williams, *The Triple Challenge* (London: Heinemann, 1948), 50–51.

2. Christopher Hollis in the *Spectator*, 13 October 1967; Michael Foot, *Aueurin Bevan* Vol. II (London: Davis-Poynter, 1973), 30–31; Williams, *Triple Challenge*, 56; Patricia Strauss, *Bevin & Co.* (New York: Putnam, 1941), 90.

3. W. Golant, 'The Early Political Thought of Clement Attlee', in *Political Quarterly* (1969), 246–255.

4. C. R. Attlee, *The Labour Party in Perspective* (London: Gollancz, 1937), 15, 145, 153.

5. Williams, *The Triple Challenge*, 52–3, 53–4.

6. Kingsley Martin, *Harold Laski* (London: Jonathan Cape, 1969), 152.

7. Foot, *Bevan* Vol, II, 155.

8. Foot, *Bevan* Vol, II, 60–102.

9. Bernard Donoughue and G.W. Jones, *Herbert Morrison* (London: Weidenfeld & Nicolson, 1973), 353.

10. Samuel H. Beer, *Modern British Politics* (London: Faber, 1965), 194; Donald Winch, *Economics and Policy* (London: Fontana, 1972), 296, 299.

11. Butler, *The Art of the Possible* (London: Hamish Hamilton, 1971), 146.

12. Arthur Marwick, *Britain in the Century of Total War* (London: Bodley Head, 1968), *passim*.

13. Calder, *The People's War* (London: Jonathan Cape. 1969), 18.

14. Pelling, *Britain and the Second World War* (London: Fontana, 1970), 326

15. Eckstein, *The English National Health Service*, (Harvard University Press, 1960), ix–x.

16. Rodney Barker, *Education and Politics 1900–1951* (Oxford University Press, 1972), 81–97.

17. Richard Crossman, 'The Lessons of 1945', in Perry Anderson et al. *Towards Socialism* (London: Fontana, 1965) 155.

18. C. R. Attlee, *As It Happened* (London: Heinemann, 1954), 23, 166.

Bibliography

1 *Unpublished papers*
  I have listed here all private collections which have been cited in the text, and a few other collections which have provided useful background information. In the case of Public Record Office documents I have listed a number of complete Cabinet series which I have searched and drawn material from, as well as individual files from the Prime Minister's office or particular departments.

A *Papers in the Public Record Office*
Minutes (W.M. series) and Papers (W.P. series) of the War Cabinet, September 1939 to May 1945.
Minutes and Papers of the War Cabinet Sub-Committee on War Aims (W.A. series), 1940.
Minutes and Papers of the Reconstruction Problems Committee (R.P. series), January 1941 to February 1942.
Minutes and Papers of the Reconstruction Priorities Committee (P.R. series), March 1942 to October 1943.
Minutes and Papers of the Reconstruction Committee (R series), October 1943 to May 1945.
Minutes and Papers of the Lord President's Committee (L.P. series), 1941 to 1945.
Minutes and Papers of the Official Committee on Internal Economic Policy (I.E.P. series), 1941.
Minutes and Papers of the Committee on Social Insurance and Allied Services (S.I.C. series), 1942.
Minutes and Papers of the Official Committee on Post-War Employment (E.C. series), 1943.
PREM 1/238; 1/251; 1/264; 1/359; 1/404.
PREM 4/6/2; 4/6/9; 4/14/5; 4/14/13; 4/21/3; 4/36/3; 4/57/7; 4/64/2; 4/65/4; 4/88/1; 4/89/2; 4/100/5.
CAB 89/26; 117/209.
Board of Education: ED 136/22; 136/131; 136/212; 136/215; 136/217; 136/278; 136/378; 138/20; 138/21.
Foreign Office: FO 371/29523; 371/29602; 371/29634; 371/32960; 371/36973; 800/310; 800/322.
Ministry of Health: MH 77/25.

Ministry of Information: INF 1/177; INF 1/264, Home Intelligence daily reports 27 May to 3 June 1940; INF 1/292, Home Intelligence weekly reports January 1941 to October 1944; INF 1/293; INF 1/849; INF 1/862.

B *Private collections*

Sir Richard Acland diary; in the possession of Sir Richard Acland.

L. S. Amery diary; in the possession of the Rt. Hon. Julian Amery, M.P.

Nancy, Viscountess Astor papers; Reading University Library.

Waldorf, Viscount Astor papers; Reading University Library.

Earl Attlee papers; University College, Oxford, and Churchill College, Cambridge.

R. M. Barrington-Ward diary; in the possession of Mrs Adele Barrington-Ward.

Beaverbrook papers; formerly at the Beaverbrook Library, now transferred to the House of Lords Record Office.

Collin Brooks diary; in the possession of Miss Vivian Brooks.

Viscount Caldecote (Sir J. Inskip) diary; Churchill College, Cambridge.

Viscount Cecil of Chelwood papers; British Museum.

Neville Chamberlain papers; Birmingham University Library. Mrs Dorothy Lloyd kindly gave me permission to read through the unpublished letters of Chamberlain to his sisters in 1939 and 1940. By agreement, I have not quoted from the papers, barring one extract, but they have provided important background information.

Common Wealth party minutes and papers. In the possession of Dr D. Bannister, secretary of Common Wealth.

Lord Croft papers; Churchill College, Cambridge.

Viscount Crookshank diary; Bodleian Library, Oxford.

Hugh Dalton diary; British Library of Political and Economic Science.

Geoffrey Dawson diary; in the possession of Mr Michael Dawson.

Earl Lloyd George of Dwyfor papers; formerly at the Beaverbrook Library, now transferred to the House of Lords Record Office.

Admiral J. H. Godfrey memoirs, unpublished; Churchill College, Cambridge.

Sir Patrick Hannon papers; formerly at the Beaverbrook Library, now transferred to the House of Lords Record Office.

Sir Basil Liddell Hart papers; in the possession of Lady Liddell Hart.

Sir Cuthbert Headlam diary; Durham Public Record Office.

Hickleton (Viscount Halifax) papers; formerly available by arrangement at York Public Library, now transferred to Churchill College, Cambridge.

Labour Party National Executive Committee minutes and papers 1940–1945; Transport House.

Marquess of Lothian (Philip Kerr) papers; Scottish Record Office, Edinburgh.

Viscount Margesson papers; Churchill College, Cambridge.

Lt-General Sir F.N. Mason-MacFarlane memoir, unpublished; formerly in the possession of Mrs MacFarlane Hall, now at the Imperial War Museum.

Mass-Observation file reports numbers 725, 905, 1014, 1166, 1361, 1649, 2265, 2268 and 2545.

Gilbert Murray papers; Bodleian Library, Oxford.

Sir Harold Nicolson, unpublished diary; loaned to me by Mr Nigel Nicolson and now available at Balliol College, Oxford.

Political and Economic Planning papers; in the possession of P.E.P.

Viscount Simon papers; in the possession of Viscount Simon.

Viscount Templewood (Sir Samuel Hoare) papers; Cambridge University Library.

The Times papers; in the possession of *The Times* archive.

Euan Wallace diary; Bodleian Library, Oxford.

Beatrice Webb diary; British Library of Political and Economic Science.

2   *Contemporary record and opinion*

Attlee, C. R., *The Labour Party in Perspective* (London: Gollancz, 1937).

Baldwin, Stanley, *This Torch of Freedom* (London: Hodder & Stoughton, 1935).

Barnes, Leonard, *Soviet Light on the Colonies* (Harmondsworth: Penguin, 1944).

Beveridge, William, *Pillars of Security* (London: Allen & Unwin, 1943).

———, *Why I am a Liberal* (London: Herbert Jenkins, 1945).

Lord Beveridge, *Full Employment in a Free Society* (London: Allen & Unwin, second ed. 1960).

Bevin, Ernest, *The Job to be Done* (London: Heinemann, 1942).

British Institute of Public Opinion, *The Beveridge Report and the Public* (London: 1943).

'Cato' (Michael Foot, Peter Howard, and Frank Owen), *Guilty Men* (London: Gollancz, 1940).

Eade, Charles (ed.), *The War Speeches of Winston S. Churchill*, Vol. I (London: Cassell, 1951).

Churchill, Winston S., *The Unrelenting Struggle* (London: Cassell, 1943).

———, *The End of the Beginning* (London: Cassell, 1943).

———, *Onwards to Victory* (London: Cassell, 1944).

———, *Victory* (London: Cassell, 1946).

Cole, G. D. H., *The People's Front* (London: Gollancz, 1937).

Cole, G. D. H. and M.I., *The Condition of Britain* (London: Gollancz, 1937).

Davenport, Nicholas, *Vested Interest or Common Pool?* (London: Gollancz, 1942).

The Economist.

Eden, Anthony, *Freedom and Order* (London: Faber, 1946).

The Elector 1936–8 (continued as) *The Onlooker* 1939–45.

Fyfe, Hamilton, *Britain's Wartime Revolution* (London: Gollancz, 1944).

Gollancz, Victor (ed.), *The Betrayal of the Left* (London: Gollancz, 1941).

Hall, J. E. D., *Labour's First Year* (Harmondsworth: Penguin, 1947).

Harrisson, Tom, 'Who'll Win?' in *Political Quarterly*, xv (1944).

Daily Herald.

Hodson, J. L., *The Home Front* (London: Gollancz, 1944).

——, *The Sea and the Land* (London: Gollancz, 1945).

House of Commons Debates.

Jewkes, John, *Ordeal by Planning* (London: Macmillan, 1948).

Keynes, J. M., *The General Theory of Employment Interest and Money* (London: Macmillan, 1936).

——, *The Collected Writings of J. M. Keynes Vol. IX: Essays in Persuasion* (London: Macmillan, 1972).

Labour Party, *Report of the Annual Conference of the Labour Party, 1939–1945.*

——, *Labour's Immediate Programme* (1937).

——, *Labour's Aims in War and Peace* (London: Lincolns-Praeger, 1940).

——, *The Old World and the New Society* (1942).

——, *National Service for Health* (1943).

——, *Let Us Face the Future* (1945).

——, *Labour Organiser*, 1944-5.

Laski, Harold, *Where Do We Go from Here?* (Harmondsworth: Penguin, 1940).

——, *Reflections on the Revolution of Our Time* (London: Allen & Unwin, 1943).

Madge, Charles, *Industry after the War* (London: Pilot Press, 1943).

Manchester Guardian.

Mass-Observation, *Us* Nos. 1 to 6, February and March 1940.

——, *War Begins at Home* (Harmondsworth: Penguin, 1940).

——, 'Social Security and Parliament', in *Political Quarterly*, XIV (1943).

——, *The Journey Home* (London: John Murray, 1944).

Morrison, Herbert, *Looking Ahead* (London: Hodder & Stoughton, 1943).

The Next Five Years: An Essay in Political Agreement (London: Macmillan, 1935).

New Statesman.

Orr, John Boyd, *Food Health and Income* (London: Macmillan, 1937).

Parliamentary Papers, PP 1939–40 Cmd 6153: *Report of the Royal Commission on the Distribution of the Industrial Population* (H.M.S.O., 1940).

——, PP 1941–42 Cmd 6386: *Report of the Committee on Compensation and Betterment* (Uthwatt Report) (H.M.S.O., 1942).

——, PP 1942–43 Cmd 6404: *Report of the Committee on Social Insurance and Allied Services* (Beveridge Report) (H.M.S.O., 1942).

——, PP 1942–43 Cmd 6458: *Educational Reconstruction* (H.M.S.O., 1943).

——, PP 1943–44 Cmd 6502: *Statement on a National Health Service* (H.M.S.O., 1944).

——, PP 1943–44 Cmd 6527: *Employment Policy* (H.M.S.O., 1944).

——, PP 1948–49 Cmd 7700: *Report of the Royal Commission on the Press 1947–49* (H.M.S.O., 1949).

'Politicus', 'Labour and the War', in *Political Quarterly*, X (1939).

Priestley, J. B., *Postscripts* (London: Heinemann, 1940).

——, *Here are Your Answers* (Common Wealth, 1943).

Rathbone, Eleanor, *Family Allowances* (London: Allen & Unwin, 1949).

Rowse, A. L., *Mr Keynes and the Labour Movement* (London: Macmillan, 1936).

Strauss, Patricia, *Bevin & Co.* (New York: G. P. Putnam's Sons, 1941).

The Times.

Tracey, Herbert, *Trade Unions Fight — for What?* (London: Labour Book Service, 1941).

Tribune.

Wells, H. G., *'42 to '44* (London: Secker & Warburg, 1944).

Williams, Francis, *The Triple Challenge* (London: Heinemann, 1948).

Young, G. M., *Country and Town* (Harmondsworth: Penguin, 1943).

3 *Memoir and biography*

Amery, L. S., *My Political Life Vol. III: The Unforgiving Years* (London: Hutchinson, 1955).

Angus, Ian and Orwell, Sonia (eds.), *The Collected Essays, Journalism and Letters of George Orwell*, Vols. I and II (Harmondsworth: Penguin, 1970).

Attlee, C. R., *As It Happened* (London: Heinemann, 1954).

——, *Clem Attlee: the Granada Historical Records Interview* (London: Panther Record, 1967).

Beveridge, Lord, *Power and Influence* (London: Hodder & Stoughton, 1953).

Beveridge, Janet, *Beveridge and His Plan* (London: Hodder & Stoughton, 1954).

Birkenhead, Earl of, *Halifax* (London: Hamish Hamilton, 1965).

Blackburn, Raymond, *I am an Alcoholic* (London: Allen Wingate, 1959).

Bruce Lockhart, R. H., *Comes the Reckoning* (London: Putnam, 1947).

Bullock, Alan, *The Life and Times of Ernest Bevin Vol. I: Trade Union Leader* (London: Heinemann, 1960); *Vol. II: Minister of Labour* (London: Heinemann, 1967).

Butler, R. A., *The Art of the Possible* (London: Hamish Hamilton, 1971).

Chandos, Viscount (Oliver Lyttelton), *The Memoirs of Lord Chandos* (London: Bodley Head, 1962).

Chatfield, Lord, *It Might Happen Again Vol. II: the Navy and Defence* (London: Heinemann, 1947).

Churchill, Winston S., *The Second World War:*
  Vol. I: The Gathering Storm (London: Cassell, 1948);
  Vol. II: Their Finest Hour (London: Cassell, 1949);
  Vol. III: The Grand Alliance (London: Cassell, 1950);
  Vol. IV: The Hinge of Fate (London: Cassell, 1951);
  Vol. VI: Triumph and Tragedy (London: Cassell, 1954).

Churchill, Randolph S., *Winston S. Churchill Vol. I: Youth* (London: Heinemann, 1966).

Churchill by his Contemporaries: An 'Observer' Appreciation (London: Hodder & Stoughton, 1965).

Citrine, Lord, *Two Careers* (London: Hutchinson, 1967).

Clay, Henry (ed.), *The Inter-War Years and Other Papers* (Oxford: Clarendon Press, 1955).

Cole, Margaret, *The Life of G. D. H. Cole* (London: Macmillan, 1971).

Cooper, Duff, *Old Men Forget* (London: Rupert Hart-Davies, 1953).

Cooke, Colin, *The Life of Richard Stafford Cripps* (London: Hodder & Stoughton, 1957).

Coote, Colin, *Editorial* (London: Eyre & Spottiswoode, 1965).

Dalton, Hugh, *The Fateful Years: Memoirs 1931–1945* (London: Muller, 1957).

Darke, Sidney, *The People's Archbishop* (London: James Clarke, 1942).

Dixon, Bernard, *Journeys in Belief* (London: Allen & Unwin, 1968).

Donoughue, Bernard and Jones, G. W., *Herbert Morrison* (London: Weidenfeld & Nicolson, 1973).

Driberg, Tom, *The Best of Both Worlds* (London: Phoenix House, 1958).

Eade, Charles (ed.), *Churchill by his Contemporaries* (London: Hutchinson, 1953).

Eden, Anthony (Earl of Avon), *The Eden Memoirs: The Reckoning* (London: Cassell, 1965).

Estorick, Erick, *Sir Stafford Cripps* (London: Heinemann, 1949).

Farrer, David, *G—For God Almighty* (London: Weidenfeld & Nicolson, 1969).

Foot, Michael, *Aneurin Bevan Vol. I: 1897–1945* (London: MacGibbon & Kee, 1962); *Vol. II: 1945–1960* (London: Davis-Poynter, 1973).

Harris, Percy, *Forty Years in and out of Parliament* (London: Andrew Melrose, 1947).

Harrod, R. F., *The Life of John Maynard Keynes* (London: Macmillan, 1951).

Harvey, John (ed.), *The Diplomatic Diaries of Oliver Harvey 1937–1940* (London: Collins, 1970).

Hill, Lord, of Luton, *Both Sides of the Hill* (London: Heinemann, 1964).

Iremonger, F. A., *William Temple* (London: Oxford University Press, 1948).

Ismay, Lord, *The Memoirs of Lord Ismay* (London: Heineman,, 1960).

James, Robert Rhodes (ed.), *Chips: the Diaries of Sir Henry Channon* (London: Weidenfeld & Nicolson, 1967).

Jones, J. Harry, *Josiah Stamp, Public Servant* (London: Pitman & Sons, 1964).

Jones, Thomas, *Lloyd George* (London: Oxford University Press, 1951).

Kilmuir, Earl of, *Political Adventure* (London: Weidenfeld & Nicolson, 1957).

King, Cecil H., *With Malice Toward None* (London: Sidgwick & Jackson, 1970).

Lindsay, Kenneth, 'Early Days of P.E.P.', in *Contemporary Review*, Vol. 222 (February 1973).

Low, David, *Low's Autobiography* (London: Michael Joseph, 1956).

MacDonald, Malcolm, *Titans & Others* (London: Collins, 1972).

Mackintosh, J. M., *The Nation's Health* (London: Pilot Press, 1944).

McLachlan, Donald, *Room 39* (London: Weidenfeld & Nicolson, 1968).

——, *In the Chair: Barrington-Ward of 'The Times' 1927–1948* (London: Weidenfeld & Nicolson, 1971).

Macleod, R. and Kelly, D. (eds.), *The Ironside Diaries 1937–1940* (London: Constable, 1962).

Macmillan, Harold, *The Blast of War* (London: Macmillan, 1967).

Maisky, Ivan, *Memoirs of a Soviet Ambassador: the War 1939–1945* (London: Hutchinson, 1957).

Martin, Kingsley, *Harold Laski* (London: Jonathan Cape, 1969).

——, *Editor* (Harmondsworth: Penguin, 1969).

Meynell, Francis, *My Lives* (London: Bodley Head, 1971).

Middlemas, Keith and Barnes, John, *Baldwin* (London: Weidenfeld & Nicolson, 1969).

Moon, Penderel (ed.), *Wavell: the Viceroy's Journal* (London: Oxford University Press, 1973).

Moran, Lord, *Winston Churchill: the Struggle for Survival 1940–1965* (London: Constable, 1966).

Morrison, Herbert, *Autobiography* (London: Odhams, 1960).

Mosley, Oswald, *My Life* (London: Nelson, 1970).

The Letters of Lewis Mumford and Frederic J. Osborn (Bath: Adams & Dart, 1971).

Nicolson, Nigel (ed.), *Harold Nicolson: Diaries and Letters 1939–1945* (London: Collins, 1967).

Reakes, G. L., *Man of the Mersey* (London: Christopher Johnson, 1956).

Reith, J. C. W., *Into the Wind* (London: Hodder & Stoughton, 1949).

Reynaud, Paul, *Mémoires Vol. II* (Paris: Flammarion, 1963).

Robbins, Lord, *Autobiography of an Economist* (London: Macmillan, 1971).

Salter, Sir Arthur, *Personality in Politics* (London: Right Book Club, 1947).

Sampson, Anthony, *Macmillan* (London: Allen Lane The Penguin Press, 1967).

Sieff, Israel, *Memoirs* (London: Weidenfeld & Nicolson, 1970).

Spears, Sir Edward, *Assignment to Catastrophe Vol. I: Prelude to Dunkirk* (London: Heinemann, 1954).

Spier, Eugen, *Focus* (London: Oswald Wolff, 1963).

Stocks, Mary, *Eleanor Rathbone* (London: Gollancz, 1949).

Strauss, Patricia, *Cripps — Advocate and Rebel* (London: Gollancz, 1943).

Summerskill, Edith, *A Woman's World* (London: Heinemann, 1967).

Taylor, A. J. P., *Beaverbrook* (London: Hamish Hamilton, 1972).

Thomas, Hugh, *John Strachey* (London: Eyre Methuen, 1973).

Webb, Beatrice, *Our Partnership* (London: Longmans, Green, 1948).

Wheeler-Bennett, J. W., *John Anderson, Viscount Waverley* (London: Macmillan, 1962).

——, (ed.), *Action This Day* (London: Macmillan, 1968).

Williams, Francis, *A Prime Minister Remembers* (London: Heinemann, 1961).

Winter, J. M. and Joslin, D. M. (eds.), *R. H. Tawney's Commonplace Book* (Cambridge University Press, 1972).

Wrench, John Evelyn, *Geoffrey Dawson and our Times* (London: Hutchinson, 1955).

4 *Secondary and other works*

Abrams, Mark, 'The Labour Vote in the General Election', in *Pilot Papers*, Vol. 1, No. 1 (1946).

Addison, Paul, 'Political Change in Britain September 1939 to December 1940', unpublished Oxford Ph. D. (1971).

Aldcroft, Derek H., *The Inter-War Economy* (London: Batsford, 1970).

Ashworth, William, *The Genesis of Modern British Town Planning* (London: Routledge & Kegan Paul, 1954).

Barker, Rodney, *Education and Politics* (London: Oxford University Press, 1972).

Beer, Samuel H., *Modern British Politics* (London: Faber, 1965).

Bonham, John, *The Middle Class Vote* (London: Faber, 1954).

Brady, Robert A., *Crisis in Britain* (University of California Press, 1950).

Briggs, Asa, *A History of Broadcasting in the United Kingdom Vol. III: The War of Words* (London: Oxford University Press, 1970).

Brittan, Samuel, *Steering the Economy* (Harmondsworth: Penguin, 1971).

Butler, David, 'Trends in British by-elections', *Journal of Politics*, IX (1949).

Butler, David, and Stokes, Donald, *Political Change in Britain* (London: Macmillan, 1969).

Butler, J. R. M., *Grand Strategy*, Vol. II (London: H.M.S.O., 1957).

Calder, Angus, 'The Common Wealth Party 1942–1945', unpublished Sussex University Ph.D., Vols. I and II (1968).

——, *The People's War* (London: Jonathan Cape, 1965).

Cantril, Hadley, *Public Opinion 1939–1946* (Princeton University Press, 1951).

Cantwell, Frank V., 'The Meaning of the British Election', in *Public Opinion Quarterly*, IX (1945).

Chester, D. N., 'The Central Machinery for Economic Policy', in D. N. Chester (ed.), *Lessons of the British War Economy* (Cambridge University Press, 1951).

Cohen, Percy, *Disraeli's Child: A History of the Conservative and Unionist Party Organisation Vol. II: 1924–1961* (unpublished MS., Conservative Research Department).

Cole, G. D. H., *History of the Labour Party since 1914* (London: Routledge & Kegan Paul, 1948).

Crossman, Richard, 'The Lessons of 1945', in Perry Anderson et al., *Towards Socialism* (London: Fontana, 1965).

Cullingworth, J. B., *Town and Country Planning in Britain* (London: Allen & Unwin, 1972).

Documents on German Foreign Policy 1918–1945, Series D, Vol. VIII (London: H.M.S.O., 1957).

Eckstein, Harry, *The English Health Service* (Harvard University Press, 1964).

Feiling, Keith, *The Life of Neville Chamberlain* (London: Macmillan, 1946).

Foreign Relations of the United States 1940, Vol. I (Washington: United States Government Printing Office, 1959).

Gilbert, Bentley B., *British Social Policy 1918–1939* (London: Batsford, 1970).

Golant, W., 'The Early Political Thought of Clement Attlee', in *Political Quarterly*, XL (1969).

——, 'The Emergence of C. R. Attlee as Leader of the Parliamentary Labour Party in 1935', in *Historical Journal*, XIII (1970).

Goodhart, Philip, *The 1922* (London: Macmillan, 1973).

Hancock, W. K. and Gowing, Margaret, *The British War Economy* (London: H.M.S.O., 1949).

Harris, Nigel, *Competition and the Corporate State* (London: Methuen, 1972).

Liddell Hart, Basil, 'Churchill in War', in *Encounter*, April 1966.

Hoffman, J. D., *The Conservative Party in Opposition 1945–1951* (London: MacGibbon & Kee, 1964).

Inman, P., *Labour in the Munitions Industries* (London: H.M.S.O., 1957).

Keable, Gladys, *Tomorrow Slowly Comes* (Town and Country Planning Association, 1963).

Kopsch, Hartmut, 'The Approach of the Conservative Party to Social Policy during World War Two', unpublished University of London Ph.D. thesis, (1970).

McCallum, R. B. and Readman, Alison, *The British General Election of 1945* (London: Oxford University Press, 1947).

MacLaine, Ian, 'The Work and Archives of the Ministry of Information', unpublished paper.

Mansergh, Nicholas (ed.), *Constitutional Relations between Britain and India. The Transfer of Power 1942–1947 Vol. I: the Cripps Mission* (London: H.M.S.O., 1970).

Manvell, Roger, *Film* (Harmondsworth: Penguin, 1946).

Marder, Arthur, 'Winston is Back', in *English Historical Review Supplement 5* (London: Longman, 1972).

Marwick, Arthur, 'Middle Opinion in the Thirties', in *English Historical Review* (April 1964), 285.

——, 'The Labour Party and the Welfare State in Britain, 1900–1948', in *American Historical Review*, LXXIII (1967).

——, *Britain in the Century of Total War* (London: Bodley Head, 1968).

Middlemas, Keith, *The Diplomacy of Illusion* (London: Weidenfeld & Nicolson, 1972).

Parker, H. M. D., *Manpower* (London: H.M.S.O., 1957).

Peacock, A. J. and Wiseman, J., *The Growth of Public Expenditure in the United Kingdom* (London: Allen & Unwin, 1967).

Pelling, Henry, *The British Communist Party* (London: Adam & Charles Black, 1958).

——, *A Short History of the Labour Party* (London: Macmillan, 1968).

——, *Britain and the Second World War* (London: Collins, 1970).

Pollard, Sidney, *The Development of the Modern British Economy* (London: Edward Arnold, 1968).

—— (ed.), *The Gold Standard and Employment Policies* (London: Methuen, 1970).

Rasmussen, Jorgen S., 'Party Discipline in War-Time: The Downfall of the Chamberlain Government', in *Journal of Politics*, 32 (1970).

Richards, Jeffrey, *Visions of Yesterday* (London: Routledge & Kegan Paul, 1973).

Richardson, H. W., *Economic Recovery in Britain 1932–1939* (London: Macmillan, 1967).

Ross, James Stirling, *The National Health Service in Great Britain* (London: Geoffrey Cumberledge and Oxford University Press, 1952).

Runciman, W. G., *Relative Deprivation and Social Justice* (London: Routledge & Kegan Paul, 1966).

Samuelson, Kurt, *From Great Power to Welfare State* (London: Allen & Unwin, 1968).

Sayers, R. S., *Financial Policy* (London: H.M.S.O., 1956).

Silvey, R. J., 'Some Recent Trends in Listening', in *B.B.C. Year Book 1946* (London: B.B.C., 1946).

Simon, Brian, *The Politics of Educational Reform 1920–1940* (London: Lawrence & Wishart, 1974).

Skidelsky, Robert, *Politicians and the Slump* (London: Macmillan, 1967).

Stone, Richard, 'The Use and Development of National Income and Expenditure Estimates', in D. N. Chester (ed.), *Lessons of the British War Economy* (Cambridge University Press, 1951).

Taylor, A. J. P., *English History* (Oxford: Clarendon Press, 1965).

Thompson, Laurence, *1940* (London: Collins, 1966).

Thompson, Neville, *The Anti-Appeasers* (Oxford: Clarendon Press, 1971).

Titmuss, R. M., *Problems of Social Policy* (London: H.M.S.O., 1950).

White, A. T. C., *The Story of Army Education* (London: Harrap, 1963).

Wilkinson, Ellen, *The Town that was Murdered* (London: Gollancz, 1939).

Winch, Donald, *Economics and Policy* (London: Fontana, 1972).

Woodward, Sir L., *British Foreign Policy in the Second World War*, Vols. I and II (London: H.M.S.O., 1970 and 1971).

Worswick, G. N. and Ady, P. H., *The British Economy 1945–1950* (London: Oxford University Press, 1952).

Index

Robert Hewison
UNDER SIEGE
Literary Life in London 1939–45

Under Siege is the first comprehensive study of the arts in Britain during the Second World War.

Drawing on a rich store of wartime writing and on the memories of survivors, Robert Hewison brilliantly describes the difficulties of being a writer, painter or composer under both military and civilian conditions.

Despite, or because of, the harsh realities of war, a flourishing literary society developed, for under siege conditions fiction, poetry, music and painting became more, not less, important.

'A remarkable reconstruction of the period' Philip Toynbee

ISBN 0 7043 3283 3 *History/Literature* £2.95 *Illustrated*

Aneurin Bevan
IN PLACE OF FEAR

'This book has been a delight and an inspiration. It will continue to be that for anyone who will give a day of their life to reading it' From Neil Kinnock's foreword.

Aneurin Bevan was the most fascinating of politicians; *In Place of Fear* was his only book. First published in 1952, it is a series of superbly written essays on many of the key issues faced by the Labour movement in Parliament. His book should be read by anyone who wishes to understand the struggles and achievements of British democracy for it is as relevant today as it was thirty years ago.

'A must for all those who would study the socialism of our time. His criticism of capitalism is trenchant' Jack Jones

'One of those rare books by a politician which gives equal weight to idealism and practical politics' *Sunday Press*, Dublin

ISBN 0 7043 3239 6 *History/Politics* £2.25

Phillip Knightley

THE FIRST CASUALTY
The War Correspondent as Hero, Propagandist and Myth Maker

From the Crimea to Afghanistan, Phillip Knightley, himself Journalist of the Year in 1980, examines the role of the war correspondent. *The First Casualty* is a disquieting book. It suggests that our attitudes to history are moulded by what we read in wartime, and that what we read too often bears little resemblance to reality.

'Fascinating, disturbing, and long overdue' Arthur Cooper, *Newsweek*

'Entertaining, lively, exasperating. . . It will be read with admiration for his devotion to his journalistic duty of revealing the truth' Jasper Ridley, *The Times Literary Supplement*

'The events are momentous. As for the correspondents, they are an irresistible assortment of idealists, artists, cads, hustlers, violence junkies and necrophiles' R.Z. Sheppard, *Time*

ISBN 0 7043 3195 0   *History/Journalism*   £4.95   *Illustrated*

Joe Ashton

GRASS ROOTS
A political novel

'It's the story of a young northern steelworker who becomes the Labour candidate for his home town, fights a difficult by-election, then rebels when he gets to Westminster. There have been . . . smoother novels about politics, but this is the first I've read that's about politics as she is lived in the pubs and clubs and the streets of a working class town. . . It's packed with detail, as rich as a slice of fruit-cake, and as vivid and exciting as an eve-of-poll rally' Simon Hoggart, *Guardian*

'Compelling and penetrating . . . compulsive reading' *Tribune*

'*Grass Roots* is the clearest guide to British party politics since *Phineas Phinn*' *The Times*

ISBN 0 7043 3328 7   *Fiction*   £2.95